Instructor's Manual to accompany

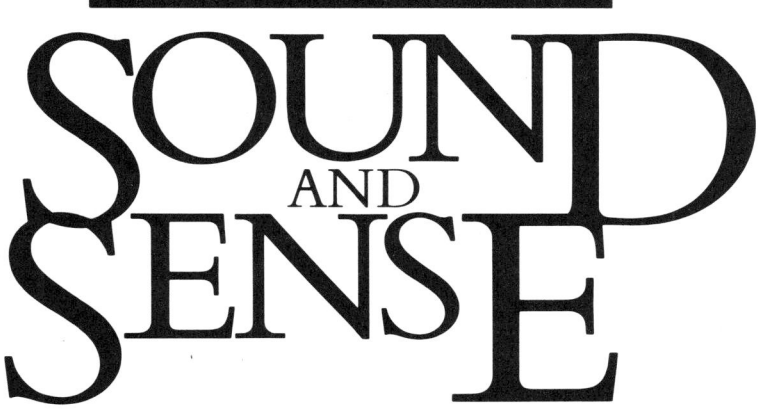

AN INTRODUCTION TO POETRY

SEVENTH EDITION

Laurence Perrine
and
Thomas R. Arp

Southern Methodist University

HARCOURT BRACE JOVANOVICH, PUBLISHERS
San Diego   New York   Chicago   Austin   Washington, D.C.
London   Sydney   Tokyo   Toronto

Copyright © 1987, 1982, 1977, 1973, 1969, 1963, 1956
by Harcourt Brace Jovanovich, Inc.

All rights reserved. No part of this publication may be
reproduced or transmitted in any form or by any means,
electronic or mechanical, including photocopy, recording, or
any information storage and retrieval system, without permission in writing from the publisher, except that, until further
notice, the contents or parts thereof may be reproduced for
instructional purposes by users of *Sound and Sense: An Introduction to Poetry,* Seventh Edition, by Laurence Perrine, provided
each copy contains a proper copyright notice as follows:
© 1987 HBJ.

ISBN: 0-15-582609-3
Printed in the United States of America

FOREWORD

This Instructor's Manual includes some commentary on every poem in the Seventh Edition of *Sound and Sense*. With some discussions we have included bibliographical references to other discussions, but we have not done this uniformly or systematically. Instructors wishing to locate other discussions should consult critical books on the poet in question (especially those that have indices) and Joseph M. Kuntz and Nancy C. Martinez, *Poetry Explication: A Checklist of Interpretation Since 1925 of British and American Poems Past and Present* (Boston: G. K. Hall, 1980), which lists explications through 1977. The annual bibliographical issues of *The Explicator* and *PMLA* may be checked for explications from 1977 to the present.

We should be foolish to expect universal agreement with the interpretations and judgments offered here; indeed, we have not always agreed with each other, and for that reason, though we have checked and criticized each other's work throughout, we have appended after each discussion the initials of its main author. These discussions will serve their purpose if they provoke a more careful scrutiny of the poems and an intelligent dissent. Certainly, the approach we take to any poem is only one of various possible approaches. Jupiter does not speak in any of these comments. Jupiter speaks in the poems. The oracles that report him here are neither priests nor prophets, but fallible human beings like yourselves.

Laurence Perrine
Thomas R. Arp

Contents

Foreword iii

Part 1 The Elements of Poetry 1

Chapter one What Is Poetry? 1
1. Alfred, Lord Tennyson *The Eagle* 1
2. William Shakespeare *Winter* 1
3. Wilfred Owen *Dulce et Decorum Est* 1
4. Lawrence Ferlinghetti *Constantly risking absurdity* 2
5. Emily Dickinson *A bird came down the walk* 3
6. John Donne *The Triple Fool* 3
7. William Carlos Williams *The Red Wheelbarrow* 5
8. A. E. Housman *Terence, this is stupid stuff* 6

Poems for Further Reading 7

Chapter two Reading the Poem 8
9. Thomas Hardy *The Man He Killed* 8
10. A. E. Housman *Is my team ploughing* 8
11. Robert Frost *Mowing* 8
12. John Donne *Break of Day* 9
13. Emily Dickinson *There's been a death* 10
14. Mari Evans *When in Rome* 12
15. George Gascoigne *And if I did what then?* 12
16. Edwin Arlington Robinson *The Mill* 13
17. Sylvia Plath *Mirror* 14
18. Philip Larkin *A Study of Reading Habits* 14

Poems for Further Reading 15

Chapter three Denotation and Connotation 16
19. Emily Dickinson *There is no frigate like a book* 16
20. William Shakespeare *When my love swears that she is made of truth* 16
21. Robert Graves *The Naked and the Nude* 17

Exercises 18

22. Edwin Arlington Robinson *Richard Cory* 18
23. Henry Reed *Naming of Parts* 19
24. Ezra Pound *Portrait d'une Femme* 20
25. Langston Hughes *Cross* 21
26. William Wordsworth *The world is too much with us* 21
27. John Donne *A Hymn to God the Father* 23
28. Siegfried Sassoon *Base Details* 23

Poems for Further Reading 24

Chapter four Imagery 25
29. Robert Browning *Meeting at Night* 25
30. Robert Browning *Parting at Morning* 25
31. Richard Wilbur *A Late Aubade* 25

32. Robert Frost *After Apple-Picking* *26*
33. Emily Dickinson *A narrow fellow in the grass* *28*
34. Adrienne Rich *Living in Sin* *29*
35. Robert Hayden *Those Winter Sundays* *29*
36. Thomas Hardy *The Darkling Thrush* *30*
37. Gerard Manley Hopkins *Spring* *30*
38. John Keats *To Autumn* *31*
Poems for Further Reading *32*

Chapter five Figurative Language 1: Metaphor, Personification, Metonymy *33*

39. Frances Cornford *The Guitarist Tunes Up* *33*
40. Robert Francis *The Hound* *33*
41. Robert Frost *Bereft* *33*
42. Emily Dickinson *It sifts from leaden sieves* *34*
43. George Herbert *The Quip* *35*
44. Edwin Arlington Robinson *The Dark Hills* *36*
45. Emily Dickinson *A Hummingbird* *37*
Exercises *38*
46. Thomas Campion *There is a garden in her face* *39*
47. Robert Frost *The Silken Tent* *39*
48. Sylvia Plath *Metaphors* *40*
49. Philip Larkin *Toads* *41*
50. John Donne *A Valediction: Forbidding Mourning* *42*
51. Andrew Marvell *To His Coy Mistress* *42*
52. John Keats *To Sleep* *44*
53. A. E. Housman *Loveliest of trees* *45*
54. Langston Hughes *Dream Deferred* *46*
Poems for Further Reading *46*

Chapter six Figurative Language 2: Symbol, Allegory *47*

55. Robert Frost *The Road Not Taken* *47*
56. Dorothy Lee Richardson *At Cape Bojeador* *47*
57. William Blake *The Sick Rose* *48*
58. Archibald MacLeish *You, Andrew Marvell* *48*
59. Robert Herrick *To the Virgins, to Make Much of Time* *48*
60. George Herbert *Redemption* *49*
61. Robert Frost *Fire and Ice* *50*
62. Rupert Brooke *The Dead* *50*
63. Alfred, Lord Tennyson *Ulysses* *51*
64. Alastair Reid *Curiosity* *52*
65. Alan Dugan *Love Song: I and Thou* *53*
66. John Donne *Hymn to God My God, in My Sickness* *54*
67. Christina Rossetti *Uphill* *55*
68. Robert Frost *Dust of Snow* *56*
69. William Blake *Soft Snow* *56*
Poems for Further Reading *57*

Chapter seven   Figurative Language 3: Paradox, Overstatement, Understatement, Irony   58

70. Emily Dickinson *My life closed twice*   **58**
71. John Donne *The Sun Rising*   **59**
72. Countee Cullen *Incident*   **60**
73. Alexander Pope *On a Certain Lady at Court*   **61**
74. William Blake *The Chimney Sweeper*   **61**
75. Percy Bysshe Shelley *Ozymandias*   **61**

Exercise   **62**

76. John Donne *Batter my heart, three-personed God*   **63**
77. John Frederick Nims *Love Poem*   **63**
78. Sir John Harington *On Treason*   **64**
79. Donald W. Baker *Formal Application*   **64**
80. W. H. Auden *The Unknown Citizen*   **65**
81. Robert Frost *Departmental*   **66**
82. M. Carl Holman *Mr. Z*   **67**
83. Robert Browning *My Last Duchess*   **68**

Exercise   **70**

Poems for Further Reading   **70**

Chapter eight   Allusion   71

84. Robert Frost *"Out, Out—"*   **71**
85. William Shakespeare *Excerpt from* Macbeth   **72**
86. e. e. cummings *in Just-*   **72**
87. John Milton *On His Blindness*   **72**
88. John Donne *Hero and Leander*   **74**
89. Keith Jennison *Last Stand*   **75**
90. Edwin Arlington Robinson *Miniver Cheevy*   **75**
91. William Butler Yeats *Leda and the Swan*   **76**
92. T. S. Eliot *Journey of the Magi*   **77**
93. Emily Dickinson *Abraham to kill him*   **78**
94. Emily Dickinson *Belshazzar had a letter*   **78**
95. Anonymous *In the Garden*   **79**

Exercises   **79**

Poems for Further Reading   **80**

Chapter nine   Meaning and Idea   81

96. Anonymous *Little Jack Horner*   **81**
97. Sara Teasdale *Barter*   **81**
98. Robert Frost *Stopping by Woods on a Snowy Evening*   **81**
99. William Cullen Bryant *To a Waterfowl*   **81**
100. Robert Frost *Design*   **81**
101. John Donne *The Indifferent*   **83**
102. John Donne *Love's Deity*   **83**
103. Gerard Manley Hopkins *The Caged Skylark*   **85**
104. Philip Larkin *Aubade*   **85**
105. Archibald MacLeish *Ars Poetica*   **86**

Chapter ten   Tone   88

106. W. H. Davies *The Villain*   **88**

107. Emily Dickinson *Apparently with no surprise* 88
108. William Butler Yeats *The Coming of Wisdom with Time* 88
109. Michael Drayton *Since there's no help* 88
110. Robert Frost *The Telephone* 89
111. John Wakeman *Love in Brooklyn* 90
112. Emily Dickinson *One dignity delays for all* 91
113. Emily Dickinson *'Twas warm at first like us* 91
114. Alfred, Lord Tennyson *Crossing the Bar* 93
115. Thomas Hardy *The Oxen* 93
116. John Donne *The Apparition* 94
117. John Donne *The Flea* 94
118. Alexander Pope *Engraved on the Collar of a Dog Which I Gave to His Royal Highness* 98
119. Anonymous *Love* 98
Exercise 1 98
A Further Exercise 99
Poems for Further Reading 99

Chapter eleven Musical Devices 100

120. Ogden Nash *The Turtle* 100
121. W. H. Auden *That night when joy began* 100
122. Gerard Manley Hopkins *God's Grandeur* 101
123. A. E. Housman *With rue my heart is laden* 102
124. Gwendolyn Brooks *We Real Cool* 103
125. Emily Dickinson *As imperceptibly as grief* 103
126. Carl Sandburg *The Harbor* 104
127. John Crowe Ransom *Parting, Without a Sequel* 105
128. Ralph Pomeroy *Row* 107
129. Edna St. Vincent Millay *Counting-Out Rhyme* 107
130. William Stafford *Travelling Through the Dark* 108
131. Robert Frost *Nothing Gold Can Stay* 109
Poems for Further Reading 110

Chapter twelve Rhythm and Meter 111

A Note on Scansion 111
132. George Herbert *Virtue* 111
Exercise 112
133. William Blake *"Introduction" to* Songs of Innocence 113
134. Robert Frost *It takes all sorts* 113
135. A. E. Housman *Epitaph on an Army of Mercenaries* 114
136. e. e. cummings *if everything happens that can't be done* 115
137. A. E. Housman *Oh who is that young sinner* 116
138. William Butler Yeats *Down by the Salley Gardens* 117
139. Walt Whitman *Had I the Choice* 117
140. Robert Frost *The Aim Was Song* 117
141. Samuel Taylor Coleridge *Metrical Feet* 117
Exercise 118

Chapter thirteen Sound and Meaning 119

142. Anonymous *Pease porridge hot* 119
143. William Shakespeare *Song: Hark, Hark!* 119

144. Carl Sandburg *Splinter*   **119**
145. Robert Herrick *Upon Julia's Voice*   **119**
146. Robert Frost *The Span of Life*   **119**
Exercise   **120**
147. Alexander Pope *Sound and Sense*   **121**
148. Emily Dickinson *I like to see it lap the miles*   **123**
149. Ted Hughes *Wind*   **124**
150. Gerard Manley Hopkins *Heaven-Haven*   **125**
151. Wilfred Owen *Anthem for Doomed Youth*   **125**
152. A. E. Housman *Eight O'Clock*   **127**
153. James Joyce *All day I hear*   **128**
154. Emily Dickinson *I heard a fly buzz when I died*   **129**
155. William Carlos Williams *The Dance*   **131**
Exercise   **132**
Poems for Further Reading   **132**

Chapter fourteen   Pattern   **133**

156. e. e. cummings *the greedy the people*   **133**
157. Anonymous *I sat next the Duchess at tea*   **134**
158. John Keats *On First Looking into Chapman's Homer*   **134**
159. William Shakespeare *That time of year*   **135**
Exercise 2   **137**
160. By various hands *A Handful of Limericks*   **138**
161. Dylan Thomas *Poem in October*   **138**
162. Matsuo Bashō/Moritake *Two Japanese Haiku*   **139**
163. William Shakespeare *From* Romeo and Juliet   **140**
164. John Donne *Death, be not proud*   **141**
165. Martha Collins *The Story We Know*   **143**
166. Randolph Stow *As he lay dying*   **144**
167. Anonymous *Edward*   **144**
168. Maxine Kumin *400-Meter Freestyle*   **146**
169. William Burford *A Christmas Tree*   **146**
Exercise   **146**
Poems for Further Reading   **146**

Chapter fifteen   Bad Poetry and Good   **147**

170. Anonymous *God's Will for You and Me*   **147**
171. Gerard Manley Hopkins *Pied Beauty*   **147**
172. Robert Francis *Pitcher*   **148**
173. George E. Phair *The Old-Fashioned Pitcher*   **148**
174. Walt Whitman *Come Up from the Fields Father*   **150**
175. J. H. McNaughton *The Faded Coat of Blue*   **150**
176. William Blake *A Poison Tree*   **153**
177. Granfield Kleiser *The Most Vital Thing in Life*   **153**
178. Richard Middleton *On a Dead Child*   **155**
179. John Crowe Ransom *Bells for John Whiteside's Daughter*   **155**
180. Emily Dickinson *Some keep the Sabbath going to church*   **157**
181. Anonymous *My Church*   **157**
182. Malcolm Cowley *The Long Voyage*   **159**

183. Sir Walter Scott *Breathes there the man* **159**
184. Eugene Field *Little Boy Blue* **160**
185. Coventry Patmore *The Toys* **160**

Chapter sixteen   Good Poetry and Great   162

186. John Donne *The Canonization* **162**
187. Robert Frost *Home Burial* **162**
188. T. S. Eliot *The Love Song of J. Alfred Prufrock* **163**
Poems for Further Reading   **163**

Part 2   Poems for Further Reading   164

189. Joan Aleshire *Slipping* **164**
190. A. R. Ammons *Providence* **164**
191. Matthew Arnold *Dover Beach* **165**
192. W. H. Auden *Musée des Beaux Arts* **167**
193. D. C. Berry *On Reading Poems to a Senior Class at South High* **167**
194. Elizabeth Bishop *One Art* **168**
195. William Blake *The Garden of Love* **168**
196. William Blake *The Lamb* **169**
197. William Blake *The Tiger* **169**
198. Lucille Clifton *Good Times* **171**
199. Samuel Taylor Coleridge *Kubla Khan* **172**
200. Emily Dickinson *Because I could not stop for Death* **173**
201. Emily Dickinson *I taste a liquor never brewed* **174**
202. Emily Dickinson *In winter in my room* **175**
203. John Donne *The Good-Morrow* **175**
204. John Donne *Song: Go and catch a falling star* **176**
205. Keith Douglas *Vergissmeinnicht* **177**
206. Carolyn Forché *The Colonel* **178**
207. Robert Frost *Acquainted with the Night* **179**
208. Robert Frost *Mending Wall* **180**
209. Isabella Gardner *Gimboling* **184**
210. Christopher Gilbert *Pushing* **184**
211. Robert Graves *Down, Wanton, Down!* **185**
212. Thomas Hardy *Channel Firing* **185**
213. A. E. Housman *Bredon Hill* **187**
214. A. E. Housman *To an Athlete Dying Young* **187**
215. Randall Jarrell *The Death of the Ball Turret Gunner* **189**
216. Ellen Kay *Pathedy of Manners* **190**
217. John Keats *La Belle Dame sans Merci* **191**
218. John Keats *Ode on a Grecian Urn* **192**
219. John Keats *Ode to a Nightingale* **194**
220. Galway Kinnell *Blackberry Eating* **195**
221. Etheridge Knight *The warden said to me* **196**
222. George MacBeth *Bedtime Story* **197**
223. Naomi Long Madgett *Midway* **197**

224. Andrew Marvell *A Dialogue Between the Soul and Body*
225. Cleopatra Mathis *Getting Out* *200*
226. Marianne Moore *Nevertheless* *201*
227. Ogden Nash *I Do, I Will, I Have* *201*
228. Howard Nemerov *Grace to Be Said at the Supermarket* *202*
229. Naomi Shibab Nye *Famous* *203*
230. Sharon Olds *The Connoisseuse of Slugs* *203*
231. P. K. Page *The Landlady* *205*
232. Linda Pastan *Ethics* *206*
233. Dudley Randall *Ballad of Birmingham* *207*
234. Alberto Ríos *Nani* *208*
235. Edwin Arlington Robinson *Mr. Flood's Party* *208*
236. Theodore Roethke *I Knew a Woman* *210*
237. Theodore Roethke *The Waking* *211*
238. William Shakespeare *Fear no more* *212*
239. William Shakespeare *Let me not to the marriage of true minds* *212*
240. William Shakespeare *My mistress' eyes* *214*
241. Gary Soto *Small Town with One Road* *214*
242. Wallace Stevens *The Death of a Soldier* *215*
243. Wallace Stevens *The Snow Man* *216*
244. May Swenson *Question* *217*
245. Jonathan Swift *A Description of the Morning* *218*
246. Dylan Thomas *Do Not Go Gentle* *219*
247. Dylan Thomas *Fern Hill* *220*
248. Jean Toomer *Reapers* *221*
249. John Updike *Ex-Basketball Player* *222*
250. David Wagoner *Return to the Swamp* *223*
251. Derek Walcott *The Virgins* *223*
252. Marilyn Nelson Waniek *Old Bibles* *224*
253. Robert Penn Warren *Boy Wandering in Simms' Valley* *225*
254. Walt Whitman *A Noiseless Patient Spider* *226*
255. Walt Whitman *There Was a Child Went Forth* *227*
256. Walt Whitman *When I Heard the Learn'd Astronomer* *228*
257. Richard Wilbur *The Mill* *229*
258. Nancy Willard *A Wreath to the Fish* *230*
259. Miller Williams *A Poem for Emily* *231*
260. William Wordsworth *I wandered lonely as a cloud* *232*
261. William Wordsworth *The Solitary Reaper* *233*
262. William Butler Yeats *Sailing to Byzantium* *234*
263. William Butler Yeats *The Second Coming* *235*
264. William Butler Yeats *The Wild Swans at Coole* *237*

part 1
THE ELEMENTS OF POETRY

Chapter one
What Is Poetry?

1. *Alfred, Lord Tennyson* **THE EAGLE** (page 5)

The first stanza presents what one sees looking at the eagle, perhaps looking up at him, with the sun above him and the blue sky around him. The second stanza is more concerned with looking down from the eagle's vantage point; it presents what *he* sees. The first stanza is more static (with "clasps," "close," "stands"), the second stanza more dynamic (with "crawls," "watches," "falls"). These are small points, but they help to organize the poem. The expressions mentioned in the first study question are all figurative. LP

2. *William Shakespeare* **WINTER** (page 6)

The words "merry" and "sings" are used *ironically* (see page 102).* LP

3. *Wilfred Owen* **DULCE ET DECORUM EST** (page 8)

The poem makes its bitter protest against the idea that dying for one's country is "sweet and becoming" by describing the agonizing death of one soldier caught in a gas attack during World War I. (We infer from the last two lines that the soldier is dead; what we witness in the poem is the anguish and horror of his dying.)
The speaker is a fellow-soldier, a member of the same patrol, and a witness of the dying. His account is given some time after the event (as measured by weeks or months), for he has re-experienced it in recurrent nightmares ever since (15–16).

---

*Unless otherwise specified, all page references in this manual are to the text of *Sound and Sense*, Seventh Edition.

From our knowledge of World War I and of the poet's own experience, we may infer that the speaker is English, that the gas shells were German, and that the action occurred in France or Belgium. The speaker has probably been furloughed back to England at the time of his account, for the person he ironically addresses as "My friend" would seem to be an older man who is patriotically recruiting teen-aged boys into the service of their country, or into readiness for it (the word "children" is undoubtedly an overstatement of their youth).

The simile in line 1 compares the soldiers' packs to sacks carried by beggars. The word "softly" (8) is particularly sinister, for it connotes something gentle but here denotes something deadly. The phrase "sick of sin" (20) means "sick from sin." The most remarkable image in the poem is the simile in lines 13-14. The mustard gas used in World War I was greenish in color, hence the man caught in it seems "as under a green sea . . . drowning." The under-ocean effect is enhanced by the fact that he is viewed by the other soldiers through the misty panes of their gas masks, which were like the goggles in the helmets used by deep-sea divers at the time. Finally, the man is literally drowning (being suffocated) in that his lungs are being deprived of oxygen; but the mustard gas also corrodes the lungs, thus leading to the uglier imagery in lines 21-24.

The theme of the poem is obvious: It is NOT sweet and becoming to die for one's country in modern warfare. LP

4. *Lawrence Ferlinghetti* **CONSTANTLY RISKING ABSURDITY** (page 11)

The poem compares the poet to a circus performer and entertainer—high-wire artist, acrobat, and clown ("a little charleychaplin man") who, apparently, will try to catch the leaping form of Beauty while balanced on the high wire of truth—an almost impossible feat. The extended simile (which includes metaphor and personification) emphasizes that the poet must be constantly entertaining (poetry must give pleasure), but that he is also concerned with such higher realities as truth and beauty. It also emphasizes that the poet's task demands the utmost skill and precision and involves constant risk: a false step by the high-wire artist can cause death; a slip by the poet in published work involves public exposure of ineptitude. The sublime and the ridiculous are often narrowly separated, but in their reviews critics are quick to flay the poet who strives for the first and falls into the second. Ferlinghetti shows his own agility as a performer with a constant flow of double meanings and "sleight-of-foot" tricks (the play upon "sleight-of-foot" is appropriate both for the high-wire artist who performs magic with his feet and for the poet who does it with metrical feet). Serious? Yes. Solemn? No.

The arrangement of words on the page mimics the succession of short hurried steps that the acrobat takes across the wire before pausing to balance himself anew. LP

5. *Emily Dickinson* **A BIRD CAME DOWN THE WALK** (page 12)

Besides its marvelously exact observation of a bird's behavior*, the poem shows the immense distance between the natural world of the bird and the human world of the speaker, as Charles R. Anderson points out in his excellent discussion [*Emily Dickinson's Poetry: Stairway of Surprise* (New York: Holt, 1960), pp. 117-19]. As long as it is unaware of the human presence, the bird goes naturally about its affairs. It eats an angle-worm, raw, as a human being would never do, and hops aside for a beetle, something normally beneath human notice. Then it drinks "*a* dew" from "*a* grass" (from the human perspective, dew and grass are collective entities: we speak of "the dew" and "the grass" and must specify "a drop of dew" or "a blade of grass" to see them as the bird habitually does. Notice how similarity of sound here suggests an unstated metaphor: the blade of "grass" is the bird's "glass" from which he drinks). In stanza 3 the bird intuits an alien presence, glances nervously all around, and stirs his head "like one in danger." When the human observer tries to bridge the gap between their two worlds, cautiously offering a friendly crumb, the bird's instinctive impulses take command, and it flies off swiftly, literally putting a distance between itself and the human observer.

In sound the first fourteen lines of the poem are unremarkable. There are a few mildly harsh words: "walk," "angle," "drank," "hopped," "beads," "crumb"; and there is an appropriately awkward juxtaposition of two stressed syllables in "hopped sideways." When the bird takes flight, however, moving into its natural element (line 15), the language turns magically euphonious: a succession of long *o*'s, "unrolled," "rowed," "home," "oars," "ocean") is combined with liquid *r*'s, *l*'s, *m*'s, and *n*'s, and with soft *v*'s and *f*'s, to create a beautiful flow of sound. The one slight interruption of this euphony comes in the last two lines with the alliterating *b*'s of "butterflies" and "banks" and the repeated *p*'s of "leap" and "plashless." The metaphorical image suggested is of a swimming hole in which butterflies leap off the banks of a pool into water; but since the "banks" and the pools are both really air, they make no splash and what we hear in the alliterative *b*'s and repeated *p*'s is those imaginary, nonexistent splashes.   LP

---

*Though never named, the bird is surely a robin. It eats worms; it has beady eyes and a velvet head; it is the right size; it is not one of a flock (like sparrows); and it allows the human presence nearer before taking flight than any other nontame, nonflocking bird. Robins were plentiful in Amherst (Dickinson's village) in spring and summer and are a favorite subject in her nature poems.

6. *John Donne* **THE TRIPLE FOOL** (page 13)

The speaker is (a) a poet and (b) a rejected lover. The complaint of a spurned lover was one of the commonest subjects for poetry in Donne's time; but, as so often in his poetry, Donne here takes a thoroughly conventional subject and gives it a thoroughly original treatment. Part of his originality is that, instead of complaining about his lady's coldness, he turns the blame for his unhappiness upon himself, calling himself a "triple fool." Another part of his originality is his exploitation of the modern idea that writing about one's suffering in a structured form has therapeutic value for the poet. But the originality is also manifest in finer details of the poem; for instance, in the choice of the unusual epithet "whining" attached to "poetry" (is he characterizing *all* poetry with this epithet or just the kind that complains about the cruelty of the poet's beloved?), and in the use of a "scientific" analogy for explaining the healing effect of expressing his grief in verse: ocean water (grief), he claims, is purged of its salt (bitterness) in its passage through narrow, crooked, underground ways ("rhyme's vexations") to freshwater lakes and streams (psychological health). (The word "rhyme" may be read literally here but is more profitably taken as a metonymy for verse in general; "rhyme's vexations" are the difficulty of finding words which exactly fit the writer's meaning and at the same time fulfill the requirements of both meter and rime.) But the main power of the comparison lies in the implicit link between the salt of ocean water and the salt of tears. In speaking of grief Donne mentions neither tears nor salt, but he knows that his readers will make the connection. But, having admired Donne's analogy, how do we judge it when we learn that Donne's "science" is false? Although Donne used the standard scientific explanation of his time for the difference between salt water and fresh water, we now know that the real explanation is almost the opposite of his: the salt in the ocean is deposited there by streams which dissolve it from the earth on their way from the lakes to the seas. How does this knowledge affect the worth of the poem? It may be too early to take up this discussion now, but at some time the differences between scientific truth, historical truth, and poetic truth must be confronted. It will be germane to other poems in our study, such as Donne's "A Valediction: Forbidding Mourning" (No. 50) and Keats's "On First Looking into Chapman's Homer" (No. 158).

It is important in reading this poem to determine with some accuracy how serious the poet or the speaker (are they the same?) is in calling himself a "triple fool." A careful reading reveals, I think, that the tone of the poem is relatively light. The speaker bears his follies lightly, humorously exaggerating each of his three claims for being a fool. He is not in despair. First, he claims that he is a fool for loving someone who does not return his love: "she" (the beloved woman) denies him; consequently, he asserts, he suffers "pains" and "grief." But he reneges on this assertion before he has finished making it, by saying, in lines 4-5:

> But where's the wiseman that would not be I
>   If she did not deny?

This purely rhetorical question pays extravagant tribute to the beloved, implying that she has so many desirable qualities that nowhere in the world could a wise man be found who would not want to trade positions with the speaker if the woman did not "deny" him. The speaker's folly is thus substantially diminished. He can hardly be thought too great a fool for seeking the love of so desirable a woman.

Second, he claims that he is a fool for expressing his grief in "whining poetry." But nothing he says in the rest of the first stanza supports this initial declaration. He develops the idea of the therapeutic value through a beautifully apt and ingenious comparison. The poet ends the stanza with a direct statement of his belief in the power of poetry to alleviate grief:

> Grief brought to numbers cannot be so fierce,
> For he tames it that fetters it in verse.

Third, he claims he is a fool because some musician may set his poem to music and sing it in a public concert. This song, while delighting other members of the audience, starts the poet's grief flowing again. But at this point he makes the most illogical statement in the poem. Love and grief are proper subjects for poetry, he claims, but not if it is *good* poetry—not if it pleases when it is heard; for then the triumph of love and grief over him are published abroad, and he becomes a "triple fool": first, for loving a woman who does not return his love; second, for expressing his grief in verse which alleviates the pain; third, for thus opening the possibility that his poem may be set to music and sung publicly, thereby (a) arousing once more his grief and (b) subjecting him to the embarrassment of letting the whole world know of his "folly."

The poem ends with a generalization: The biggest fools are not congenital idiots, but those who are "a little wise"—wise enough, perhaps, to perceive their folly. The speaker, basing this generalization on his own experience, has been wise enough to choose an extremely attractive and virtuous woman to fall in love with, is gifted enough to write a good poem about his grief, but is unlucky enough to prompt a gifted composer to set his words to music and sing them in public. We must quarrel, however, even with this last assertion. If he really is grieved and embarrassed by this third event (no act of his own), why does he write *this* poem ("The Triple Fool"), which can only make his follies even more widely known? Is he not sucking pleasure out of his grief? LP

7. *William Carlos Williams* THE RED WHEELBARROW (page 14)

The simplicity of this free verse poem inevitably leads students to question "What *does* depend upon these things, and *how* much is so much?" The answer is "human life," both as physical existence and as aesthetic experience.

Momentarily ignoring the visual details—"red," "glazed," and "white"—one might investigate the importance of the objects. A wheelbarrow is a basic farm implement associated with the most primitive stage of human toolmaking, only one step advanced beyond the use of sledges or unwheeled barrows for dragging heavy loads. Rain water is obviously an essential for farming as for all life, and chickens provide two common foodstuffs in their flesh and in their eggs. The objects, that is, can be seen as among the most basic in providing physical sustenance, and much therefore "depends upon" them.

By contrast, the visual imagery is nonutilitarian. Although paint does protect against rot and rust, the color red has no specific usefulness. The glazing of rain (and the potential rotting of wood that it implies) is more potentially harmful than beneficial, and a chicken is an egg-layer and a source of meat whatever its color. These visual references thus run counter to the utilitarian functions of the objects they adorn. But they provide contrasts and harmonies of color, shape, and texture, basic to aesthetic enjoyment. White and red are clear contrasts, as are a shiny glaze contrasted to the downy softness of a chicken's feathers. While there is a contrast between the living and nonliving objects, one may also see a vague similarity in the triangular shapes of a wheelbarrow and a pecking chicken. (It helps students to see this if blackboard sketches are provided.)

The poem thus offers two distinct dependences: we depend upon farmers for our food (and they depend upon nature in producing it), and as sensitive observers we depend upon visual perceptions to feed us aesthetically. TRA

8. *A. E. Housman* TERENCE, THIS IS STUPID STUFF (page 14)

Housman's poem compares the efficacy of three things for helping one lead a satisfactory life: cheerful poetry, liquor, and pessimistic poetry. The first two, by making one "see the world as the world's not," arouse expectations that life can rarely fulfill. The result is disappointment and disillusionment. Pessimistic poetry, by truly picturing a world containing "much less good than ill," prepares one for the troubles that are sure to come. Thus fortified, one can withstand their shock and lead a satisfying life.

In the first verse-paragraph a friend playfully criticizes Terence (Housman) for the kind of poetry he writes and gives a delightful parody of it in the two lines (7-8) about the cow. Reading his poetry, the friend claims in a humorous overstatement, is driving Terence's friends mad and causing them to die before their time. He pleads with Terence to write cheerful poetry instead.

Terence replies that if his friend wants gaiety and cheer, liquor is more efficacious than poetry. It makes the world seem a "lovely" place and oneself a "sterling" lad. The only trouble is that this picture is "all a lie." By implication, cheerful poetry likewise misrepresents the world. Liquor and optimistic poetry are for "fellows whom it hurts to think." Their effect is temporary and ultimately enfeebling. They offer escape, not a solution.

In the first six lines of the third section Terence sums up his philosophy. To train for ill is to prepare oneself for the world as it is. One can do this by reading the kind of poetry Terence writes. It will strengthen "heart and head" and prepare one's soul for adversity. Many students misread the poem at this point. They fail to see that "the stuff I bring for sale" is Terence's poetry, metaphorically compared to a bitter brew that is "not so brisk" (so intoxicating) as the literal ale of the second-verse paragraph. Its "smack is sour" because it was wrung out of bitter experience.

In the final section Terence clinches his point by telling a parable. Mithridates immunized himself to poison by first taking a little and then gradually increasing the dosage. As a result Mithridates lived a long and satisfactory life. Similarly, Terence implies, one can immunize oneself against the troubles of life by reading the kind of poetry Terence writes.   LP

POEMS FOR FURTHER READING

Poems 245 and 260 from Part Two provide additional illustrations of topics presented in this chapter.

Chapter two
Reading the Poem

9. *Thomas Hardy* THE MAN HE KILLED (page 19)

The hesitations and repetitions of stanza 3 beautifully reflect the thought processes of the speaker. The pause after "because" (9) occurs because he is groping for an explanation. When he finds one, he must repeat the "because." He then has to convince himself that this answer is correct and sufficient. He does this (or tries to do it) by telling himself three times emphatically that it is: (1) "Just so"; (2) "my foe of course he was"; (3) "That's clear enough." But despite this triple emphatic effort at self-assurance, we know that the attempt is unsuccessful, as it trails off into "although..." LP

10. *A. E. Housman* IS MY TEAM PLOUGHING (page 21)

The word "bed" signifies literally the bed that the living man sleeps in, metaphorically the grave that the dead man lies in, and symbolically a lot in life, or condition of existence. The word "sleep" has corresponding meanings: of sleeping, of being dead, and of having a certain lot. In addition, it gathers up from the last stanza the meaning of sleeping with a woman, that is, of making love.

The poem at first seems cynical, suggesting, as it does, the transience of human loyalties. On reflection, however, few people expect a man or woman not to remarry after a first mate has died. (Housman's poem probably doesn't refer to marriage, but the principle is the same.) In general, Housman's poetry is pessimistic about man's chances for happiness, but Housman is not cynical about human courage or human virtue. LP

11. *Robert Frost* MOWING (page 25)

The effectiveness of line 13 proceeds from the shock of paradox. Paradox, discussed in Chapter 7, is an apparent contradiction which is nevertheless somehow true—a self-contradictory truth. The statement in line 13 identifies two things usually regarded as opposites: *fact* and *dream*. It says that fact *is* a dream ("the sweetest dream," *in fact*, that "labor knows"). The paradox is resolved when we realize that the word "dream" has two different meanings. In one sense a dream is an illusion, something insubstantial and untrue ("He woke in the morning and found it was only a dream"). In this sense "dream" is indeed the opposite of "fact," fact being something irreducibly true or certain. But, in another sense, a dream is something we ardently wish for, a desire whose fulfillment seems out of our reach, unattainable yet not impossible (all that is meant in that trite phrase "making our dreams come true"). It is in this sense that the speaker in Frost's poem discovers that the "fact" (in this case the labor of mowing) is the sweetest thing he could wish for. The sheer joy of performing this task, and performing it well (laying the swale "in rows"), exceeds any pleasure that might proceed from "idle hours" or "easy gold"—whether as a lucky gift or as the wages of his labor. The work is its own reward.

The period at the end of line 13 is significant. First, it separates this line from the rest of the poem (since it follows a period as well as ends with one), thus giving the line the weight it deserves in summing up the theme of the poem. More importantly, it raises a question. Who speaks the line? A comma at the end would have reduced the answer to a single possiblity—the scythe. But the period gives it additional possibilities: It may be spoken (or left unspoken) by the scythe, the speaker, or the poet. (Or may the speaker here be taken as the voice of the poet?)

The orchises and the snake? Some readers, whenever a snake appears in a poem, will automatically identify it as a symbol of evil; and, indeed, the flowers and the snake here may remind any reader of Eden. But this snake, "bright green," is of a harmless garden variety, hardly the kind whose form Satan took in the Garden. Indeed, it enhances by its bright coloring the satisfactions gained by the speaker. The orchises add another element of beauty, though their "spikes" are "feeble-pointed," neither dangerous nor spectacularly beautiful, unlike the flowers in the Garden. We notice also that the man working "by the sweat of his brow" is not doing so as a *punishment*; rather, he finds *rewards* in his work. If one insists on reading a reference to Eden in the poem (and indeed we should not be dogmatic here), one can say that the poem says that the Edenic experience can be duplicated or enjoyed at times in *this* life—times when the human being feels in harmony with his surroundings, can rejoice in the beauty of a snake and of flowers, and finds joy in the work by which he earns his bread.

Some critics will find in the man's work with the scythe (laying the swale "in rows") a symbol of the poet's work in making a poem (laying out his material in lines). Indeed, the mower's work in this poem is an analogue of any creative labor where the worker finds his deepest gratification in the work itself. LP

12. *John Donne* **BREAK OF DAY** (page 26)

The situation presents two lovers in bed. The man has just remarked "It's day!" (or something of the sort) and has made a gesture toward getting up. The woman's reply is a protest against his leaving. In the three stanzas of the poem she suggests three reasons why he might be thinking of leaving (because it's light; because he fears to expose their relationship; and because he has business to attend to; and shows each in turn to be invalid. The second of these concerns shows that the lovers are unmarried.

The speaker is conclusively proved to be the woman by her use of the pronoun "him" in line 12. Additional evidence is offered by the following considerations: (a) it was the woman who, under the double standard of morality, risked her reputation ("honor") in an illicit relationship; (b) a man would have been more likely than a woman to be drawn away by "business"; (c) the speaker makes her complaint against "the busied man," not the busied *person*; (d) the speaker compares the offender to a "married man" who woos another, not a married *person*, married *woman*, or *wife*.

Lines 15-16 may be read as meaning either (a) Love (personified as a sovereign) can admit the poor man, the foul man, even the false man into her province, but cannot admit "the busied man," or (b) The poor man, the foul man, and the false man can admit love into their lives, but "the busied man" cannot. We do not have to choose between these two readings. Both make sense.

The woman clearly has a scale of values that puts love at the top. She is not ashamed of her relationship with the man (as shown in the second stanza). She has committed herself to him and expects an equal commitment from him. His "business" threatens that commitment, and she is jealous of it as she would be jealous of any rival. Their love is as sacred to her as if legitimatized by marriage; he cannot have *two* mistresses: "business" and her.

Though the arguments of the three stanzas are logically discrete, they are verbally linked. Stanza 1 is connected to stanza 2 by the repeated image of "light," stanza 2 to stanza 3 by the contrast of her "being well" and his having (possibly) "the worst disease of love." The poem's title not only means *Morning* but suggests the threatened separation ("break") between the lovers. Students may have to be guided through the figurative legerdemain of line 11. Light is personified (as a mute, unable to speak); it is metonymically linked with its source, the sun; and the sun is metaphorically compared to a large eye (which is in turn referred back as the sole anatomical feature of the personified Light). The sun may discover the two lovers in bed together but, having no tongue, it can spread no scandal; but, *even if it could* (the woman declares), she would not be shamed by anything it could say. LP

13. *Emily Dickinson* **THERE'S BEEN A DEATH** (page 27)

The speaker in this poem has not been informed of the death across the way and apparently does not know who has died. He is not one of the neighbors who "rustle in and out." Probably he is a visitor in the house from which he watches. But he is no stranger to the ways of country towns: he knows by the signs immediately and intuitively that a death has occurred. He is a sensitive observer, able to report and to interpret precisely and imaginatively what he sees and to enter empathetically into the thoughts and feelings of the children who hurry past.

What he focuses on is the difference that the death makes in the ordinary life of a house. The house itself seems to have a "numb" look, as if stunned by the unusual occurrence. Neighbors—mostly women, for their skirts "rustle"—come and go, offering help and sympathy. The sick room is ventilated, a mattress hung to air across the window sill. The children hurry by, scared, for death to them is mysterious and vaguely terrifying: they can think of the corpse only as "it," not as a person, and they wonder if "it" died on the mattress they see. The minister enters "stiffly," not relaxed: this is a solemn occasion, and he will be the most important person in the funeral ritual. He immediately takes command. The milliner and the undertaker arrive to measure—between them—the corpse for the coffin, the mourners for black veils and other mourning apparel, and the house itself for getting the coffin in and out and perhaps for hanging with crepe bunting. (The word "house" is used, throughout the poem, as a metonymy to indicate, not just the house itself, but the activity and the people around and within it, including the corpse. It is not the house itself that is "numb" but the people within it; but the house itself seems to reflect this numbness in the way its window opens. Even the minister reflects it in his stiffness.) The speaker concludes with an account, not of what he sees, but of what he knows will soon be seen—the funeral procession of black coaches hung with tassels that will take the body and the mourners to the cemetery. He then generalizes his opening observation—how easy it is to tell when a death has occurred in a country town.

Some students will have difficulty with the tone of this poem, seeing it or the people in it as regarding death callously, impersonally, or coldly. The mistake may result from misinterpreting the role of the speaker (who is an observer, not a participant) or from misconceiving the "numb" look (which signifies, not lack of emotion, but the stunned state following or accompanying too much emotion) or from identifying the attitude of the children toward the corpse with that of the adults or the observer. The poem focuses on the outside of the house, not on the dead person, because that is what the observer sees; but all of the activity he sees results from the presence of the dead person within. The tone of the poem reflects the awesomeness of death and its solemnity. Part of the speaker's attitude is revealed in his reference to the undertaker as the man of the "appalling" trade (in the double sense of "horrifying" and "putting a pall on" a coffin) and to the funeral procession as a "dark" parade (dark literally because of the black badges of mourning but with the additional connotations of mystery and awesomeness).

Though written by a woman, this poem has a male speaker. Donne's "Break of Day," though written by a man, has a female speaker. An instructive point can be made from this juxtaposition. LP

14. *Mari Evans* **WHEN IN ROME** (page 28)

The first speaker is a white woman, the second her black maid. We are given only the unspoken thoughts of the second speaker, hence the inclusion of her words in parentheses.

Though the white employer's words take the outward form of affection and solicitude ("Mattie dear . . . take / whatever you like"), their tone, without her realizing it, is subtly patronizing. The invitation to take "whatever you like" is qualified by "don't / get my anchovies / they cost / too much!" And her utter ignorance of what the black servant likes to eat betrays the essential emptiness of her solicitude. The phrase "take / whatever you like / to eat" functions on two levels: *take whatever you wish to take*, and *take whatever you like to eat*. (There is almost nothing in the icebox that the black woman really *likes*.)

The black woman's attitude is one of repressed antagonism. Consciously or unconsciously, she knows she is being patronized, and though she is accustomed to speaking outwardly in terms of respect ("yes'm"), her resentment expresses itself through the use of irony: "what she think, she got— / a bird to feed?" and "yes'm. just the / sight's / enough!" The last phrase can be read in two ways.

The title and the conclusion are an allusion to the familiar saying "When in Rome, do as the Romans do." Rome in the poem serves as a metaphor for the white world, and the speaker is tired of having to eat what whites like to eat rather than what blacks like to eat.   LP

15. *George Gascoigne* **AND IF I DID WHAT THEN?** (page 29)

The first speaker is the mistress, quoted by the lover who goes on to narrate his reaction and quote his response to her. This little drama begins in the middle (after she has said—and perhaps done—something to make the speaker suppose she has been unfaithful to him) and concludes before its final outcome, for we cannot know either her response to his statements nor what actions if any they provoked. The focus, then, is not on the *actions* performed either before or after this exchange, but on her statement, his confusion, and his statement.

"There are plenty of fish in the sea" is an ancient phrase of consolation for loss: you've lost this fish, but there are plenty of others for you to catch. This the mistress says, and adds that anyone who counts on catching and keeping a particular fish is only causing himself grief. But we shouldn't overlook the conditional "if" with which she begins: he has accused her of infidelity, but she neither denies nor confesses, only says *if* she has been unfaithful, any grief he feels is his fault and not hers: he should never have counted on exclusive possession of her.

This aggressive behavior of hers completely confuses him, for he was apparently ready to argue against a denial or to forgive a confession—he was at least not at all prepared to be asked to defend *his* attitude. And so, with more force than the words now have, he is amazed with doubt (good sixteenth-century meanings would yield the paraphrase "panic-stricken with fear") when she pops her casual and insignificant question. After some moments of perplexity, he manages to pick up on her use of the trite metaphor, and extends it to the end of the poem, affirming that he will live with his loss, refuse consolation, and await the day when he can ridicule other men who discover her infidelities as he has done.

As a noun, "fish" is a metaphor for woman, as a verb it is a metaphor both for courting and for capturing; "the sea" is a metaphor for the social world. The sobriety of a poem about losing (or supposing one has lost) the love of a mistress is tempered by the speaker's wit in extending her cliché at such length: if the speaker was momentarily nonplussed, he quickly managed to find his tongue, and to exploit the situation wittily. As the curtain does not fall on this drama, we cannot know whether such sprightly word-play leads her to a pleasant rejoinder—but we might notice that all this exchange occurred "once" (5) in the past, with the potential implication that such an event is now the material for recollection and amusement. Such an implication would be consistent with court-poetry of Gascoigne's sort.   TRA

16. *Edwin Arlington Robinson*   THE MILL (page 30)

"The Mill" was first published in 1920. Its setting is earlier, sometime during the industrial revolution, probably late in the nineteenth century. The miller's remark (5) means that individual millers are no longer able to make a living: they are being replaced by industrialization.

This poem furnishes a good opportunity for taking up the issue of clarity and obscurity. Clarity is a supreme virtue in expository prose: we want our students to be perfectly lucid in their own writing. In poetry and fiction clarity is still a virtue, but not a supreme one. It takes second place to power and richness of meaning. A poem should be as clear as it may be without sacrificing something more important.

Certainly, Robinson has not been at pains to be perfectly clear about what happens in this poem. The miller's remark (5) is cryptic. We are not told "what else there was" (13) in the mill, or "what was hanging from a beam" (15), or where the miller's wife went (16), or what kind of "way" she is thinking of (19), or what ruffles the water (23). But surely this story of a double suicide gains in power exactly *because* it is not at first perfectly clear. The reader feels a growing horror as its meaning gradually dawns on him, as bewilderment shifts to suspicion and suspicion to certainty. If we change "what was hanging from a beam" to "his body hanging from a beam," the poem is made clearer, but its effect is greatly weakened. We no longer experience the terror of the half-seen.

Obscurity in a poem may arise from various causes, including the poet's ineptitude. It is not always as integral a part of meaning as it is here. But it can be. The point can be driven home by analogy to the person who spoils a joke by explaining it. A joke, too, is a small work of art. It must not be made so clear that its effect is destroyed.

This poem is briefly discussed by Wallace L. Anderson in *Edwin Arlington Robinson: A Critical Introduction* (Boston: Houghton Mifflin, 1967), pp. 103-04. LP

17. *Sylvia Plath* MIRROR (page 31)

Although the speaker is the personified mirror, who in the second stanza goes on to personify itself as a lake, the subject of the poem is the woman who looks into the mirror and learns the truth of the changes in her appearance that time brings. Like a person, the mirror looks outward, observing—and meditating about—the objects that come into view. But unlike a person, the mirror has no preconceptions, does not distort its vision with emotional responses. It is godlike in its detached truthfulness, even if it is a little god with a limited area of observation.

As a lake (and perhaps like a pool into which Narcissus plunged in adoration of his own beauty), the mirror still will give only the truth about the surface of reflections, no matter how the woman might want to find a deeper truth. Candlelight and moonlight, which cast flattering dim gleams of romantic imagination, are by comparison with the mirror's faithful images "liars."

What the searching woman finds in the truthful reflection is the sad fact of aging: the little girl that she was is now dead, and the old woman that she will become lurks in the depths of time, waiting to appear and terrify her. TRA

18. *Philip Larkin* A STUDY OF READING HABITS (page 31)

Even the slow student should see that neither the language nor the attitudes of the speaker in this poem could possibly be those of a poet. To clinch the case, one can point out that Philip Larkin was by profession a librarian.

The speaker is a weak person, unable to face reality, who escapes reality as boy and adolescent by reading "escape" fiction, either in pulp magazines or in paperbacks. As a boy (stanza 1) he identifies himself with the virtuous hero, the man who overcomes villainy by physical force. As an adolescent (stanza 2) he vicariously engages in sex escapades by identifying with the bold villain (Dracula type) or the picaresque hero (James Bond type). As a young man he reaches a stage at which reading no longer conceals from him his own failures—he now recognizes himself in the weak secondary characters—and he must find escape in alcohol.

Even better than Hardy's "The Man He Killed" (page 19), this poem demonstrates that poetry need not be made out of lofty, dignified, exquisite, or even original language. The language here is vulgar, slangy, and trite; yet it is perfectly chosen to express the intellectual poverty of its speaker. The good poet chooses his words, not for their beauty or elegance, but for their expressiveness—that is to say, their maximum appropriateness to subject, situation, and speaker. Trite language need not make a trite poem, as this piece effectively demonstrates. And even working within the limitations of deliberately trite language, Larkin achieves striking effects. The word "ripping" (10), for instance, has not only its slang meaning of "exciting" or "great" but also its literal meaning (here) of "ripping the clothes off of"—a doubleness of which the poet was probably aware, the speaker unaware. The student might be asked to paraphrase this poem in genteel or "correct" literal English, to see what it loses by such treatment.

In "Terence, this is stupid stuff," Housman agrees with the speaker that "ale's the stuff to drink" for "fellows whom it hurts to think" and that one should "Look into the pewter pot / To see the world as the world's not"; but for wiser fellows, Housman recommends reading. However, Housman is recommending quite a different kind of reading from that engaged in by Larkin's speaker; he is recommending a kind in which one can "see the world" as the world *is*. Thus, Housman is in diametrical disagreement with Larkin's speaker, and probably in perfect agreement with Larkin himself. LP

POEMS FOR FURTHER READING

Poems 198 and 222 from Part Two provide additional illustrations of topics presented in this chapter.

Chapter three
Denotation and Connotation

19. *Emily Dickinson*   **THERE IS NO FRIGATE LIKE A BOOK** (page 34)

Miles suggests a measurable and therefore a lesser distance than "lands"; also, it suggests distance only. "Lands" suggests not only distance but difference—not only far lands, but foreign lands, perhaps even fairylands. The connotations of *cheap* are unfavorable; of "frugal," favorable. "Prancing," besides participating in the alliterative sequence of "a page / Of prancing poetry," brings to mind the metrical effects of poetry and the winged horse Pegasus, symbol of poetry in Greek mythology. LP

20. *William Shakespeare*   **WHEN MY LOVE SWEARS THAT SHE IS MADE OF TRUTH (Sonnet 138)** (page 35)

Because of the pun on *lie*, students frequently misconceive the tone of this sonnet as light. It might better be called dark. The pun is grim, not merry. Trapped in a love affair that he knows to be unworthy of him, too weak to break loose, the speaker cynically resigns himself to continuing it, though he knows his mistress is unfaithful. He cannot leave the honey-pot; it has become a "habit."

The attraction of the affair is sensual, as shown by the two meanings of "lie"—conjunction at the physical level, separateness at the spiritual. Not only do the two lovers lie to each other, the speaker lies to himself, and *knows* that he lies to himself. He *pretends* to believe the woman's lies (2) in the hope that she will think him young and naive (3-4), and he makes himself think in one part of his mind that the deception works (5) though he knows in another part that it does not (6). A no-longer young man—one who is fully learned in "the world's false subtleties," including his own—he has ambivalent feelings toward his mistress and toward himself. Line 11 is not mature wisdom but rationalization. Love's *best* habit is trust, not *seeming* trust. Mature lovers can accept each other's faults without needing to lie to each other about them, and the speaker would not feel insecure about his age if he were confident of his mistress' love for him.

The speaker is a number of years older than the woman and is uneasy about the discrepancy. He cannot be really *old*, else he would have no chance even in his own mind of making her think him young.

"Simply" (7) carries its older meaning of "foolishly" (cf. the nursery rhyme "Simple Simon met a pieman") while "simple" (8) means "plain" or "unadorned."

"Vainly" (5) primarily means "futilely" (cf. "in vain") but with overtones of "in such a way as to please one's vanity." "Habit" (11) is a garment or clothing and also a customary practice. "Told" (12) means both "spoken" and "counted." LP

21. Robert Graves   THE NAKED AND THE NUDE (page 36)

In "The Naked and the Nude" Graves is concerned with both semantic and human values. Though seemingly he uses differences in human behavior only to illustrate differences in the connotations of two words often regarded as synonyms, actually he is as much concerned with moral as with lexical values. This ambiguity begins in the first stanza. If Graves were talking only about words, his proper beginning would be "For me, *naked* and *nude* . . . ." or "For me, the words 'naked' and 'nude' . . . ." By introducing two definite articles and omitting italicization or quotation marks, Graves forces us to take "the naked and the nude" as people. At the same time, by having them "construed / As synonyms," he forces us to consider them as words. This duality of interest persists throughout the poem.

The moral qualities characteristic of the opposed kinds of people connoted by the two words are in part named in the last line of stanza 1 and in part suggested by the kinds of behavior shown in stanzas 2 and 3. In general, the naked are natural, honest, unashamed, unselfconscious, undesigning; they are swayed by some passion (love, truth, or justice) which carries them beyond mere self-concern. The nude, in contrast, are deceptive, sly, and designing; by artifice and trickery they seek to attract attention to themselves and arouse prurient desire for their own pleasure or profit.

But ambiguities and paradoxes abound. In stanza 2 Graves's three examples are lovers, doctors, and a Goddess. The lovers are deeply consumed by physical desire, but reciprocally and unashamedly so; their passion is a natural part of their love. The physicians, on the other hand, in their passion for diagnostic knowledge, are completely beyond physical desire. Notice, however, that, though the physicians illustrate the moral quality concerned, it is their patients who are "naked." Finally, the Goddess, nonhuman and immortal, will not be among those sent to the underworld by death in the final stanza. The shifts of category in the second and third examples are explainable by Graves's dual interest in lexical and moral values.

In stanza 3 the nude both boldly flaunt and slyly conceal their charms, like a dancer with fans or veils, to entice and hold the gaze of onlookers. "Draping by a showman's trick / Their dishabille in rhetoric," they are paradoxically both clothed and unclothed, nude but not naked. Thus arrayed in illusory attire, the nude assume a holier-than-thou attitude and pretend to be more modest than the plainly naked, while actually more seductive. The reference to "rhetoric" keeps the interest focused on semantic as well as moral values; the word "rhetoric" suggests verbal embellishment of the plain and unvarnished, just as "nude" suggests embellishment of the "naked."

Though, in stanza 4, both the naked and the nude tread the "briary pastures of the dead," it is clear that the nude, who in this world defeat the naked in terms of material reward, in the underworld will get their comeuppance. At this point, Graves is clearly talking about people, not about words. But, in this stanza, the poet keeps his interest in words alive by giving the word "naked" a brilliant new twist in connotation: in the last line of the poem it means, not just "unclothed," but "unprotected"—cruelly exposed to the lashes of the Gorgons' whips. Though both the naked and the nude may be pursued by the Gorgons (whose "long whips" suggest serpents torn from their hair), it is the nude who will suffer cruelly from their exposure.*

*This commentary is adapted and abridged from an item in *The Explicator*, 39 (Fall 1980), 36–38, by Laurence Perrine and Margaret Morton Blum.

EXERCISES (page 38)

1. (a) steed, (b) king, (c) Samarkand.
2. (a) mother, (b) children, (c) brother.
3. (a) slender, (b) prosperous, (c) intelligent
4. having acted foolishly.
5. A fast *runner* is one who runs swiftly; a fast *color* is one that doesn't run at all.
6. In the first example *white* suggests rare beauty; in the second it suggests extreme fear.

22. *Edwin Arlington Robinson* **RICHARD CORY** (page 39)

Despite the popularity and apparent simplicity of this poem, it is often badly misread by students, who reduce it to the platitude that "great wealth does not guarantee happiness." Such a reading ignores nine-tenths of the poem. What the poem actually says is much more terrifying: that good birth, good looks, good breeding, good taste, humanity, *and* wealth do not guarantee happiness. The poem establishes all these qualities as being Cory's, and the "people on the pavement" thought that Cory "*was* everything" (not "*had* everything") to make them wish that they were in his place. This larger meaning must be insisted on. "Richard Cory" may not be as great a poem as, say, Robinson's "Mr. Flood's Party," but it is a genuine poem, neither superficial nor cheap.

The word "gentleman" is used both in its modern sense of one who is well behaved and considerate of others and in its older sense of one who is well born. The first meaning is established by Cory's courteous and uncondescending "good morning" to the "people on the pavement" and by his being "admirably schooled in every grace." The second meaning is established by a constellation of words that, by their primary or secondary meanings, suggest aristocratic or royal privilege:

"crown," "favored," "imperially," "arrayed," "glittered," "king," "grace," "fine" ("crown" here means "top of the head," but it also a symbol of royalty; "clean favored" means "clean-featured," but "favored" is also "privileged"; "grace" means a "social nicety," but it is also the term used for addressing a duke; "in fine" means "in sum," but "fine" implies also a quality of character and dress. Notice how the adjective "quietly" before "arrayed" imbues Cory with good taste: he dresses finely but unostentatiously).

Cory's first name has as its first syllable the word *rich* and is the name of several English kings, including the gallant Richard *Coeur de Lion*. His last name has a sonorous sound and is a good English name such as might belong to the New England landed gentry. It is in addition suggestive of such French words as *cor*, hunting horn; *coeur*, heart; and *cour*, royal court.

It is not just that "pavement" alliterates with "people." A pavement is lower than a sidewalk: it establishes the commonness of the "people" in contrast with the higher status of Cory; it has the "people" looking up at him.

The surprise ending is not there for its own sake. By setting up an ironic contrast, it suggests a number of truths about life: that we cannot tell from outside appearance what may be going on inside a person; that often the people we envy have as many troubles as we, or more; that, as has been said above, birth, wealth, breeding, taste, and humanity do not ensure a happy life.

There is an excellent discussion of this poem in Norman C. Stageberg and Wallace L. Anderson, *Poetry as Experience* (New York: American Book Company, 1952), pp. 188-92. I expand slightly on the present discussion in *The Art of Total Relevance: Papers on Poetry* (Rowley, Mass.: Newbury House, 1976), pp. 97-99.
LP

23. *Henry Reed* NAMING OF PARTS (page 40)

The poem presents a corporal or sergeant giving instruction to a group of army trainees. There are two "voices" in the poem, but their dialogue is conducted within the mind of one person, probably that of a recruit. The first three-and-a-fraction lines of all but the last stanza are the spoken words of the sergeant as heard by the recruit. The last two-and-a-fraction lines of these stanzas, and the whole of the final stanza, are the unspoken thoughts of the recruit. This interpretation can be disputed, for there is some ambiguity about the "speaker" in the poem. Exact determination, however, is unimportant. Whoever the "speaker" is, he is a sensitive person. His unspoken thoughts furnish a comment on the instruction he receives or is compelled to give.

The instruction takes place out-of-doors. It is spring. Not far off are gardens in blossom, with bees flying back and forth, cross-pollinating the flowers. The time apparently is just before or just after the outbreak of a war, during a period of rapid mobilization, for the equipment of the recruits is incomplete. Their rifles have no slings and no piling swivels.

The meaning of the poem grows out of the ironic contrast between the trainees and the gardens, both of which have symbolical value.

Besides lacking slings and piling swivels, the trainees have not got a "point of balance," in one sense the point on the rifle at which it balances on the finger, in another sense a psychological point of balance in their lives. Living in barracks, apart from wives and sweethearts, they are living an unnatural kind of life. Their lives are incomplete, like their equipment. By learning the parts of the rifle, they are preparing to kill and be killed. They are living a regimented life. Being raw recruits, they are awkward. Their lives are tedious, as expressed by the repetition of dull phrases. The rifle is a mechanical instrument, and their lives are likewise mechanical.

The gardens represent the natural, the free, the graceful, the beautiful, the joyous—everything that is missing from the lives of the trainees. The bees, by fertilizing the flowers, are helping to bring about new life. The trainees and the gardens thus symbolically represent a series of opposites: death versus life, incompleteness versus completeness, the mechanical versus the natural, regimentation versus freedom, awkwardness versus grace, drabness versus beauty, tedium versus joy—the list can be extended. Through this ironic juxtaposition, the poet indirectly makes a statement about the kind of life imposed on man by war and preparation for war.

The poem is heavy with sexual implications, and, if handled with tact, discussion of these will open up a further dimension of meaning. If handled clumsily, such discussion will give this aspect of the poem a false emphasis and send students away thinking it a "dirty" poem. Men segregated from women tend to become obsessed with sex and to think of women as sexual objects rather than as persons. The absence of normal contacts between the sexes is one reason for the lack of a "point of balance" in the recruits' lives. Many words and phrases in the poem symbolically or connotatively suggest sexual "parts" or actions: "thumb," "bolt," "breech," "rapidly backwards and forwards," "assaulting and fumbling," "cocking-piece." The instructor must rely on his own discretion as to how explicit to be about these matters, remembering that they are properly overtones and undertones, not the burden of the poem.

The language and rhythm of the poem beautifully support its central contrast. The words of the sergeant are prosy, and their rhythm is a prose rhythm, frequently faltering and clumsy. In the lines about the gardens, the words are beautiful, and the rhythm flows. The abrupt change in rhythm from smooth to halt is especially striking in the middle of line 17.

The poem is discussed by Richard A. Condon in *The Explicator* 12 (June 1954): 54. LP

24. *Ezra Pound* **PORTRAIT D'UNE FEMME** (page 41)

In fact the Sargasso Sea is a large area of relatively still water in the North Atlantic, bounded by rotating currents, notable for its great abundance of floating seaweed. In legend it is a place where ships have become hopelessly entangled in seaweed, a place where the ocean floor is littered with the half-buried hulks of ancient caravels, Spanish galleons, pirate ships, and men-of-war, a place which, originating nothing, has collected treasures from all over the earth and from all its centuries.

As such, it is the perfect image for the mind of the woman Pound is describing. A person of no original thought but of wonderfully quick and retentive memory, a good talker and listener and a charming companion, she has collected treasures from the minds of all the great men who have sought her out—not for a wife, but for a companion or mistress. Living, as it were, no life strictly her own, having no husband and no children, she has yet participated richly in the lives of others, and now her mind is full of entertaining anecdotes, curious suggestions, strange bits of knowledge, "Ideas, old gossip, oddments of all things." She has thus become an even more entertaining companion, and her conversation repays richly those who seek her out, though she is "second always"—has never been the emotional center of any one man's life. Her knowledge, furthermore, serves no practical use, but only makes her delightful company.

One dominating metaphor makes the poem. Weaving skillfully back and forth between literal statement and its figurative counterpart, Pound paints beautifully the strange wonder of the underwater world with its shifting half-lights and collected treasures, and gives at the same time an exact accounting of the life and mind of this woman in whom nothing, as Shakespeare puts it,

> But doth suffer a sea-change
> Into something rich and strange.

"You are a person of some interest," Pound says to the woman, "one comes to you / And takes strange gain away." The use of the word *interest* both in its ordinary and in its financial meanings illustrates Pound's unerring sense of diction. His words fit their context exactly, usually in more than one way. Here, the financial meaning fits into a series of other words suggesting money—*fee, price, pay, gain, riches.* The other meaning pertains literally to the attractions of her mind. LP

25. *Langston Hughes*   CROSS (page 42)

The speaker is a "cross" (literal) between black and white, and this is the "cross" (metaphorical) that he has to bear. There is also an overtone of the adjectival meaning "angry" in the title. LP

26. *William Wordsworth*   THE WORLD IS TOO MUCH WITH US (page 43)

This sonnet juxtaposes nineteenth-century Christian English faith in industrial development and mercantile values with a primitive faith in the pagan deities of nature. As one scholar puts it, it is in the traditional mode of the conflict between Christ and Pan, but the conflict is exacerbated by identifying Christianity with modern materialism and urban insensitivity to nature. Wordsworth places his speaker at a fulcrum: he is forlornly identified with the modern, and his own way of "glimpsing" natural vitality and harmony is by wishing he could be a pagan—though he knows intellectually that the beliefs of ancient Greece are "outworn."

The speaker stands in a grassy meadow on a calm moonlit night, in view of the sea. This placid and unspectacular situation makes him forlorn as he thinks of the worldliness that destroys emotional and imaginative responses to natural beauty. "We," including the speaker, have traded away the real power of imagination that we possessed; we "get" wealth, but we "spend" our hearts for it. Nature is no longer ours, nor we hers.

The opening quatrain abstractly generalizes, withholding the motive for the generalizations. It contrasts the presumed power of trade with the internal power of the imagination, and declares that the real cost of a materialistic value system is our hearts.

The second quatrain begins to set the scene, establishing the time and place: it is night, the sea is calm, the moon is bright, and the expected high winds of the seaside are subdued. The speaker poetically personifies sea and winds, an imaginative contrast to the philosophical generalizations of the first quatrain, representing the speaker's attempt to display his own sensitive image-making powers—but his images tend toward triteness, as lines 8-9 suggest by abruptly changing the tone to straightforward colloquialism. The phrase "for this, for everything" reveals a loss of imaginative concreteness, and the cliché "out of tune" emphasizes the speaker's failure either to feel or to create. As a transition from octave to sestet, these lines appear to give up the attempt to counter crass materialism with poetic originality.

Instead, beginning in line 9, the speaker swears (by his Christian God) his preference for a "pagan creed" that would allow him to believe in such mythical nature deities as Proteus and Triton, as antidotes for his forlornness. But in fact he was not "suckled" in such a creed and can summon up only a glimpse of these nature gods. ironically created for him by great Christian English poets of the past. "Pleasant lea" is quoted from Spenser's "Colin Clouts Come Home Again," a description of Colin's first view of England (line 283); the reference to Proteus alludes to Milton's *Paradise Lost* (III.603-604); and line 14 refers again to "Colin Clout": "Triton blowing loud his wreathèd horn" (line 245). Desiring to reach backward to a natural paganism, the speaker must rely on his Christian poetic heritage. Furthermore, he realizes that he cannot actually hold such beliefs, and is wistful about the "outworn" but imaginative mythological personifications of sea and wind, visible Proteus, audible Triton, representing a lost harmony between man and nature.

For further discussion of the mythical and literary allusions, see Douglas Bush, *Mythology and the Romantic Tradition in English Poetry* (Cambridge, Mass.: Harvard Univ. Press, 1937), pp. 58-59. TRA

27. *John Donne* A HYMN TO GOD THE FATHER (p. 44)

According to Izaak Walton, Donne's first biographer, this poem was written during a severe illness in 1623. It is a *confession* of sin and a *prayer* for forgiveness; but by its acknowledgment of the power and mercy of God, it becomes a *hymn* as well.

The first two lines refer to *original sin*, the sin we are all guilty of, by inheritance from Adam's sin in the Garden. Having "spun my last thread" means roughly "having reached the end of my life." The image derives from the Greek myth of the three Fates—Clotho, who spun the thread of life; Lachesis, who twisted it; and Atropos, who cut it short; but Donne has effectively simplified the myth. The *shore* is the shore on *this* side of the river or water which one must cross to reach eternal life.

The poet puns on his own name in the penultimate line of each stanza. In the first two stanzas the first *done* means "finished"; the second means both "finished" and "Donne." In the third stanza the first *done* means "performed" (as also in line 2), and the second again means both "finished" and "Donne."

In line 15 *thy Sun* is an obvious pun on "thy Son." It is particularly relevant because Jesus was God's agent to bring mercy to mankind, and this poem is a prayer for forgiveness.

In the final line of each stanza, the word *more* is a pun on the maiden name of Donne's wife. We must not think, however, that Donne regarded his marriage as a mistake or counted it among his sins. Rather, he subscribed to the "Neoplatonic belief that to rise to the love of God one must leave behind the love of 'creatures'"*; thus his continuing love for Anne is an obstacle to his reaching heaven.

It is worthy of notice that this eighteen-line poem involves only two rimes; and that the word *forgive* occurs four times, the word *sin* eight times, and the word *done* seven times. These repetitions along with the two-line refrain account for much of the poem's power. LP

*Two worthy articles on this poem, especially as to the pun on *more*, are "John Donne's Terrifying Pun," by Harry Morris, in *Papers on Language and Literature*, 9 (Spring 1973), 128-37; and "Donne's 'A Hymn to God the Father': New Dimensions," by David J. Leigh, in *Studies in Philology*, 75 (Jan. 1978), 84-92. My quotation comes from the first of these, p. 132.

28. *Siegfried Sassoon* BASE DETAILS (page 45)

The poem expresses the resentment of a front-line soldier in the First World War, exposed to the constant dangers, discomforts, and deprivations of trench warfare, toward the frequently casual attitudes and soft lives of officers assigned to staff duty at the base, safely located miles behind the front. Although we can't know his rank, the speaker is almost certainly an officer and is perhaps, like the poem's author, a captain. Company commanders (captains) and platoon commanders (subalterns) suffered the highest mortality rate during World War I because they had to lead their men "over the top" on charges across "No Man's Land" against withering enemy fire. The speaker expresses his bitterness through irony; he is really strongly averse to being the kind of person and living the kind of life he describes so deprecatingly.

The title expanded to manifest both its meanings might read "Ignoble Particulars about Officers Detailed for Duty at the Base."

"Fierce" is used ironically (fierce manner, inward timidity). "Scarlet" suggests the red face of someone who is choleric, acts fiercely, is short of breath, and drinks too much, as well as implying the red lapel tabs and cap bands worn by staff officers in the British army. "Puffy" means both short-winded and fat. "Guzzling and gulping" connotes gluttony. "Scrap" minimizes the seriousness and horror of battle by reducing it in importance to a street-corner altercation between kids. "Youth stone dead" has ambiguous reference: it may refer either to the utterly vanished youthfulness of the returning majors or to the young men left literally dead on the battlefields. "Toddle" suggests second childhood and senility. LP

POEMS FOR FURTHER READING

Poems 220 and 251 from Part Two provide additional illustrations of topics presented in this chapter.

Chapter four
Imagery

29. *Robert Browning*   MEETING AT NIGHT (page 47)

30. *Robert Browning*   PARTING AT MORNING (page 48)

The auditory imagery of "Meeting at Night" is strongly reinforced by onomatopoetic effects. In lines 5-6 the sound of the boat's hull grating against the wet sand of the beach seems echoed by the series of *sh, ch,* and *s* sounds in "pu*sh*ing . . . quen*ch* . . . *s*peed . . . *slushy* sand." In line 9 the sharp *p* of the onomatopoetic "ta*p*" is repeated in "*p*ane," and the *-tch* of the onomatopoetic "scra*tch*" is partially anticipated in "*sh*arp" as well as repeated in the rime.

Both meanings suggested for the last line of "Parting at Morning" are applicable. The "world of men" does need the contributions of the male speaker to its daily labors; and the speaker himself—as Browning's answer implies—needs the companionship of men as well as the love of a woman.   LP

31. *Richard Wilbur*   A LATE AUBADE (page 49)

An *aubade* (from a word meaning dawn) is a sunrise love song, a morning serenade, a lyric addressed at dawn to one's sweetheart. The word is used whimsically here, for, though the lovers have recently awakened, the time is almost noon. It is a very late aubade indeed. The woman has apparently made some gesture toward rising. ("It's almost noon," she has said. Implication: it's time to get up and go about one's business.) The man is pleading with her to stay in bed with him a while longer, and then to cap their lovemaking with some delicious snacks from the icebox.

Are these lovers unmarried? The question is irrelevant to the theme of the poem, and ought not to be raised. If students insist on bringing in a moral issue, however (and some will), one should be prepared to point out that the poem does not answer the question one way or the other. The lovers might be a recently married couple with no children as yet. They are in a house with two stories, not in a bachelor apartment, and the woman knows her way to the refrigerator.

The poem is a celebration of the delights of the senses. Both the woman, who would rather "lie in bed and kiss / Than anything," and the man, who orders up a connoisseur's menu from the kitchen, know how to savor these delights. The images chosen appeal to touch (kisses, chilled wine), to taste (wine, cheese, crackers, pears), and to sight. (Though white wine and blue cheese refer more to kinds than to colors, they suggest, when combined with "ruddy-skinned pears," a visual as well as a gustatory treat. The arrangement of items indeed suggests the eye of a painter, a Cézanne or Renoir, as well as the palate of an epicure.) All the images suggest a keen appreciation of such delights by the lovers, not coarse sensuality or gross overindulgence.

The poem belongs to the *carpe diem* tradition, famously exemplified by Herrick's "To the Virgins, to Make Much of Time," with its opening line "Gather ye rosebuds while ye may" (page 86). The theme of such poems is "Time flies; therefore enjoy to the fullest each moment as it passes."

The speaker in the poem is a cultivated person, familiar with "centuries of verse," with Schoenberg's music, with the appearance of old books ("liver-spotted pages"), and with the manner of library research ("sitting . . . in a carrel"). It is clear that he is thoroughly acquainted with the life of the intellect, but has not allowed intellectual interest to dull or dry up his delight in the senses. In listing the activities that the woman might otherwise be engaged in, he manifests a wry wit and describes each in a manner that makes it seem unattractive ("liver-spotted," "cage," "raucous," "screed," "unhappy," "bleak") beside the pleasure he proposes. The woman, we may infer, has qualities of mind and imagination similar to his own. He does not need to explain to her the "rosebuds-theme of centuries of verse"; he knows she will understand his references to "Schoenberg's serial technique" and to carrels and old books. He can apparently count on her for an appreciative response to his quiet humor. There is between them a mutuality of mind and taste. LP

32. *Robert Frost*   AFTER APPLE-PICKING (page 50)

Let us be clear from the start about one thing. The speaker in this poem has had a richly satisfying experience. He may be "overtired," but it is that good kind of overtiredness that comes when a man has worked hard and long at a task he loves and does well. There may be two or three apples he has overlooked somewhere, but what is that to the thousands he has harvested? No human task is done perfectly. The love he has felt for his task and the care he has put into doing it well are best expressed in lines 30–31:

> There were ten thousand thousand fruit to touch,
> Cherish in hand, lift down, and not let fall.

His love and the care he takes with each apple are beautifully expressed by the grammatical pauses, which slow down the rhythm and divide line 31 into three infinitive phrases, and seem to divide the action itself into separate phases, emphasizing each. His love for the task shines out radiantly from the word "Cherish." His care and concern are indicated by the paradoxical phrase "lift down." His conscientiousness for the quality of his work is further shown by his sending to the cider-apple heap every apple that falls to the ground, no matter how unblemished it appears on the outside. The whole harvesting experience is symbolized by the ladder which, one end planted firmly on earth, points with the other end "toward heaven." Like the speaker in "Mowing," this speaker can find in his work here on earth an almost heavenly joy.

Repetitive labor brings repetitive dreaming. When the speaker tells what form his dreaming is about to take, his dream continues the labor of the day, but on a larger scale: "Magnified apples appear and disappear / Stem end and blossom end, / And every fleck of russet showing clear." The dream experience blends into the working experience, so that in the lines that follow he is describing both. A rich use of imagery makes the experience vivid and exact: the visual imagery of the magnified apples; the tactile and kinesthetic image in "My instep arch not only keeps the ache, / It keeps the pressure of a ladder-round"; the kinetic image of "I feel the ladder sway as the boughs bend" (where the rhythm makes the line itself sway); the auditory image of "The rumbling sound / Of load on load of apples coming in." These figures of dream experience are one with the work experience. We are reminded again of "Mowing," where "The fact is the sweetest dream that labor knows." Earlier in the poem we have the olfactory image of "the scent of apples" together with the visual and tactile images of the thin ice skimmed from the drinking trough.

The time of the poem is the end of the day, the end of a season ("Essence of winter sleep is on the night"), and the end of the harvest. These endings, plus the drowsiness of the speaker and the six-times repeated reference to sleep, inevitably invite the reader to read symbolically. The symbolic implication is that sleep after a day's work represents death after a life's work. Four of the six references to sleep come in the last five lines of the poem where the speaker wonders whether his oncoming sleep ("whatever sleep it is") is like the woodchuck's sleep (hibernation) or "just some human sleep." The speaker does not answer the implied question, but insofar as the poem suggests an answer it is that, if there is a life after death, it will not differ much from the life lived here on earth, perhaps only as much as his dream differs from his waking life. The speaker has fulfilled his life here, and does not need a future life to complete it. The poem does not *say* that; it suggests it.

The phrase "ten thousand thousand" (30) is overstatement. The phrase "just some human sleep" (42) is understatement. At the literal level, the woodchuck's hibernation lasts much longer than man's winter sleep, but the hibernation is a comatose, torpid, dreamless state. Human sleep is shorter, but dream-filled.

This poem is iambic in meter but with irregular line lengths (ranging from six feet in line 1 to one foot in line 32) and with irregular riming: every line in the poem rimes with some other line, but without a fixed pattern. The longest separation of end-rimes is that of "heap" (35) and "sleep" (42) but internal rimes in between help bridge the gap.

The following discussions of this poem are useful: Robert Penn Warren, "Themes of Robert Frost," *The Writer and His Craft: Hopwood Lectures, 1932-1952* (Ann

Arbor: Univ. of Michigan Press, 1954) pp. 218-33; Reuben A. Brower, *The Poetry of Robert Frost: Constellations of Intention* (New York: Oxford Univ. Press, 1964), pp. 23-27; John Robert Doyle, Jr., *The Poetry of Robert Frost: An Analysis* (Johannesburg: Witwatersrand Univ. Press, 1962), pp. 26-31. LP

33. *Emily Dickinson* A NARROW FELLOW IN THE GRASS (page 52)

The subject of the poem is snakes and the (male) speaker's fear of them, and it is vividly rendered through Dickinson's effective use of visual, tactile, and visceral imagery and through her consistently surprising but precise word-choices.

The word "fellow" (twice used for the snake), when contrasted with nature's "people" (17), suggests someone of inferior class and breeding. The adjective "narrow" is exactly right for a snake, but who ever used it to describe one before? "Rides" suggests effortless motion, without legs. But the characteristic of the snake principally emphasized in the first two stanzas is the suddenness of its appearance. (The departure from normal word order in line 4 not only provides an oblique rime for line 2 but gives unusual emphasis to "sudden.") One is not aware of the snake's presence until the grass parts unexpectedly at one's feet and one catches a fleeting glance of "a spotted shaft"; then the grass closes again and opens further on, this time without revealing the snake. (The grass is not that of a mown lawn, but the ankle- or calf-deep grass of a field.)

Stanzas 3-4 indicate how alien to man is the snake's habitat and emphasize the suddenness of the snake's *dis*appearance. Though "occasionally" snakes come out to forage in a field or enjoy the sun, their preferred habitat is the swamp, land too wet and cool for man to use even for agricultural purposes. Yet the speaker "more than once" when "a boy, and barefoot" (thus vulnerable to snakebite) had come across one basking in the sun and, mistaking it for a discarded whip-lash, had stooped to pick it up, when it suddenly "wrinkled" and vanished.

The first two pairs of stanzas indirectly suggest the power of the snake to startle the speaker, whether by sudden appearance or disappearance. The last two stanzas, partly through effective contrast with each other, reveal the snake's power to inspire deep fear in him. With several of "nature's people" (e.g., squirrels, birds) he has struck up an acquaintance, and he feels for them "a transport / Of cordiality." But he has never met "this fellow" (the snake), either by himself or in the company of friends, "Without a tighter breathing / And zero at the bone." The images in the final two lines strike home with the shock of pure terror. "Tighter breathing," with its unexpected adjective, is precisely accurate for that feeling of constriction in the chest which makes it difficult to breathe. And to contrast with "cordiality" (warmth of heart) in stanza 5, we are given—not just a chill, or cold, or even freezing—but "zero" (the lowest point on the centigrade scale), and not at the heart but at the "bone" (cold piled upon cold).

Many students will have difficulty with the image of the "whip-lash / Unbraiding in the sun," the participle suggesting motion to them. But the basking snake is motionless. A whip-lash of braided leather left out in the sun too long will begin to dry out and disintegrate, its thongs loosening and cracking. The snake, with its mottled leather back, has a similar appearance. When the boy stoops to pick up what he thinks is a whip-lash, it suddenly comes to life and hurries off. LP

34. *Adrienne Rich*   LIVING IN SIN (page 53)

The central contrast of the poem is between glamorous expectation and realistic fulfillment. The central emotion is disillusionment. The woman had thought that "living in sin" with an artist in his studio would be romantic and picturesque. The phrase "living in sin" suggests (here) the free, unconventional Bohemian life. The word "studio" connotes something appealing, not just a top-story room in a walk-up flat. The sentence in lines 4-7 gives the picture that had arisen in the woman's mind when he had urged her to come live with him. She had not foreseen that the apartment might be dirty, creaky, and bug-infested, with noises in the plumbing—that furniture would have to be dusted, windows cleaned, beds made, and dishes washed—and that her lover would not be romantic all the time. The irony of the situation is that "living in sin" with an artist in his studio proves not much different from marriage to a workingman in a run-down apartment. LP

35. *Robert Hayden*   THOSE WINTER SUNDAYS (page 54)

The central images evoke coldness and heat, and are extended into the emotions reported and experienced by the speaker: his sense of cold indifference to his father in contrast to the emotional warmth expressed in the father's loving care, and in contrast to the warmth the speaker feels for his father now.

The father's actions all imply love: even on Sundays, when he need not rise early to work for his family's sustenance, he is the one who undertakes the task of driving coldness from the house. And he goes beyond the necessity of providing warmth, adding the care of his son's appearance (the "good shoes" that need to be polished for church).

The coldness is made especially vivid in the sensory images which describe it—"blueblack" in the pre-dawn darkness, and so solid and brittle that its retreat from the heat causes it to splinter and break. But the physical warmth of the house cannot dispel the emotional chill: the speaker flatly asserts that "no one ever thanked him," and the household continues to suffer from "chronic angers."

The poem moves from past to present time, and from memory to self-castigation, with the repeated lament "What did I know, what did I know." Thoughtless and indifferent childhood gives way before the mature knowledge "of love's austere and lonely offices," and the poem ends in regret and remorse. TRA

36. *Thomas Hardy* THE DARKLING THRUSH (page 54)

The end of the day, the end of the year, and the end of the century symbolically unite with the bleakness of the imagery in the first two stanzas of this poem to evoke a mood of utter desolation and hopelessness. The contrast between this desolation and the apparently unlimited joy of the thrush's song is the pivot on which the poem turns, and the contrast is so striking that it leads many students to read into this poem an optimism that is in fact not there. Conditioned by earlier experience with more cheerful poets and with sentimental cliché, they see in this poem the dark cloud with a silver lining, the tale of woe with a happy ending, darkness giving way to light, despair overcome by hope.

What the poem actually presents is subtler and less cheerful. The speaker is overcome with wonderment at the joy of the thrush's song, and momentarily—but only momentarily—he is prompted to wonder whether the bird may not know of some "blessed Hope." But, notice, he does not say that the thrush knew of some blessed Hope. He does not even say, "I thought [did think] . . . he knew," but only, "I *could* think . . . ." That is, it's *as if* the bird sang out of some blessed Hope. The speaker *could*—but didn't—think so. The thought has crossed his mind, but transiently, too swiftly to take up residence there. The speaker, after all, sees no cause for joy or hope "written" on the world around him. In the last line he flatly states that he is unaware of any hope. The bird sings, really, out of instinct, not out of knowledge, and at the bottom of his mind the speaker knows this. The poem concludes, than, not with hope, but only with the wistful wish that there *were* some reason for hope, and with wonderment at the mystery of the bird's joyous song. The conclusion of "The Oxen" (page 150) evokes a similar mood and presents a similar interpretive problem.

Image and mood blend perfectly in this poem. The simile of the "tangled bine-stems" that score the sky like "strings of broken lyres" is marvelously effective, both visually and emotionally exact, giving a sense of music destroyed, of something else come to an end—like the day, the year, the century. LP

37. *Gerard Manley Hopkins* SPRING (page 56)

Hopkins's poem is an Italian sonnet. The octave is descriptive, the sestet makes a religious application. The abstract statement of the first line is made concrete with rich particularized imagery in the rest of the octave, and this richness of imagery is supported throughout the poem by richness of sound—alliteration, assonance, consonance, interior rime, end rime.

In the sestet Spring is compared to the Garden of Eden, and this in turn to childhood. The three things thus compared have at least three things in common: (1) they are characterized by abundant beauty, sweetness, and joy; (2) they each occur at the beginning of something—the year, human existence, individual life;

(3) they are innocent, free of sin. But the mention of Eden reminds the poet that human beings were thrust out of paradise through the sin of Adam and Eve. He therefore exhorts Christ, the innocent "maid's child," to capture the minds of girls and boys before they too spoil their lives by sinning. The poem is—or ends in—a prayer.

The poem is as rich in associational connections as it is in imagery and sound. For example, blue, the color of thrush's eggs, is the color of the sky, thus of "heaven," and is also the Virgin Mary's color, symbolic of purity. White, the color of lambs and pear blossoms, symbolizes innocence, as do lambs themselves, which in addition have symbolic association with Christ. Thus religious connotations are already implicit in the octave, ready to be activated by the explicit references in the sestet.
LP

38. *John Keats* TO AUTUMN (page 56)

Opulently rich in imagery, "To Autumn" is also carefully structured. The first stanza deals with the ripening process, the second with harvesting activities, the third with natural sounds. Although each stanza blends various kinds of imagery, each gives prevalence to one kind. The first stanza is dominated by images of fullness and tension, a kinesthetic-organic imagery apparent in such words as "load," "bend," "fill," "swell," "plump," "budding," and "o'er-brimmed." The second stanza places greatest emphasis on visual imagery. The third stanza stresses auditory images, some of them onomatopoetic ("wailful," "bleat," "whistles," "twitter").

The poem is also structured in time, the three stanzas presenting a progression both in the season and in the day. The first stanza presents early autumn: fruit and nuts are coming to ripeness. The second stanza presents mid-autumn: harvesting is in process. The third stanza presents late autumn: the harvest over, stubble-plains remain, and the swallows gather for their migration southward. In parallel movement, the first stanza presents morning: mists are on the fields and the sun is "maturing" (perhaps in the triple sense of climbing the sky, moving toward the winter solstice, and bringing the fruits to maturity). The second stanza presents midday and afternoon: the reaper, overcome by lassitude and the fume of poppies, sleeps on a "half-reaped" furrow, and the worker at the cider press watches "the last oozings hours by hours." The third stanza presents evening: sunset streaks the clouds and touches the stubble-plains "with rosy hue," crickets and birds resume their songs.

This double movement in time toward endings, plus the question asked at the beginning of stanza three, points to the theme of the poem—Keats's most persistent theme—that of transience. In this poem, however, Keats does not regard transience with the anguish manifested in "Ode on a Grecian Urn" and "Ode to a Nightingale." Autumn (symbolic of the latter part of life) has its beauty (its "music") as well as Spring (symbolic of youth); and the images of the third stanza, though touched with melancholy (the day is "soft-dying," the small gnats "mourn," the light wind "lives or dies," the swallows gather to depart) are as lovely as those in the first (when one thinks "warm days will never cease"). The mildness and beauty of the images throughout the poem, the peacefulness especially of those in the third stanza, and the assurance that Autumn has its music too, all reveal a serene acceptance of passing life.

The poem is a sustained apostrophe, addressed to a personified Autumn. Though this personification is most explicit in the second stanza, where Autumn is pictured in various roles as a harvest worker, it is manifested also in the first stanza (where Autumn is "bosom-friend" of the sun, conspires with him, and blesses the vines) and in the third (where it is exhorted not to "think" of the songs of Spring). The sun is also personified, and the fecundity of nature in stanza 1 results apparently from the union of female Autumn and male sun. LP

POEMS FOR FURTHER READING

Poems 199, 213, 220, 241, 243, 248, 250, 255, 260, and 264 from Part Two provide additional illustrations of topics presented in this chapter.

Chapter five
Figurative Language 1:
Metaphor, Personification, Metonymy

39. *Frances Cornford*   THE GUITARIST TUNES UP (page 59)

The guitarist is compared negatively with a "lordly conqueror" and positively to a lover or husband; but, since all three are men, the figurative element in this simile is slight. It is strong, however, in the other half of the comparison—that of a guitar with "a loved woman." Here there is no question of the essential unlikeliness of the things compared. (The similarities exist in the curved shape, in the capacity to utter sweet sounds, in responsiveness to the man's touch, and, most of all, in the way they are approached by the man—with "attentive courtesy.")

The literal and figurative terms of the simile come together in the pun on the word "play"—meaning (a) to perform music and (b) to engage in sexual play.   LP

40. *Robert Francis*   THE HOUND (page 60)

The dual possibilities of the "hound's intent" are underscored by the poet's craftsmanship each of the three times they are mentioned. (1) The four-syllable word "equivocal" occupies a whole line of the poem. (2) The opposed possibilities in lines 4-5 are given in a riming couplet (the only one in the poem) and by the exact duplication of the meter in the two lines (the only adjacent lines in the poem that match each other exactly). (3) In line 10 the two possibilities are designated by two alliterating monosyllabic nouns ("teeth," "tongue") naming parts of the dog which serve as metonymies respectively for a hostile or friendly intent.

The basic meter of the poem is iambic dimeter, though only lines 2, 7, and 10 are perfectly regular. All lines rime, but in an irregular pattern.   LP

41. *Robert Frost*   BEREFT (page 60)

Time: a fall evening. Place: an isolated house with a wooden front porch in disrepair on a hillside overlooking a lake. The speaker has opened the front door to inspect the weather. A storm is coming up. The door tugs at his hand. The wind swirls the leaves up against his knee like a striking snake. There are waves breaking in foam and spray against the shore of the usually placid lake.

There is "something sinister" in the tone of the poem as well as of the wind. The title, the imagery, the massed rimes all give the poem such ominousness and weight as to overbear any comfort the speaker may hope to give himself in the last two words.

The sounds of the poem reinforce the oppressive tone. Although the poem is sixteen lines long, it uses only five rime sounds, almost only three. Ten lines end in rimes containing long -o- sounds, reinforcing the onomatopoetic "roar" and the desolation of the twice-repeated "alone" (see discussion of phonetic intensives on page 189). Four lines end in rimes with prominent -s- sounds reinforcing the onomatopoetic "hissed." The two remaining lines end only in an approximate rime ("abroad"-"God"), further weakening the force of the last line to reassure the speaker or the reader. The onomatopoeia of "hissed" is supported not only by the rimes, but by the repeated -s- alliterations in the lines following; it is anticipated in the repeated -s- sounds of the lines preceding.

The wind in line 3 would seem to be compared to a wild beast. The "restive" door is personified—as if it had a will of its own. The speaker's "life" (15) is like some habitation he lives in larger than his house—but no stronger. LP

42. *Emily Dickinson* IT SIFTS FROM LEADEN SIEVES (page 61)

The subject of "It sifts from leaden sieves" is snow, though nowhere is this subject named. Instead, it is developed through a series of metaphors in which the literal term is represented by the pronoun "it." Most of these are metaphors of the third form in which only the figurative term is named ("alabaster wool," "fleeces," "celestial veil"). In lines 1-2 and 17-18, however, not even the figurative term is named. In 1-2 it is flour; in 17-18 it is some kind of soft white cloth or lace. These are metaphors of the fourth form.

The "leaden sieves" refer to the darkened sky or clouds from which the snow is falling (a metaphor of the third form). But kitchen sieves were ordinarily (during Emily Dickinson's time) tinware; hence another metaphorical process is involved in the substitution of "leaden," with its connotations of heaviness and darkness in the weather, as opposed to the lighter, shinier connotations of tin. "Wool" as a figurative term for snow suggests softness and whiteness, but the introduction of "alabaster" as an adjective brings in an additional comparison, making the snow whiter and giving it a surface crustiness or hardness.

"Face" is an appropriate metaphor for a natural surface (even a dead metaphor in such phrases as "the face of a cliff"), but faces are seldom "even"—so this is a special face, a face compared to something having a smooth, flat surface. "Unbroken forehead" works in a similar way: this is an unwrinkled or unfurrowed forehead. The harvested field of "stump and stack and stem" is metaphorically compared to a room once inhabited (before the harvest) by a personified "summer" but now "empty" (no longer filled with growing grain). The "artisans" are snowflakes, the ghost-like weavers of the fleeces, veils, ruffles, and laces. At the end of the poem the snowflakes stop falling, but their creation—the variegated designs of snow on the ground—remains. LP

43. *George Herbert*   THE QUIP (page 63)

A "quip" is nowadays any play on words—a synonym for "pun." But in Herbert's day and earlier, it had the connotative suggestion of a sharp or sarcastic jibe (the *OED* even guesses that its *-ip* ending is a phonetic intensive linking the word to *clip, nip, snip,* and *whip*, and conveying the idea of something sharp or cutting). In another definition current in the sixteenth century, it meant equivocation or quibbling, the purposeful creation of ambiguous statements to confuse or evade. In this poem it seems to have the power of both definitions: it has a sharp, jibing purpose (to "answer home" the jeers of the world), and it has ambiguous reference.

The ambiguous quip in Herbert's poem is in line 23, disclosed by answering study question 4 regarding the antecedents of the two pronouns: Is the speaker asking the Lord to say "This man is mine," or "I am this man's"? Both, and either, since the quip permits of both interpretations equally. The theological meaning is embodied in the quip, for a virtuous person dedicates his life to the Lord, in exchange for which the Lord sacrifices Himself as the salvation of the virtuous. As the speaker indicates, one need only rest on this mutual relationship, without arguing "at large" (lengthily) in answer to the temptations and taunts of the "merry world."

This little allegory presents the personified temptations of this world ("merry," because it is trying to play a trick, and because it is devoted to pleasure—though of course to the speaker "merry" is verbal irony), embodied in four abstractions each of which has been shunned by the speaker and has therefore joined in sport to taunt him. The manner of their jeering varies, but the speaker's response in the refrain is steadfast. For example, Beauty presents herself as a rose who wonders what has robbed the speaker of the power to command his own hands, discrediting his abstention as implying his weakness. Money again belittles him by suggesting that the speaker has not really learned his music if he cannot recognize the alluring "tune" of chinking gold. And Glory tries to tempt by superciliously parading his superiority. Herbert uses more ingenuity on "quick Wit and Conversation," ironically undercutting him in several ways: verbal irony in *quick* and *to be short*, since in fact this character is neither quick nor brief, but makes "an oration," and dramatic irony in presenting a character who supposes himself to be a comfort but who is rather a bore.

The tactic used by the "merry world" and his mates—to "jeer at" the speaker as a means of luring him into joining them—seems foredoomed. Yet Beauty's approach probably best represents the purpose of their sport: if the speaker were to yield to temptation, he might both gain what they have to offer and avoid their taunting at his refusals.

In any case, Herbert opposes these talkers to the taciturn speaker (we should probably take the italicized lines to be unspoken thoughts, a rejoinder never uttered aloud), for the answer is not to be made by man but by the Lord, who accepts and approves his actions. And rather than draw out any argument to support this, the speaker produces his quip, for debate and argument are the modes of the world. (The refrain line may be an allusion to Psalms 38:15 as translated in the Psalter included in the Anglican Book of Common Prayer [this differs from that in the King James Version]: "For in thee, O Lord, have I put my trust: thou shalt answer for me, O Lord my God." The context of Psalm 38, in either translation, is relevant to Herbert's allegory.)

The biographical information in study question 5 suggests that if Herbert may be identified as the speaker, his renunciation of worldly goods and pleasures should be recognized as temptations truly overcome, rather than as the rejection of things which he has never experienced. Helen Vendler (see below) would even suggest that this allegorical drama should be read as spiritual autobiography—that the temptations of the world are "self-lacerations" which are not merely recorded as former obstacles to his piety but which continue in "the roots of his being," and thus the poem (like "Redemption," No. 60) must be read as an event situated both in the past and in a continuing present. It is a repudiation of worldliness which continues to tempt.

Two useful readings of this poem are contained in the following books: Arnold Stein, *George Herbert's Lyrics* (Baltimore: Johns Hopkins Press, 1968), pp. 147-48, and Helen Vendler, *The Poetry of George Herbert* (Cambridge: Harvard University Press, 1975), pp. 184-85. TRA

44. *Edwin Arlington Robinson* THE DARK HILLS (page 64)

One sentence, one poem. Grammatically the sentence curls easily and without distortion into a pattern in which all lines rime alternately and each line is measured against a metrical framework of four iambic feet. The grammatical kernel of the sentence—"Dark hills . . . You fade" (1, 7)—indicates the subject of the poem: a description of a sunset in the west. The first four lines consist of modifiers attached to "hills," the last four lines of modifiers attached to "fade." The whole poem describes the dark hills, outlined against the lingering sunset glow, gradually fading as the light disappears, and sky and hills blend into the darkness of night.

But just as a sunset has many tones, so does this poem. Its life lies in its metaphors, in the modifiers. In the first four lines we are told that the light of the sunset seems to hover or linger as do the prolonged tones of trumpets blown at a military burial. The simile catches up not only the lingering quality of both sunset light and trumpet tone, but also their richness: the light of the sunset is golden, the sonorous tones of the trumpet seem golden and are blown from golden trumpets. (The resonance and sonority of these tones are echoed by the four long *o*'s, the rolling *l*'s, the lingering *n*'s, the concealed half-rime, and the final consonant correspondences of the two phrases "golden horns" and "old bones.") In the last four lines we are told that the dark hills are now fading far from the bright skies of the midday sun. But again a military figure is used: the bright noonday skies are "the bannered ways," the sun's rays transversing them "the legions of the sun." "Banners" and "legions," "warriors" and "horns," all suggest the colorful pomp of ancient warfare explicitly indicated by "old": the effect would have been quite different had the poet used *flags* and *regiments, soldiers* and *bugles*: words suggesting a more modern warfare and drab uniforms, inappropriate to the rich colors of the sunset.

All the material imagery prepares us for the final simile. The dark hills fade into dark night as if daylight were ending forever and history were done. Some day-ends do give this impression of utter finality. And the poet adds, "as if . . . all wars were done." Now we see the meaning of the poem complete. Literally, it describes a sunset behind dark hills. But through the quality of its imagery—the metaphor and similes contained in the modifiers—are added larger overtones of meaning. War, the poem suggests, is a condition of human life. We have had wars since the beginning of recorded history (a second reason is now apparent for the poet's using the imagery of *ancient* warfare). We shall continue to have wars until the fading of "the last of days"—till history is done.

The poem is an extended apostrophe but contains no hint of personification. The apostrophe helps give the impression of a solitary speaker brooding over the sunset. A sunset poem is appropriately a somber poem. The darkness of the hills serves not only as a visual image but as an emotional symbol. LP

45. *Emily Dickinson* **A HUMMINGBIRD** (page 66)

"Route" and "rush" are metonymies, naming the direction and the motion of the bird as a substitution for the bird itself; "resonance" presents the metonymy "emerald," referring to part of the bird's coloration with an aural term; "revolving wheel" metaphorically represents the rapid motion of the bird's wings, comparing them to the disappearing spokes of a whirling wheel, for the speed of a hummingbird's wing-beats causes the optical illusion that they have disappeared.

While the first quatrain refers to the motions of the bird, it is itself static, a collection of nouns and prepositional phrases without predication. These phrases thus refer to two characteristics of a hummingbird in flight: its ability to hover motionlessly in the air and its sudden, almost magical disappearance from sight as it speeds away. These lines *name* motion, but do not have the completeness of sentences moving through grammatical correctness.

Lines 3-4 also contain examples of synesthesia, the substitution of one sense for another. "Resonance" is an auditory phenomenon that is here attributed to sight or color, while "rush" implies the sensation of motion and is applied to another visual phenomenon, the color "cochineal." These substitutions intensify the sensations, and create the mystery that is solved in the concluding four lines, which answer the implied question "What *was* that?" The poem is in the form of a riddle (one of the poet's regular tactics) presenting first a series of vivid sense impressions, then a hypothetical solution—but never, in the body of the poem, identifying the hummingbird by name. The opening quatrain is also made compact by the four alliterated *r*'s and the two *e*'s.

These first four lines seem to exist all in a moment of stopped motion, and give way to the slower motion of the next image. The observer turns to look at "every blossom," and takes note of the time required for them to return to their normal positions. The "tumbled heads" of the flowers are childlike, and the speaker in the last two lines seems to offer them an explanation for the tumbling they have just gone through, an explanation drawn from Shakespeare's play of magic and reconciliation. The bird that has ruffled their hair is as swift—and as magical—as a postman who travels thousands of miles in a single morning.

For a full discussion of this poem, see Charles Anderson, *Emily Dickinson's Poetry: Stairway of Surprise* (New York: Holt, 1960), pp. 114-16. TRA

EXERCISES (page 68)

1. Personification and metaphor: day = a man; sky = a blue urn; sunlight = fire. ("Ode")
2. Simile: words = sunbeams.
3. Personification: Joy, Temperance, Repose = persons.
4. Metonymy: pen = literature or persuasive writing: sword = armed might or armies. (*Richelieu*, II, ii)
5. Metaphor: oaths = straw; human desire or impulse = fire in the blood. (*The Tempest*, IV, i)
6. Metaphor: conventional minds or souls = furnished rooms. (Nothing in a furnished room belongs to or is original with its occupant.) "The Cambridge ladies . . .")
7. Literal.
8. Metaphor: the desert = a lion. ("Sister Songs," II)
9. and 10. When asked the difference between these two statements, students usually say that the first expresses certainty, the second possibility. The real difference is that the first is metaphorical, the second is literal; that is, it is literally true that we *may* die tomorrow, but it is literally unlikely that we *shall* die tomorrow. Tomorrow = the day of death; the underlying metaphor is a *lifetime* = *one day*; and the meaning is "Life is very short; therefore we should enjoy it while we can." The imaginative force that shrinks the span of a lifetime to a single day is destroyed, and the statement rendered drab and prosaic, when this passage is misquoted, as it so often is. "Eat and drink," of course, is somewhat more than literal in both 9 and 10. The sense is "Let us be merry and enjoy our-

selves" (we are being urged to drink wine, not water). Eating and drinking may be taken as a symbol, or a metonymy, for living the good life. LP

46. *Thomas Campion* THERE IS A GARDEN IN HER FACE (page 69)

The lady is praised for her beauty and for her modesty, honor, or chastity—it is difficult to find one word which precisely sums up the second quality; but it is the quality which will let neither "peer nor prince" buy her lips for any price and which is embodied in the angels with bended bows threatening to kill anyone who would try to kiss her without her permission.

In stanza 1 the "roses and white lilies" may be taken as the colors of her complexion, the "pleasant fruits" as matured and appealing features, and the "cherries" as her lips. In stanza 2 the pearls and the "snow" are her teeth; the "rosebuds" are her lips. The pearls constitute the one metaphor which does not fit in with the central metaphor of the garden. In stanza 3 the lady's brows are likened both to "bended bows" and to the bowmen who guard her with these bows. The arrows are the maiden's "piercing frowns." The plain sense of the concluding couplets is that no one may kiss the lady's lips until she herself issues the invitation or at least gives her consent. This plain sense is rendered through three form 4 metaphors. Kissing is compared to purchasing cherries. An invitation or consent to a kiss is compared to calling out "Cherry-ripe." And the lips that call out "Cherry-ripe" are not only cherries to be sold but the cherry-vendor who sells them.

The "garden" of the poem could be any garden, but it can also be taken as the Garden of Eden if the reader wishes. It is called a "heavenly paradise" in stanza 1; it is guarded by angels in stanza 3; the cherries within it are referred to as "sacred" (line 17); and the maiden who dwells in it is innocent. But this is a love poem, not a religious poem. Its focus is not on piety but on the beauty of a woman's face. There were no cries of street vendors in the Biblical Eden, nor were there peers or princes there. The Eden overtones are just that—overtones, not the subject of the poem.

All four forms of metaphor are found in this poem. The central metaphor equating a garden and a face belongs to form 1. The comparison of the woman's laughing lips to "cherries filled with snow" is a simile, as is the comparison of her "brows" to "bended bows." The likeness of her "piercing frowns" to arrows is a form 2 metaphor. The "roses and white lilies," the "pleasant fruits," and the "cherries" are all form 3 metaphors. The form 4 metaphors in the concluding couplets have already been discussed. LP

47. *Robert Frost* THE SILKEN TENT (page 70)

The poem consists of a single simile sustained through fourteen lines comparing a lovely and loving woman to a silken tent. It also consists of a single sentence winding easily and gracefully through the strict formal requirements (meter and rime scheme) of an English sonnet. It thus exemplifies in its form the paradox which is central to its content—the idea of freedom achieved within bondage.

Many students have preconceptions about tents that may interfere with their reading of the poem, and it may be wise to start discussion by exploring what kind of tent the woman is being compared to. It is a tent made not of coarse canvas, but of silk. Silk suggests beauty and fineness. The silken fabric of the tent is supported by a "central cedar pole." Cedar is a durable, aromatic wood, and its Biblical associations ("cedars of Lebanon") make it suggest worth and value. This upright pole ("pointing heavenward") is itself supported by silken guy-ropes that are staked to the ground around it. The tent is circular, for it is bound to earth "the compass round" (both words suggest circularity). When its guy-ropes are slack, the tent "gently sways at ease," and the tent-pole, though not "strictly held" by any single guy-rope, is yet "loosely bound" by all of them. It enjoys the freedom of a bondage that becomes apparent only when one of the ropes goes taut. (It may be helpful to take some pictures of such tents to class. There is a small one in *The American Heritage Dictionary*, p. 1327.)

What kind of woman is portrayed in this comparison to a tent? The first four lines suggest outward beauty, delicacy, gentleness, freedom, and composure. The next three lines suggest strength and sweetness of soul, and a firm dedication to spiritual values. The second half of the poem develops the paradox that, though apparently free and independent, the woman is "bound / By countless silken ties of love and thought / To everything on earth . . ." "Countless" and "everything" are overstatements (at least as applied to the tent); literally she is attached by love and concern to many, many people—family, friends, neighbors, children, fellow human beings. Some students will be thrown off by the word "capriciousness," associating it with "feminine caprice." The capriciousness, however, is not in the tent (the woman) but in the "air" (her environment). Some change of circumstance, a sudden gust of wind, causes a tug or pull on her, to which she responds. In human terms, she is needed, and responds to the need.

Frost's poem is a lovely tribute to a lovely and loving woman who exemplifies Frost's belief that worthwhile freedom consists in bondage to what one deeply loves or cares about. Elaine Barry has an excellent discussion of this poem in her book *Robert Frost* (New York: Frederick Ungar, 1973), pp. 94-97. LP

48. *Sylvia Plath* METAPHORS (page 70)

The speaker is a pregnant woman. The "loaf" is the growing fetus (an allusion to the common euphemism for pregnancy, "she's got a loaf in the oven"). The "fat purse" is her belly, swollen as if she had eaten a bag of green apples. The "red fruit" (like the "yeasty rising" and the "new-minted" money) is the unborn child; "ivory" refers to its skin, "fine timbers" to its delicate bones. The "train" is pregnancy; the "nine syllables" are the nine months of pregnancy. The poem has nine lines. Each line has nine syllables. LP

49. *Philip Larkin*   **TOADS** (page 71)

Toads are squat, cold-blooded, warty creatures, and, though they can be handled quite harmlessly, their warts do contain a poisonous fluid that oozes out when they are attacked and makes the attacking animal sick. The speaker in this poem, no doubt the poet himself, lugubriously but humorously complains that he is encumbered with *two* toads. The first, specifically identified as work, squats *on* his life, binding him down to a repetitious six-day routine, all for the sake of the weekly or monthly paycheck and an old-age pension. The second toad, left unidentified, squats *in* him, and represents those internal qualities that prevent his throwing over his job and using his wits to live a day-by-day existence, choosing the risky free life over the safe unfree one.

Why is the second toad not identified? Because it represents no single nameable quality but a combination of qualities that the speaker himself might find it difficult to specify with any exactitude: timidity, prudence, middle-class morality, love of material comforts, perhaps even conscience (though the speaker would be slow to claim this last).

In the final stanza the speaker won't go so far as to say that the first toad embodies the second toad's spiritual truth, but neither does he deny it, and pretty clearly it at least comes close to doing so. That is why he will probably never rid himself of either toad. As so often in Larkin's poetry, the speaker finds himself in a dilemma, caught between alternative choices neither one of which is fully attractive to him.

The poem is remarkable for its use of an expressive colloquial diction that can modulate through the plain, the slangy, and the vulgar (*"Stuff your pension!"*) yet gracefully pun on that vulgarity with an allusion to one of Shakespeare's most exquisite passages—Prospero's speech in *The Tempest* that includes the lines ". . . We are such stuff / As dreams are made on, and our little life / Is rounded with a sleep."

The phrasing "Lots of folk . . . Lots of folk" (*not* "Lots of folk . . . These folk") seems to indicate that the people mentioned in stanza 3 are not quite the same as those mentioned in stanzas 4-5. Those in stanza 3 "live on their wits" and probably make a fair go of it, perhaps even blarneying their way to fame or the girl or the money, if not all three. "Lecturers" seldom "live up lanes." The people in stanzas 4-5 are paupers, still they don't actually starve, and the toad *work* doesn't squat on their lives. LP

50. *John Donne* A VALEDICTION: FORBIDDING MOURNING (page 72)

Izaak Walton, Donne's first biographer, tells us that Donne wrote this poem to his wife and gave it to her before leaving on an embassy to the French court, a project that would separate them for two months. His wife, who was with child at the time, had been reluctant to let him go, as she feared some ill during his absence.

Without this biographical information, however, we can know that the speaker in the poem is not dying. In the famous simile that concludes the poem, it is the traveling foot that "comes home" to the fixed foot, not the fixed foot that follows after the traveling foot to join it in some other place (such as heaven). Students often get the wrong notion of this poem, partly because of the title, partly because of the death-image in the first stanza. It should be pointed out to them that the dying "virtuous men" in this stanza belong to the figurative part of a simile, not to the literal referent. The sense is "Let us part from each other as silently and imperceptibly as a dying virtuous man parts from his soul."

The love of the true lovers (members of the "priesthood") is a love of souls and minds rather than primarily of senses; therefore they can never be truly parted, and they do not "carry on" (like "lay" lovers) when they are physically separated. Donne has skillfully managed his meter so as to force an equal accent on both syllables of *absence* (15), thus bringing out the pun. Absence, for the "laity," is literally *ab* + *sense*: to be away from sense, to be separated from "eyes, lips and hands."

Three similes compare the parting of true lovers to the parting of virtuous men from life, to the expansion of gold beaten into gold leaf, and to the separation of the legs of a pair of drawing compasses. A metaphor compares it to the almost imperceptible "trepidation" (trembling) of the spheres (as contrasted to the gross movements of the earth—flood, tempest, and earthquake). LP

51. *Andrew Marvell* TO HIS COY MISTRESS (page 74)

Perhaps the greatest obstacle to student understanding of this poem is its title. The word "mistress" has none of its most common modern meanings: the "lady" (2, 19) of the poem is, in fact, a virgin (28). Also, the word "coy" means no more than *modest* or *reluctant* without its usual modern connotations of teasing or playing hard-to-get. The lady is reluctant to accede to her lover's pleas because of "honor" (29), which requires that she preserve her virginity until marriage. But the young man is not proposing marriage. In short, this is a seduction poem. It is also a *carpe diem* poem. The speaker belittles the lady's "honor" as of no importance in the face of the brevity of life and the imminence of death. Life being so short, they must enjoy their pleasures NOW! He puts his argument into syllogistic form: (1) *If* we had time enough, your coyness would not be a crime; (2) *but* time rushes on, death comes quickly, and nothing follows; (3) *therefore* we should make love *now*.

The poetic force of the poem derives, not from the cogency of the syllogism, but from the fancy, wit, and imaginative force with which it is presented. First, the speaker elaborates the temporal with a spatial dimension. If they had "world enough, and time" (he says), not only could they stretch out his courtship from "ten years before the Flood" (an immeasurably distant time in the past) till "the conversion of the Jews [to Christianity]" (an inconceivably remote time in the future), but they could pass their time separated by oceans and continents (she looking for rubies along the river Ganges in India; he complaining, in verse or song, of her coldness by the river Humber in England). He could allow his "vegetable love" to grow "Vaster than empires, and more slow." (The phrase "vegetable love," suggesting a love bloodless and unimpassioned, capable only of growth, subtly makes such a prospect seem undesirable.) He could also spend the amount of time praising her beauty that each of its features deserves, and would end up praising her heart (implying that his love for her is more than physical, as he would be glad to demonstrate if he had time). The tone of this first section is fanciful and playful; it is appropriately the longest of the poem's three sections for it depicts a state of nature in which there is no need to hurry.

At line 21 the tone changes dramatically. It becomes urgent. The speaker constantly feels "Time's winged chariot" about to overtake him. Time is at his back; and ahead (after death) he sees nothing but "Deserts of vast eternity" (eternity is a desert, a vast blank, a place without life). In the grave, she will lose her beauty; he will no longer be able to sing her love songs; she will lose her "long-preserved virginity" ("You're going to lose it anyway," the lover implies; "would you rather lose it to me—or the worms?"); her "quaint honor" will turn to dust (the word "quaint" has a slightly deprecatory connotation here, suggesting something without real importance; and a sexual pun buried beneath the word further trivializes the "honor" it is attached to); and, finally, his "lust" will turn to ashes (the speaker is quite frank here in confessing that his desires are physical). This section ends with a wry irony: the grave would seem a perfect place for making love—dark, quiet, private—but, strangely, no one makes love there.

Therefore, says the speaker, let us make love while we are young and eager, desiring and desirable. Let us love, not with a "vegetable love," but like "amorous birds of prey" (fiercely, like hawks or eagles). Let us devour time before time devours us. Rather than remaining as far apart as the Ganges and the Humber, "Let us roll all our strength and all / Our sweetness up into one ball" (a sphere is the most compact concentration of matter) "And tear our pleasures with rough strife / Thorough the iron gates of life." (There is considerable disagreement about the exact meaning of the "gates of life" image, but the tone and meaning of the lines are clear enough. The tone is resolute and determined; the meaning is, Let us love, not passively and delicately, but passionately and actively.) Thus, though we cannot make time stand still (we cannot hold back death), we can make it seem to pass very quickly (excitingly, vitally, rather than dully or monotonously).

The poem concerns time more than love. It is perhaps the intensest, most urgent *carpe diem* poem in English. The poet has chosen love-making as a symbol for any activity which involves living intensely. As an argument for seduction, the poem is certainly specious. The lady, by waiting till she can fulfill her desires honorably, may save herself fifty years of misery. Conceived of, more generally, as an argument for spending one's hours in pleasurable, useful, or rewarding activities, the argument has greater force. The person who has to "kill time" out of boredom is a pitiful failure. The speaker is determined to master time rather than let it master him. LP

52. *John Keats* TO SLEEP (page 76)

The central metaphor is derived from the age-old analogy of sleep to death—but extended in such detail that it gains a new vitality. The apostrophe begins by personifying sleep as an "embalmer" whose office it is to shut the eyes of people who have passed into the divine forgetfulness of death. The first quatrain is given over to defining the general attributes of this personification—what it does to all of us. In the second quatrain, the poem switches to the first person singular as the speaker requests that sleep grant him the benefit of its acts, either immediately, in the midst of the hymn he is singing in praise of sleep, or after he has completed his song and said "Amen" to it. Although "poppy" is a metonymy for an opiate, and thus figurative (the speaker does not literally wish for a flower), it is not possible to determine whether he is literally talking about a drug or is only comparing the state of sleep to a state of druggedness: he may indeed have taken a sedative before retiring.

Through the first eight lines the poem implies a question: *why* does the speaker wish so to achieve sleep and loss of consciousness? Why does he identify himself among the "gloom-pleased," why does darkness seem to him a bower protecting him from light, why is "forgetfulness divine," why will it be a charity to him to be lulled into unconsciousness? Considering the link that he draws between sleep and death, is he in fact desiring a final escape from wakefulness, a literal death? The intensity of his desire through line eight makes that seem a reasonable conjecture (although we must be careful not to take a figurative term literally)—but still, *why* does he desire it?

Lines 9-10, formally singled out by their unexpected break from the rime pattern (see below), provide a generalized explanation: daylight, and the memory of "the passed day," breed "many woes." The speaker needs to be saved from what in wakefulness he would remember, and from the "burrowing" of "curious conscience." This last phrase is evocative and intriguing, for both words possess multiple denotations which point the poem in various directions. "Curious" may mean strange, odd, queer; it may mean overly scrupulous; it may mean inquisitive and prying—denotations that bear varying connotative weight. But the noun "conscience," in its several denotations, has positive connotations, whether it means the moral sense of right and wrong, or the inner compulsion to behave morally, or (in an older but still extant definition) consciousness or self-consciousness. We would normally suppose that it is better to possess the mental qualities embodied in the word—moral standards, moral compulsion, and consciousness. Yet clearly, to the *speaker*, this phrase is negative in its implications—it is what he wants to be saved from.

Because Keats takes the speaker no further, it is not possible to determine any specific cause for the desire for sleep, though of course we can rule out some simplistic explanations: he is not insomniac; he is not weary after great physical labors; he does not need to sleep now so as to wake early. For him, sleep is a salvation from what consciousness, conscience, and daylight represent, "many woes" of an unspecified sort. (Lines 9-10 contain a metaphor complementing the central sleep/death comparison: the still and loving darkness of sleep and death are contrasted to the busy "breeding" of daylight.) Readers of Keats will notice, of course, a parallel to the desire for death as an escape from the miserable conditions of human existence expressed in "Ode on a Grecian Urn" (page 277), "Ode to a Nightingale" (page 278) and elsewhere, though this sonnet refrains from defining such "woes" as physical disease and debilitation as reasons for wishing to escape. The open-endedness of the desire, here, is part of the appeal of this sonnet, which focuses more on the desire than on the motive.

As an example of a Shakespearean sonnet, this poem represents one of Keats's several experiments with the form. Strikingly, he eliminates the concluding couplet (which to him and many others has seemed too likely to be glib and superficial as a resolution), and instead interrupts the orderly progression of heroic quatrains with anomolous rimes at lines 9-10: abab cdcd bc efef. As pointed out, lines 9-10 seem to begin a rationale for the speaker's deep desire for sleep, and in their concluding phrase approach the most teasing of the questions in the poem—what *are* the "woes" which so fret the speaker? TRA

53. *A. E. Housman* LOVELIEST OF TREES (page 76)

"Loveliest of trees" (*A Shropshire Lad, II*) is a *carpe diem* poem expressing the philosophy that life is short and that one should therefore enjoy it fully while one can, wasting no moment that might be filled with pleasure. The pleasure proposed in this poem is the enjoyment of beauty, especially of natural beauty, as symbolized by the blossoming cherry tree.

In assuming that the natural life span of man is seventy years, the speaker *alludes* to the Old Testament (Psalms 90:10): "The days of our years are three-score years and ten." The speaker is twenty. Normally one would think of a young man at that age as having ample time left for pleasure and enjoyment. His "only" and "little" therefore come as small shocks of surprise, emphasizing how little fifty years really are for something so wonderful as the enjoyment of nature. This is not verbal irony, for the speaker means what he says, but irony of situation—a discrepancy between what the reader anticipates and what he actually hears.

"Snow" (line 12) is metaphorical, representing the masses of white bloom with which the cherry trees are hung at Eastertide. The critical argument concerning this point is summarized in Laurence Perrine, "Housman's Snow: Literal or Metaphorical?" *The CEA Critic* 35 (November 1972): 26-27.

The speaker is not Housman but a Shropshire lad (for Housman was older than twenty when he wrote this poem), but he undoubtedly speaks *for* Housman, or one aspect of him. But this aspect should be contrasted with other aspects, as expressed, for instance, by the speaker in "To an Athlete Dying Young" (page 273). LP

54. *Langston Hughes* **DREAM DEFERRED** (page 77)

Specifically the "dream deferred" is that of full and equal participation of blacks with whites in the political and economic freedoms supposedly guaranteed by the Constitution. Metaphors, because more condensed, are (other things being equal) more "explosive" than similes. The metaphorical comparison of black frustration to a bomb (metonymically representing a race riot or even armed revolution) is therefore appropriately placed in the climactic position. LP

POEMS FOR FURTHER READING

Poems 191, 193, 247, 258 from Part Two provide additional illustrations of topics presented in this chapter.

Chapter six
Figurative Language 2:
Symbol, Allegory

55. *Robert Frost* **THE ROAD NOT TAKEN** (page 78)

Since the publication (1970) of the second volume in Lawrance Thompson's three-volume biography of Frost, there have been an increasing number of different interpretations of "The Road Not Taken." These interpretations see the poem principally as an example of dramatic irony rather than of symbol. They are perhaps best summed up in Elaine Barry's discussion (in *Robert Frost* [New York: Frederick Ungar, 1973], pp. 12-13) by her statement that "the poem is a gentle parody of the kind of person whose life in the present is distorted by nostalgic regrets for the possibilities of the past, who is less concerned for the road taken than for the 'road not taken.'" The impetus for these interpretations was provided by Thompson's revelation that Frost himself regarded the poem as a gentle spoof of his English friend Edward Thomas and thought of Thomas rather than of himself as the speaker in the poem (*Robert Frost: The Years of Triumph* [New York: Holt, 1970], pp. 87-89, 544-48). After a careful review of the evidence, both external and internal, I find myself unable to accept these ironic interpretations. (I fall back on D. H. Lawrence's adage, "Never trust the artist. Trust the tale"; and I hope sometime, time permitting, to argue the case in an article.) However, the instructor should know of the existence of these other interpretations, and may wish to raise them for discussion in the classroom. LP

56. *Dorothy Lee Richardson* **AT CAPE BOJEADOR** (page 80)

There is no silken tent physically present in Frost's sonnet. The speaker thinking of his lady, is *reminded* of a silken tent and uses "as" to express the comparison. Richardson, on the other hand, comes upon an actual, physically present sea urchin, and is reminded by it of a woman—of women—not physically present. The next morning she finds the sea urchin again, this time literally crushed in a footprint, and she is reminded again of the vulnerability of fragile women, but is reminded of it by the sea urchin, not vice versa. It is principally the physical presence of the sea urchin that makes it a symbol. Richardson also compares women to eggshells, in a metaphor that emphasizes their fragility. This comparison in the first stanza anticipates the destruction in the second stanza. The phrase "thin bone mixed with sand" is effective in numerous ways, not least because it may remind the reader of an hourglass in which the flow of sand measures time.

The fact that the speaker *knows* and *admires* the woman of whom the sea urchin reminds her suggests that the woman has something more than physical beauty to commend her. LP

57. *William Blake* THE SICK ROSE (page 81)

The "night" and the "howling storm" are part of the symbolic design of the poem: they give it depth and resonance and they *may* be assigned a specific meaning. (The "howling storm" is materialism, say a couple of critics; and I have no objection.) In general, however, there is a danger that the student (and sometimes the professional critic), once the powers of symbolism have been discovered, will want to press down all the buttons, to find an equivalent for every noun in the story or poem. At this point, reading the poem becomes an exercise in ingenuity rather than one in understanding and enjoyment. Symbol-hunting is a practice no less bad, perhaps, than moral-hunting. The symbol-hunter tends to restrict rather than expand the meaning of a poem by converting a symbolic story into an allegory. LP

58. *Archibald MacLeish* YOU, ANDREW MARVELL (page 83)

The implicit metaphor running throughout the poem compares the coming of darkness to the rising of flood waters. The night comes on steadily, without interruption or pause; the absence of punctuation and the repetition of "and" embody that unceasing, uninterrupted movement in the form of the poem. The substitution of suspension periods for a single period at the end indicates that the movement continues beyond the end of the poem. LP

59. *Robert Herrick* TO THE VIRGINS, TO MAKE MUCH OF TIME (page 86)

The rosebuds in the first stanza symbolize pleasures. The general meaning of the poem is to enjoy life while one can, for life is short, and the capacity for enjoyment is progressively and sharply reduced in middle age and old age. The last stanza specifies one kind of pleasure—but an important kind: sexual fulfillment in marriage. The use of "virgins" instead of *maidens* underscores the sexual significance.

The meaning of a symbol, like the meaning of a word, is largely controlled by context. Herrick's rosebuds are generalized by the author's emphasis on the swift passage of time, and by his use of the plural rather than the singular. *Gathering* rosebuds suggests getting as many as possible, and thus the rosebuds suggest a variety of pleasures—including, of course, the pleasure of gathering rosebuds.

"Smiles" (3) personifies the flower that is dying, thus adding poignance to its death and preparing us for the idea that it is the death of persons, not of flowers, that Herrick is really concerned about. "Race" (7) emphasizes swiftness. "Spent" (11) has the connotation of exhausted or wasted, whereas "use" (13) suggests making a profitable or worthy employment of. LP

60. *George Herbert* REDEMPTION (page 88)

The first clue that this sonnet is not merely a dramatic narrative is not a forceful one: the title ambiguously refers to a business transaction and to a religious concept. Similarly ambiguous, "Lord" at the end of the first line may refer to a landlord or to God (the capitalization is retained from the first printing of the poem, but there was little consistency in the use of capitals in the seventeenth century). Only in the fifth line does the poem assert the break from superficial meaning, placing the manor house of the lord "in heaven." Even that phrase could be read as a metaphor (the manor house is so grand that it seems heavenly to the tenant) until the contrast in line 8 makes it clear that heaven and earth must be taken literally.

The poem allegorically presents what Herbert and other Puritans of the period called the "New Covenant," or the "Covenant of Grace," between God and man. The old covenant, the "Covenant of Works," had come into effect with the creation of Adam; it left man wholly responsible, and punishable, for his sins, and at Adam's fall it condemned mankind to death. By the Covenant of Grace, God sent his son to offer redemption of sin, a new contract by which man could be gathered into heaven as an act of God's grace rather than by his own deserts.

This allegorical meaning is made clear in a very early commentary on the poem, by George Ryley, at the beginning of the eighteenth century, as quoted by Joseph H. Summers, *George Herbert: His Religion and Art* (Cambridge: Harvard, 1968), pp. 60-61:

> The first lease this great landlord gave to man, his tenant, was the covenant of works, by which man was bound to yeild all the profits of the land to his landlord's use; the condition being, *he that doth them shall live in them, and the soul that sinneth shall dye*. Man breaking the articles of this once, rendered himself for ever incapable of retrieving that loss, or of keeping them for the future; so by these articles he could never *thrive*, that is, never be *justified*. *But what the law* (that is, this law of works) could not do, God, sending his own Son, & c. hath wrought for us, that is, our Redemption: making us free from the law of sin and death, and granting us a new *small-rented lease*. This was purchased for us by, and granted to us att, the death of Christ. These premises will lead us into the plain sence of this poem.

The allegorical form permits Herbert to relate the narrative of "history" to the spiritual reality of every person's life. As Summers says, "the speaker is both one man in the present and all mankind from the Fall to the Crucifixion; the search is the search of the Jews until Calvary and it is also the search of every man who wishes to be a Christian; the discovery was made by humanity at one moment in the past, but it is also made by individuals at every moment, present and future" (p. 182).

This explanation helps us to understand the time reference in lines 7-8, "which he had dearly bought / Long since on earth." The event is obviously the Crucifixion, when the lord paid "dearly" (both at great expense, and with great love) to save mankind. As an historical event that occurred in the first century, it was "long since"; but as a continuing redemption, it occurs over and over in the lives of individual people. As Herbert would have seen it, the Crucifixion is a recurring event manifested to the spiritual life of each person, so the concluding image of the poem is both historical and present, and the "ragged noise and mirth" of the multitude re-enacts the scene of the original Crucifixion.

Students who may not have examined the metaphorical texture of Christian terminology may at first be shocked or affronted by Herbert's handling of the action of redemption in commercial terms; they can be led to see that the concept of heaven as *reward*, of Christ's *payment* for the sins of the world, and many others that they might contribute, rest on similar mercantile phrasing, justified by the need to express metaphysical truth in physical terms comprehensible to mankind. TRA

61. *Robert Frost*   FIRE AND ICE (page 88)

Scientists have made various predictions about how the world will end, most of them involving either a fiery or an icy terminus. At the time that Frost published this poem (December, 1920), probably the two leading theories were (1) that, as the earth gradually loses momentum in its orbit, it will be drawn by gravity closer and closer to the sun, until finally it plunges into the sun, and (2) that, as the sun gradually cools, or as the interior of the earth itself cools, the earth will get colder and colder, until finally all life is extinguished in a new ice age. Both theories still have many supporters.

Frost makes symbolic use of these theories. Fire becomes a symbol for desire or passion, ice a symbol for hate, the earth a symbol for human or civilized life ("world" means both physical and social world). The poet has experienced enough of desire and hate within himself to recognize that both passion (e.g., desire for sensual gratifications, possessions, or power) and hate (e.g., between nations, classes, or races) are forces strong enough to bring an end to mankind.

The last line is understatement. Instead of saying that desire or hate could ruin, wipe out, or annihilate mankind, he says only that either would "suffice." LP

62. *Rupert Brooke*   THE DEAD (page 89)

"Hearts" (1) is a metonymy for the lives of those young men killed in war; it leads to the definition of these men as sensitive, emotional beings whose lives were characteristically full of mixed contradictions—joy, care, sorrow, mirth, dawn and sunset, slumber and waking, friended and alone, and so forth—what might seem the whole compendium of experience of the young. Note, however, that they are not given some of the less admirable qualities such as selfishness, lust, spitefulness, and others equally characteristic of young men. In paying his respects to the fallen, Brooke purposely sets out with the word "hearts," a slightly sentimental approach. (Even though we know about "hard-hearted" or "black-hearted" people, the unmodified word seems to point connotatively toward the "kindness" which Brooke singles out as the gift of the years: "kind-hearted" would be the modified term in this poem.)

The symbols in the poem are introduced in the sestet with the images of water, wind, sunlight, and of frost, stillness, darkness. The "laughter" of line 9 is a metaphor for the appearance of sunlit waves on a lake. The literal process presented in the sestet is the freezing over of a lake that was brilliantly active in the sunlight, and now is brilliantly still in the moonlight. The sunlit lake is a symbol for the lives of these young men, and the frozen lake a symbol for their deaths. They are equally beautiful, though completely opposite. TRA

63. *Alfred, Lord Tennyson* ULYSSES (page 90)

Ulysses represents and recommends a life of continuous intellectual aspiration; he has an avid thirst for life and experience that finds fulfillment primarily in the life of the mind rather than in the life of the senses (his concluding injunction is "to strive, to seek, to find," not "to taste, to touch, to smell"). Geographical exploration in the poem symbolizes intellectual exploration. The key lines for this interpretation are lines 30-32: "And this grey spirit yearning in desire / To follow *knowledge* like a sinking star / Beyond the utmost bound of human *thought*." But throughout the poem are words and phrases that reinforce this reading. In line 5 Ulysses characterizes Ithacans as a savage race that "hoard, and sleep, and feed, and know not me" (that is, a people who live a materialistic and physical life and know not the excitement of the intellectual life). In line 13 he says, "Much have I seen and *known*." In line 46 he addresses his mariners as souls that "have toiled, and wrought, and *thought* with me."

The westward journey has a double symbolism that is also congruent with this reading. In sailing westward (toward the setting sun), Ulysses is sailing toward death (going west is a traditional symbol for death); he is also sailing from what, for the Greeks, was the *known* world (the Mediterranean world) into what was for them the *unknown* world (the world of the Atlantic, beyond the Strait of Gibraltar). The meaning is that Ulysses will continue to seek new knowledge, new discovery, until his death. The continuing nature of this search is also indicated in the images of following knowledge "like a sinking star" and of sailing "beyond the sunset, and the baths / Of all the western stars." One cannot, of course, ever catch up with a sinking star or with the setting sun; no matter how far west one sails, they still set beyond a horizon still farther west. Likewise, no matter how much knowledge one gains, there is still further knowledge to be sought. Thus Ulysses' quest is truly one of continuing aspiration: his thirst for new knowledge will never be satisfied; he will continue to seek new knowledge until he dies. What will become of him *after* death, he does not know (lines 62-64), but his program for life before death is clearly mapped out.

The image in lines 18-21 includes the idea of a horizon that is always to be sought, never to be reached—that is, the idea of knowledge that is never to be exhausted. Lines 26-29 tell us that every hour of life brings new experience, new knowledge. (Grammatically, the subject of "is saved" is probably to be construed as "something more," with "a bringer of new things" in apposition and "every hour" treated as an adverbial modifier; but the ambiguity of the construction suggests the wisdom of saving every hour possible from death, of living as long as possible in order to learn new things.) Thunder and sunshine are symbols for adversity and good fortune. Hearts and foreheads are metonymies for wills and minds (the meaning is "We confronted the thunder and the sunshine with free wills and free minds"). The poem celebrates strength of will as much as it does the intellectual quest. The metaphor in line 23 compares a person to a sword or a shield.

In recent years "Ulysses" has been the subject of considerable critical controversy, some of it captious, and some oversubtle. Extreme views are presented by E. J. Chaisson in "Tennyson's 'Ulysses'—A Re-Interpretation," *University of Toronto Quarterly*, XXII (1954), pp. 402-409, and by Paul F. Baum in *Tennyson Sixty Years After* (Chapel Hill: University of North Carolina Press, 1948), pp. 92-95, 299-303. John Pettigrew, in "Tennyson's 'Ulysses': A Reconciliation of Opposites," *Victorian Poetry*, I (January, 1963), pp. 27-45, gives an overview and seeks to reconcile conflicting viewpoints; and Charles Mitchell, in "The Undying Will of Tennyson's Ulysses," *Victorian Poetry*, II (Spring, 1964) pp. 87-95, adds still another point of view. The critical pendulum continues to swing, however; in his prize-winning book, *The Poetry of Tennyson* (New Haven: Yale Univ. Press, 1977), A. Dwight Culler presents persuasive evidence for the traditional (and I think correct) interpretation. LP

64. *Alastair Reid*   **CURIOSITY** (page 92)

In its own sardonic and humorous fashion, this poem has much the same message as Tennyson's "Ulysses." Cats and dogs symbolize two different kinds of people: cats, the intellectually curious, the adventurous, and the unconventional; dogs, the incurious, the prudent, and the conventional. Though the parallel is not to be pressed too hard, Ulysses is a cat, Telemachus a dog. The poet's sympathies are with cats. (Tennyson regards Telemachus more favorably, however, than Reid regards dogs.)

The poem utilizes two folk sayings: "Curiosity killed the cat" and "Cats have nine lives." The poem says that curiosity is dangerous, but that one cannot really *live* without it. Curiosity leads to suffering and discomfort; nevertheless, it is the condition of being really alive. Intellectual curiosity is the kind in question.

"Death" in line 3 means literal, physical death. "To die" in line 16 means to die intellectually, emotionally, and spiritually; that is, to exist in a merely physical sense, like Tennyson's Ithacans—or like dogs. "To die" in lines 34-35 means to suffer, and "dying" in lines 41-42 means suffering. Thus "to die" has exactly opposite meanings in lines 16 and 34-35, and these two opposite meanings, being both figurative, are in turn both opposite to the literal meaning of "death" in line 3. These contradictory meanings are not a sign of the author's confusion, as they would be in a logical treatise or in any discursive prose; they are what give life and interest to the poem. Manifested in metaphor, and resulting in paradox, they help the poet probe the real significance of living. He is firmly in control; he knows what he is doing. LP

65. *Alan Dugan*   LOVE SONG: I AND THOU (page 93)

Dugan's "house" is his life, and I classify this poem as allegorical. The speaker swears "by Christ" because Christ *was* a carpenter, and he is pointing up a contrast. Nevertheless, the speaker will be metaphorically "crucified" in his life (that is, he will suffer), as Christ was literally crucified. He needs someone who will "help" him suffer. The word "help" (31) works two ways: the wife will help him to suffer in the sense of causing additional suffering (she will nail his right hand to the right-hand cross-piece); but also, and more important, she will help him *in* his suffering— by sharing it, she will alleviate it, she will make his life supportable, and she will even, by introducing love, bring a little heaven into his life. The word "prime" has at least three relevant meanings: foremost or principal, of best quality (as applied to whiskey), and primitive or original (tying rage in with original sin).

Martin Buber's book has especially influenced the Protestant theologians classified as Christian existentialists. The movement of the poem supports the general tenor of this body of thought. Suffering and imperfection are inescapable conditions of human life ("God damned it. / This is hell"); nevertheless, life is made meaningful as man forms "I-Thou" relationships. Shared suffering is bearable; unshared suffering is not. The speaker in the poem finds that he cannot build a satisfactory life simply as an "I"; he must enter into an "I-Thou" relationship. Essentially the poem begins as an account of the speaker's attempt to build a life for himself and by himself; it ends up as a proposal of marriage.

There are additional remarks about this poem on page 113 of this manual (j). LP

66. *John Donne* HYMN TO GOD MY GOD, IN MY SICKNESS (page 95)

Because of the personal reference in lines 28-30, we may not unfairly take Donne himself as the speaker in this poem. In stanza 1 he is preparing his soul ("tuning the instrument") for his entry into heaven, where he will become part of that holy choir which not only furnishes but *is* God's music.

In stanza 2 the dying poet initiates the extended geographical metaphor which governs the poem's four central stanzas—for which the first stanza and the last provide a frame. Lying flat on his sickbed, with his doctors bent over him trying to make a proper diagnosis and prescribe a suitable treatment, he compares himself to a flat map of the earth stretched out on a table with geographers bent over studying it. The explorers of Donne's day were fervently seeking a "Northwest Passage" or strait which would give merchants easier access to the treasures of the Orient. A strait is of course a narrow and difficult passageway connecting two larger bodies of water, and Donne makes it symbolize the confining, difficult fever which he must pass through from this life to eternal life. In these straits, he sees his "west," a natural and traditional symbol for death (because it is there that the sun sets).

He is not afraid of death, however, for he is confident that it is closely followed or accompanied by resurrection. He illustrates this belief by reference to the map. On a flat map (containing, from left to right, eastern Asia, the Americas, Europe, Africa, the Middle East, and central Asia), if you trace a line *westward* from the righthand edge of the map to the lefthand edge, you arrive finally again at eastern Asia or the Orient, at the same meridian from which you started, demonstrating that west and east are one. In the same way, Donne argues, death and resurrection are one.

Illustrating from the map again, he shows that its three principal straits all lead to places that, in one way or another, may be taken as symbols of heaven, the realm of resurrection. The Anyan (Bering) straits lead ultimately to "the Eastern riches" (that is, the precious spices of the East Indies); the straits of Magellan lead from the stomy Atlantic Ocean to the peaceful "Pacific Sea"; and the straits of Gibraltar (entered from the Atlantic) lead through the Mediterranean to the Holy City, "Jerusalem." Moreover, the three straits lead to the three continents that were thought, in the medieval period, to constitute the whole world, and which were peopled (according to Christian legend) by the descendents of the three sons of Noah. The whole world and its riches, material and spiritual, in turn are symbols of the glories of heaven. The symbology here is rich and complex and perhaps needs a chart to clarify it:

Anyan Straits — "Eastern riches" — Asia — Shem ⎫ Riches ⎫ Glories
Straits of Magellan — "Pacific Sea" — Africa — Ham ⎬ of the ⎬ of
Straits of Gibraltar — "Jerusalem"* — Europe — Japhet ⎭ world ⎭ Heaven

*Jerusalem, as part of the Mediterranean world and a "center" for Christianity, was probably considered by Donne more European than Asian. It was certainly not oriental.

The Biblical names in the last line of this fourth stanza provide a transition to the Biblical and Christian geography of the fifth stanza. Speculative Christian writers had proposed that the Garden of Eden had been located at the same spot where Jesus was later crucified, thus giving a neat formal design to the Christian story. The place where Adam had sinned by eating the forbidden fruit was the same as that where Christ had redeemed mankind from the eternal consequences of that sin. Christ's "tree" (the cross) stood in the same place as Adam's tree (the tree of the knowledge of good and evil). This identification endorses the identification of the first Adam and the last Adam (Christ).

The last eight lines of the poem are a prayer. The first Adam, because of his sin, had been condemned by God to get his bread by the "sweat" of his face (Genesis 3:19); the last Adam (Christ) had redeemed that sin by shedding his blood on the Cross. Donne prays that the Lord will find "both Adams" met in him. The anguish of his fever has brought beads of sweat to his brow, and he prays he may be saved by the blood of the Redeemer. "Purple" (a word which in Donne's day applied to any color between modern purple and crimson) was a metonymy or symbol for royalty (being the color of kings' robes), and was also the color of blood (compare "The Flea," page 153, line 20). Thus the poet wishes to be received by the Lord wrapped in Christ's "purple" (the blood of Christ the redeemer and the robe of Christ the King). He also wishes to exchange the "crown of thorns" which had mockingly been put on Christ at the crucifixion (and which in Donne's case is a symbol of suffering) for Christ's "other crown"—the golden crown that Christ wears enthroned at the right side of God in heaven (and which for Donne is a symbol for salvation). The last three lines identify the speaker as the Dean of St. Paul's who preached God's "word" to others' souls and now wishes to preach it to his own. As traditionally all sermons elaborate on a Biblical text, he appropriately chooses for his sermon to himself a passage from Psalms, roughly paraphrased in the final line. It is an appropriate choice for Donne, for it repeats one of his favorite themes (compare "Batter my heart, three-personed God," page 108).

For a brilliant and much fuller discussion of this poem, see Clay Hunt, *Donne's Poetry: Essays in Literary Analysis* (New Haven: Yale Univer. Press, 1954), pp. 96-117. There is also an excellent but shorter discussion in Charles B. Wheeler, *The Design of Poetry* (New York: W. W. Norton, 1966), pp. 192-95. LP

67. *Christina Rossetti* UPHILL (page 96)

The two speakers are a weary traveler and a comforter, and the central event is the traditional symbol of life as a difficult journey that will end with rest and comfort. The identity of the answerer is not clear-cut: Is he Christ, promising rest after a weary life, or only someone who knows the answers posed by the traveler? And— as the first study question hints—are there *really* two speakers here, since their questions and answers are not placed in quotation marks, or is this to be regarded as an internal question-and-answer monologue, a symbolic catechism in which the speaker rehearses the age-old questions and their simple but slightly riddling answers?

The riddling tone of the poem arises out of the simplicity of the symbols. Rather than identify the process as living and dying, the destination as heaven, the journey as a life well and truly lived, the poem's naive tone is childlike in its questions, for which there is much precedent in the teachings of Jesus. TRA

68. *Robert Frost*   **DUST OF SNOW** (page 97)

69. *William Blake*   **SOFT SNOW** (page 97)

"Dust of Snow" describes a literal incident, "Soft Snow," an allegorical incident.

"Dust of Snow," except for the muted metaphor in its title, may be taken quite literally. The beauty of the scene (powdery white snow, black crow), the animation provided by the movement of crow and snow, the suggestions of cheeriness and humor (as if the crow were greeting the speaker or playing a sly practical joke on him)—all combine to give a lift to the speaker's heart and to change his mood from one of sorrow, resentment, frustration, or whatever, to one of delight.

Other readers have read this poem rather differently, seeing sinister connotations in "crow," "dust," and "hemlock." I strongly disagree. If one insists on calling the crow a symbol, it is a life symbol, not a death symbol. In two published notes I have attempted to refute what I consider overingenious and mistaken interpretations of the poem, using my own arguments in one and quoting Frost's remarks on the poem in the other. Whoever wishes to acquaint himself with both sides of this controversy should consult the following: Edgar H. Knapp, in *The Explicator* 28 (September 1969), item 9; Laurence Perrine, in *The Explicator* 29 (March 1971), item 61; Norbert Artz, "The Poetry Lesson," *College English* 32 (April 1971): 740-42; Laurence Perrine, "Dust of Snow Gets in Our Eyes," *College English* 33 (February 1972): 589-90. Whatever its symbolical implications, the *incident* in the poem may be taken literally.

The last line of Blake's poem cannot be interpreted literally, and it forces us to look for a metaphorical or allegorical interpretation of the whole. (I would myself classify "Soft Snow" as allegory—one of the shortest in existence.) The clues to the allegorical meaning are the personification of the snow as "She"; the possible sexual connotations of such words as *soft, play, melt,* and *prime*; the fact that the speaker doesn't play *in* the snow but *with* the snow, or, rather, the snow plays with *him*, after he has first *asked* it ("her") to play with him; the moral judgment implied by "dreadful crime." The snow (in her prime) is a maiden. The speaker asks her to "play" (amorously) with him. The maiden consents and "melts" (yields her virginity). Conventional society ("winter") calls it a "dreadful crime."

It is clear that Blake takes an unconventional stance. He regards sexual desire and fulfillment as natural and innocent. By identifying society with "winter" he suggests that its judgment is cold and harsh, and by identifying sex with "play" and the melting of snow he implies that society's judgment is not only harsh but absurd. Blake expressed similar unconventional judgments in a number of poems; for example, "The Garden of Love," "Ah! Sun-flower," "Abstinence sows sand," and "The Lilly." LP

POEMS FOR FURTHER READING

Poems 195, 196, 197, 200, 202, 207, 208, 210, 211, 217, 218, 219, 224, 232, 242, 244, 254, 257, 262, and 263 from Part Two provide additional illustrations of topics presented in this chapter.

Chapter seven
Figurative Language 3:
Paradox, Overstatement, Understatement, Irony

70. *Emily Dickinson* **MY LIFE CLOSED TWICE** (page 99)

Most readers have little difficulty with the first paradox. The speaker, while living, suffered two metaphorical deaths through the loss of persons dearly beloved by her. Many readers, however, go on to interpret the possible "third event" as another event of the same kind: the loss of another dear friend.

The "third event," however, must be an event of a different order, an event contingent on her own death—for three reasons. (1) The use in line 1 of the past tense (rather than the present perfect) indicates that the speaker is at or near the point of her death: her life has come to its literal close now, and she is therefore in a position to make this definitive statement. (2) The two previous events had been "unveiled" to her by life (losing friends to death is an inescapable part of life); this third event (if it occurs) will be unveiled to her by Immortality. (3) An event of a different order is aesthetically required by the necessity of bringing the poem to a climax: otherwise it could go on forever: ". . . a fourth event . . . a fifth event, etc."

Both interpretations suggested in the first study question for lines 2-6 are viable: (a) This speaker is uncertain whether Immortality awaits her and will unveil a "third event" to her; (b) She does not know whether any "third event" unveiled to her by Immortality can have an emotional magnitude for her equal to that of the two losses she suffered during her life. She suggests, in other words, that the deaths of her two precious friends were so painful to her that even the bliss of her own entry into heaven (or the horror of her entry into hell) may seem trivial by comparison. (Or does she perhaps suggest that Immortality, by separating her from friends still living, may be as painful to her as mortality twice was, by separating her from friends newly dead?)

The last two lines, by using "heaven" and "hell" simultaneously in both their literal and metaphorical senses, sum up the themes both of uncertainty about the future (we do not know whether life on earth will be followed by a continued existence in heaven or hell) and of the tremendous emotional impact of separations suffered during life. Parting is "all we need of hell." Loss of a loved person is so painful that any further suffering for any sins we have committed in life is entirely unnecessary. "Parting is all we know of heaven." This line is subject to two interpretations: (1) The closest we can come to knowing heaven is when our friends depart for it—which is to say, we can know nothing of it as long as we are still living and our friends have gone there without us. (2) Though we do not know whether there is an afterlife of bliss after death, we have a foretaste of what heaven will be like (if it does exist) in the emotions we feel at parting from loved ones during life. Parting is a sweet experience as well as painful one: it is sweet because, at the moment of parting, one's whole heart flows out to the departing friend; at the moment we feel our love (because we are about to lose its object) more fully and intensely than ever before. Thus, at parting, deep love and deep grief commingle, offering a possible foretaste of heaven and enough of "hell" to be sufficient forever. LP

71. *John Donne*   THE SUN RISING (page 100)

Like many other Donne poems in this text, this presents the dramatic situation of a speaker addressing a second party (in this case, the personified sun) from an easily identified place and time: he is in bed, with his love, at break of day. Like "Batter my heart, three-personed God" (page 108), "The Flea" (page 152), and "Song: Go and Catch a Falling Star" (page 266), the poem has a sense of immediacy arising from the speaker's apparent change of heart or mind as he is speaking, so that these poems have the effect of motivating their own conclusions out of the ideas with which they begin.

In the impertinent and colloquial opening lines, the speaker angrily chides the busybody sun for interrupting the lovers. Let him go elsewhere, remind other people for whom punctuality is a necessity (schoolboys, apprentices, courtiers, farmers) that it is time for them to be up and busy. Lovers, he says, are not governed by the sun with his "rags of time," seasons, hours, days, months; his peeping through their curtains is improper and rude (as rude as is the speaker in addressing the interloper).

While the first stanza insists that this is neither the time nor the place for the sun to intrude, it does acknowledge the sun's power in keeping the world on time. But in the second stanza the speaker denies that the sun's beams do have the power to control mankind: he can shut them out merely by blinking, though he won't do so because that would mean not looking at his love. With a traditional overstated metaphor, he suggests that his love's eyes are so bright that they might blind the sun himself; but if they have not, then the sun should go off on his daily inspection of the world, and return—tomorrow (as he inevitably will)—to report whether the East and West Indies, sources of spices and gold, haven't left their accustomed places to gather into the person of his love, here in the bed. And if the sun in his journey should ask for all the kings of the world, he will be told that they too have left their kingdoms, and are gathered into the person of the speaker.

The third stanza extends the metaphor of the world contracted into the one bedchamber. The woman is all the nations, the speaker all their rulers—and there is nothing left out there for the sun to shine upon. All those who call themselves princes are imitations, as is their honor and their wealth. Having reduced the world to that point, the speaker then pityingly tells the weary old sun that he can do his job of warming the world merely by shining on the two lovers, as he invites him to do.

Thus the initial attitude, chasing away the powerful sun, changes to welcoming his warmth and attention. What does the speaker really want, then? (And does he, literally, have any choice in the matter?) Most of all he wants his lady to overhear the extravagance of his praise for her and his claims of the importance of their love. The changes in attitude, from chiding the sun to denigrating his power to welcoming him into the chamber, while they are inconsistent, have in common the theme that he and his love are superior to the whole world, to the sun itself. The intellectual playfulness of his dialogue, the wide-ranging references, even the inconsistencies, mean "this woman means more to me than the whole world." The sprightliness of this "overheard" speech might have his lady laughing at his outrageousness, but she could not help being flattered by it. TRA

72. *Countee Cullen* INCIDENT (page 101)

Good poetry may be simple or complex. This poem relates a simple incident simply, in simple stanza form, without elaboration of metaphor or simile. And yet, in twelve lines, it sums up the poignant tragedy of the black experience in America —friendliness rebuffed, the childish hurt that leaves a scar, happiness turned to ashes.

Simple as the poem is, we should not regard it as artless. Notice how the four mouth-filling syllables "heart-filled, head-filled" in line 2 are counterpointed against the five skipping syllables of "Baltimorean" in line 3. Because the two hyphenated words are jammed with consonants and separated by a comma, and because they spread two metrical accents evenly over four syllables, they take twice as long to pronounce as the five syllables and three accents of "Baltimorean." The emphasis is appropriate to their emotional importance and gives them the sense of *fullness* required by the meaning. Notice also how the climactic incident of the poem is set off by the rhythm. The other lines of the poem are all to some degree end-stopped; even line 3 is followed by a natural pause. But lines 7 and 8 break in the middle, and line 7 is the one line in the poem which demands that the voice rush on to the next line without pause. Thus the contemptuous action and the contemptuous epithet are isolated by the rhythm. Finally, notice how the significance of the incident is brought home by understatement. We are not told that the speaker's glee was turned to pain, that the contemptuous epithet went through him like a sword or rankled in his consciousness, or that he felt suddenly crushed and humiliated. We are told only: "Of all the things that happened there / That's all that I remember." Need we be told more?*

*Reprinted from Laurence Perrine and James M. Reid, *100 American Poems of the Twentieth Century* (New York: Harcourt Brace Jovanovich, 1966), pp. 190-91.

73. *Alexander Pope* **ON A CERTAIN LADY AT COURT** (page 103)

Pope's poem is ironic, but the very opposite of sarcastic or satiric: it employs irony to pay a graceful and beautiful compliment to the lady in question; it employs irony for purposes of praise, not detraction. The ironic line is line 10, for the one fault that the poet avers against the lady turns out to be her crowning virtue: modesty, lack of vanity. "Deaf" (line 12) is overstatement: literally the lady does not listen, or, rather, she makes no egotistic response to praise of herself. "All the world" (line 11) is also overstatement. "Envy" (lines 2, 9) is personification. LP

74. *William Blake* **THE CHIMNEY SWEEPER** (page 105)

Blake uses dramatic irony here for sympathetic rather than detractive purposes. In line 3 the boy, too young to articulate clearly, is calling out his trade in the streets—sweep, sweep, sweep, sweep—but the poet is telling us that we should weep over his pitiful plight. In lines 7-8 the innocent boy is genuinely trying to comfort his friend and does not recognize, as the poet does, the ironic discrepancy between the comfort he intends and the lack of comfort he actually offers, for not being able to have one's hair soiled is hardly consolation for having it shaved off! In line 24 the boy's words are an expression of a childlike trust that the poet, with more experience of the world, knows to be unfounded: the poem, in fact, is a protest against the harm that society causes its children by exploiting them for labor of this kind. In each case the dramatic irony arises from the poet's knowing more or seeing more than the child does, but in each case also the boy's ignorance testifies to his good heart and likable innocence.

The dream in lines 11-20 is obviously a wish-fulfillment dream, though Blake would not have been familiar with this Freudian terminology. It is also a miniature allegory, capable of two interpretations, one applying to this world, the other to the next. On the first level—most obviously the wish-fulfillment level—the "coffins of black" are the chimneys the boys work in, the Angel who releases them is a wise legislator or rich benefactor (like Oliver Twist's Mr. Brownlow) who releases them from the bondage of their labor with the key of social legislation or of wealth, and the green plains represent a happier future. At this level, the dream represents only a wish or a hope. On the second and perhaps more relevant level, the coffins are real coffins and the Angel is one of God's angels who releases the boys into heaven with the key of death. At this level, the poet is saying that the only release for these boys, under the then existing conditions of society, is through death. LP

75. *Percy Bysshe Shelly* **OZYMANDIAS** (page 106)

The central theme of "Ozymandias" is the vanity of the claims of human tyrants to enduring glory. It is brilliantly conveyed through irony of situation: the overturn of expectation by fulfillment. After reading the inscription on the pedestal, the second line of which may be paraphrased, "Look on my works, ye mighty (but lesser) kings, and despair of ever equaling them," one expects to look up and see a great imperial city with marble palaces, temples, hanging gardens, monuments, and fortified walls; instead, as far as the eye can reach, one sees only emptiness and sand.

Increasing the irony is the fact that the sole remaining work of this self-proclaimed "king of kings" is a huge broken statue (its hugeness manifesting his megalomania), carved by an artist who saw through the self-deluding egocentrism of the ruler and recorded it in stone, mocking Ozymandias, as it were, to his face. In the "frown, / And wrinkled lip, and sneer of cold command," the sculptor knew that his imperceptive and arrogant master would see only the signs of his awesome authority and power whereas the more perceptive viewer would note the absence of joy, wisdom, compassion, and humility—the marks of true greatness—and see only crude ambition and cruel passions. The insight of the artist has outlasted the power of the conqueror.

The emptiness of Ozymandias's pretensions to everlasting fame is further increased by the fact that this whole account has been related to the speaker by "a traveler from an antique land." That is, the speaker would never have heard of Ozymandias at all had it not been for his chance encounter with a desert explorer. (And most of us, in our turn, would never have heard of Ozymandias had the poet Shelley, another artist, not written a poem about the incident.)

No English reader in 1817 could have read this poem without thinking of Napoleon, who had made himself conqueror and ruler of almost all Europe before he was defeated at Waterloo in 1815 and exiled on the barren island of St. Helena in 1817. In more recent times we may be reminded of Hitler, Mussolini, Stalin, or Mao.

Except for the awkwardness caused by the separation of the transitive verb "survive" (7) and its objects "hand" and "heart" (8), the poem is brilliantly written. In "Nothing beside remains" (12), the word "beside" means both "beside" and "besides." The alliterating *b*'s, *l*'s, and *s*'s of the last two lines put a heavy emphasis on the words that re-create the vast level emptiness, and the final unstopped vowel sound allows the voice to trail off into infinity.

Two pitfalls for the student: (1) The "hand" that mocked the passions of Ozymandias is the sculptor's; the "heart" that fed those passions was Ozymandias's. The passions depicted in the stone visage have outlasted both the artist and the tyrant. (2) The words on the pedestal were not composed by the sculptor. Ozymandias commanded the sculptor to inscribe them there. The scupltor "mocked" Ozymandias by his frank portrayal of the ruler's character in the sculptured visage. LP

EXERCISE (page 107)

1. Paradox. 2. Irony. 3. Overstatement. 4. Understatement. 5. Paradox. 6. Overstatement. 7. Paradox ("immortal" is ironical). 8. Overstatement (containing also metaphor and personification). 9. Literal (but "soul" is a metonymy). 10. Paradox.

76. *John Donne* BATTER MY HEART, THREE-PERSONED GOD (page 108)

In the first quatrain Donne metaphorically compares God to a tinker who is trying to mend a metal utensil such as a kettle. Donne (the kettle) cries out to God that he needs to be made anew, not just repaired. It is not enough for God to "knock, breathe, shine," He must "break, blow, burn," and batter. The parallel series of verbs reflect the three persons of the Trinity. The verbs "knock" and "break" belong to the Father (representing Power); "breathe" and "blow" belong to the Holy Spirit (the word *spirit* comes originally from a Latin word meaning "to breathe"; cf. *respiration*); "shine" and "burn" belong to the Son, a concealed pun on *sun*.

In the second quatrain Donne compares himself to a town "due" to God but "usurped" by Satan (or sin), who has taken captive God's viceroy, Reason.

The "enemy" (10) again is Satan (or sin). LP

77. *John Frederick Nims* LOVE POEM (page 109)

The title may lead us to expect something about moonlight and roses, sighs and a broken heart. Instead, we are given taxicabs, streetcars, coffee, lipstick, and bourbon whiskey. But this is a modern love poem. It is appropriately placed among the realities of modern times (though streetcars have vanished since the poem's publication in 1947), and is more real in its passion because it is so.

Love poems traditionally praise the beloved, and so does this one. But it does not place her on a pedestal. She is clumsy, careless, unpredictable, never on time, "A wrench in clocks and the solar system." In short, she is also real—a human being, not a goddess. We love her the more for it. For her clumsiness with things is balanced by her deftness with people. The poem pivots on this contrast. She is hopelessly inept moving in traffic, but she maneuvers expertly "in traffic of wit." She may break cups, rip cloth, upset coffee, smear lipstick, and spill bourbon, but she knows how to put the nervous at their ease, to make the homeless feel at home, to steady the unsteady, and to join diverse people in a circle of good will, good conversation, gaiety, and love. She merits her lover's praise and devotion.

We may not expect to find wit in a love poem. But Shakespeare and Donne proved long ago that wit and deep feeling are compatible. The lover here, like his sweetheart, is able to maneuver expertly in traffic of wit: to speak of "The drunk clambering on his undulant floor," of lipstick "grinning" on a coat, of the "apoplectic streetcars" (the image is of the streetcar's madly jangling its bell at pedestrians or cars in its path), and of souls floating "on glory of spilt bourbon." Earlier poets loved to write about the soul, but seldom placed it in a context like this.

Overstatement is the traditional language of love poetry. The overstatements in this poem are as extravagant as any, but are used in dispraise as well as praise. The sweetheart is her lover's "clumsiest dear"; beneath her hands "*all* glasses chip and ring"; yet if her hands dropped "white and empty / All the toys of the world would break."

If his sweetheart died, her lover would be heartbroken. This is what the last line means. But it says it so as to make us *feel* it.*

*Commentary adapted from Laurence Perrine and James M. Reid, *100 American Poems of the Twentieth Century* (New York: Harcourt Brace Jovanovich, 1966), pp. 165-66.

78. *Sir John Harington* ON TREASON (page 110)

The verbal irony is in the first phrase, "treason doth never prosper," since the poem proceeds to explain what happens if it *does* prosper. One might also find situational irony in the final phrase, since it indicates an outcome contrary to truth or fact: that treason must be called by another name if it succeeds, even though it remains by definition what it is. This final phrase puts irony to the service of satire, pointing an accusing finger at those who for the sake of expedience (or out of fear) will avoid stating the truth.

The word "prosper" is the only equivocal term in the epigram, because it carries with it two relevant meanings—to succeed in an endeavor and to achieve wealth. One might conceive of a successful act of treason that does not bring with it wealth —that of the Minutemen in the American Revolution, for example, who were traitors to the British crown not for personal gain but for an idealistic goal. Harington's epigram, because of the ambiguities of "prosper," seems clearly to suggest a self-interested treason, perhaps the venality of an ambitious usurper.

Harington's wit thus plays with two aspects of language—the ambiguities that allow a single word to radiate meanings and connotations, thus enlarging its application; and the dicta of the powerful, who may suppress the use of a word, thus diminishing its ability to present truth, so that political success determines linguistic limits. TRA

79. *Donald W. Baker* FORMAL APPLICATION (page 110)

Occasion: The poet reads in *Time* that "poets apparently want to rejoin the human race." Perhaps startled to learn that he does not already belong to it, he decides to submit a formal application for membership. Examining recent history (World War II was its central event), he finds that modern man has devoted his major energies to devising ingenious methods of subjugating and destroying other men. The chief qualification for membership, then, is to be a crafty killer. In his application (the poem) he therefore describes the program he proposes for himself in order to acquire the requisite skills.

The poem divides into three equal sections of three three-line stanzas each, marked off by "I shall begin," "Meanwhile," and "Finally." The first section describes how he will master the skill of knife-throwing; the second, how he will acquire the craft of deceit, teaching the birds to trust him; the third, how he will combine these skills to "qualify as Modern Man." He brings his application to a vivid climax in the central stanza of this section through the use of a bold figure of rhetoric in which he addresses the reader as if the reader were actually on the spot, and directs his attention to the "splash of blood and feathers" pinned by his knife to the tree, thus demonstrating that he has already acquired the requisite skills. To identify this gruesome exhibition more closely with other modern artifacts and accomplishments of modern man, he gives it a euphemistic label: "Audubon Crucifix."

The poem as a whole is an exercise in verbal irony. The poet's petition for membership in the human race is a mock-petition. His program for qualifying himself is one that he does not intend to carry out. If the human race is what it appears to be, and if he indeed has the option of belonging or not belonging, he chooses not to belong. In addition, the poem is filled with ironic contrasts between appearance and reality—between the "pleasing (even pious) connotations" of some of its phrases and the brutal realities that lie beneath them. The progress from primitive savagery to civilization implied by the capitalized term "Modern Man" contrasts with the greatly increased scale of terror and destruction actually characterizing the modern world. The technical phrases "conditioned reflex" from modern psychology and "functional form" from modern aesthetic criticism here disguise the nature of the skills they actually refer to. The contrasts between connotation and reality in the terms "Audubon Crucifix," *Arbeit Macht Frei*, "Molotov Cocktail," and *Enola Gay* are obvious.

The title embodies two distinct meanings. It refers not only to the official petition for membership that the poet pretends to be making, but also to the disciplined effort he mockingly proposes to undertake in acquiring a precise coordination of wrist and fingers in throwing the knife: that is, a rigorous application of himself to the mastery of "form." LP

80. *W. H. Auden* **THE UNKNOWN CITIZEN** (page 111)

The title alludes to the "Unknown Soldier." It is ironic because *everything* is known about the "unknown" citizen—except, apparently, his name. The information about him is filed under a code number. The citizen has been reduced to a set of statistics. The loss of his name symbolizes the loss of his individuality. The unknown soldier's *body* had been blown to bits; the unknown citizen's *soul* has been blown to bits.

In the old sense, a "saint" was a person who served God (line 4). In the "modern" sense, he is a person who serves "the Greater Community." The old-fashioned saints, to serve God, often had to defy the world—and in doing so, they found their souls. The modern saint, to serve "the Greater Community," must only do everything he is told to do—and in doing so, he loses his soul. The things "necessary to the Modern Man" are purely materialistic things—"a phonograph, a radio, a car and a frigidaire"—and they are "necessary" not mainly to serve the man but to keep the economy going. The unknown citizen had no opinions of his own, but adopted those of the State—that is, he accepted State propaganda. He "never interfered" with the education of his children: what his children really received was indoctrination, not education, and the unknown citizen never questioned the rightness of what his children were taught.

For Auden himself the questions "Was he free? Was he happy?" are the important questions, not absurd ones, and in his eyes *everything* was wrong. The answers to the questions are that the unknown citizen was *not* free, though he never realized his lack of freedom, and that he was neither happy nor unhappy, for it takes a *man*, with a soul, to be happy or unhappy—and to be a man, one must be free, at least in his soul. The unknown citizen did not live; he existed. He was not a man but a statistic, a comfortable conformist, a pliant tool in the hands of the State.

The satire in the poem is against several tendencies of modern life: its increasing demands for conformity, uniformity, and collectivization; its materialism; and its disposition to do everything by statistics, to exalt the "average," and to put life into the hands of social scientists and managers. The old-fashioned saint was an extraordinary man; the modern one is an average man—if he can be called a man.

Be sure to ask students, "*Was* he free? *Was* he happy?"   LP

81. Robert Frost   DEPARTMENTAL (page 112)

The poem is a gentle satire—not against mankind or human nature—but against the increasingly departmentalized structure of the modern bureaucratic state, in which all human functions and needs are provided for by the state, with a resultant depersonalization of human relationships, specialization in human interests, and loss of individuality.

The satire is gentle because it is comic, and it is comic partly because the society actually observed is an ant society (we can be amused by behavior in ants that would be unamusing to us in human beings) and partly because of Frost's comic treatment (playful riming, humorous personifications, constant flow of whimsy). But this ant society is symbolic of modern human societies.

"Ants are a curious race" (13)—This generalization coming at the conclusion of the first example of ant behavior (the discovery by an ant of a huge dormant moth) and serving as introduction to the second illustration (the discovery of a dead ant by another member of the colony) is literally true in one sense of the word "curious"; but, ironically, what is curious about them is that, in another sense, they are an extremely incurious race: they have no curiosity about matters unrelated to their own assigned duties in the colony. The ant who discovered the moth "showed not the least surprise. / His business wasn't with such." The ant who discovers his dead fellow isn't "given a moment's arrest— / Seems not even impressed." But both ants pass the word along to the proper authorities, and the second illustration concludes with a "solemn mortician" heaving the dead ant "high in air" and carrying him away. "No one stands round to stare. / It is nobody else's affair." It is not that ants are apathetic or lazy (each is extremely busy pursuing his own assignment, and the whole society seems to function fairly efficiently); it is just that they are so extremely specialized. (No provision is made for grief, wonder, or personal relationships in the efficiently organized bureaucracy.) Nor is it that ants are selfish or self-centered: the adjective "selfless" (24) implies just the opposite: they devote their whole energies to serving the welfare of the colony (the "Greater Community" of Auden's poem); but, in doing so, they have become selfless in another sense: lacking selfhood. To shift metaphors violently, they are cogs in a machine.

The poem begins with the poet's having just observed the behavior of an ant on his dining table. (The interest shown by the poet in the much smaller ant contrasts with the lack of interest shown by the ant in the much larger moth.) This observation leads him to ruminate about ants in general, and to provide a second illustration of their behavior from past observations. The whimsy in the first observation about "the hive's inquiry squad / Whose work is to find out God / And the nature of time and space" is perhaps a thrust at the departmentalized University. The whimsy in the second illustration about the state burial is clearly aimed at the bureaucratic nation-state. For further discussion, see John Robert Doyle, Jr., *The Poetry of Robert Frost: An Analysis* (Johannesburg: Witwatersrand Univ. Press, 1962), pp. 92-99. LP

82. *M. Carl Holman*   MR. Z (page 113)

M. Carl Holman is a black poet, and "Mr. Z" is the ironic portrait of a black man who attains distinction in life by disowning his own racial and cultural heritage and adapting himself to the manners and values of the white world. He is apparently light-skinned, for he is able to do this quite successfully, and he marries a white woman who, out of a similar motivation, has disowned her Jewish heritage and is adapting herself to the manners and values of the gentile world. The marriage is a marriage of convenience for both of them, for through the marriage, they are both enabled to shake off some of the social stigma of their own backgrounds. There is also the suggestion that neither of them could have acquired a purely white gentile mate of respectable social pretensions: they have had to settle for the second best, which is nevertheless better, in their eyes, than marriage within their own cultures.

In giving Mr. Z only an initial, not a name, the poet suggests that Mr. Z has lost personal identity by disclaiming racial identity. In choosing the last letter of the alphabet for that initial, the poet suggests his own low opinion of Mr. Z. The satire of the poem is directed mainly at Mr. Z and the type of person he represents. But the satire also hits, secondarily, at the snob values of a WASP society that make people like Mr. Z and his wife possible. Mr. Z is clearly a person of considerable ability, and in a healthy society he could have remained himself and still have acquired the kind of recognition he needed.

The obituary notices cruelly reflect the false values of this society by making Mr. Z's distinction relative, not absolute. There is subtle though probably unconscious condescension in the statement that Mr. Z was "one of the most distinguishd members of his race." (Implication: He did pretty well for a black person. Further implication: Blacks are inferior.) But the obituary notices are particularly cruel for Mrs. Z, for they implicitly reveal the fact which all their lives she and Mr. Z labored to conceal. This is irony of situation.

There is muted irony throughout the poem: "perfect part of honor" (2), "faced up" (7), "exemplary" (9), "profane" (10), "right" (17), "not one false note" (23). The first ironic note is in the first line, and it might be labeled either verbal or dramatic. The reader realizes, as Mr. Z's "teachers" and Mr. Z do not, that an accident of birth cannot possibly be a "sign of error." (One infers, incidentally, that Mr. Z was lighter skinned than his mother, and that his father may have been white.) LP

83. Robert Browning   MY LAST DUCHESS (page 114)

Speaker: The Duke of Ferrara. Time: Late Italian Renaissance, probably mid-sixteenth century. Place: An upper room or corridor in the Duke's palace. Audience: An envoy from the Count whose daughter the Duke plans to marry. Occasion: The Duke and the Count's emissary have just concluded negotiations over the terms of the marriage and the dowry which the Duke expects to receive with his bride. (Students need to know that a duke of Ferrara was a supremely powerful figure, equal in status to a king.) On their way to join the company of guests and courtiers in the assembly hall below, they pass a portrait of the Duke's former duchess, and the Duke pauses to display it for the emissary, engaging him now in what seems purely social talk.

The primary subject of the poem is the character of the Duke, but Browning is interested in his character also as it reflects his period in history (the pride and arrogance of the aristocracy, its system of arranged marriages, its enthusiasm for art and artists). A secondary and pendant point of interest lies in the character of the duchess.

The Duke is characterized, first, by pride—pride of birth and station. He is a duke—let no one forget it!—and one with "a nine-hundred-years-old name!" His dissatisfaction with his former wife (but he refers to her always as his "duchess") is that she forgot it. Instead of being lofty and reserved like himself, saving her smile only for him, thus enhancing the eminence of his station, she treated social inferiors as equals, blushed when they complimented her, was too visibly pleased when they did her favors. She did not comport herself like a duchess! And why didn't he try to correct her? Because to have done so would have been to "stoop." Even if she had accepted his tutelage without making excuses or arguing back (the ultimate humiliation)—"E'en then would be some stooping; and I choose / Never to stoop!" A proud purchaser doesn't haggle over defects in the merchandise; he simply sends it back and demands replacement.

Second, the Duke is cruel. Were it not for the "stooping," the Duke would not hesitate to tell his wife "This . . . in you disgusts me." But since he wouldn't stoop, he "gave commands;/ Then all smiles stopped together." What were the commands? Browning doesn't tell us, and doesn't need to, for the very tone in which the words are uttered sufficiently underlines the Duke's cruelty and arrogance. But probably they were to have the duchess put to death. In the opening lines, "That's my last duchess painted on the wall, / Looking as if she were alive," the subjunctive mood implies that she is no longer living—a suggestion repeated in line 47.

Third, the Duke is a connoisseur of art. There is no need to believe that his love of art is not genuine: love of art can coexist comfortably with egotism and cruelty in some natures (read *The Autobiography of Benvenuto Cellini*); and this was a time of great enthusiasm for art and artists. The Duke is a patron and collector of art. He speaks appreciatively of the merits of Fra Pandolf's painting and keeps a protective curtain in front of it which he allows no one but himself to draw. Nevertheless, his love of art is not pure; it too reflects his pride. He is proud of having commissioned work from painters and sculptors of such eminence as Fra Pandolf and Claus of Innsbruck and he carefully drops their names into his conversation ("I said Fra Pandolf by design"). Part of the value of his Neptune taming a sea-horse is that it is "thought a rarity," and that Claus of Innsbruck cast it in bronze "for me!"

Finally, the Duke is shrewd. He knows what he wants, and he knows how to get it. While apparently simply making pleasant conversation about the shortcomings of his former duchess, he is indirectly informing the envoy what he expects in his new duchess, knowing that the envoy will report it back to the Count. Primary evidence of the Duke's shrewdness is his skill in speech. His disclaimer of such skill (35-36) is part of the evidence for it, and should remind the reader of a similar disclaimer by Shakespeare's Mark Antony in his oration on Caesar, which serves a similar purpose. It is a rhetorical trick, designed to throw the listener off his guard. The Duke's momentary gropings after words (21-23, 31-32) by no means support this disclaimer, for the words he eventually comes up with are exactly the right words, and the hesitation in his speech only serves to give them added emphasis. But the conclusive proof of the Duke's skill in speech is the beautifully modulated passage (48-53) in which he couches his demand for dowry. Clearly the dowry is his main motivation in this new marriage (he is driving a hard bargain: his rank and nine-hundred-years-old name for her money), but he is too polished to avow this openly, so he adds, "Though his fair daughter's self, as I avowed / At starting, is my object." The words "I repeat" and "as I avowed / At starting" show that the

Duke has mentioned both of these matters before, in reverse order; he is now driving them home in the order of their real importance, making sure he is clearly understood. The passage is a masterpiece of diplomatic circumlocution. Though the nature of the demand is made perfectly clear, it is gloved in a sentence softened by a double negative and by a skillfully tactful and euphemistic choice of diction: not "riches" but "munificence"; not "proves" but "is ample warrant"; not "my demand" but "no just pretense of mine"; not "refused" but "disallowed." The hard bargaining is thus enveloped in an atmosphere of perfect courtesy. The Duke's diplomatic skills are also shown throughout in his treatment of the emissary, which is subtly designed to flatter. After the business conference, he gives the emissary a private showing of his prized portrait and chats in a friendly manner about personal affairs. This courtesy, from the man who is accustomed to give commands and who objected to too much courtesy in his Duchess, is apparent throughout the interview: "Will't please you sit and look at her? . . . Will't please you rise?" And when the envoy, having risen, waits respectfully for the Duke to precede him downstairs, as befits his eminence, the Duke tells him, "Nay, we'll go / Together down, sir." And so the envoy walks side by side down the stairway with the possessor of a nine-hundred-years-old name who has just said, "I choose / Never to stoop." How can he do other than return a favorable report to the Count?

So much for the Duke; what about the Duchess? The Duke paints her as being frivolous, trivial, too free in manner, "too easily made glad." The reader's reaction to her, however, is controlled by the genuine pleasure she takes in compliments; by her graciousness to all, regardless of station; and especially by the simple things she takes delight in: the beauty of a sunset, a gift of a bough of cherries, a ride round the terrace on a white mule. Her response to these indicates a warm, sensitive nature which takes joy in natural things rather than in gauds and baubles or the pomp of position and power which attract the Duke.

The poem is a masterpiece of dramatic irony, a dramatic irony which is manifested chiefly in the whole tone of the poem rather than in specific passages. The Duke speaks all the words. He seeks to give a favorable impression of himself (and no doubt succeeds with the envoy, who belongs to his world and has not our advantage of perceiving him through the lens of art) and an unfavorable impression of his last duchess. What Browning conveys to the reader is exactly the opposite. LP

EXERCISE (page 116)

11. Irony. 12. Paradox. 13. Paradox. 14. Paradox. 15. Irony. 16. Paradox.

POEMS FOR FURTHER READING

Poems 201, 203, 204, 205, 214, 216, 221, 224, 227, 228, 233, 249, and 256 from Part Two provide additional illustrations of topics presented in this chapter.

Chapter eight
Allusion

84. *Robert Frost* "OUT, OUT—" (page 118)

A newspaper account would have given us facts—the boy's name, his age, the exact place and time of the accident. The poet, as omniscient narrator in this poem, is interested in communicating experience. The first six lines provide a vivid sense of the setting through combined images of sight (sawdust, stove-length sticks of wood, five mountain ranges under the sunset), of smell (the resinous scent of new-cut timber), and of sound (the onomatopoetic snarling of the buzz-saw as the timber is pushed through it, its onomatopoetic rattling as it waits for the next load). Vivid visual imagery continues through the poem (the boy holding up his injured hand, the boy under ether puffing his lips out with his breath). The poem also provides dialogue (as a newspaper account wouldn't except in the form of a witness's answers to a reporter's questions) and includes the poet-narrator's own comments ("Call it a day, I wish they might have said . . ."; "the saw, / As if to prove saws knew what supper meant, / Leaped out at the boy's hand . . ."; "No more to build on there").

The role of chance is underscored in the poem in that the boy's death is really a double-accident. The cutting of the hand is caused by a moment of inattention, but moments of inattention rarely have such a dire consequence. The boy's death is caused by shock, but fatal shock infrequently follows such a "minor" accident. The boy does not expect it. The attendants can't believe it. There is indeed a terrible situational irony involved in the swift progression from the boy's first reaction ("a rueful laugh") to his perception that the accident may cost him his hand to the ending that no one anticipates.

The abruptness of the last line-and-a-half misleads some students into thinking the central theme of the poem identical with that of Housman's "Is my team ploughing" (page 21): namely, that life goes on without us when we are gone just as it did before. To be sure, these lines do embroider the central theme with the truth that individual death does not bring human life to a halt. But Frost deliberately leaves the antecedent of "they" ambiguous, and he does not say how quickly "they . . . turned to their affairs." We should not assume that the sister returned to the normal course of her life as quickly as did the doctor, or that the unseen parents immediately resumed their lives as if nothing had happened. LP

85. *William Shakespeare* Excerpt from **MACBETH** (page 120)

The importance of recognizing Shakespeare's poetic rhythms is made clear in the punctuation and scansion of the third line of this passage. A prosaic reading, emphasizing the dictionary stresses only, sounds like this: toMORrow and toMORrow and toMORrow. But the commas fall between the syllables of iambic feet, throwing greater stress on the normally slurred syllable "and," to this effect:

to- MOR- / row, AND / to- MOR- / row, AND / to- MOR- / row.

That boring, eventless regularity imitates the apathy that has hardened Macbeth's heart and poisoned his mind. TRA

86. *e. e. cummings* **IN JUST-** (page 121)

In this little poem about "Just- / spring"—that is, the very first beginning of spring—Cummings captures the perennial delight of the children in a world that is "mud-luscious" and "puddle-wonderful" and in which they can again play outside at marbles and piracies and hop-scotch and jump-rope. The setting is urban, and the whistle of the balloonman advertising his wares in the park or along the sidewalks brings the children running.

The description of the "little / lame balloonman" as "goat-footed" links him (or identifies him) with Pan, half-man, half-goat, the Greek god of nature and legendary inventor of the panpipes. When Pan blew on his pipes in the spring, all the little creatures of the field and wood came running. Thus Cummings's city scene reenacts ancient ritual, and the "queer / old balloonman" ushers in the season that begins life anew as he has done each spring since the beginning.

Though the poem is written in free verse, it is organized into alternating four-line and one-line "stanzas" with a floating refrain in the thrice-repeated "balloonman whistles far and wee" each time preceded by an announcement that it's spring. The hyphenated adjectives "mud-luscious" and "puddle-wonderful" express exuberance in the assonance of their principal vowel sounds and echoing *d*'s and *l*'s; the hyphenated nouns "hop-scotch" and "jump-rope" display assonance and consonance respectively; the lines "luscious the little / lame balloonman" glide on alliterating *l*'s; and breathless "eddieandbill" and "bettyandisbel" echo each other in both vowel and consonant sounds. The whole builds up a celebration of spring and the children's delight in it. Cummings called it a "Chanson Innocente." LP

87. *John Milton* **ON HIS BLINDNESS** (page 122)

The three parables grouped together in Chaper 25 of Matthew's Gospel teach the necessity of being prepared for the day of judgment, for the coming of the Lord.

They emphasize chiefly two aspects of preparedness: that the Lord's arrival will be sudden and without warning, and that the actions of the waiting life are an enactment of the judgment to be made (and, as in the third parable, verses 31-46, that men cannot recognize the meanings of all their actions). The middle parable to which this poem alludes teaches that the state of being prepared for the Lord's return is an *active* state, which insofar as possible requires the servants to perform as their master has performed—even if, to their limited understanding, the master has seemed a sharp dealer more interested in profit than in justice.

The parable of verses 14-30 contrasts the behavior of servants of a lord who in his absence are entrusted with sums of money. Two of them employ the money as their lord had, in trade and usury, and double their sums, while the third buries the one talent he has been given. When the lord returns from his travels, the two who have doubled his money are rewarded, but the one who has only the single talent to surrender back is cast "into outer darkness." The parable has been interpreted to equate the talent with faith, and to mean that one must not merely possess faith, but employ it in the manner God intends. (Taken literally, of course, it seems to teach the value of investing and taking risks, and castigates the person who merely hoards and saves.)

Milton had begun going blind in the late 1640s; this sonnet has been dated variously from 1652 to 1656, while Milton was actively involved in his duties as Oliver Cromwell's "Latin Secretary," a position roughly equivalent to secretary of state, explaining and justifying Cromwell's Puritan regime to the monarchies of Europe. In the sonnet he ponders his future life and work, contrasting the possible use of his literary talent (and his faith) in ways far different from writing public statements and pamphlets supporting the Cromwellian theocracy. The poem seems to report a crisis in his life, examining the alternatives for a writer who wants his gift to fulfill God's plan for him.

In his blindness (both physical and, momentarily, spiritual) Milton laments that he is not employing his talent, which he supposes useless to do the Lord's work, and fears that when he is confronted by his Maker and made to render his account, he will be cast away. He is foolishly about to ask how a man whose sight has been taken by God can be expected to do the same work as others. But his patience, personified, forestalls the question, telling him that his affliction is not a heavy burden and that his service to God may be merely to "stand and wait" rather than to pursue a life of action.

The word "wait" has several relevant denotative meanings (this poem might be used as the occasion for students to learn to consult the *Oxford English Dictionary,* with its full historical definitions). It may mean to await—that is, to stand in readiness for the master's arrival; or to wait upon—to attend to less active tasks than the "thousands" who range over the world carrying out the Lord's commands, as Milton figuratively is doing for Cromwell. In obsolete meanings current in Milton's time, it also meant to hope or to expect, or—a definition that returns to line 1—to consider. Patience is thus counseling him to accept his less spectacular tasks, to be ready for whatever God intends, to live in Christian hope and expectation of his salvation, and to return to the starting point of the sonnet—to consider again.

In the octave, Milton appears to misunderstand the meaning of the parable, thinking it unfair of God to expect "day-labor" from one who has been deprived of eyesight. But like the verbal echoes of the language of trade, the objection to the parable is literal-minded; properly understood, as Patience instructs him, it teaches him to bear what he must, to stand in readiness, and not to believe that only great activities gain God's grace, for the best service is performed by those who accept their limitations and maintain an active faith.

The word "prevent" is the hinge of the sonnet, occurring at the point separating the octave from the sestet. In its sense of "forestall" it reveals that the ideas of the sestet prevent him from voicing the foolish question to which his considerations have led him. In its further reference to the concept of "prevenience," it suggests that the advice of Patience is an action of God predisposing him toward performing God's will. In both senses, it reveals a circularity in the poem: "as I was about to murmur my complaint, Patience counseled me to consider again." This circularity is also suggested in the obsolete meaning of "wait," to consider. In effect the poem says that a reading of the parable momentarily led the poet to a misunderstanding of God's purposes, but God's prevenience checked him in time to see what those purposes really are. The half-rebellious mood of the octave never turns into open rebellion.

For further discussion of this sonnet, see: Marjorie Nicolson, *A Reader's Guide to John Milton* (New York: Farrar, Straus and Giroux, 1963), pp. 152-55; E. M. W. Tillyard, *Milton* (New York: Collier Books, 1967), pp. 160-62; and Macon Cheek, "Of Two Sonnets of Milton," reprinted in *Milton: Modern Essays in Criticism*, ed. Arthur E. Barker (New York: Oxford University Press, 1965), pp. 125-35.   TRA

88. *John Donne*   HERO AND LEANDER (page 122)

Greek philosophers believed that the universe is composed of four basic elements: air, earth, fire, and water. Donne uses this scientific concept as a basis for celebrating the legendary love of Hero and Leander, who, separated from each other by the wide waters of the Hellespont and by the opposition of Hero's parents to their union, nevertheless managed to meet secretly every night by Leander's feat of swimming the Hellespont guided by Hero's signal light. On one stormy night, however, Hero's light was blown out by the fierce winds and Leander was drowned by the fierce waves. When Hero saw Leander's body wash ashore, she threw herself too into the water and later was buried by his side.

Of the four elements uniting the lovers in the poem, "air," "ground," and "water" are all literal, but "air" is part of a form 2 metaphor which compares it to a commodity or possession of which one can be "robbed." "Fire," on the other hand, is the figurative term in a form 3 metaphor, whose literal term is passion.   LP

89. Keith Jennison   LAST STAND (page 123)

The title makes us think of Custer; the last line, of *Don Quixote*. Both allusions are ironic, for the courage of Custer and Quixote, however foolish or "quixotic," is in contrast to the timidity of the poem's subject. Quixote charged the windmills; this man waits, trembling, for the windmills to charge him. Like Quixote, he is foolish; but, unlike Quixote, he is a coward.

Triteness is the point of the poem, for this man has a trite mind; he thinks in clichés: "sound the alarm," "saddle up your steed," "take the bit in your teeth," "put your ear to the ground." Line 2 mixes a metaphor. In line 6, the image of someone sitting on a fence with his ear to the ground is visually absurd, but poetically valid, for it expresses the triteness and the confusion of the subject's mind. People who think in slogans are seldom logically consistent, or even logical.

A good poem can be made out of trite language when the trite language is used consciously for ironic effect.   LP

90. Edwin Arlington Robinson   MINIVER CHEEVY (page 123)

"Miniver Cheevy" is a portrait etched in irony. Misfit and failure, unable to adjust to the present, Miniver escapes reality by dreaming of a romantic past, and by drinking. Miniver longs for "the good old days" (or "bad old days"), which are more highly colored in his imagination than they were in actuality.

"Child of scorn"—this deliberately ambiguous phrase suggests a mythological paternity, Miniver's father was Scorn personified, and Miniver is his father's son. Miniver scorns the present: its art, its warfare, its materialistic aims, its drabness. But Miniver is also the target of scorn. His own scorn of the present is a rationalization of his failure to adjust to it, a defense against the scorn of others. The word *child* points up his essential immaturity.

The triteness of "days of old," "swords . . . bright," "steeds . . . prancing," "warrior bold" signals the superficiality of Miniver's idealization of the past, and its source in romantic literature. The homely word "neighbors" next to "Thebes and Camelot" makes Miniver's dream ludicrous, and the ironic juxtaposition of "grace" with "iron clothing" brings out a clank. That Miniver, if he could have chosen, would have belonged to one of the wealthiest families of history—the Medici—reveals the falsity of his contempt for gold; that then he would have "sinned incessantly" exposes the cheapness of all his values. Notice how the collocation of "ripe" and "renown" makes the first word suggest "overripe" and the second "notoriety." "Fragrant," because it follows, brings to mind not springtime and blossoms but fall and decaying fruit.

Robinson achieves his effect through form as well as diction. The repetition of Miniver's name at the beginning of each stanza reinforces the self-centeredness of his dreams. The short last line and feminine ending of each stanza furnish an anticlimax that jars Miniver's romantic idealization. The hissing *s* sounds in "assailed the seasons" and "sinned incessantly" echo Miniver's scorn and his evil glee in the prospect of sin. Robert Frost has expressed his delight in the second to last stanza: "There is more to it than the number of 'thoughts.' There is the way the last one turns up by surprise around the corner, the way the obstacle of verse is turned to advantage." The last "thought," of course, is the drop that overflows the bucket, emphasizing the futility of Miniver's thinking. In the final stanza the alliteration of key verbs—*kept, coughed, called, kept*—reasserts the continuance of the activity. The last line is brilliant poetic economy. Robinson first tells us that Miniver has been drinking by telling us that he "kept on" drinking. And the parallelism of "kept on drinking" with "kept on thinking" makes us supply a "drank, and drank, and drank, and drank" to match the previous repetitions of "thought."

Born too late? Miniver would have been "born too late" whenever he had been born. [This discussion is condensed from a much more detailed analysis in the *Colby Library Quarterly*, 6 (June 1962), 65-74.]   LP

91. *William Butler Yeats*   LEDA AND THE SWAN (page 124)

What this sonnet describes is, quite literally, a rape. The action of the rape is indicated precisely through sexual terms and symbols. The first quatrain describes the fierce assault and the foreplay; the second quatrain, the act of intercourse; the first part of the sestet, the sexual climax; the last part, the languor and apathy following the climax. But this is no ordinary rape: it is a rape by a god, by divine power temporarily embodied in the majestic form of a swan. And so it is described in terms that bring out awesomeness, not sordidness. The divinity appears as a "feathered glory" and its assault is "a white rush." It is also a momentous rape: it has large consequences for the future. And so the climax is described in terms that convey not only the experience of orgasm but also its remote consequences: the destruction of Troy, the death of Agamemnon. And then, after the moment of passion is over, and its results indicated, Yeats asks a question about the significance of the act: "Did she put on his knowledge with his power?"

Neither the word *swan* nor the name *Zeus* is mentioned in the body of the poem. We must rely on the title for our cues to the mythological event. Leda was a mortal princess by whose beauty Zeus, king of the gods, was smitten, and with whom he consummated his passion in the form of a swan. There are several versions of this story, but in all of them Helen of Troy was one offspring of this union, and in the version used by Yeats, Clytemnestra was another. [See William Butler Yeats, *A Vision* (New York: Macmillan, 1956), p. 51.] The later abduction of Helen by the Trojan prince Paris from her husband the Greek king Menelaus led, of course, to the ten-year siege of Troy by Greek forces under the command of Agamemnon and to the ultimate defeat of the Trojans and the burning of Troy by the Greeks. On his return from Troy, Agamemnon was murdered by his wife Clytemnestra and her lover. (It matters little which version of the Leda story we know, the ultimate results are the same.)

In her union with the god, Leda clearly took on some of the power of the godhead, for she bore in her womb the forces that were to shape the future. Did she also take on his knowledge? The question can be formulated in different ways. Can human sexual passion ever foresee its consequences? Can power and wisdom coexist in human life? Can man ever combine the vitality and passion of youth with the knowledge and wisdom of age (cf. "The Coming of Wisdom with Time," page 145)?

The question posed is left unanswered. Critics differ over whether an answer is implied. Some say the question is left open: that it is unanswerable. Others claim that it is the third of three rhetorical questions asked in the poem, all implying a negative answer (lines 5-6: "They can't"; lines 7-8: "It can't help but feel"; lines 13-14: "No."). Others suggest that power and knowledge can be combined in moments of artistic inspiration. This is a rich poem. For three provocative discussions, see Arnold Stein, in *Sewanee Review*, 57 (Winter 1949), 617-20; Hoyt Trowbridge, in *Modern Philology*, 51 (Nov. 1953), 118-29; Leo Spitzer, in *Modern Philology*, 51 (May 1954), 271-76. LP

92. *T. S. Eliot* JOURNEY OF THE MAGI (page 125)

The traditional story tells of the three Magi, journeying from the East, following a star, bearing gifts of gold, frankincense, and myrrh, to worship the child in the stable. When the star stopped over Bethlehem, the Bible tells us, "they rejoiced with exceeding great joy." Eliot's poem undercuts our sentimental anticipation almost immediately. It doesn't mention the star; it says nothing of gold, frankincense, and myrrh; above all, it doesn't represent the experience as one of transforming joy.

Eliot's narrator, one of the Magi, is remembering the journey a long time after it happened, perhaps dictating it to be put in writing by a scribe (33-35). He begins with a description of the hardships of the journey: freezing weather, bad roads, refractory camels, unreliable camel men, hostile cities, unfriendly towns, dirty villages, high prices. Instead of following a star with unwavering confidence and joy, they are plagued by doubts telling them this journey is "all folly." As they near their destination, they encounter indications suggesting hope of something better—a temperate valley, a running stream, a white horse; but these indications are balanced by less hopeful ones—"six hands at an open door dicing for pieces of silver." (The images here anticipate events or symbols connected with the life and death of Christ—the three trees, the three crosses on Golgotha; the white horse, the first of the four horses of the Apocalypse, a symbol of Christ; the vine leaves and wineskins, the wine of the Eucharist; the six hands dicing, the soldiers who diced for Christ's garments; the pieces of silver, the thirty pieces for which Judas betrayed Christ.) When they finally reach the stable, instead of presenting a glorified vision of a haloed Christ child surrounded by adoring shepherds and angels, the narrator can only say, "It was (you may say) satisfactory."

This poem is concerned with the experience of conversion, of spiritual rebirth. Conversion, as Eliot depicts it and as he knew it, is not necessarily a sudden transcendent experience accompanied by light from heaven and "exceeding great joy." It may instead be a slow painful process, accompanied by doubt of its validity, by spiritual agony and perplexity. It means destruction of one's former beliefs and way of life and their replacement by a new, more demanding way of life. "This Birth," the speaker says (he is referring both to the birth of Christ and his own rebirth), was "hard and bitter agony for us, like Death, our death." It made them no longer able to live comfortable lives among their people, whose beliefs they no longer shared. Yes, he would do it again, he says; but he does not say so eagerly. He yearns, in fact, for another death—physical death—to put an end to a difficult, demanding life.*

*This commentary is adapted from Laurence Perrine and James M. Reid, *100 American Poems of the Twentieth Century* (New York: Harcourt Brace Jovanovich, 1966), pp. 133-34.

93. *Emily Dickinson* **ABRAHAM TO KILL HIM** (page 127)

94. *Emily Dickinson* **BELSHAZZAR HAD A LETTER** (page 127)

These two poems illustrate a use of allusion in contrast to Milton's in "On His Blindness" (page 122), for while Milton's sonnet applies the meaning of his allusive source to the reality of a modern man's spiritual condition, taking the Biblical story "straight," Dickinson re-examines the scriptural stories and finds certain ironic meanings which may be applied to modern life in non-religious ways. In brief, she does not expect or require faith in the original meanings of the stories, but revises their significance for a less credulous age.

In the first of these two poems, Dickinson ironically presents the sovereignty of a testy "mastiff" of a God over a totally compliant servant and his "urchin" son. Abraham was unthinkingly, unhesitatingly obedient to God's pointless command; the heavenly tyrant was flattered, and so withdrew the command, allowing the urchin to grow into maturity and fatherhood. The "moral," tacked on as if the poet were paraphrasing Aesop rather than Moses, alliteratively jokes about the way God's creatures can learn how to placate Him to their own best interests. One might notice, though, that the speaker keeps her fingers crossed: she refrains from naming God or the Lord, whose orders are cast into the passive voice, and whose metonymous label ("Tyranny") and metaphoric incarnation ("mastiff") carefully sidestep direct delineation. And there is more fun in the poem arising from the elliptical way in which the events are narrated: you really do have to know (or consult) Genesis in order to understand what events are being alluded to—and when you do, you see that the detachment achieved by the cool latinisms of the second stanza (contrasted to the earthiness of lines 3-4 and the cliché of line 10) wryly deflates the incident. Does the poem have a "moral"? Probably "don't take that old Thunderer so seriously—His growl is worse than His bite."

The lesson originally taught by the story of Abraham and Isaac is not particularly appealing to the poet: unhesitating obedience to a tyrant's whimsy will placate a god of vengeance. But the moral of Daniel's story of Belshazzar (and his father Nebuchadnezzar) seems to have been more to the poet's liking. Belshazzar had not learned the lesson taught to his father, that the sacred vessels should not have been stolen from the temple in Jerusalem; he callously and impiously feasted from the holy kitchenware, and was informed by the finger of fire that his wickedness had been judged, and that he and his kingdom were to be destroyed—a prophecy fulfilled that very night. The tale presents the punishment of arrogance, willful refusal to learn, and luxurious sinfulness; from this the poet draws a moral for us all: conscience is a reliable guide to conduct. Yet the poem is not without ironic detachment in the understated metaphor of a "letter" from a "correspondent"; the point of the poem is that a person of conscience can dispense with such an interpreter as Daniel. We "can read without . . . glasses" and perhaps without recourse to holy scripture as well. TRA

95. *Anonymous* IN THE GARDEN (page 128)

If the answer to the question is not immediately forthcoming, it should be possible to elicit it from any class by means of a leading question or two. For example, the instructor may ask: Why does the poet say "the garden" instead of "a garden"? Is any garden so famous that one may refer to it as "the garden" and count on being understood?

It is also useful to ask why (besides for rime) the poet compares the maid to "flowers of the morn" instead of to flowers at noon or flowers at evening, for this question points up the difference between ordinary logic and poetic logic. Morning, noon, and evening flowers are equally fair, but there is a symbolic connection between the morning of a day and the morning of human life. Poetic logic calls for as tight a coherence of all details in the poem as possible. Emotional connections are more important than strictly logical ones.

A few students may need to have it explained that Eve was never "born." LP

EXERCISES (page 128)

1. The speaker is quite clear: she rejects the advice "When in Rome, do as the Romans do"—or at least she rejects the "Roman" diet of her white employer, as she silently satirizes her mock-generosity. The poet is more harsh than her obsequious speaker, for rather than thinking "yes'm," she displays the white woman's insensitivity and condescension. There are *no* values in this "Rome" that she would adapt to.

2. The types of fiction the speaker read in his "growth" are presented by the poet with dramatic irony. Although the speaker liked to identify himself with the heroes and villains—and regretfully came to recognize himself in the ineffectual cowards—the poet makes it clear that to have found such books satisfying was at least one of the speaker's mistakes: those books are indeed "a load of crap," but not for the reasons the speaker intends.
3. The three allusions that conclude the poem, as the footnote to the poem says, moving "backward in time through the historic, the legendary, and the prehistoric," offer support to the poem's theme: mankind from its earliest traces through its historical glory and in its creative imagination has consistently demonstrated its bellicosity, its tendency "to make / Red war yet redder." The allusions are offered in comparison to the theme, although the fact that the poet is stating what he sees as an irony of our race may momentarily mislead the student.
4. Ruth's sad, forlorn condition—"sick for home . . . amid the alien corn," listening to the song of the bird—is offered by the speaker as evidence of the immortality of the nightingale's song, a parallel to himself. That Ruth is also alone, forlorn, and unhappy, further reinforces the speaker's situation both before his imaginative transport and after he returns to the reality of his "sole self."
5. Frost regrets that beauty is a function of changes in time, transitory and fleeting; Ammons claims that this is a condition ordained for our benefit by "Providence," for our greater pleasure. This poem alludes ironically to Frost's, contradicting it. TRA

POEMS FOR FURTHER READING

Poems 190, 192, 203, 209, 235, and 250 from Part Two provide additional illustrations of topics presented in this chapter.

Chapter nine
Meaning and Idea

96. *Anonymous* **LITTLE JACK HORNER** (page 129)

"Little Jack Horner," of course, presents an example of dramatic irony—a boy who sticks his thumb in a pie is *not* a good boy. LP

97. *Sara Teasdale* **BARTER** (page 131)

98. *Robert Frost* **STOPPING BY WOODS ON A SNOWY EVENING** (page 131)

The statement that the reader should be able to enjoy both of these poems does not imply that they are of equal poetic value. Frost's poem is by far the richer, more resonant, more tightly structured of the two. Teasdale's poem is unified by its central metaphor of buying and spending. Its first two stanzas, after their opening thematic statement, comprise a brief catalogue of beautiful things, all lovely in themselves, but with no ordering principle beyond that dictated by the rime scheme. Frost's poem has a tight narrative and dramatic, logical, and psychological organization in which no lines or images could be interchanged without loss. There is further discussion of "Stopping by Woods . . ." on pages 142-43. LP

99. *William Cullen Bryant* **TO A WATERFOWL** (page 133)

100. *Robert Frost* **DESIGN** (page 134)

Bryant's and Frost's poems both begin with an observation from nature and end with an idea about God, but their conclusions are diametrically opposite. Bryant observes the solitary waterfowl at sunset as it flies on its annual spring migration to its summer breeding grounds in the North. Though the air through which it flies is "pathless," empty, and "illimitable," the bird is not lost (Bryant tells us), for there is "a Power [God] whose care" teaches it its way through "the boundless sky" and "guides" it safely to its destination. The poet concludes optimistically that he can safely entrust his own life to the guidance of the same Power.

The connotations in Frost's poem work in two opposite directions. First, there is a series of words and images suggesting innocence—"dimpled," "heal-all," "morning," "right," "snow-drop," "flower," "blue," "innocent," and the five-times repeated "white." Second, there is an equally impressive sequence suggesting evil—"spider," "death," "blight," "witches' broth," "dead," "night," "darkness," "appall." The collocation of these two kinds of words seems to pose a question.

The design indicated by the title is formed by three things—a white heal-all, a white spider, a white moth. The heal-all, a wild flower with medicinal virtues, is usually blue. Spiders are ordinarily black or brown. What has brought together these three white things, two of them so rarely white? It would seem the work of a conscious artist. But what is the consequence of this artistry? Death. The white moth, lured by the usually protective kindred color of the heal-all, has been trapped by the spider and killed. It is held now "like a white piece of rigid satin cloth" (the image not only describes a dead moth exactly but suggests the lining of a coffin). The three white things are thus "like the ingredients of a witches' broth." The suggestion that these ingredients have been mixed "to begin the morning right" (rite?) is ironical. There is irony also in the connection of the innocent color white with this sinister enterprise of death.

In the eighteenth century, a favorite argument for the existence of God was the so-called "argument from design." The intricate construction of the universe, it was held, with all of its stars and planets whirling in mathematically chartable courses and regulated by the law of gravity, testified to the existence of an infinitely wise creator, for how could there be design without a designer? As the nineteenth Psalm so eloquently expresses it, "The heavens declare the glory of God, and the firmament showeth his handiwork."

Frost's title alludes to this famous argument in a grimly ironical fashion. For the design, Frost points out, in nature is that of "a witches' broth." Thus the poem asks a terrible question,

What brought the kindred spider to that height,
Then steered the white moth thither in the night?
What but design of darkness to appall?—

Perhaps the universe is governed, not by infinite goodness, but by infinite evil. The poem does not assert this proposition as an actuality, merely suggests it as a possibility. And the suggestion is immediately softened, apparently, by the provision of another possibility—that perhaps design does not govern in a thing so small. But the afterthought, tossed in so casually, when examined closely turns out to be not very comforting either. If nature is not governed by design, then it is governed merely by chance, coincidence, anarchy, chaos—certainly not by the traditionally omnipotent benevolent God who is concerned over the smallest sparrow's fall.

Cast in the sonnet form but confining itself to only three rime sounds (the title might refer to the pattern of the poem as well as to the design made by the three white things in nature), Frost's brief poem chillingly poses the problem of evil.

Bryant's use of the verb "guides" (30) and Frost's of "steered" (12) makes Frost's poem seem almost a reply to Bryant's. The waterfowl's instinct in Bryant's poem guides it unerringly to its distant destination. Conclusion: a benevolent God presides over the universe and protects His creatures. The white moth's instinct in Frost's poem steers it unerringly into the spider's trap. Conclusion: perhaps the Power which presides over the universe is malevolent rather than benevolent, evil rather than good. Bryant offers reassurance; Frost offers terror. Frost's terror is more authentic than Bryant's reassurance, for Bryant ignores the fact that many waterfowl do *not* escape the fowler (5). (Whooping cranes were almost extinguished in the nineteenth and twentieth centuries to provide feathers for ladies' hats.)

Bryant's poem has been called a "great lyric" by Yvor Winters [*In Defense of Reason* (New York: Alan Swallow & W. Morrow, 1947), p. 239]; it was greatly admired by Matthew Arnold, and was once enthusiastically described by Hartley Coleridge as "the best short poem in the English language" [John Bigelow, *William Cullen Bryant* (Boston: Houghton Mifflin, 1890), pp. 42-43]. "Design" is surely one of the most powerful sonnets in the language.*

*This commentary is partially adapted from Laurence Perrine and James M. Reid, *100 American Poems of the Twentieth Century* (New York: Harcourt Brace Jovanovich, 1966), pp. 46-47.

101. *John Donne* **THE INDIFFERENT** (page 135)

102. *John Donne* **LOVE'S DEITY** (page 136)

The irony in "The Indifferent" depends on a simple reversal of what human beings usually call vice and virtue. For the speaker, constancy in love is a vice, promiscuity is a virtue. Love's "sweetest part" is variety, not fidelity. In the speaker's "religion" any woman who is faithful to one mate is a "heretic." The goddess of this religion is Venus (Aphrodite), who in classical mythology was herself unfaithful to her husband Vulcan (Haephestus) through affairs with Mars (Ares), Mercury (Hermes), Bacchus (Dionysus), and others, by one of whom she was mother of Cupid (Eros). When Venus hears the speaker's complaint that modern women are guilty of heresy (that is, of fidelity to one man), she forms herself into a one-person investigating committee and finds that the report is greatly exaggerated—she has found two or three faithful women, but no more, and she will punish them by giving them unfaithful mates.

The speaker in "Love's Deity" suffers from unrequited love and accuses "Love's deity" (Cupid) of having overreached his assigned duties. He wishes he could speak to the ghost of some lover who died before Cupid ("this child") was born, in order to confirm his charges. He believes that the older gods, who put Cupid in office, intended that his duties be restricted to assisting mutual lovers and bringing together young persons who could and would reciprocate each other's love. But, like other ambitious bureaucrats, Cupid has enlarged the powers of his office beyond its intended limits; he has tyrannically seized powers not meant to be his and aspires to powers equal to those of Jove himself. Instead of presiding over and helping to create a realm of harmonious and reciprocated feeling, Cupid has introduced obsession, lust, intrigue, and betrayal into his domain. Worst of all, the speaker seems to feel, Cupid has caused *him* to be in love with someone who does not return his love. This is the burden of his complaint through the first three stanzas. In the third stanza he becomes openly rebellious and blasphemous, proposing that if humankind were sufficiently aroused "by this tyranny / To ungod this child again, it could not be / I should love her who loves not me."

In the final stanza, however, shocked by the violence to which his thought has risen, he returns to a more moderate dissatisfaction. Addressing himself as "Rebel and atheist" (for wanting to "ungod" the child again), he reproaches himself for complaining; as he realizes, there are two worse fates that Love could have made him suffer Love could have (a) made him cease loving or (b) made her return his love.

But is this not an almost complete reversal of his previous thought? Indeed it is. Are these worse fates not paradoxically the very solutions he had earlier been desiring for his problem? Indeed they are. How do we explain them then? First, by understanding that the speaker, psychologically, must first give vent to his pain (as he does in the first three stanzas) before he can view his situation more calmly and philosophically. Second, by absorbing the new information (withheld until the final stanza) that the woman loved by the speaker is already attached to another man (she is probably a married woman; but at least she is fully committed elsewhere and was so before the speaker fell in love with her).

What, then, are the philosophical beliefs or values which serve to moderate, though not to obliterate, the speaker's suffering? First, that there is value in *all* loving. Although unrequited love involves deep anguish, there is a richness of feeling in this anguish that makes it better to have experienced it than never to have felt at all. Second, that infidelity in love is a grave moral deformity. "Falsehood [infidelity]," the speaker says, "is worse than hate." He would rather endure the pangs of unreciprocated love than enjoy the favors of a faithless woman.

[*Note:* Donne's favorite figurative devices are paradox and overstatement. It is probable that "hate" (27) and "scorn" (4) are both overstatements of her lack of responsiveness to any suit of adulterous love; or perhaps they literally express her feeling toward infidelity itself rather than her feeling toward the speaker.]

But now that we have resolved the contradictions and paradoxes in "Love's Deity," how do we resolve the contradictions between "Love's Deity" and "The Indifferent," both composed by the same poet? The speaker in "Love's Deity" regards fidelity in love as a virtue; the speaker in "The Indifferent" regards it as a "dangerous" vice. The two recommendations are polar opposites.

The easiest and best way of explaining the contradiction is simply to say that the two poems, though written by one poet, have two different speakers, neither one necessarily speaking for Donne himself. Donne in many of his poems seemed to be exploring different ways of regarding love by deliberately expressing disparate views through disparate speakers.

It should be noted that the speakers in these two poems mean different things by the word "love." The speaker in "The Indifferent" consistently uses the word to mean physical love—copulation. Nothing in the poem suggests that he recognizes any further dimensions of meaning for the word. The speaker in "Love's Deity" consistently means something more by the word: something perhaps combining warm affection, admiration, and physical desire. He makes a distinction, as the other speaker does not, between "love" and "lust." LP

103. *Gerard Manley Hopkins* THE CAGED SKYLARK (page 137)

"The Caged Skylark" is an Italian sonnet. The octave concerns the relationship of the spirit and the body in life, the sestet, the relationship of the spirit and the resurrected body in eternity. The basic analogies may be expressed thus:

1. spirit-in-life : body = caged skylark : cage
2. immortal spirit : resurrected body = wild skylark : nest = meadow-down : rainbow

Both a rainbow and a shadow are perfect images for weightlessness, but a shadow suggests evil, fear, darkness, death, whereas a rainbow suggests hope, joy, beauty, God's compact with man in the Bible. Hopkins's rainbow beautifully demonstrates how a poet gets extra dimensions of meaning out of his words and images. LP

104. *Philip Larkin* AUBADE (page 138)

While the irony in Richard Wilbur's title "A Late Aubade" (page 49) merely overturns a reader's expectation of a poignant dawn parting of lovers, Larkin's irony reaches deeper: his dawn song is not wistful about separating from a mistress, but terror stricken at the prospect of the inevitable parting from life itself.

Larkin does not make that life attractive, but tedious and mundane. It is a life of work, offices, and telephones, with only drink and "people" to relieve the boredom or the lurking fears of death. The emphasis is not on beauty or pleasure or love, all to be lost in the obliteration of death, but on the fear of nothingness. The images associated with life provide the only defense against the thoughts of death, and they are images of social connection, culminating in the last line: "Postmen like doctors go from house to house." All of us, that is, share in the disease of fearing death, and the cure comes in links with other people. But communication is a temporary cure, an alleviation of the *fear*, but certainly no defense against death itself or the knowledge of its inevitability.

The time of the poem, four o'clock in the predawn morning, is a time of total darkness and silence. Staring into "soundless dark" is like staring at death, for the two primary senses of hearing and sight have been lost. Deprived of physical sense, the speaker must "see" what his mind knows, "the total emptiness for ever, / The sure extinction."

Neither the rich, elaborate fabric of religion—now tattered and "moth-eaten"—nor the fallacious plausibility of the plainer fabrics of rationalism is sufficient to hide the naked fact of fearfulness; rich or plain, these are mere covers or garments, incapable of disguising the reality at such a time as this.

And "courage is no good" at such times, because it cannot alter the fact the speaker is staring at. Since he defines life in its social connections, "to love or link," courage seems only a matter of social behavior that has value in the impressions one gives to other people. "It means not scaring others" with the horrifying truth that the speaker understands and faces. He does display another kind of courage, though —the courage to acknowledge to himself his fears and to look into the darkness with honesty.

The final stanza, in which the dawn slowly comes, restores the speaker's physical senses, and leads him to project the resumption of daylight activities. The terror subsides and the fact of "what we know," though it is as plain and as familiarly unremarkable as a piece of furniture, may be ignored in the workaday world. The knowledge that he has faced when alone can be put aside; the dilemma of knowing that "we can't escape" death and "yet can't accept it" can be postponed another day.

The poem carries the additional richness of its verbal echoes of two well-known passages from Shakespeare, Hamlet's soliloquy beginning "To be, or not to be" (III. i. 55-89) and the conclusion of Jaques' speech on the seven ages of man (*As You Like It*, II. vii. 162-65). The allusions to Hamlet's speech occur in lines 8, 17, 18-19, and 30, and to Jaques' in lines 27-28. These allusions in effect re-open the questions raised in Hamlet's meditation, and in several other themes in that play— courage, friendship, even drink—as if Larkin's speaker were being forced to reexamine Hamlet's condition for himself. What he finds, in his modern (and more squalid) experience is a similar dilemma: although being alive is fraught with pain and misery, chiefly because of fear and loneliness, the alternative "not to be" is worse, and so like Hamlet he will have to live with his "indecision."

Because these allusions are only faintly signalled, by little more than a single word or phrase, Larkin is relying on a reader's thorough recall of the Hamlet soliloquy and of the whole play, and most students are not likely to make the connection for themselves. If the instructor wishes to use the poem for a further lesson in allusion, the class should probably be supplied in advance with copies of the Shakespeare passages, and asked to find the verbal echoes. TRA

105. *Archibald MacLeish* ARS POETICA (page 140)

The poet's philosophy of his art is summed up in the opening and closing lines of the poem's third section. A poem is concerned with experience, not with propositional statements. When it is successful, it is "equal" to the experience it creates; the reader properly responds to it by imaginatively "living" that experience, not by judging the content of the poem as right or wrong, true or false. To create experience, the rest of the poem tells us (and illustrates in its telling), the poet must rely upon images and symbols.

"Ars Poetica" has three sections, each of which starts with what seems a paradox or a violation of common sense. Section one declares that a poem should be "palpable" and "wordless." Yet if we run our fingers over this poem as printed on the page, the only palpable thing is the page; our fingers make no distinction between recipe, advertisement, poem, or blank sheet of paper. And does not MacLeish's statement that a poem should be "wordless" run directly counter to Wallace Stevens's (in "The Noble Rider and the Sound of Words," *The Necessary Angel*) that "Poetry is a revelation in words by means of the words"? No, I think not. What MacLeish means is that the "experience" or "revelation" created is wordless. When we read a poem, we must be acutely sensitive to the words used, but with the final result that we are drawn into an imaginative experience in which we see "globed" peach or pear, or draw our thumb over an old medallion, or feel the soft moss and worn stone of an ancient casement ledge, or watch a flight of birds crossing the sky.

Section two asserts that a poem "should be motionless in time, / As the moon climbs," which seems contradictory in itself, for how can something be "motionless" and yet climb? Yet the moon "climbs" so slowly that its motion is imperceptible except when it can be related to some earthly object, such as the horizon or a "night-entangled tree," and watched for some time. What is this section saying about a poem then? That when we read it, we are so caught up in the experience created that we are unconscious of the passage of time? Or that the experience it creates lingers in the mind and fades from memory slowly and almost imperceptibly? An excellent case for the latter reading is made by Edwin St. Vincent, in *The Explicator*, 37 (Spr. 1979), 14-16, through a detailed analysis of the difficult syntax of this section.

And so we come to the summary third section which says that a poem should be "equal to: / Not true," and "should not mean, / But be." Does this mean that a poem should be meaningless? No, only that its "meaning" (what I have called in this chapter its "total meaning") is an *experience*, not an idea or propositional statement, and is expressed through images and symbols. The symbolic image of an "empty doorway and a maple leaf" (suggesting absence, loneliness, and the transitory quality of life) creates "all the history of grief," and the images of "leaning grasses and two lights above the sea" (suggesting perhaps a summer field where two lovers might lie overlooking the ocean) create the experience of love. LP

Chapter ten
Tone

106. *W. H. Davies* **THE VILLAIN** (page 143)

107. *Emily Dickinson* **APPARENTLY WITH NO SURPRISE** (page 143)

The title and the image in the last two lines of Davies's poem both suggest stage melodrama, and therefore a kind of theatricality exaggerated or remote from reality.

Dickinson's poem may profitably be compared with Frost's "Design" (page 134), for both poems raise similar issues, and both (like Melville in *Moby-Dick*) make the color white, usually associated with purity and innocence, take on exceedingly sinister connotations. LP

108. *William Butler Yeats* **THE COMING OF WISDOM WITH TIME** (page 145)

Yeats associates youth with "leaves," "flowers," and "sun," which are agreeable, and with "lying," which is disagreeable. He associates age with "truth," "wisdom," and "oneness," which are agreeable, and with "wither," which is disagreeable. Thus be carefully balances youth and age as to favorable and unfavorable qualities. Yeats is neither exulting over a gain nor lamenting a loss; but he *is* lamenting the fact that one can't have everything at once—beauty, vigor, and enthusiasm, *and* wisdom. Life is never complete: one gains some desirable qualities at the expense of losing others. LP

109. *Michael Drayton* **SINCE THERE'S NO HELP** (page 146)

From the first eight lines of this sonnet it seems apparent that the speaker (the male, as we shall see) and his beloved are breaking off their relationship. Does the speaker want to break it off? He asserts quite positively, perhaps too positively, that he does (3-4), but even in these first eight lines this assertion is undercut by the implication that he is acting under constraint ("Since there's no help") and by the suggestion that at any future meetings they may have difficulty disguising their still-existent feelings for each other. If any doubt remains that he does not really want to break off, it should be dissolved by the sestet, especially the last two lines, where he declares that she could still bring their love back to life, if she only would. He obviously hopes that she will. The rich allegorical and poetic language of the sestet, as opposed to the clipped, prosaic language of the octave, indicates that his true feelings come out here, feelings that he deliberately falsified in the octave.

Does *she*, then, want to break off the relationship? Although she is given no words in the poem (he is the speaker throughout), the "Nay" beginning in line 2 is a clear signal that this line is spoken in response to some gesture or word of protest made by her against his pronouncement in line 1. She does not want to "kiss and part." A further clue to her feelings is provided by his including her along with himself in his forecast of the difficulty *both* will have in concealing their feelings at future meetings.

But if neither of them *wants* to break off the relationship, *why* are they breaking it off? To answer this question, we must examine the allegorical death scene depicted in the sestet. When asked how many figures are involved in this scene, students initially answer four. But do we then have two dying figures, two deathbed scenes? Or are not "Love" and "Passion" two different names (suggesting the spiritual and the physical aspects) for one dying figure? Clearly they are one person, most fittingly called "Love-Passion." There is only one deathbed (11), and the dying figure is referred to by a singular pronoun in each of the last four lines ("his," "his," "him," "him"). The masculinity of the pronoun suggests that the dying Love-Passion is *his* (the speaker's). The logic of the situation suggests that the two attendants at the bedside, Faith kneeling in prayer, Innocence pulling down the eyelids of the presumably dead figure, are *hers*. By a subtle associative logic these two attendants, ostensibly present to ease the death, are made to appear the causes of the death. Her innocence is closing up the eyes of his passion; her faith (religious scruple) is assisting at the bedside. Yet, he asserts, if she would, she might at the very moment of death—"Now," in an instant—bring his love-passion quite suddenly back to life. Surely, the situation is clear. Though the woman wishes to retain his love, she also values and wishes to preserve her innocence (her purity, her chastity); her faith tells her that fornication is a sin. He claims that, by refusing to satisfy his passion, she is causing both it and his love (they are one and the same) to die. LP

110. *Robert Frost* **THE TELEPHONE** (page 146)

The poem is a dialogue between two lovers at the close of day upon his return from an all-day walk set out on in the morning. Whether the lovers are a married couple or are still in the courtship stage of their relationship is uncertain, but he has returned to the "here" (2)—home, summer hotel, village, or whatever—where both are living. At the farthest point of his walk, there had been an hour "all still" (probably about noon) during which he had felt a strong urge to be with his beloved and had felt intuitively that she was feeling a simultaneous wish to have him with her; now he is back and is trying to confirm the truth of that intuition. He goes about it playfully but delicately, inventing a fanciful story of her calling him on her telephone—the flower on the windowsill—and his receiving the call on a telephone—a flower—in a field where he was resting. (Early telephones were comparable in shape to daffodils, and the two flowers may, though need not, be taken as daffodils.) But of course he has made up this fantasy, and, as soon as he says "I heard you talk," he interrupts himself to say "Don't say I didn't," in order to keep her from denying it before he has well begun. Then, because he does not want to embarrass her or himself by putting words in her mouth that she might be forced to deny, and because he really wants to hear from *her* lips the confirmation that he was wanted, he breaks off from telling her what he heard her say, to ask, "Do you remember what it was you said?" But she is cautious too, unwilling to commit herself to the role until she knows more fully the part he has imagined for her. "First tell me what it was you thought you heard," she says. So the lover elaborates on his story, completing the metaphor of the telephone call; but again, when he gets to the crucial point, he hesitates to put words in her mouth and still wants *her* to say them, so he turns again to questions—"What was it? Did you call me by name? Or did you say—" And then he sees how to handle the problem—by saying what he wants her to admit having felt, but without himself putting the words in her mouth: "*Someone* said 'Come.'" It works. "I may have thought as much," she confesses, "but not aloud." Then joyously and triumphantly (though quietly) he affirms the truth of his fiction: "Well, so I came."

"The Telephone" is a poem of subtle dramatic interplay, delicate fancy, shared feeling, and deep tenderness. The two lovers are dramatically differentiated—the male ardent, fanciful, playful, but also diffident; the female more down to earth but open and responsive. Whether a telepathic message has actually been communicated between the two lovers—as he wants to believe, and as the title perhaps implies—is left open for the reader to decide. It is, in any case, not unusual for two lovers simultaneously to wish to be together.* LP

*This discussion is adapted from an item in *Notes on Contemporary Literature*, 10 (May 1980), 11-12, by Laurence Perrine.

111. *John Wakeman* **LOVE IN BROOKLYN** (page 147)

The man—middle-aged, fat, lonely, employed by a large Brooklyn business firm at a desk job which requires him to write correspondence. The woman—younger, physically attractive, sent up from the Payroll Department within the year to be the man's secretary-typist.

The man, smitten, inexperienced with women, vulnerable, has after several months summoned up courage to invite the woman out for a drink and to declare his feelings for her. He does so ineptly, blurting out the words, addressing her by her last name, blowing his nose. The woman, though neither insensitive nor unintelligent, is hard and experienced, has undoubtedly been propositoned many times, and has developed defensive tactics. Her immediate response, splashing her drink, is "The hell you say." But then she senses there is something different about this case; she lights a cigarette, thinks hard, and explains a difference she has probably not had occasion to put in words before: there is a difference between loving a woman as a person and mere sexual desire combined with gratitude for good typing.

But she has underestimated his feeling. "You wanna bet? You wanna bet?" he blurts out in protest against her suggestion that he has just "drunk" his drink "too fast." Then, trying to articulate his feelings, he makes an almost grotesque comparison. Seeing her swing round on her typing chair made him "shake" like he did in World War II when he first saw a tank slide through some trees "like it was god." Somehow the very grotesqueness of the double comparison testifies to its sincerity. He means it.

Her response, conditioned by past behavior, is jocular, fending the propositioner off in a kind of ritualized game which she must not take seriously. Playfully she swings full circle on her bar stool, mimicking the motion of her typing chair which had "shaken" him so. "You think I'm like a tank, you mean?" she says, deliberately misinterpreting his meaning; "Some fellers tell me nicer things than that." But then she sees his face and realizes that this is no time to kid. The man is not only earnest, he is highly vulnerable.

The last four lines express the depth and hopelessness of the man's emotion, and the pity she is capable of beneath her hard outer shell. Though there is little prospect that she can return this man's feeling, she recognizes its extent and helplessness, and she presses his trembling hand hard to express her pity.

This, according to the poet, is love "in Brooklyn." In contrast to Frost's poem, Wakeman's is deliberately unromantic, even antiromantic. The bar setting, the crude colloquial language, the grotesqueness of the man, the hard outer shell of the woman—all remove it from the delicate pastoral world of "The Telephone." Even the girl's name, Horowitz, is chosen for its unromantic connotations. Though probably common in Brooklyn, it is decidedly uncommon in poems about love. The man's feeling for the girl is not one based on a mutuality of mind and spirit, as in "The Telephone"; yet it is a powerful and sincere gut feeling which is a good deal more than an itch. The poem portrays genuine feelings: the hopeless if grotesque yearning and vulnerability of the fat man have pierced the woman's defensive armor and moved her, if hardly to a reciprocated feeling, at least to profound pity. LP

112. *Emily Dickinson* ONE DIGNITY DELAYS FOR ALL (page 148)

113. *Emily Dickinson* 'TWAS WARM AT FIRST LIKE US (page 149)

The theme of "One dignity delays for all" is that all of us, no matter how humble, will one day be honored and treated like nobility—namely, on the day of our burial. In the second stanza the funeral procession through the streets of the village is compared to the progress of a king, duke, or bishop through his domain. The hearse is a carriage, the casket is the royal chamber, the undertaker and his assistants are footmen, bells toll in the church towers, crowds stop to watch on the sidewalks or follow behind the hearse. In the third stanza the procession stops at the graveside, the officiating clergy ("dignified attendants") conduct a funeral ceremony (like a coronation ceremony or an official welcome to a visiting prince), and everyone takes off his hat as prayers are read and the casket is lowered into the grave. (The above account may be overspecific in its point-to-point comparisons, but the general meaning is valid.)

"Meek escutcheon" combines oxymoron and metaphor. Metaphorically it represents our humanity. Just as a coat of arms entitles its bearer to ceremonial treatment on all occasions, so our common humanity entitles us to ceremonial treatment at death. We may all look forward to this moment of grandeur. It "delays" (waits) for all.

"'Twas warm at first like us" describes the changes that take place in a body between death and burial. The poem begins its description at a point a split-second after the instant of death. Though still warm, the body has already become an "It," is no longer a *he* or *she*. Then, in almost clinical detail, are shown the loss of body warmth, the vanishing of expression from face and eyes, the stiffening of rigor mortis, the increasing and finally utter separation between the worlds of the dead and the living. In the final stanza, as it is lowered into the grave, the corpse is a mere thing, a weight, unable by any sign to assent or demur to what is happening. The final word "adamant" underscores its stoniness.

Written in Dickinson's characteristic elliptical style, the poem demands for grammatical completeness that we supply an *it* at the end of line 2, an *if* after "as" in line 12, and a completing verb (*show? manifest? manage?*) at the end of line 12. But the meaning is clear without these additions. Dickinson's omissions simply compact her meaning.

There may be a latent irony in the fact that the "dignity" that "delays for all" does not occur till we can no longer be conscious of it, but in the poem this irony is muted. The tone of the poem is generally one of excited anticipation, marked by the exclamatory elation of the last two stanzas, and by words like "dignity," "mitred," "purple," "crown," "state," "grand," "pomp," "surpassing," "ermine," and "escutcheon." Death in this poem is not the great democratizer, leveling all ranks, but the great "aristocratizer," elevating all to the status of nobility.

The tone of "'Twas warm at first like us," on the contrary, is one of unrelieved and increasing horror. Concentrating not on the funeral ceremonials but on the physical facts of death, it projects not an elevation in status but a reduction in status, from human being to thing. Its tone is determined by words like "chill," "frost," "stone," "cold," "congealed," "weight," and "dropped like adamant." Instead of "pomp surpassing ermine," it presents us with a dead body crowding "cold to cold."   LP

114. *Alfred, Lord Tennyson* **CROSSING THE BAR** (page 149)

115. *Thomas Hardy* **THE OXEN** (page 150)

Despite the fame and popularity of "Crossing the Bar," students often have difficulty with it, and it is well to make sure that they understand it. The two complementary sets of figures used to express approaching death are the coming of night and setting out on an ocean voyage. The moment of death in the first set is the disappearance of the last light of day: the arrival of "the dark." In the second set it is the moment of "crossing the bar": leaving the harbor, which belongs to the land, and setting out on the ocean. As the land represents temporal life, the ocean—"the boundless deep"—represents eternity. "That which drew from out the boundless deep" is the soul: in Tennyson's thought the soul comes from eternity, takes fleshly embodiment during life, and returns to eternity upon death. Tennyson wants no "moaning of the bar"—no lamentation over his death—for his soul is returning "home," is passing on to eternal life, and will see its "Pilot" (God) "face to face" after death. The occasion should therefore be one for joy rather than for sadness.

The whole poem expresses Tennyson's faith in immortality. Despite its popularity, which stems largely from its message, the poem is a good one. An oversubtle cavil about the image of the pilot, raised by Brooks and Warren in their manual for *Understanding Poetry*, 3rd ed. (New York: Holt, Rinehart & Winston, 1960), is satisfactorily answered by G. Geoffrey Langsam in *The Explicator* 10 (April 1952): 40. For a debate about the tone of the poem, see James R. Kincaid, "Tennyson's 'Crossing the Bar': A Poem of Frustration," *Victorian Poetry* 3 (Winter 1965): 57-61, and Laurence Perrine, "When Does Hope Mean Doubt?: The Tone of 'Crossing the Bar,'" *Victorian Poetry* 4 (Spring 1966): 127-31.

"The Oxen" divides exactly in the middle, the first two stanzas presenting a scene from the speaker's childhood, the second two, one from his adult life. If we take the speaker as Hardy himself, or as a contemporary of Hardy, the two scenes are divided by Darwin's *Origin of Species* (1859) and by the dramatic decline of religious faith that it accelerated. In the poem the superstition of the kneeling animals is symbolic of the whole system of Christian belief that Hardy was taught as a boy and that he gave up as a man, but that, like Matthew Arnold (see "Dover Beach," page 256), he never ceased to regret. Though he can no longer subscribe to Christian doctrine or to its world view, he regrets the loss of the emotional security and comfort provided by that world view.

In emotional tone the two halves of the poem differ sharply. In the first two stanzas, there is a sense of warmth, of comfort, and of community. Young and old sit "in a flock / By embers in hearthside ease," and the speaker uses the plural pronoun "we." In the last two stanzas, there is isolation and darkness. The speaker uses the singular pronoun, refers to the barton as "lonely," and with the word "gloom" refers not only to the darkness of the night but also to the spirit of the times—the desolation caused by the loss of religious faith. The superstition of the kneeling oxen—and with the divine birth and the resurrection—is dismissed as a "fancy," one that few people any longer accept, but that was nevertheless "fair" (attractive).

The word "hope" in Tennyson's poem and in Hardy's has opposite meanings relative to the expectations involved. Tennyson's *hope* expresses expectation without real doubt. Hardy's expresses a wish without real expectation. Tennyson's poem expresses confident faith that it will be so. Hardy's expresses a wistful yearning that it might be so. Hardy does not say that he would go out to the barton to see the oxen kneel. He says (in effect), "I *feel* I would go *if* someone asked me." But no one will ask him, and it doesn't occur to him to go alone. Moreover, if someone did ask him, he wouldn't really go. The feeling is an ephemeral one that would not survive the invitation. Hardy (or the speaker) is an intellectually sophisticated twentieth-century man who would feel himself a goose to go on such a fool's errand. To put this point across to a class, it might be useful to ask: Would Hardy go if someone asked him? Would *you* go? Today Charlie Brown may wait in the pumpkin patch on Halloween to see the Great Pumpkin, but he won't when he is five years older, and no one of high school or college age in America today would be caught dead waiting for Santa Claus to come down the chimney. Hardy's "hope" is a wistful yearning, not a hope.

Reading Tennyson's poem aloud, one should read the word *hope* very quietly; without emphasis, for to emphasize it is to express doubt, and the serenity and beauty of the preceding imagery indicate absence of doubt. One need not, in reading Hardy's poem, put artificial emphasis on "hoping": the inversion of accent (a trochee instead of an iamb) forces an emphasis on it. Hardy's poem, in its own way, is as quiet and as beautiful as Tennyson's, but the quietness comes from resignation rather than from faith. (For further comment, see the discussion of "The Darkling Thrush," page 30 of this manual.) LP

116. *John Donne* **THE APPARITION** (page 151)

117. *John Donne* **THE FLEA** (page 152)

"The Aparition" has frequently been misread as an expression of hate and revulsion in which the motive of the speaker, a rejected lover, is revenge. It is, in reality, a poem of thwarted love and unspent desire in which the speaker is making a last desperate effort to obtain his lady's favors. In doing so, he adopts a new strategy. In the past, he has presumably tried and failed with all the usual methods—praising the lady's beauty, flattering her in various ways, declaring the strength and depth of his love for her, and so on. This time he attempts to *frighten* her into his arms. He works on various anxieties he *hopes* she may have. Instead of telling her how much he loves her, he tells her that his love "is spent." (By portraying himself as having slipped the hook, he may make himself seem more valuable in her eyes than when she was assured of his devotion.) He predicts that, if she rejects him, she will in the future have to settle for a much inferior lover. He attempts to frighten her with the prospect of his ghost appearing at her bedside, scaring her to death. But, most of all, he tries to terrify her by threatening that his ghost will utter some unspecified but awful pronouncement or curse upon her, possibly capable of damning her soul for eternity, but the nature and content of which he will not reveal to her now, because (he says) he wants revenge—and if he told her now, she would do anything necessary to avoid it.

But the speaker's assertion that his love (*desire* would be a more accurate term) "is spent" is undermined by the whole tone and intensity of the poem. If he no longer cares about her, why should her "scorn" be killing him? Would it not be more logical for him to say he was "cured"? And why should he send his ghost to her bedside? Obviously he has intense feelings concerning her still.

Most misreadings of the poem misinterpret "feigned vestal" as meaning "feigned virgin." But why should Donne use the fancier term if a simpler one means the same? The speaker, having unsuccessfully solicited the woman many times, has no personal grounds for doubting her virginity. What he accuses her of is not that she has falsely claimed to be a virgin, but that she falsely thinks herself capable of *sustaining* the state of virginity as the vestal virgins did. Inferentially she has rejected his advances in the past by claiming that she wants to preserve her virginity or that she is by nature virginal. (The word *feigned*, spelled *fain'd* in the manuscripts of Donne's poems, is a pun blending the meanings of *feigned* ["pretended"] and *fained* ["wished for"]. The speaker in effect is telling her, "Don't deceive yourself. You have the same strong carnal desires as I have, and if you do not take me, you will eventually settle for someone much less capable than I of satisfying your sexual needs." This "someone," tired out from their earlier love-making, will think, when she tries to wake him to protect her from the ghost, that she wants *more* love-making, and he will pretend to be asleep. Thus she will have to face the scary ghost alone. Trembling like an aspen tree and bathed in cold sweat, she will be "scared to death." Her "sick candle" will blink out, and she will become hyperbolically a "verier ghost" than her visitant. The "sick taper" is metaphorically her life (see "Out, out, brief candle" from *Macbeth*). It could be taken literally as well if we assume that a couple would go to bed leaving a candle burning by the bedside. It was commonly believed that a candle would dim in the presence of a ghost.

The speaker will not tell her what his ghost would say because, he says, he wants her to "painfully repent" her mistreatment of him, and if she knew *now* what it would say, that knowledge would "preserve" her and keep her "innocent." Innocent of what? Innocent of the one crime that has been alleged against her in the poem—that of being a murderess—of "killing" the speaker by her scorn. She can remain innocent of this crime only by ceasing to "kill" him—that is, by granting him her favors. What could the ghost say that would be terrible enough to accomplish this end? We do not know—nor does the speaker know. If he did, he would say it now. But he is gambling on the psychological principle that an unknown threat is more frightening than a known one. It is the darkness at the top of the stairs which daunts us. It is more frightening to hear a strange cry in the dark than to face five armed men by daylight. Thus the speaker does not reveal what the ghost will say, first because he does not *know*, and second because not telling will be more frightening than telling. In short, he *wants* her to remain "innocent" of the crime of "killing" him. He *wants* her to fulfill his unspent desires.

Donne here uses the cliché of Renaissance poetry which makes a woman "kill" a man by refusing to satisfy his desires, but he here gives it an original twist by taking the metaphor literally and developing the whole poem on its literalness. It is important that the speaker accuses the lady of "killing" him, not having "killed" him. He is not *yet* "dead"; therefore there is still time for her to revive him and remain innocent of "murder."

In "The Flea" a young man attempts to seduce a young woman by the use of highly ingenious but highly sophistical reasoning. Basically, his argument is that losing her virginity will be no more damaging to her than a flea bite.

Before the first stanza, a flea has bitten the young man and then has jumped to the young woman and begun to bite her. The young man sees an opportunity and seizes it. He points to the flea and remarks that it has innocently mingled their bloods within itself, which is no more than sexual intercourse does (according to a traditional belief), and yet is more than she will allow to him. (When he says "more than we would do," he means, of course, more than *she* would do, for he is eager enough himself.) His remark that the flea's action cannot be called a "sin" or "shame" or "loss of maidenhead" indicates that she is a virgin and wishes to preserve her virginity until she can surrender it without sin.

Between the first and second stanzas the young lady raises her finger to squash the flea. The young man protests, urging her to spare the flea, in which, because of their commingled bloods, they "almost, yea more than married are." With dazzling sleight-of-wit he has parlayed his claim that the mingling of their bloods within the flea is tantamount to a sinless act of sexual intercourse into a claim that it is tantamount to marriage. The flea is their "marriage-bed" and "marriage-temple." If she kills it, he claims, she will be destroying three lives—his, hers, and its—and committing three sins—murder, suicide, and sacrilege. (The line "Though use [habit] makes you apt [habitually disposed] to kill me" indicates that the speaker has already attempted many times to seduce the young woman and has failed. He is metaphorically playing with the poetic lover's traditional complaint that he is "dying" of his unrequited love and therefore that the lady is "killing" him by withholding her favors.)

But the young lady pays no attention to the speaker's protest. Between the second and third stanzas she has cruelly (according to the young man) killed the flea—has "purpled [crimsoned]" her nail with "blood of innocence." The flea's only guilt, the speaker claims, was contained in the drop of blood it sucked from its murderess, and now she declares triumphantly to the young man that neither he nor she has been injured (let alone "killed") by the flea's death. With one quick stroke of her finger she has indeed thoroughly discredited the young man's "logic."

But the young man is not for a moment discountenanced. Nimbly, he turns his defeat into a further argument for his original design. Because his fears proved false, he contends, *all* fears are false, including hers that she will lose honor in yielding to him. She will lose no more honor in submitting to his desires, he claims, than she lost life in killing the flea. This argument (a generalization from a single instance) is, of course, as specious as those that have gone before, yet we have to admire the young man's mental agility in turning the tables and putting the young woman on the defensive once again.

Though one cannot make a dogmatic statement about what action follows the conclusion of the poem, evidence favors the inference that this attempt on the young lady's virginity is as unsuccessful as those that have preceded it. We know from lines 2, 9, 14, and 16 (we are given the information four times) that the young lady has previously denied the young man, and not just once but many times. Presumably this young man has also tried with no success the ordinary tactics of seduction—protestations of adoration, lavish compliments to the lady's charm and beauty, and pleas for pity—so he now turns to witty casuistry. We also know on what grounds the young lady has turned him down. She would consider the loss of her chastity a "sin" and a disgrace (line 6); she is concerned for her "honor" (line 26). In addition we see that the young lady is not taken in for a moment by the young man's preposterous "logic" in stanza 2. She calls his bluff, kills the insect, and laughs in his face. True, the young man is undismayed by this refutation and turns it immediately to his advantage. But are we to believe that the girl suddenly turns gullible or loses concern for her honor just because the young man has made a clever answer? If we extrapolate from the evidence given *in* the poem as to her past behavior, her intelligence, and her morality, we must conclude that she is a sensible young lady, not at all deceived by the young man's sophistry, and that she is holding out for honorable marriage, whether with this young man or another. The young man may have "won" this skirmish between the sexes, but only at the verbal level.

In a previous manual I wrote that this poem is "not to be taken too seriously as a reflection of human life, but to be enjoyed for what it is—a virtuoso display of ingenuity and wit." On further reflection I would modify that statement. It may be truer to life than at first appears. We are given a situation where a young man has attempted many times to obtain the woman's favor but has always been refused. Yet the woman by all indications enjoys his company. She has never told him, "Begone, vile seducer, never darken my doorway again!" And, indeed, why should she not enjoy the company of such a witty and clever young man? Is it not quite possible that the "seduction attempt" has become a little game they play? That after the first rejection or so, the young man has realized that her virtue is unshakable, yet keeps on inventing more and more preposterous reasons why she should yield to him, not expecting her to do so, but for the "fun" of the thing? A student of mine once declared indignantly that no man could ever win *her* heart with an analogy drawn from a *flea*! Exactly. But if we see the seduction attempt as a "game" which neither of its two players takes very seriously, it becomes quite believable.

Both "The Apparition" and "The Flea" present an often-rejected lover taking a new and "far-out" approach to winning a woman's favors. But in tone the two poems are radically different. In tone "The Apparition" is dark and menacing; "The Flea" is light and playful. The speaker in "The Apparition" attempts to attain his goal by threats, the speaker in "The Flea" by obviously specious reasoning. The speaker in "The Apparition" attempts to win his lady's favors by maximizing her fears of what will happen to her if she refuses. The speaker in "The Flea" attempts to win them by minimizing his lady's fears of what will happen if she consents. Fear is the weapon of a rapist. The methods used by the speaker in "The Apparition" are ingenious and sinister. The methods used by the speaker in "The Flea" are ingenious and witty. LP

118. *Alexander Pope* **ENGRAVED ON THE COLLAR OF A DOG WHICH I GAVE TO HIS ROYAL HIGHNESS** (page 153)

The *speaker's* tone is plain enough: it is one of supreme *hauteur*. The *poet's* tone is more complex. Is there a bit of pride expressed in the title at being on such close terms with the King? A bit of flattery for the King in the implication that no higher honor could befall a dog than to belong to him? But surely some irony too in having dogs take pride in the station and birth of their owners. How much more snobbish can a creature get! Yes, a sly dig at snobbery in any station of life. LP

119. *Anonymous* **LOVE** (page 154)

There is a brief comment on these verses on page 227 of the text. LP

EXERCISE 1 (page 154)

The three *carpe diem* poems differ chiefly in the sense of urgency with which their message is communicated, which in turn develops largely from the differing speaker-audience relationships and situations in the three poems, although other factors (diction, imagery) are also important.

The most urgent—one might almost say desperate—is "To His Coy Mistress" (page 74). Here the speaker is a young man addressing a young lady, urging her to make love with him. There is, he claims, no afterlife ("yonder all before us lie / Deserts of vast eternity"), and there is no love-making after death ("then worms shall try / That long-preserved virginity, / And your quaint honor turn to dust, / And into ashes all my lust"). They must therefore fulfill their strong physical desire for each other *now!*

In "To the Virgins, to Make Much of Time" (page 86) the speaker is no longer a young man urging his own passionate desire upon his mistress *now*; rather, the speaker seems to be a disinterested older man advising, not a specific young woman, but young women in general. He urges them, not to satisfy their senses *now*, in an illicit relationship, but to "go marry," a process which they may set in motion now but which may demand several weeks to consummate.

In "Loveliest of trees" (page 76) the sense of urgency almost vanishes, disappearing into a tone of serenity and fulfillment, for this time the speaker, a young man of twenty, is not urging anyone, not even himself (and he appears to be addressing only himself) to do something; he is doing it, or preparing to do it. He is simply announcing his intention to do now and his resolve to do in the future what he would undoubtedly advise others to do, if asked. And the desire he is about to fulfill is nothing illicit, like fornication, nor momentous and perhaps irreversible, like marriage; it is an act entirely innocent, one that no one would protest against or advise against, namely, enjoying beauty, in particular natural beauty, while he has the opportunity to do so.   LP

A FURTHER EXERCISE

The following exercise does not appear in the text, because its usefulness will vary with the maturity of the students and the skill of the instructor. If the instructor can use it without embarrassment, it provides an excellent exercise for teaching differentiation of tone.

Dickinson's "In winter in my room" (No. 202), Graves's "Down, Wanton, Down!" (No. 211), and Olds's "The Connoisseuse of Slugs" (No. 230) treat the same object with great differences in tone. Explain. (The editors' discussion is given with the last of these.)

POEMS FOR FURTHER READING

Poems 190, 192, 203, 209, 235, and 250 from Part Two provide additional illustrations of topics presented in this chapter.

Chapter eleven
Musical Devices

120. *Ogden Nash* **THE TURTLE** (page 156)

One might also ask why Nash chose to write about a turtle rather than a tortoise. The anatomical problem is the same for each. LP

121. *W. H. Auden* **THAT NIGHT WHEN JOY BEGAN** (page 158)

The two people in the poem have been disillusioned by their experiences with love. They have found that it is not lasting and that it ends in disappointment. They have been "burnt" by it. Thus they are deeply skeptical about their present affair. It begins, as have past affairs, in the joy of sexual excitement; they are prepared to find in the morning that their attraction has little or no other basis, but in the morning they are still in love; days pass, then weeks; they begin to realize that they have found a true human relationship, one rooted in something deeper than sexual attraction.

The basic metaphor presents two foot travelers cutting across fields that they hope are the public fields of love where all may travel but that they fear may be private lands where they will be shot or apprehended for trespassing. The metaphor in lines 3-4 beautifully combines the visual image of the sun's horizontal rays awakening them from their dream and the metaphorical idea of the landowner's shooting them for trespassing—that is, destroying their temporary illusion of love. But as they hike for additional miles (days), they outgrow their nervousness and begin to believe in spiritual peace, for they are not reproached for trespassing and they can see in the future (through love's field glasses) nothing that is not genuine and lasting love.

The rime pattern:

Lines 1 and 4 (of each stanza): alliteration and consonance
Lines 2 and 3 (of each stanza): alliteration and consonance
Lines 1 and 3 (of each stanza): assonance
Lines 2 and 4 (of each stanza): assonance

In line 10 the last syllable must be thought of as beginning with *r* rather than with *p* to preserve the integrity of this pattern, and in line 12 the final syllable must be thought of as including the final *s* (really a *z*) of *his*. The whole is ingeniously worked out, along with the extended metaphor; and the poet's pleasure (and ours) lies partly in the working out of this design. LP

122. *Gerard Manley Hopkins* GOD'S GRANDEUR (page 160)

The theme of the poem might be stated in some such words as these:

The natural world is filled with the beauty and energizing power of its Creator. But men, ignoring God's authority, through their commercial and industrial activities, have despoiled and polluted this beauty and separated themselves from its spiritually regenerating power. Nevertheless, this power is never used up; through God's love for his world, nature's beauty is continuously renewed.

How pale and flat this prose statement is as compared to the poem's "grandeur"!

In line 1 the word "charged" because of its associations with electricity and gunpowder, has many times the force of *filled*. In line 2 the image is of crinkled metallic foil (gold, tin, silver, or lead) being shaken in the sun and flashing light-reflections from each of its multifold creases and facets. In line 4 "rod" is a metaphor or symbol for God's authority and chastening power. In lines 7-8 the soil is "bare" because man has pitted it over with his heaps of coal and iron ore and paved it over with streets and walks; and man cannot feel the grass underfoot anyway because his feet are cased in shoes. (We need not assume that Hopkins denounces the wearing of shoes, though he may indeed think it good sometimes to walk barefoot in the grass.) Pavement and shoe leather serve the poet here as symbols for man's twofold separation from nature. In lines 11-12 the image of the sun's light disappearing in the west only to reappear next morning in the east is a symbol for the perpetual renewal of nature. And this renewal springs from the love of the Holy Ghost (third member of the Trinity) in His traditional metaphoric embodiment as a dove (symbol of gentleness and tenderness) brooding over the world (as over a nest) with warm breast and bright wings. The word "bent" means both that the earth is curved (as suggested by the preceding image of the sun's apparent travel around it) and bent out of shape from man's misuse of it.

Just as the world is charged with the grandeur of God, so this sonnet is charged with a rich verbal music appropriate to its subject. In its end-rimes it follows the strictest and most demanding pattern for the Italian sonnet (four rime sounds). Alliteration is apparent in almost every line, perhaps most brilliantly in the three two-word clusters of line 14 (*w*orld *b*roods—*w*arm *b*reast—*b*right *w*ings). Assonance is especially apparent in line 11 (bl*a*ck-l*a*st, W*e*st-w*e*nt) and line 13 (H*o*ly Gh*o*st *o*ver). Consonance is prominent in line 1, where each stressed syllable ends with a *d* (wor*ld*-charge*d*-grandeu*r*-Go*d*). In the question in line 4, where nine short monosyllables (all but two of them stressed) are spat out in rapid succession like bullets from a machine gun, there is internal rime (men-then), alliteration (now-not, reck-rod), and assonance (not-rod, reck-men-then); except for the initial "Why," each stressed syllable in the series gets into the act once if not twice. In line 5 the triple repetition of a whole phrase ("have trod") emphasizes the repetitiousness of the action described. In lines 6-7 two sets of internal rimes (seared-bleared-smeared; wears-shares) combined with the three *sm-* alliterations (smeared-smudge-smell) put such an emphasis on words of disagreeable meaning as to give one a feeling of almost physical revulsion. But we leave this analysis incomplete; the reader's patience will be "spent" long before the poem's "music" is.

An interesting thematic comparison may be made between this sonnet and Wordsworth's "The world is too much with us" (poem 26). LP

123. *A. E. Housman* WITH RUE MY HEART IS LADEN (page 161)

The poem is an expression of grief for all good friends the poet had who died in their youth. Though neither the word *died* nor *death* is used in the poem, the fact is conveyed through "had," "are laid," and "are sleeping." The brevity and apparent simplicity of the poem make its poignancy seem almost magical. It results from an exquisite choice of diction and a classical perfection of form. The compound adjectives "rose-lipt" and "lightfoot" are both particularized and universal in their application to the blooming beauty and athletic vitality of the maidens and youths they modify. Their reversed repetition in the second stanza, attached to different nouns, balances the two stanzas against each other and binds them together in a pattern of parallelism and opposition. The word "rue," meaning sorrow, is also the name of an herb with bitter leaves, which readers of *Hamlet* may remember as one of the flowers distributed by the young Ophelia in her mad scene (IV, 5) shortly before her death. The connotations of "golden"—precious, bright, shining, pure, true, young—are enriched and deepened for the reader who recalls the dirge from *Cymbeline* (poem 238), addressed to another youth who has died young.

The landscape of the second stanza is not literally that of the churchyard cemeteries where these lads and girls are buried; the point is that after death *all* brooks are too broad for leaping and that in the grave *all* beauty fades.

The ear picks up much of the rich alliteration in the poem on a first reading. Analysis discloses that every stressed word or important syllable (I include the unstressed halves of the two compound adjectives) in the poem except one alliterates with another:

rue (1), rose- (3), rose- (7), roses (8);
heart (1), had (2);
laden (1); -lipt (3), light-, lad (4), leaping (5), light-, laid (6), -lipt (7);
golden (2), girls (7);
friends (2), -foot (4), -foot (6), fields, fade (8);
many, maiden (3), many (4);
brooks, broad (5), boys (6).

The one exception is "sleeping," and it, of course, is a rime word. Though the full extent of this alliterative network is apparent only on analysis, its presence contributes to the beauty of the poem. LP

124. *Gwendolyn Brooks* WE REAL COOL (page 162)

The placement of the pronouns in this poem gives its rhythm a syncopated effect appropriate to the jazz culture of the speakers.

The critic who called the poem immoral was oblivious to its dramatic irony (its tone). The poet does not share the opinion of the speakers that they are "real cool," nor does any moderately good reader, which obviously the critic was not. LP

125. *Emily Dickinson* AS IMPERCEPTIBLY AS GRIEF (page 162)

The subject of the poem is ambivalence about seasonal change. The initial simile sets the tone: summer lapsed away imperceptibly, as *grief* lapses imperceptibly; were the diminution of grief consciously perceived, its passing would seem to be a perfidious betrayal of the person for whom we grieve. So, the simile says, the passing of summer evokes an emotion which includes one's love and loyalty, the sadness of loss, and the consciousness of separation. But how can these emotions be identified with summer, the season of richness and growth, the apogee of the year to which spring climbs and from which autumn (in the distinctly American term) falls? If summer is like grief, what are we grieving *for*? "Spring" might be one logical answer—the loss in summertime of the exuberant excitement of that early time—yet the terms of the poem do not invite such a comparison.

The grief, rather, is associated with summer's relationship to us: it is summer that passes so imperceptibly that its betrayal *of us* is almost overlooked. This personification (overtly revealed in the feminine pronouns) and the constant tone of regret imply the imaginative act of the speaker: we long for the personal, permanent love for us of what we love. Why does the summer betray us by leaving us? The two middle stanzas present a series of appositives for the diminution of the season, presenting it in terms of its voluntary withdrawal and increasing alienation yet without showing any ill will toward those it leaves behind. These two stanzas also present a series of attempts to pinpoint or define the precise feelings excited by the imminent departure of summer: Is it like an intensification of quietness? Has nature withdrawn from us as a person might shut herself up for a long, quiet afternoon (the metaphor must be especially poignant when we recall Emily Dickinson's own sequestration)? The factual evidence is that both the coming on and the departure of night, at dusk and daybreak, seem strangely changed, an earlier darkness and a foreign sunrise. The process resembles the ambivalence of a dear guest "who would be gone," whose gracious behavior is both full of courtesy and deeply distressing.

These attempts at definition reveal the ambiguities of feeling already noted in the simile of grief in line 1: the increased beauty of "quietness distilled," the sense of being excluded mixed with an understanding approval of nature's sequestration, and most of all (placed in the climactic position), the paradoxical combination of "a courteous, yet harrowing grace." But this is a poem about the "imperceptible," and it is to that quality that the poem returns for its conclusion. Without any of the "perceptible" (and humanly comprehensible) means of transportation, neither the wing of the bird nor the keel of the boat, two silent means of departing, "summer made her light escape / Into the beautiful." The guest, though gracious, does not live with us, but elsewhere, and finally manages to escape. The final line, "Into the beautiful," has been criticized for its abstract vagueness, but the sense of an ideal, abstract realm of beauty as the proper "home" for this sojourning visitor, this sequestered captive, may be appropriate in its vagueness. If the process of its departure is "imperceptible," so too may be its destination.

The music of this poem is muted, as befits its subject. Approximate rimes, subtle consonant links, delicately unobtrusive alliteration, and the poet's marvelous ear for related vowel sounds all reinforce the elegiac tone. For example, in the last stanza, the phrase "without a wing" alliterates the initial *w* followed by the assonance of short *i*—but the effect is softened by the fact that the syllable *with-* is metrically unstressed, while *wing* is stressed. The preponderant consonant sounds in the stanza are the sibilant *s* of "thu*s*," "*s*ervice," "*s*ummer," and "e*s*cape," the crisp *t* of "withou*t*," "ligh*t*," "in*t*o," and "beau*t*iful," and the *k* of "*k*eel" and "es*c*ape"—consonants that with the *w*'s and *l*'s underscore the quickness and lightness of the action being described.

But perhaps the most interesting example of the use of musicality is to be heard in the key term, "imperceptibly," a word so proper to its purpose that the poet reiterates a form of it two lines later. The word has the flickering of its consonant sounds—*mp*, sibilant *c*, *pt*, and *bl*, all rapidly unobtrusive—and the light swiftness of its collection of short vowels. It also has an intrinsic rhythm that finds echoes throughout the poem in words with an elegiac "falling" rhythm: IM-per-*CEP*-ti-BLY and IM-per-*CEP*-ti-BLE both alternate stressed and unstressed syllables, and both occur in perfectly regular iambic lines. The stresses within the words, however, are not equal: in both, the syllable *-cep-* is more heavily stressed than the initial *im-*, and both of those syllables receive greater stress than the final stressed *-bly* or *-ble*. Both words, that is, are rapid in pronunciation (owing to their vowel and consonant combinations) and rise to a central stress before falling off in a final, very lightly stressed syllable. This falling effect in a final light stress can be heard as well in such key words as *PER*-fi-DY and *BEAU*-ti-FUL; the elegiac tone is also reinforced by the high incidence of words that are individually trochaic in rhythm (though they usually function in regular iambic foot patterns): summer, twilight, nature, spending, earlier, morning, foreign, and so forth. TRA

126. *Carl Sandburg* THE HARBOR (page 163)

This poem presents two contrasting scenes: a city slum (in the first five lines) and its harbor (in the last seven). The pivotal line (6) presents the speaker, who is out walking, passing from the first scene to the second. The city, we infer, is large (to have such extensive slums), and so is the lake (to have a harbor where long waves break and fling spray on the shore). (If we know anything about Carl Sandburg, we have no trouble in identifying the city as Chicago and the lake as Lake Michigan; the poem was first published in Sandburg's *Chicago Poems*, 1916.) The contrast between the two scenes is one of closeness vs. openness, subjection vs. freedom, ugliness vs. beauty, the man-made vs. the natural.

It should be clear to any reader, upon examination, that these contrasts are created not only by the denotations and connotations of the poet's words, but also by their sounds. The first five lines are dominated by the repetition of short *u* vowel sounds—*huddled, ugly, hunger-, hunger-, huddled, ugly*. The prevailing consonant sounds are *h, d,* and *g.* Of the words just cited, *huddled* has an initial *h* and two *d* sounds (medial and terminal), *hunger* has an initial *h* and a *g, ugly* has a *g*. This repetition of unappealing sounds, in addition to their unappealing sense, accounts for the poet's using each of the three words twice, and augmenting them with words like *haggard* and *haunted*.

In the last seven lines of the poem, though we still encounter the short *u*'s (*under, sun, -flung, fluttering, gulls*), they seem less dominant; we are struck instead by the rich assonance of long vowels—long *a* as in *lake waves breaking, spray-, great gray;* long *i* as in *flying white;* and long *e* as in *veering, wheeling free* in the culminating line of the poem. We are also pleased by the alliterations (*blue burst, Long lake, flung... fluttering, great gray*), and by the internal rime (*lake, break-*).

In summary, the first five lines are harsh in meaning and harsh in sound; the last six lines are pleasing in meaning and pleasing in sound. Line 6 is transitional. LP

127. *John Crowe Ransom* PARTING, WITHOUT A SEQUEL (page 164)

The disappointment of first love bears a slightly comic aspect when viewed from the outside or when looked back on over a perspective of years, but to those who are actually suffering it, it is undiluted tragedy. We may try to talk "wisdom" to the disappointed youngster, but how can she understand? Or how can *we* understand? "She just doesn't realize," the oldsters say; "this will be nothing to her in a few months or years." "They just don't *know*," the youngster thinks; "how can they know what I feel?"

John Crowe Ransom catches both the comedy and the tragedy in this wryly poignant little poem. Observing the termination of a first attachment from a point of view partly inside and partly outside the heartbroken girl, he is able both to *feel* the tumultuous suffering of the girl and to note its theatrical exaggerations and its humorous ambivalences. The comic aspects are reflected in the double and triple rimes, many of them slant; in the melodramatic triteness of the phrase describing the girl's attitude toward her letter "which he so richly has deserved"; in her gloating satisfaction with the letter's crushing language ("And nothing could be better"):

in the stagy *hauteur* of her command as she delivers it to the messenger boy—"'Into his hands'"; in the solemn pretentiousness of the epithet for the messenger boy—"the blue-capped functioner of doom"; in her mixed feelings as she watches the messenger boy ride off (hoping at once that he will deliver the letter promptly, which will put her errant lover in his place, and that it will get lost, allowing one more chance for reconciliation); and in her exaggeration of the episode's significance—"the ruin of her younger years." It is also reflected in the title, where the phrase "without a Sequel" suggests the theatrical component of the affair ("Final Parting" would have been more straightforward).

But if we allow ourselves amusement at the girl's expense, we must also bleed with her. The parting *hurts*. We are moved to pity as the blood drains from her face and she goes to seek comfort from her father. The fourth and fifth stanzas are ambiguous. Is it her father or a tree she goes to? Either reading is possible. The "oak" may be a metaphor for her father, chosen to connote his strength and pride. Or it may be literally an oak, one perhaps that her father has planted by the front door ("lintel") of the house, a tree which embodies his strength and through which his spirit seems to speak. At any rate the father, or the father's presence in the oak, tries to calm the daughter, gently reproaching her for the foolishness of her despair. In vain, of course. His talk is like the sound of leaves as it ceases and begins again. There are several double meanings here. The word *sere* means old and dry, but also suggests wise (*seer*). Is there something dry and meaningless in the wisdom of the father? The word *vaunting* applied to a tree would mean large and spreading; applied to a man, proud. Combined with *sere-seer* it suggests a gently wry ironic comment on the father's "wisdom." Wisdom comes easily to an old man who is himself past the storms of youth.

The use of figurative language is imperative if we are to be faithful to the full truth and complexity of human feeling. The bitterness of the girl's feeling is summed up in the marvelous metaphor of the last stanza comparing the tread marks of the bicycle tire to the track of a snake (and to the pattern on the back of the snake). Both visually and emotionally the metaphor is exact. The girl has been venomously bitten by her disappointment and hopes that her letter, whose characters are also snakelike, will bite the offending young man. The physical effects of the bite (i.e., of her emotion) are accurately conveyed through the paradox of the last two lines: "she stood there hot as fever / And cold as any icicle." Logically the statement is contradictory and impossible, but in the epistemology of human feeling it is not only true but could be conveyed in no other way.*

---

*This commentary is reprinted, with a slight alteration, from Laurence Perrine and James M. Reid, *100 American Poems of the Twentieth Century* (New York: Harcourt Brace Jovanovich, 1966), pp. 139–41.

128. *Ralph Pomeroy* **ROW** (page 165)

The speaker is rowing a flat-bottomed boat on a shallow lake surrounded by pines. The lake is swampy, with water-lilies, croaking frogs, and turtles so fearless that they seem tame. The day is sunny with the slight breeze that makes the water surface seem dappled with "shingles," a "roof" over the "murky floors" of the lake.

The preponderance of imagery in the poem is visual; the only auditory images are in the onomatopoeia of line 1 ("Slap. Clap.") and lines 4 and 6 (the repeated "croak"), and in the metaphorical "singing" in the final line. But because the poem so abounds in internal rime, alliteration, assonance, and consonance—that is, in suggestive sound effects—a reader might readily *feel* that sound imagery predominates. The only line without internal or connecting sound repetitions is line 19, "roof of the water," an important line conceptually because it imaginatively reinforces the distinction between the speaker's position atop the water and the rich activity *of* the water and its denizens. So much of the punctuation occurs within rather than at the ends of lines (this is particularly true of the periods) that the poem may seem to imitate the action of rowing, the bisecting activity of dipping the oars into the water, and then pushing on the "cut" to propel the boat.

The metaphor comparing the shining appearance of the pines to the singing of a "green creed" presents the theme of the poem: to the human observer, interposing himself and his actions into the self-contained natural world, the harmonies of that world seem like a faith or religion shared only by nature. Nature in its self-preserving defense metaphorically marshals its forces: they slap, they send out flotillas, they flare (and—punning—they have "moats"), they flame, they have dreadnoughts, and no amount of human digging can really destroy the roof that protects the water-world. The only two repeated words are "croak" (4 and 6) and "water," (8 and 19), key terms since they link the warning sound and the well-defended liquid environment. The title pun reinforces the impression of noise and motion as representation of a struggle between the speaker and this world: he can "row" his boat across its surface, but in so doing he provokes a hubbub of activity, he raises a "row" (rimes with *cow*) directed against his intrusion.

But it is probably too sober-sided to insist on major themes in this poem, for its greatest pleasures derive from the multiple, playful manipulations of sound. TRA

129. *Edna St. Vincent Millay* **COUNTING-OUT RHYME** (page 166)

A counting-out rhyme, as its name implies, is a verse (usually for children) which involves counting things, often using numbers ("1, 2, Buckle my shoe / 3, 4, Knock at the door . . ."), but just as often not ("Eeny, meeny, miny, mo, / Catch a Dutchman by the toe . . ."). They are usually passed down from obscure origins by oral tradition through generations of children, and they are usually nonsensical in content.

Millay, however, gives the form artistic treatment. First, she gives it unity of content. She counts the parts (bark, leaf, wood, stem, twig), usually distinguished by their color (silver, sallow, yellow, green, pale), of different species of trees (beech, birch, willow, maple, apple, popple, oak, hornbeam, elder). Second, she gives her verse a subtler and more sophisticated form than the usual clunking iambic or trochaic rimed couplets. She invents a three-line stanza with a strict pattern of feminine half-rimes, using trochaic trimeter in the first two lines and dimeter in the third, varying this with a high percentage of run-on lines. Third, obviously enchanted by the sounds of words, Millay enchants the reader with a dense variety of sound-correspondences (alliteration, assonance, consonance, internal rime, feminine half-rime), made more striking by their skillful juxtaposition of euphony (*silver, yellow, willow*) and cacophony (*oak for yoke and barn-beam*).

This poem, all said, may not "say" much, but what it does say, it says enchantingly. It delights by its sheer love of language and sound. LP

130. William Stafford TRAVELING THROUGH THE DARK (page 166)

Line 3 makes clear that it is not unusual for dead deer to be found on the Wilson River road. The only inference to be drawn is that they are hit by autos as they cross the road on their way to the river, but that most drivers, after the impact, leave the carcass where it falls and drive on. That the speaker stops—even though he was not the one who hit the deer—shows him to be an unusually responsible person. He has carefully driven around in front of the animal, has turned down his headlights—another responsible action—but has left the motor running, hoping to make quick work of pushing the carcass over the edge, not stopping too long on the dangerous unlit road.

That he recognizes an ethical dilemma when he discovers the unborn fawn still living inside the dead doe particularly marks him out as a thoughtful person concerned with the preciousness of all life; and that he hesitates—thinking hard "for us all"—again reveals his deep sense of involvement. Who are the "us all" for whom the speaker thinks? Himself surely, the unborn fawn surely, other motorists traveling the Wilson River road, and, beyond that, all humanity, perhaps all life, which needs relationships with other forms of life in order to exist.

But what are his options? There is no way he can deliver the unborn fawn: he is hardly equipped to perform a Caesarean in the middle of the road. Nor could he mother the fawn, were it born. He must either take responsibility for killing the fawn by pushing its dead mother over the edge, or walk away and leave the dead doe there, endangering other lives—motorists who might be killed while swerving to miss the body. There is no choice really. The second alternative would be equivalent to washing his hands of moral responsibility—like Pontius Pilate in the Bible. The fact that he hesitates, however—considering the options—makes us like him. That one "swerving" from what should and must be expeditiously done makes him fully human.

Many of the images have symbolic implications, though perhaps not of the kind that benefit from being pinned with a label and spelled with a capital "S." The image of "Traveling through the dark" (how different in effect from "Driving at night"!) suggests the difficulties of living life and having to make moral decisions with only limited knowledge and with no certain moral guidance. The cold of the doe's body and the warm spot in its side are *signs*, not symbols, of death and life. The car, its steady engine purring, its parking lights "aimed ahead," suggests a kind of automated life which never hesitates, does not make decisions, and is always ready for action. Its purring engine contrasts with the stillness of the wilderness (and of the unborn fawn), which has its own claims on the speaker, and which seems to "listen" (16), as if for his decision. The red taillight of the car is a conventional symbol of danger, and "the glare of the warm exhaust turning red" in which the speaker stands (15) almost symbolizes his dilemma. He must choose between spilling the warm blood of the unborn fawn over the edge of the canyon or endangering the lives of other human beings.

"Canyon" (3) is the only line-end in the poem without any correspondence in sound to another line-end in its stanza, and even it alliterates with the first line-end in the following stanza, just two lines away. LP

131. *Robert Frost* NOTHING GOLD CAN STAY (page 167)

The paradox in line 1 is to be explained by the fact that, when leaves first bud in the spring, they have a golden tint, more gold than green, which they lose as the leaves grow larger.

The paradox in line 3 has been explained by Alfred R. Ferguson as referring to much the same thing: "The earliest leaf unfolds its beauty like a flower," but I believe it refers to something different. Some trees and shrubs blossom in the spring before they bear leaves (the plum, for example; also the redbud and some species of peach and cherry). In botanical language, however, the term *leaf*, in its broadest sense, includes all foliar structures of the higher plants, including the sepals, petals, pistil, and stamens of a flower: all parts of the blossom, technically, are modified leaves. For trees like the plum, therefore, it is literally true that the "early leaf's a flower." That it remains so only "an hour" is an overstatement, but the blossoming period of these trees is brief at best; then the flowers drop off and the ordinary leaves begin.

Frost's poem, then, lists four things that have an early but brief period of perfect beauty (or happiness): the foliage of trees; the plants which blossom before they bear leaves; the course of human history (as storied in the Eden myth—or other myths of a "golden age"); and a day (which begins with the fresh gold-tinted air of sunrise). It ends with a generalization: "Nothing gold can stay." But by this time Frost's examples have assumed the force of symbols: they remind us as well of the year (which begins with spring), of the individual human life (which blooms in youth), and perhaps of love (most blissful in its early stages). Frost's "gold" is a symbol of perfection, and his theme is that most things reach their moment of perfection early and retain it briefly. His poem is about the transiency of beauty, bliss, youth, spring, and the transport of early love.

For another treatment of this theme in Frost, see his poem "The Oven Bird." For another poet's response to Frost, see A. R. Ammons's "Providence," page 255. For additional perspectives on "Nothing Gold Can Stay," see Lawrance Thompson, *Fire and Ice* (New York: Holt, 1942), pp. 169-70; Charles R. Anderson, in *The Explicator*, 22 (Apr. 1964), item 63; Alfred R. Ferguson, in *Frost: Centennial Essays* (Jackson: Univ. Press of Mississippi, 1974), pp. 436-39; and John Robert Doyle, Jr., *The Poetry of Robert Frost* (Johannesburg: Witwatersrand Univ. Press, 1962), pp. 174-76. For a possibly fuller analysis than you may want of the musical devices in the poem (and *their* perfection), see John A. Rea, "Language and Form in 'Nothing Gold Can Stay'," *Robert Frost: Studies of the Poetry*, ed. Kathryn Gibbs Harris (Boston: G. K. Hall, 1979), pp. 17-25. LP

POEMS FOR FURTHER READING

Poems 190, 199, 209, and 215 from Part Two provide additional illustrations of topics presented in this chapter.

Chapter twelve
Rhythm and Meter

A Note on Scansion

English meter is still a matter of considerable controversy—perhaps it is becoming more so—and I do not expect everyone to agree with my own scheme. In fact, I do not agree with part of it myself. But I believe that *serious* students of poetry need some familiarity with traditional terms. If they don't know what iambic pentameter is, they will be handicapped in reading about poetry.

Many writers, for purposes of scansion, prefer to use x for an unstressed syllable and an accent mark (′) for stressed syllables. I find this system clumsy for classroom use. The x's take too long to write on the board (two strokes instead of one) and the accent marks get confused with uprights dividing the feet. An additional merit of the horizontal stroke for stressed syllables is that the stroke may be lengthened to indicate heavy stresses, shortened to indicate light stresses.

Some metrists include the pyrrhic ($\smile \smile$) and the amphibrach ($\smile - \smile$) among the kinds of feet, but I don't find them necessary or helpful. The notion of a foot without an accent violates my definition of a foot. Where scansion might seem to call for a pyrrhic, one syllable will nearly always be slightly heavier than the other and thus can be regarded as bearing a light stress. As for the amphibrach, one gets it only by dividing the feet in an unusual and unwarranted way. LP

132. *George Herbert*   **VIRTUE** (page 170)

Three stanzas presenting sweet things that die are contrasted with a fourth presenting the one thing that does not die. The first three stanzas parallel each other: each is an apostrophe beginning with the word "Sweet" and ending with the words "must die." The fourth stanza, which is not an apostrophe, reserves "sweet" for the third position in the opening line, and ends with the word "lives." The first three stanzas are interconnected because the "day" of the first stanza may be thought of as containing the "rose" of the second, while the "spring" of the third stanza contains them both. The ordering is also marked by the opening words of the fourth lines: "For thou . . . ," "And thou . . . ," "And all . . . ."

In stanza 1, the day is presented in an apt metaphor as the "bridal" (wedding) of the earth and sky, uniting them in light; the metaphor connotes a beginning, brightness, and hope. The dew is fittingly chosen to mourn the death of the day, for dew is associated with evening. The dew is both a personification and a metaphor, both the weeper and the tears that are wept. The words "to night" function both as adverb and, because the hyphen has been omitted, as prepositional phrase in which the noun is a traditional symbol for death.

In stanza 2, through a bold metaphor, the crimson rose is compared in color to the face of an angry man, and, in an even bolder overstatement, is described as so bright that it causes tears in an observer who rashly gazes at it without shielding his eyes (like looking directly at the sun). Yet, despite this dazzling brilliance, it too is doomed to die. Its "root" is ever in its "grave" (a metonymy for earth). The rose's death is a condition of its birth: it dies back into the very soil from which it sprang; its root is "ever" there.

In stanza 3, the spring is compared metaphorically to a box where "sweets" lie compacted. (For the seventeenth-century reader the connotations would suggest, not a box of candy, but a box of perfumes—rose petals, lavender, cedar sprays, etc.) But the poet's "music" shows that the spring also has its "closes" and must die like the rest. The "music" may be read literally as well as metaphorically (Herbert was a musician as well as a poet). The word "closes" has three relevant meanings: the spring ends or terminates, the metaphorical box shuts, and a "close" in music is a cadence or concluding strain.

Stanza 4 presents a contrast. A "sweet and virtuous soul," it declares, is immortal. Like "seasoned timber" it never "gives" (*buckles* or *snaps*). Even should the whole world "turn to coal," it would survive. Spiritual in its origin, and having preserved its purity and strength through virtuous discipline, it will live even more intensely after the destruction of everything physical.

Two thoughtful brief discussions of this poem, by Louis L. Martz and M. M. Mahood, may be found in *Metaphysical Poetry*, ed. by Malcolm Bradbury and David Palmer (London: Edward Arnold, 1970), pp. 109-10 and 143-44. There is an extended discussion in Helen Vendler, *The Poetry of George Herbert* (Cambridge, Mass.: Harvard Univ. Press, 1975), pp. 9-24. LP

EXERCISE 1 (page 179)

a. Blank verse. Line 15 has only three feet (a departure with a precedent in Milton's "Lycidas"). Lines 29-30 combine to make a pentameter line (page 41).
b. Free verse (page 123).
c. Blank verse (page 90).
d. Rimed iambic pentameter (page 45).
e. Blank verse. The first and last lines in this speech are trimeter, but that is explainable by its being an excerpt (page 120).
f. Blank verse. Some lines in this poem are rough and almost unscannable (especially line 2), but the majority point to iambic pentameter as the norm (page 118).
g. Free verse (page 125).

h. Iambic meter. The lines are irregular in number of feet (page 146).
i. Free verse (page 31).
j. Free verse. The lines of this poem, though all similarly short in appearance, do not manifest a consistent meter until almost their very end, and thus must be classified as free verse. In the last three lines, however, they become increasingly regular iambic tetrameter (the last line is as strongly regular as verse can get). These are also the lines in which the speaker realizes that he can't build a secure life by himself, that he must have "a help, a love, a you, a wife." Sound echoes sense as the skewed free verse of the earlier lines submits to order and regularity in the conclusion (page 93). LP

133. *William Blake* **"INTRODUCTION" TO** *SONGS OF INNOCENCE* (page 180)

The child upon the cloud substitutes for the traditional Muse. The Lamb symbolizes innocence. The poet is first inspired by an emotion or idea (stanzas 1-2), then finds words to express that experience (stanza 3), then writes down or publishes his poems for all to read (stanzas 4-5). (In the poem he fashions a pen from a hollow reed and dyes water to make ink.) In this "Introduction" Blake indicates the source of inspiration for his poems—childhood; their subject matter—innocence; their intended audience—both children and adults (the last line indicates that "Every child" may joy to hear them; but line 14 indicates that the book is for "all" to read); and their tone—pleasant (2), merry (6), cheerful (6), happy (10), joyous (20). (Actually they are all these and more.)

Lines 1-2 and 9-10 establish a regular tetrameter pattern with accents on both the first and last syllables of the line. In scansion the pressure of the pattern forces us to promote the initial prepositions (*On, In*) and the conjunctions (*And, So, While*) to accented status. *Every* (20) is pronounced essentially as two syllables. Dividing the feet *after* the stressed syllables produces one monosyllabic foot and three iambs in each line. Dividing the feet *before* the stressed syllables produces three trochees and one monosyllabic foot in each line. It is obviously duple meter, but whether one calls it iambic or trochaic is a purely arbitrary decision: it is no more one than the other. LP

134. *Robert Frost* **IT TAKES ALL SORTS** (page 181)

This couplet can be scanned either as iambic:

it TAKES / ALL SORTS / of IN- / and OUT- / door SCHOOL- / ing
to GET / a- DAPT- / ed TO / my KIND / of FOOL- / ing

or as trochaic:

> it / TAKES ALL / SORTS of / IN- and / OUT- door / SCHOOL- ing /
> to / GET a- / DAPT- ed / TO my / KIND of / FOOL- ing. /

Scanned as iambic, both lines have an unaccented syllable left over at the end of the line. Scanned as trochaic, both lines have an unaccented syllable left over at the beginning of the line. Both scansions yield an equal number of iambs and trochees. This is a pentameter couplet in duple meter. LP

135. *A. E. Housman* EPITAPH ON AN ARMY OF MERCENARIES (page 181)

In the essay cited below, Richard Wilbur identifies two important allusions in this poem: first, to *Paradise Lost*, VI, 668 ff. and 867 ff., the account of the battle in heaven which includes the phrase "the sum of things" as a term for the universe and refers to the peril applied to its "foundations" by the revolt of Satan, finally averted by God's direct intervention in the person of the Son; and second, to the myth of the mortal hero Heracles temporarily bearing the weight of the heavens on his shoulders. These allusions enrich Housman's poem, but also help to define its complex tone—for he is using the word "mercenary" and its venal connotations ironically, as a rebuttal to the sarcasm with which the German press labeled the British regulars at the Battle of Ypres. Housman adopts the slanderous word, and uses it to pay tribute to men whose professionalism led to their certain death, but who were at the time the only resistance to a force that threatened to destroy the world. But we must not misunderstand the tone of this poem: it does not say "dulce et decorum est pro patria mori," claiming selfless idealism for these dead, nor deny that these men were in the army as a job for pay; rather, Housman's point is that ordinary men, with ordinary worldly motives, were called upon to perform extraordinary self-sacrifice, and did so, to the salvation of the world—although saving the world was probably not what led them to become professional soldiers.

In Herbert's "Virtue (page 170), extra-metrical syllables at the ends of lines 9 and 11 are variants to the pattern of the poem; Housman establishes such syllables as part of his pattern, since they occur regularly at the ends of all odd-numbered lines—that is, they are a part of the rhythm, not an exception or syncopation. They contribute a "falling" rhythm to the ends of those lines, which is made more obvious by their feminine rime contrasting to the masculine, monosyllabic rime words of the even-numbered lines. And in scanning the odd-numbered lines, we may detect another pattern, the substitution of a trochaic foot at the beginning of the line:

> THESE, in / the DAY / when HEAV'N / was FALL- / ing   1
> FOL- lowed / their MER- / ce- NAR- / y CALL- / ing   3
> THEIR shoul- / ders HELD / the SKY / sus- PEND- / ed   5

Notice that in lines 1 and 3, there can be no dispute about the initial trochee, while that in line 5 might be questioned. Read as prose and out of context, the line might sound like "their SHOULders held the SKY susPENDed," with an iamb at the beginning. But the purpose of the statement is not to point to *shoulders*, but to discriminate *these* men from others who did not bear the great burden; it was *their* shoulders, the only ones available. Line 7, on the other hand, provides no such clear-cut interpretive support for reading the first foot as a trochee, and one might rather read it as an iamb—or as a spondee. This departure from the rhythms Housman has established for the odd-numbered lines is of course appropriate to this emphatically blasphemous line, this complete reverse of what God did in *Paradise Lost*. In the absence of divine protection and intervention, the world must rely on its own resources, even if that requires heroic deeds from unheroic men.

For a fuller discussion, see Richard Wilbur's essay, "Round about a Poem of Housman's," in *Response: Prose Pieces, 1953-1976* (New York: Harcourt Brace Jovanovich, 1976), pp. 16-38; also included in *A Celebration of Poets*, ed. Don Cameron Allen (Baltimore: Johns Hopkins Press, 1967), pp. 177-202. TRA

136. *e. e. cummings* **IF EVERYTHING HAPPENS THAT CAN'T BE DONE** (page 182)

The subject is love. The season is spring. The tone is ecstatic. cummings is a romantic poet for whom, if there is anything more wonderful than being a live individual with a heart and feelings of one's own (a ONE; not a cipher, a blank, a nothing, an emotionally dead person), it is being one of two such individuals (two ONES) who achieve identity through love. But being a ONE is prerequisite, and the poet devotes the first two stanzas to establishing that "there's nothing as something [so important] as one." Being a ONE, for cummings, is a function of feeling, not of intellect. The analytic reason (symbolized throughout the poem by "books" and in stanza 2 by analytic terms such as "why," "because," and "although") for cummings deadens and kills, whereas feeling (symbolized by "buds" and "birds" and "trees") enlivens and vitalizes ("buds know better than books" and "books don't grow," to expand cummings's telescoped phrase). The consummation of natural feeling comes with the mutually realized love of two individuals; and the love theme (introduced in the third stanza with "so your is a my") is explicitly stated in the fourth stanza ("now i love you and you love me") and receives its triumphant expression in the fifth (where all the pronouns have changed to "we's"), especially in the poem's final line, which incorporates, with a neat bit of word play, the mathematical equation for this identity ("we're WONderful ONE times ONE"). When such miracles happen (when "everything happens that can't be done"), as they regularly do in the spring, then even "the stupidest teacher" (representing the intellect again) will dimly guess the miraculousness of individuality, feeling, spring, life, and love.

cummings has constructed his poem on an intricate pattern. Each stanza is linked to the one that follows (like persons holding hands) by the repetition of its last word as the first word in the next. Lines 2-4 of each stanza contain a parenthesis in which life and feelings are contrasted with intellect. Lines 6-8 of each stanza contain a second parenthesis showing the participants in the poem to be engaged in a spontaneous joyous dance. Each stanza is additionally organized by a pattern of approximate and perfect rimes in which lines 1, 4, 9 rime together, and lines 5, 8. The prevailing meter is anapestic (freely mixed with iambic and monosyllabic feet, which give it spontaneity and variety), in which the nine lines of each stanza have four, two, one, one, four, one, one, two, and three feet respectively.

Had cummings printed the two parentheses of each stanza as one-line rather than three-line units, he would have had a simple five-line stanza with all lines riming (anapestic $aabb^4a^3$). But by breaking up the parentheses, he introduces into them two additional rhetorical (line-end) pauses which, without altering the meter or slowing it down, give it additional spontaneity, variety of movement, a bit of a swirl, reinforcing the dance-like quality of these lines. Indeed the joyous tone of this poem is as much the result of the meter as of the words. Notice, moreover, that line 28, which states the subject of the poem, the cause of its joyousness, consists of four regular iambic feet. Had the poem been printed, as proposed above, in five-line stanzas with the parentheses compacted into one line each, line 28, would be the only one in the poem without a single anapestic foot. This slowing down of line 28, through the use of exclusively duple feet, gives it an emphasis appropriate to its thematic importance in the content of the poem.*

*This discussion is adapted from the essay "A Look at Rhythm and Meter" in *The Art of Total Relevance: Papers on Poetry*, by Laurence Perrine (Rowley, Mass.: Newbury House, 1976), pp. 70-73.

137. *A. E. Housman* **OH WHO IS THAT YOUNG SINNER** (page 184)

The poem is satire against the prejudices that cause men to hate and persecute each other for superficial and accidental differences between them. The color of one's hair, having nothing to do with intrinsic human ability or worth, symbolizes any such difference. When I first read the poem I identified it in my own mind—because of my American experience with racial conflict—with skin color. I have since learned that the poem was occasioned by the conviction and imprisonment of Oscar Wilde for homosexuality. Either reading of the poem is legitimate, and so probably would be such religious or racial differences as presently divide Protestant and Roman Catholic in Northern Ireland and Moslem and Jew in the Middle East.

I would call the irony verbal, for the poem gives me no sense of a dramatic speaker different from the author. LP

138. *William Butler Yeats* **DOWN BY THE SALLEY GARDENS** (page 185)

The meter is basically iambic heptameter, but the fourth accent regularly falls on a pause—except that in lines 3 and 7 it *might* be taken as falling lightly on "as." By the former option, the fifth foot in these two lines is anapestic; by the latter, iambic. LP

139. *Walt Whitman* **HAD I THE CHOICE** (page 186)

140. *Robert Frost* **THE AIM WAS SONG** (page 186)

Walt Whitman defends free verse (in unrimed free verse); Robert Frost defends metrical verse—"measure" (in rimed iambic tetrameter). The verse form, in each case, is perfectly chosen for the subject matter. This may seem elementary, but what would have been the effect if Whitman had defended free verse in meter, and Frost, meter in free verse?

In Whitman's poem even the greatest poetic art is seen as pale and inferior when set beside nature. The implication for poetry is that the most desirable poetry will be that which is most natural, most *like* nature. The further implication is that free verse is natural and that metered, rimed verse is artificial. Still another implication is that metaphors, similes, and contrived paradoxes ("conceits") are artificial.

In Frost's poem successful poetry is seen as an improvement on nature. Though it uses natural materials, it orders them, imposes form on them, and thus gives them a power which they do not have in their natural state. In repeating the words "by measure" in line 13—and placing a period after them—Frost gives the phrase tremendous emphasis. Song, he insists, is "measured"; rather than taking form from nature, it gives form to nature. Thus nature is made humanly meaningful.

Readers must judge the two philosophies by their own standards. But the fact is that great poetry has been written both in meter and in free verse. LP

141. *Samuel Taylor Coleridge* **METRICAL FEET** (page 187)

Coleridge's verses are about feet both literally and metaphorically. The personified Trochee "trips," the Spondee "stalks," the Iambics "march," the Anapests proceed with "a leap and a bound." LP

EXERCISE (page 187)

Now came still Evening on, and Twilight gray
Had in her sober livery all things clad;
Silence accompanied, for beast and bird,
They to their grassy couch, these to their nests
Were slunk, all but the wakeful nightingale;
She all night long her amorous descant sung;
Silence was pleased; now glowed the firmament
With living sapphires: Hesperus that led
The starry host, rode brightest, till the Moon
Rising in cloudy majesty, at length
Apparent Queen, unveiled her peerless light,
And o'er the dark her silver mantle threw.

Chapter thirteen
Sound and Meaning

142. *Anonymous* **PEASE PORRIDGE HOT** (page 188)

This verse has been described as a "clapping game" for children. LP

143. *William Shakespeare* **SONG: HARK, HARK!** (page 189)

Even with onomatopoetic words, we must not assume an *identity* between sound and meaning. The French equivalent of "cockadoodle-doo" is *co co rico*; in German it is *ki-ke-ri-ki*; in Spanish it is *kikiriki*; and in Shakespeare's original (unmodernized) text it was *cockadiddle-dow*. LP

144. *Carl Sandburg* **SPLINTER** (page 190)

"Thin" and "splinter" (also "cricket") are phonetic intensives, and in line 4 their effect is reinforced by the short *i*'s in "singing" (and, though their effect on the ear is slight, by those in "It" and "is"). The consonance of "last," "first," and "frost" also adds to the effectiveness of this miniature. LP

145. *Robert Herrick* **UPON JULIA'S VOICE** (page 191)

"Silvery" (literally *like silver*) suggests something precious, beautiful, smooth to the touch, softly gleaming in color. Julia's voice is smooth, soft, agreeable, and precious to the speaker. "Amber" (a fossilized resin) is a translucent substance that glows with soft rich golden-yellow light. Julia is singing and accompanying herself on a lute made of wood but finished with an amber-colored varnish. More importantly, the sound of the lute under her fingers is softly and richly resonant, golden-toned, the perfect complement to her voice. It is as if the melodious words she sings each melted into a purely translucent amber lute. LP

146. *Robert Frost* **THE SPAN OF LIFE** (page 195)

No one who has ever been greeted at the door by an affectionate and enthusiastic puppy can miss the image implicit in the second line, which is all the more effective because of Frost's *understatement* (almost *un*-statement) of it. [Actually the Greeks, whose versification was based on duration rather than on accent, had a name for the second foot in the first line (it was called a *molossus*) but we see no reason to burden English students with it.] Frost's title universalizes the subject of the poem, making the dog a symbol of human as well as of animal life. LP

EXERCISE (page 196)

The letter in parentheses indicates the superior version.
1. (a) ("Independence") The linkage in sound of "*gui*de" and "*guar*d" (alliteration and consonance) emphasizes their syntactical parallelism in an iambic pentameter couplet. Version *b* takes more words (and an extra foot) to make a less forceful connection. (The Biblical allusion is to Exodus 13:21.)
2. (b) (*Comus*) This blank verse passage, after the generalization in line 1, calls for harshness in line 2 and musicality in line 3. The three hard consonant sounds of "*crabbed*" crowding around one vowel are much harsher than the soft consonants in "*rough*" (prounced *ruff*); in addition, two accents coming together on "dull fools" emphasize these words (as do their repetition of *l*'s) and strain the meter (a monosyllabic foot replaces the expected iamb in the fourth position), whereas "foolish men" is pleasant in sound and regular in meter. The name "Apollo," with its final open vowel and its mellifluous *l*'s (picking up *l*'s in "musical" and "lute") is far more melodious than "Phoebus."
3. (b) ("Mid-Winter") The core of each version is "crows croak hoarsely" with its suggestion of raucous cawing. The three sharp *k*-sounds in "*c*rows *c*roa*k*" are supported in version *b* in "out-*c*ast" and "a*c*ross"; and the hissing *s* of "hoar*s*ely" is reinforced in "out-ca*s*t," "acros*s*," and "whitene*ss*" (with the addition of three sharp *t*'s). In version *a*, "fleeing" and "over the snow" are rather pleasant in sound.
4. (b) (*Tristram,* VI) The gaps in "Your _____ how bells of singing gold / Would sound at _____ over silent water" must be filled with pleasant, musical sounds. In version *b* "low voice" is soft and lovely, "tells" provide an internal rime with "bells," and "twilight" a half-rime with "silent." In version *a* "talk attests" is noisy; "evening" is softly pleasant but provides no rime.
5. (b) (*The Princess:* "Come down, O maid") The blank verse of version *a* is metrically regular throughout. In version *b* the superfluity of unstressed syllables in line 1 (MYR-i-ads of RIV-u-lets HUR-ry-ing THROUGH the LAWN) gives the effect of speed; and the onomatopoetic words "moan" and "murmuring" are reinforced by the *m*'s, *n*'s, and *r*'s in "my*r*iads," "im*m*e*m*o*r*ial," "el*m*s," and "i*nn*u*m*e*r*able."
6. (a) (*Romeo and Juliet*, III, 5) The effect wanted is a harsh unpleasantness.

The nasal "sings so" is less pleasant and less flowing than "warbles." The metrical irregularity of "STRAIN- ing HARSH DIS- cords" strains the meter and puts heavy emphasis on harshness, whereas the smooth regularity of "with HARSH dis-CORD-ant TONES" mutes it. "Unpleasing sharps" lacks the pleasant assonance of "tones" and "doleful."

7. (b) (*Don Juan*, VII, lxxviii) The flowing rhythm and euphonious sound of version *a*—its liquid *l*'s, *r*'s, and *m*'s and its soft *f*- and *v*-sounds—make it beautiful to listen to; but this beauty is highly inappropriate to the subject. The sharp monosyllables, the clogged meter, and explosive *b*'s and *d*'s of version *b* make it far superior.

8. (a) ("Reconciliation") The repeated *s*-sounds in "si*s*ters," "incessantly," "*s*oftly," and "*s*oiled" provide the repetition called for and perhaps even the sound of hands sloshing repeatedly in sudsy water.

9. (b) ("Elegy Written in a Country Churchyard") In line 1 "tolls," like "knell," is onomatopoetic. In line 2 a spondee appropriately slows down the line by bringing three accents together (the LOW- / ing HERD / WIND SLOW- / ly O'ER / the LEA /). In line 4 a light accent on "and" in the fourth foot requires a slight compensatory pause before it (as if there were a comma after "darkness"), thus isolating the final pronoun and preparing for the meditative nature of the poem. (In version *a* lines 3 and 4 are absurdly swift for the solemnity of the subject.)

10. (b) ("Epistle to Dr. Arbuthnot") In line 1 the succession of short monosyllables with sharp endings ("let," "flap," "bug," "wings") spits out the spite of the speaker at the subject of his satire, and line 2 adds another ("child"). But the manifest superiority of version *b* is the superiority of "stinks and stings" to "smells and bites." The alliterating *st*'s, the assonance of the short *i*'s, and the sharp final consonants link these verbs in sound as well as in syntax and give them a force that the soft word "smells" lacks (though "bites" has it). LP

147. *Alexander Pope* **SOUND AND SENSE** (page 198)

Introducing his topic with the general observation that good writing is the result of art (it looks easy, but mastery is acquired only by long practice), Pope then states the thesis of his passage in line 4: In good writing "The sound must seem an echo to the sense." He elaborates and demonstrates this thesis (simultaneously) through a series of five examples, each included within an iambic pentameter riming couplet. When a poet writes about a gentle west wind and a smooth-flowing stream, Pope begins, the verse should also be soft and smooth. (The following scansions represent my sense, and may be modified to fit yours.)

SOFT is / the STRAIN / when ZEPH- / yr GEN- / tly BLOWS, /

And the SMOOTH / STREAM / in SMOOTH- / er NUM- / bers FLOWS. /

The reversal of stress in the first foot gives additional emphasis to "Soft," which is the key word in the first line. Most of the words in the line are soft in sound, especially "Zephyr," whose *z-f-r* combination of consonants is softer than the *w-st-w-nd* of *West wind* despite the latter's alliterating *w*'s. The *g* in "gently" is a *j*. The explosive *b* of "blows" is gentled by the following *l* and long vowel sounds. "Soft" and "strain" contain a gentling *f* and *n* respectively. In the second line the key word "smooth," itself a smooth-sounding word, is emphasized (a) by the meter, which joins it with "stream" (also smooth in its long vowel sound and concluding *m*), and (b) by its repetition in "smoother." The fourth foot contains the soft consonants *n* and *m*. The fifth combines the soft *fl-* with a long vowel. The repeated *s*'s in these two lines (I suspect) take on the color of their surroundings.

But WHEN / LOUD SURG- / es LASH / the SOUND- / ing SHORE, /
The HOARSE, / ROUGH VERSE / should LIKE / the TOR- / rent ROAR. /

It is arguable whether the key word "loud" is a loud sound (its vowel, of course, is a dipthong, and is the sound we use for a cry of pain—"ow!" or "ouch!"), but it is inarguable that the meter puts a stress on it appropriate to its importance in the sentence, and that its effect is intensified by its near-rime with "sounding." The onomatopoetic "roar" is emphasized by its anticipation in "shore," "hoarse," and "torrent." The alliteration of "loud" and "lash" and the consonance of "hoarse" and "verse" gives emphasis and linkage to these two pairs of words. Though none of the words in these two lines sounds particularly harsh (the roughness and hoarseness we may imagine in "rough" and "hoarse" disappear from *ruff* and *horse*), by bringing three accents together in "hoarse, rough verse," the meter puts extraordinary emphasis on words that are hoarse-meaning and rough-meaning, and pushes together three syllables that do not articulate easily. The grammatical pause contributes to this lack of articulation.

When A- / jax STRIVES / SOME ROCK's / VAST WEIGHT / to THROW, /
The LINE / TOO LA- / bors AND / the WORDS / MOVE SLOW. /

It is not just the five stressed syllables in a row that slow down the first line and give it such a sense of strain and muscular effort, it is the impossibility of sliding these words easily off the tongue, the muscular effort required in the reading. The mouth has to be reshaped for each word in the series. Even in a single word like "strives," effort is required, for we must pronounce five distinct consonant sounds *s-t-r* and *v-s* with only one vowel sound between them (*v-s* is harder than *s-t-r*). In the second line the two spondees, bringing three stresses together at two points in the line, slow the line down.

NOT so, / when SWIFT / Ca-MIL- / la SCOURS / the PLAIN, /
FLIES o'er / the un- BEND- / ing CORN, / and SKIMS / a- LONG / the MAIN. /

In each of these lines the reader has the choice of stressing the first or the second syllable in the opening foot. I have elected to stress "Not" because (a) it signals the change from the grunting effort of Ajax to lift his rock to the effortless ease of swift Camilla running, (b) the two unstressed syllables following it speed up the line, and (c) the increased distance separating the first two stresses give added emphasis to the second stress—"swift"—which is the key word in the couplet. The name "Camilla" (like "Zephyr") fits Pope's purpose perfectly, so easily do the syllables flow together. (Contrast the effort and speed involved in saying the three syllables of "Camilla" and of "rock's vast weight.") The assonant short *i*'s of "swift," "Camilla," and "skims" quicken these words, as well as link them in meaning. In the second line I stress the initial "Flies," again because the reversed stress gives added emphasis to the more important word in the meaning, and because the unstressed syllables succeeding add speed to the line. (The three unstressed syllables together were not allowed by the strict rules of Pope's day, however, nor the two consecutive vowel sounds in "the" and "un-". Pope's unmodernized text—*th' unbending corn*—blends "the" and "un-" together in one syllable.) The notable variation here, however, is the introduction of a six-foot line (called an "Alexandrine") into the pentameter pattern. The extra foot, making it possible to divide the line into two three-foot segments (separated here by a comma), gives the line additional lightness (see discussion in Exercise 1, page 179).

HEAR how / Tim- O- / theus' VAR- / ied LAYS / sur- PRISE, /

And BID / al- TER- / nate PAS- / sions FALL / and RISE! /

With no other text than that before us, the reader with a sensitive ear can confidently declare that Pope put the accent on the second syllable of "alternate." With the accent on the first syllable, the meter goes smash. Put on the second syllable, the line perfectly alternates unstressed and stressed syllables (it is the most regular line of the whole fourteen), thus echoing the alternation of passions of which Timotheus sings. (British usage, as opposed to American, even today stresses the second syllable of *alternate* when used adjectivally, as we do with the word *alternative*.)

Pope's passage is a brilliant display of technical virtuosity. LP

148. *Emily Dickinson* **I LIKE TO SEE IT LAP THE MILES** (page 198)

The basic metaphor of the poem compares a train to a horse, though neither train nor horse is named in the poem. The subject is a train because it laps miles and valleys up, feeds itself (takes water) at tanks, peers (with its headlight) into shanties by the sides of roads, hoots (with its whistle), is punctual, and stops "docile and omnipotent" (obedient to the engineer but tremendously powerful) at its stable (station or roundhouse). It is a horse because it laps, licks, feeds, steps, peers, has ribs, crawls, complains, chases itself, neighs, and stops at a stable. It is a whole train rather than just a locomotive because it chases itself downhill.

The most unusual technical feature of the poem is that each of the first three stanzas ends with a run-on line. These run-on lines give the poem, or the train, a continuous forward motion (there are no periods until the end of the poem), a forward motion that finally grinds to an abrupt halt on the word "stop" (line 16). The stop—it must be a strong one to stop a train—is made strong in a number of ways: first, the word *stop* itself stops suddenly, ending with an explosive consonant; second, though in a normally unstressed position, the word receives a strong metrical stress (with the partial exception of the preceding line, which slows the train down, this is the only line in the poem stressed on the initial syllable); third, it is followed and preceded by grammatical pauses; fourth, it is followed and preceded (on the other side of the grammatical pauses) by stressed syllables, with one of which it has assonance and with the other of which it alliterates. All these features emphasize or isolate the word *stop* in a remarkable way. The phrase that follows—"docile and omnipotent"—is a beautiful expression of power at rest.

But before the train comes to a stop, it makes a variety of motions and sounds. In the first two lines the regular meter and the predominance of *l*'s give the train speed, while at the same time the monosyllabic words ending in *p* or *k*, found throughout the first stanza, give it the clippety-cloppety-clackety sound of iron wheels going over joints in the rails. In line 4 the big word "prodigious," set off between commas, slows the line down as the train slows down to "step" around a curve—an effect that is repeated in line 6. The division of what would normally be line 9 into two lines, comma-interrupted, again slows the train down, this time to a crawl, as it goes through a tunnel, tooting its whistle each inch of the way. The three trochaic words in succession—"horrid, hooting stanza"—convey the regularity and repetition of the whistle's sound, intensified by the narrow walls of the tunnel. The onomatopoetic word "hooting" sounds like *tooting* but alliterates with "horrid," thus emphasizing the repetitiveness of the sound while also retaining the metaphoric sense that this is a creature rather than a machine.

This brief analysis by no means exhausts the adaptation of sound to sense in this poem, but it perhaps indicates the chief features.

The poem employs approximate rime (consonance) in even-numbered lines. Lines 8 and 16 contain overstatement. LP

149. *Ted Hughes* **WIND** (page 199)

The poem describes a house and the surrounding countryside during a hurricane. The wind is accompanied by rain during the night (stanza 1); the rain ceases with morning, but the wind continues throughout the day. In the last two stanzas the poet and his companion sit before the fire, presumably that evening, but can concentrate on nothing but the tremors of the house and the sounds of the storm. Throughout the poem the poet uses violent images to convey the violence of the storm.

Many of the images are sound images, and these are reinforced by the use of onomatopoetic words ("crashing," "booming," "drummed," "bang," "flap," "rang," "shatter") and effective use of sound repetitions. In the first stanza, for instance, the alliteration of w ("woods," "winds," "window," "wet") is accompanied by a remarkable series of repeated d's ("woods," "darkness," "winds," "stampeding," "fields," "window," "floundering," "astride," "blinding"), k's ("crashing," "darkness," "black"), and b's ("booming," "black," "blinding"). The w's are appropriate to the whoosh of the wind, the d's, k's, and b's to the thudding, crashing, booming, and banging noises caused by it. In line 14 the onomatopoeia is reinforced by assonance ("bang," "vanish," "flap"). In lines 15-16 rhythm also contributes in a remarkable way, the series of stressed syllables in "BLACK- / BACK GULL BENT like an I-ron BAR SLOW-ly" reinforcing the visual slowness. Similar effects may be observed throughout the poem.

The poem uses various kinds of rime, mostly very approximate, following the scheme *abba* except in stanza 3, which is *abab*. The rhythm moves very freely around what is basically a five-beat line. LP

150. *Gerard Manley Hopkins* HEAVEN-HAVEN (page 200)

The speaker is a nun taking the vows that commit her to the cloistered life of the convent. This life, dedicated to religious meditation and the worship of God, is metonymically represented by "heaven" and metaphorically represented as a "haven" or sheltered place. In the extension of the metaphor, the sea represents life in the outside world and the storms are especially violent commotions in that life—passions, desires, appetites. The "havens" are pictured in the first stanza as gardens or sheltered fields (as inside a convent wall), in the second stanza as harbors protected from the ocean swells. "Springs" (2) refers both to springs of water—sources of pure refreshment—and to the mildest season of the year, free from wintry storms. "Lilies" (4), because of the pure white color of Easter lilies, are a traditional symbol of purity, chastity, religious worship, absence of sexual passion. Be sure your students realize that "blow" (4) here means "blossom," *not* "sway in the wind."

The basic stanza pattern is iambic $a^3b^2b^5a^3$, but there are many variant feet. In the last line the substitution of anapests for iambs in the last two feet gives the line a swinging motion that imitates its meaning. The effect is enhanced by the use of monosyllables, by the extreme lightness of the unstressed syllables, and by the alliteration of "swings" and "sea." LP

151. *Wilfred Owen* ANTHEM FOR DOOMED YOUTH (page 201)

The octave has its geographical setting on the battlefield (since this is a World War I poem, in France). The sestet has its geographical setting back home (since

Owen was an English poet, in England). The octave concerns the death of soldiers in battle. The sestet concerns the bereavement of friends and families back home. The imagery of the octave is primarily auditory. The imagery of the sestet is primarily visual. The tone of the octave is angry and indignant. The tone of the sestet is tender. (Line 8 is transitional: the "sad shires" are back in England. This line connects the deaths to the bereavement and shifts the geographical locus from battlefield to home.) Both octave and sestet are introduced by questions.

Octave and sestet are unified by the central metaphorical image of an Anglican funeral service. Neither the literal terms of this metaphor (battle and bereavement) nor the figurative term (church funeral service) is named, so this is a metaphor of the fourth form (see page 61). The terms of the central metaphor are arrived at, as it were, by adding up the subsidiary figures and drawing a total. In the octave, at least, the central metaphor emphasizes contrast more than similarity, for the point is that these soldiers will never have a church funeral. Instead of the items in the second column of the list below (the figurative terms), they will have only the items in the first column (the literal terms):

literal	*figurative*
Owen's poem	anthem
monstrous anger of the guns	passing-bells
rapid rifle fire	orisons
wailing shells	choirs singing
bugles calling	voices of mourning
glimmers of good-byes in boys' eyes	candles held by altar boys
pallor of girls' brows	pall-cloth on coffin
tenderness of patient minds	flowers
dusk coming each evening	drawing-down of blinds

The last metaphor on this list does not belong to the funeral service image, but it too is associated with the formal observance of death. (In addition to the metaphors, the octave uses considerable personification: guns are angry, rifles stutter and patter out prayers, shells wail and are demented, bugles call, shires are sad. Words like "monstrous," "stuttering," and "demented" suggest that the noises of battle are like those of a madman.)

Students will have their greatest trouble with lines 10-11. Many will identify the "boys" with the "doomed youth" and read these lines as referring to the gleam in the eyes of the dying soldiers on the battlefield. Candles at a church funeral, however, are not held by the dead man but by attendants (altar boys). The logical organization of the sonnet, moreover, places this scene back home rather than on the battlefield. The boys and girls of the sestet are younger brothers, sisters, sweethearts, or other persons close to the dead.

The main point of the poem is that a church funeral service would be a "mockery" for these dead soldiers. Funeral services are a means of ritualizing or giving dignity to human death. These soldiers, however, did not die a human death; instead, they were slaughtered like "cattle." The dignity of a funeral service would be inappropriate to the indignity of their death. Owen's poem, though a tribute (an "anthem") to the dead soldiers, is mainly a bitter attack on modern war. It expresses horror, indignation, and anger at the senseless slaughter of human beings by mechanical means. Modern warfare, it implies, is mass slaughter: a mockery of human dignity. Death in modern warfare is an animal death, not a human death.

In the octave, sound is adapted to sense chiefly by the use of words and phrases whose sounds imitate meaning. The onomatopoetic series "stuttering . . . rattle . . . patter" is reinforced by the t's in "cattle," "monstrous," and "hasty." The onomatopoetic "wailing" is reinforced by the l's in "bells," "shrill," "shells," "bugles," "calling." ("Bells" and "shrill" may perhaps themselves be considered onomatopoetic.) The phrase "rifles' rapid rattle" is given speed by its pronounced trochaic rhythm (the phrasing corresponding with the meter)* and by the alliteration of the liquid r's, but the hard p and d of "rapid" reinforce the staccato quality of "stuttering . . . rattle . . . patter."

In the sestet, sound is adapted to sense chiefly by the linking together through similarity in sound of words logically connected in meaning, e.g., "candles . . . hands," "glimmers . . . good-byes," "pallor . . . pall," "dusk . . . drawing-down." LP

*The basic meter of the poem is iambic pentameter, and in *scansion* line 3 would be divided as follows:

ON- ly / the STUT- / ter- ing RI- / fles' RAP- / id RAT- / tle.

In *reading* the line, however, we hear "rifles' rapid rattle" as the three trochees.

152. *A. E. Housman* EIGHT O'CLOCK (page 201)

The place of execution is probably the courtyard of the town jail. The clock is one of those that plays a four-note tune at a quarter past the hour, extends it to eight notes at the half hour and twelve at three-quarters past, and then plays a full complement of sixteen notes before beginning the bong, bong that announces the new hour. The young man, strapped and hooded, with a noose around his neck, sees nothing, but he hears the sixteen notes (the four "quarters") of the clock's tune "tossed" down upon the town, then the noises of the clock machinery as it tightens its springs (almost literally collecting its strength) before beginning the series of eight monotone strokes, at the first of which the trap will be sprung beneath him, and he will drop the distance (carefully calculated according to his weight) sufficient to break his neck.

The stanzaic form is iambic $a^3b^5a^5b^2$, with the a-rhymes all feminine, but with considerable metrical variation. The second line, for instance, with its initial trochee and its very lightly accented "on" in the third foot, brings together a number of unstressed or lightly stressed syllables that give it a speed consonant with the indifferent brightness of the tune played by the chimes. In contrast, the two internally punctuated spondees that begin line 3 and the internally punctuated first foot of line 5 followed by an initially stressed trochee, slow these two lines dramatically in consonance with the subjective experience of the protagonist. Of particular importance is the series of sharp *k*-sounds beginning in line 6: "*c*ounted . . . *c*ursed . . . lu*ck* . . . *c*lo*ck c*olle*c*ted . . . stru*ck*," and the heavy *str*-alliteration of "*str*apped" (5), "*str*ength" and "*str*uck" (8). The syntactical displacement of "its strength" from the expected position immediately following the verb places the alliterating monosyllables "strength" and "struck" together in the final line, where the final word "struck" culminates both the *str-* and *k-* series of repetitions. In addition, the heavy metrical regularity of this line, with its internal comma isolating the final verb, gives "struck" enormous force (the result of alliteration, consonance, rime, syntax, meter, and punctuation), thus putting a heavy emphasis on its double meaning. Not only does the clock mechanically strike the hour, but it (or perhaps the whole clock tower), personified as an executioner, brings down its axe with a powerful blow on the neck of the victim, striking out his life.

The use of "morning" and "nighing" as adjectives is unusual enough that one may detect a suggestion of *mourning* and *sighing* behind them.   LP

153. *James Joyce*   ALL DAY I HEAR (page 202)

The central purpose of the poem is the evocation of mood, the objectification of inner feeling. The mood is one of sadness or desolation, and the poet projects it through both imagery and sound.

He *hears* the noise of waters and the cry of the winds. The waters seem to be "making moan" in a "monotone"—a single sustained sound. He compares himself to the sea-bird which in memory, in imagination, or in fact he *sees* "going / Forth alone," and which he assumes is sad because it is alone (as he is). He envisions the winds as "grey," not a cheerful color. He *feels* the winds as well, and they are "cold."

The dominant musical device is the repetition of the long *o* sound, phonetically linked with melancholy or sorrow (page 190). The six short lines all end in rimes containing this vowel; the six long lines end alternately with the word "waters" (three times) and with rimes containing the long *o* (three times). The sound also occurs internally in "forth" and "cold." All of these *o*'s support the poem's one onomatopoetic word, "moan."

The speaker does not tell us the cause of his desolation, but the imagery, emphasizing loneness, monotone, and lack of warmth, strongly suggests that loneliness, isolation, separation from a loved one, may be the cause.

The meter is iambic, alternating tetrameter with dimeter lines.   LP

154. Emily Dickinson   I HEARD A FLY BUZZ WHEN I DIED (page 203)

Of the more than seventeen hundred poems in Dickinson's collected work, over five hundred are on the subject of death. Over and over she pictures or imagines what the experience of dying is like, and what, if anything, exists beyond it. Her solutions to these problems are as various as Donne's on sexual love. In this poem—one of her greatest—the poet projects her imagination into the future through a speaker who is recollecting the past—a technique she also uses in "Because I could not stop for death" (page 262).

The poem presents a death-bed scene—a conventional motif in nineteenth-century fiction when people had large families and died more often at home than in hospitals. In these scenes the protagonist is shown on her deathbed, surrounded by relatives, neighbors, and friends, who have gathered to give comfort, to hear any last words, and to say farewell.

Some readers will regard the appearance of the fly as the first event of the poem because it is mentioned first, but the poem does not follow a strictly chronological order. (The answer to question 1 is *b, d, a, c*.) In line 1 the speaker announces her subject and theme, providing the poem's "topic sentence," as it were. She then goes back and relates what led up to it. (It's as if one said, "I shared a sandwich with our president once. Here's how it happened" or "Here's how it was.") Use of the past perfect tense in line 5 indicates that earlier there had been weeping and lamentation, but now the mourners have ceased weeping and are restraining external display of feeling in preparation for witnessing the solemn moment of actual death. The "stillness" (both of sound and motion) in the room is not a mere *absence* of speech and movement; rather, the atmosphere seems charged, like that lull in a storm when the air takes on a greenish tint and the silence is electric. The first "heave of storm" had been the weeping and mourning of those gathered around the the death-bed; the second will presumably accompany or immediately follow "that last onset"—the moment of death itself. In stanza 3 the speaker is not "making out her will." The formal conveyance of her larger properties (land, house, bank deposits, investments) would have been made, in the presence of a lawyer, long before. In the poem she is disposing of smaller items ("keepsakes"), saying perhaps that she wants Cousin Lizzie to have her blue scarf, her daughter to have her favorite brooch, and her son to have the family Bible. The terms "willing" and "signing away" are metaphorical.

It is at this moment ("And *then* it was"), when everyone is silently awaiting the moment of death, that the fly makes its appearance. Whether it has just arrived or has been present all along but unnoticed is an unanswerable and unimportant question. What *is* important is that the fly now dominates the dying woman's awareness and does so till her actual death in the poem's final line.

What are we to make of this fly—and of the poem?

The poem is structured on an ironic contrast between expectation and fulfillment. The imagery and language of the second stanza ("last onset," "the king," "be witnessed") indicate a confident expectation among the onlookers, and undoubtedly in the dying woman also, that some solemn and awesome event is about to occur. (Notice how much more formal and solemn is the phrase "be witnessed" than "be seen.") The *king* will appear to carry off the soul of the dying woman. And who is "the king"? The king may well be Death itself, personified as a majestic figure. Perhaps more likely the king is God, or Christ, or the Angel of Death. But, for the speaker, all that appears is a small and rather nasty domestic insect—a bluebottle or blowfly—trying to make its escape through the windows but continually bumping up against the glass, which it cannot see. It interposes itself between the light from the windows and the speaker. And perhaps the light also represents some special enlightenment the speaker had expected but failed to receive at the moment of death.

Some students will interpret the windows in line 15 as the eyes of the dying woman, but this interpretation is too allegorical. The "room" is not allegorized, why should the windows be? The windows are literal windows, but as the speaker's vision blurs and dims, they become the last thing she can discern; and then they too go dark. It is her eyesight which fails, not the windows; but it fails in the sense that her literal eyes can no longer see the literal windows. In the final line, being dead, she can no longer see at all. She cannot see to see any illumination she might have hoped for from the windows, because of the interposition of the fly, or death.

At one level, the poem may be given a purely psychological interpretation about the experience of dying. One expects it to be a momentous and illuminating experience; but, the poem hypothesizes, death may turn out to be merely the diminution and final cessation of one's sensory and physical powers. Instead of illumination at the end, the dying person's consciousness in the final moments may be unable to focus on anything more significant than the sound and movement of a blowfly.

Most readers, however, will want to give the fly more than a purely literal significance, and, indeed, one can hardly avoid seeing the fly as a symbol of death, coming not in the majestic form of a king but in the trivial and even repulsive aspect of a fly. However, if we stop with the simple assertion that the fly is a symbol of death, we will lose much of the richness of the symbol. For its fuller meanings we must examine all the connotations of the "fly" in this context, expecially as they contrast with those of "king." For fuller discussion, see Clark Griffith, *The Long Shadow: Emily Dickinson's Tragic Poetry* (Princeton Univ. Press, 1964), pp. 134-37; Robert Weisbuch, *Emily Dickinson's Poetry* (Univ. of Chicago Press, 1975), pp. 99-102; and Charles B. Wheeler, *The Design of Poetry* (New York: W. W. Norton, 1966), pp. 188-92.

In addition to the symbolic richness in this poem, we need also to appreciate the marvelous vividness with which the poet brings to life the actual, literal fly, especially in line 13 (one of the most magical lines in English poetry).

The basic rime scheme is xaxa xbxb xcxc xdxd, but the rimes are perfect only in the final stanza. The one onomatopoetic word in the poem is "buzz" at the end of line 13. But notice how this buzz is brought into the poem and gradually intensified. In line 11, the final word *was*, though unrimed in its own stanza, and unrimed in the formal rime scheme, nevertheless rimes perfectly with *buzz* in the first line of the final stanza. In line 12 the word "interposed" continues the buzzing into the final stanza. In line 13 the vowel sound of *buzz* is preceded by the identical vowel sounds in "*u*ncertain" and "st*u*mbling," making three *u* sounds in close succession. Finally, the *b* sound in "buzz" is preceded in line 14 by the *b*'s in "*b*lue" and "stum*b*ling." Thus, *all* the sounds in "buzz"—its initial and final consonants and its medial vowel—are heard at least three times in lines 11-13. This outburst of onomatopoetic effect consummates the aural imagery promised in the opening line, "I *heard* a fly buzz when I died." But line 13 combines images of color, motion, and sound. Though the sound imagery is the most important, the poem concludes with a reference to the speaker's dimming eyesight, and we may infer that she *saw* a blur of the bluebottle's deep metallic blue as well as hearing its buzz. The images of motion between "blue" and "buzz" belong to both the visual and aural modes of sensing. The speaker hears and imperfectly sees the "uncertain" flight of the fly as it bumbles from one pane of glass to another, its buzzing now louder now softer. The meter of line 13, if the poem is scanned, is perfectly regular, but the two grammatical pauses help to give it an uncertain, irregular effect. Would it be too fanciful to say that the line itself stumbles over its three *b* sounds? LP

155. *William Carlos Williams* **THE DANCE** (page 203)

The repetition of the first line of the poem as its last line gives the poem a circularity of form, which is emphasized internally by the repetition of the word round" (2, 2, 5), "around" (3), and its rimes "impound" (6), "Grounds" (9), "sound" (10), plus the assonant "about" (8). The poem lacks end rime, but is rich in internal rime, exemplified in the above; in "prance as they dance" (11); and in such approximations as "squeal"-"tweedle"-"fiddles" (3-4), "tipping"-"thick"-"hips" (5-7), "bellies"-"balance" (7), "about"-"butts" (8-9), etc. The abundance of participial verb forms—"tipping," "kicking," "rolling," "swinging," "rollicking" —contributes also to the sense of vigorous motion. The triple meter gives this motion speed, but is subject to occasional jolting irregularities (as in 5, 6, 8) which remind us that these are thick-shanked, big-bellied, heavy-butted peasants dancing, not a graceful group of nymphs on Mount Olympus. The great majority of the lines are run-on (only the last ends with a full stop, and 1 and 6 with partial stops), thus giving the poem a sense of continuous motion, especially when the lines end with such traditionally unlikely words as "and," "the," and a hyphenated "thick-," where the reader is thrown forward into the next line without even a pause to observe the line-ending. This fact is further enhanced by the fact that all but three of the lines (5, 6, 11) have feminine endings, so that the meter as well as the grammatical incompleteness throws the reader forward. A highly unusual feature of this poem is that all but three ("around," "impound," and "about") of the words of more than one syllable (there are twenty-six of them) are accented on the first syllable; and this also contributes to the sense of continuous motion. The exceptions to the foregoing observations occur just frequently enough to keep the reader a bit off-balance, like the peasants themselves.

Three onomatopoetic words provide the music for all this motion—the "squeal," "blare," and "tweedle" of the bagpipes, bugle, and fiddles. LP

EXERCISE (page 204)

11. (a) (*The Princess,* V) The four short *a*'s in succession ("clanging," "anvil," "banged," "hammer") give the effect of repeated blows. "Clanging" and "banged" are onomatopoetic.
12. (b) ("Wreck of the Deutschland") "Soft sift" is softer and more nearly silent than "quiet sand."
13. (b) ("Boot and Saddle") The basic anapestic meter enhances the speed of the action. The first line, by its meter and punctuation, gives the effect of starting from a standstill and gradually picking up speed: BOOT, / SADdle, / to HORSE / and a-WAY! /
14. (a) ("Delores") The poet contrasts virtue and vice unconventionally. The alliteration of "virtue" and "vice" makes the contrast vivid. Each is described by a symbolic flower and an abstract noun. The flower and noun ("lilies and languors," "roses and raptures") are in each case joined and made parallel by being alliterated, two-syllabled, and trochaic.
15. (a) The soft *l*'s in "still" and "lulled" are more "sleepy" than the sharp sounds in "yet" and "conjured."

POEMS FOR FURTHER READING

Poem 257 from Part Two provides an additional illustration of topics presented in this chapter.

Chapter fourteen
Pattern

156. *e. e. cummings* **THE GREEDY THE PEOPLE** (page 207)

When read in the two ways suggested, cummings's poem reveals a multiplicity of patterns. First, a rime pattern (*abcbac*), repeated in each stanza, utilizing both approximate and perfect rimes. Second, a metrical pattern, built on an anapestic base (five lines of dimeter and one of monometer), in which the corresponding lines of each stanza match each other exactly. Third, a sound pattern which relates the two chief words of each first line by assonance ("greedy"-"people"), alliteration ("timid"-"tender"), or rime ("chary"-"wary"). Fourth, a syntactical pattern which matches the corresponding lines of the various stanzas, putting identical grammatical structures and parts of speech in corresponding places. (The second line of each stanza, for instance, is always a parenthesis in which the framework "as _____ as can _____" is filled in by words related in form but opposed in meaning.) Fifth, and most important, a structural pattern, in which the meaning of the first four lines of each stanza is countered by the meaning of the last two, and within which words of similar or related meaning and forms are balanced neatly against each other (such pairings as "sell" and "buy," "don't" and "do," "when" and "how" are obvious).

The cummings trademark comes out in this poem in his imaginative transformation of the parts of speech, particularly in the final word of the fourth line in each stanza, in which conjunctions ("because"), pronouns ("which"), verbs ("seem," "must"), and prepositions ("until") are made to serve as nouns. "Because" (4) for cummings represents the cold sterility of abstract reason as opposed to the warm life of instinct and emotion (Faith asks of materialism, "Why?"). "Which" (10) is a thing rather than a person ("Who"). "Seem" (16) indicates a mere illusion of existence as opposed to real existence ("be"). "Until" (22) represents an indefinite future as contrasted to the living present ("Now"). "Must" (28) represents the restrictive authority of artificial social conventions and rules as opposed to the permissiveness of nature ("May"). cummings concludes his poem with a triumphant pun, for "May" is not only the auxiliary verb of permission; it is that season of the year which stands for youth, for growth, for nature, and for life.

The two nouns in line 1 of each stanza represent undesirables in cummings's vocabulary ["people" (1) stands for *masses* rather than *individuals*; "tender" (25) is probably meant in the sense of *tender-minded* rather than *tender-hearted*]. Of the two variables in line 2 of each stanza, the first always represents something undesirable, the second something desirable ["you're" (14) is a plural as opposed to a singular "i'm"]. The activities depicted in lines 3–4 of each stanza are undesirable ["work" (27) represents materialistic drudgery as opposed to creative play; "pray" (27) is directed toward an authoritarian god (a "must") rather than toward a God of love].

In summary, the poem opposes states of unbeing and being. The first four lines of each stanza pass in review those people who feverishly pursue materialistic goals and whose lives are governed by greed, anxiety, prudence, convention, and conformity. In the last two lines of each stanza, the steeple bell, moon, stars, sun, and earth offer a laconic comment on the these people's foolishness.*

*This commentary is adapted from Laurence Perrine and James M. Reid, *100 American Poems of the Twentieth Century* (New York: Harcourt Brace Jovanovich, 1966), pp. 156-57.

157. *Anonymous* I SAT NEXT THE DUCHESS AT TEA (page 208)

The limerick's never averse
To expressing itself in a terse
   Economical style,
   And yet, all the while,
The limerick's *always* a verse. LP

158. *John Keats* ON FIRST LOOKING INTO CHAPMAN'S HOMER (page 209)

The octave is concerned with exploration, the sestet with the experience of discovery.

The octave is an extended metaphor in which travel is the figurative term for reading, and "the realms of gold" for literature. The "goodly states and kingdoms" are various kinds of literature, and the "western islands" are specifically poetry, the domain of Apollo, god of poetry and inventor of the lyre (from which the term "lyric" is derived). Though geography should not be pressed too hard, these islands are probably called "western" to associate them with the West Indies, where many of the early English and Spanish explorers sought for gold.

The sestet consists of two similes conveying the thrill of discovery. First, the speaker compares himself to an astronomer looking through his telescope when "a new planet swims into his ken." Anyone who has looked through a good astronomical telescope can testify to the "swimming" or quaking motion that an observed celestial body has as it enters the field of vision. The word "ken" is also beautifully effective here, for it not only means "range of vision" but is associated with knowing or knowledge; and the excitement here is generated by the astronomer's discovering a planet—a whole new world—previously unknown to man.

The second simile partly derives its force from the fact that the early explorers, seeking a shorter route to the East Indies and Cathay, at first thought they had found it and did not realize that what they had actually found was a new continent separated from their destination by another whole sea. Balboa's discovery of the Pacific thus came as a surprise and vastly expanded European ideas about the size of the earth. Keats captures the exact awe-struck moment when the explorer and his men first encounter this vast, shining, and unguessed-at new ocean while crossing the mountains of a land they did not know to be an isthmus.

One would prefer poets to be historically accurate, and it would be folly to pretend that nothing is lost when they are not. Yet Keats's subject is not history but human experience, and when one contemplates the consequences of substituting the three syllables of *bal-BO-a* for the three syllables of "STOUT COR-tez," one may even be glad for the blunder. (The name "Cortez" in Spanish is accented on the second syllable, but common British pronunciation reverses the accents.) The first loss is the adjective "stout" which, along with "eagle-eyed," gives strength and stature to the discoverer. The second loss is one of sound and rhythm which support this strength. "STOUT COR-tez" with its three *t*'s, sharp *k*-sound, and two stresses, gives the adventurer just that intrepid quality which is needed, while *bal-BO-a* softens its *b*'s with a liquid *l* and trails off into two vowel sounds suggestive more of grace than of strength. The heroic description of the discoverer matches the heroic verse and voice ("loud and bold") of Chapman's translation, which for Keats first captured the heroic qualities of Homer's epic narratives.

But if this poem were only about Keats's discovery of Chapman's translation, it would be of limited interest. What gives it enduring value is Keats's transformation of his discovery into a symbol for all discovery, his magnificent success in conveying the excitement that may attend any discovery, made by any of us, whether it be of universal or only personal significance. LP

159. *William Shakespeare* **THAT TIME OF YEAR** (Sonnet 73) (page 210)

In this sonnet an aging speaker, constantly aware of his approaching death, addresses a beloved person considerably younger than himself.

The structure of thought in the sonnet is perfectly matched to the formal divisions marked out by its rime scheme. In each of the three quatrains the speaker makes a metaphorical statement of his increasing age and nearness to death, and in the concluding couplet he makes a counterstatement of his beloved's increased love for him. This structure is formally expressed in the language of the poem. Its opening line contains the words "thou mayst in me behold"; the second and third quatrains each begin "In me thou see'st"; the concluding couplet, before making its counterstatement, summarizes what has preceded in its opening words "This thou perceivest."

In the opening quatrain the speaker compares himself to "that time of year" (late autumn or early winter) when "yellow leaves, or none, or few" hang upon the trees. In the second stanza he compares himself to the dusk of day, fading from sunset into night. In the third he compares himself to a sinking fire, whose glowing embers are about to be extinguished by the ashes of the fuel which once "nourished" it. Though the quatrains (each a sentence) make parallel statements, they are arranged in a climactic order and could not be rearranged without loss. First, they are concerned with diminishing periods of time (a year, a day, the length of time that a fire will burn), and thus they bring us metaphorically closer and closer to the thought of death (weeks, hours, minutes). In addition, the first quatrain emphasizes coldness ("bare" boughs "shake against the cold"); the second emphasizes darkness (twilight fading into "black night"); the third combines cold and dark in the image of the sinking fire which is losing both warmth and light. Finally, the first quatrain looks backward in time to what has been lost, the second forward to what will be lost, and the third combines references to past and future.

Each central metaphor is complicated by an additional metaphor or metaphors. In the first, the tree's leafless boughs are called "bare ruined choirs." A choir is that section of a church or chapel containing wooden choir stalls, and the sight of "bare ruined choirs" would have been familiar to every reader of Shakespeare's time because of the confiscation of Roman Catholic monastic properties throughout England by Henry VIII some half-century earlier and the subsequent spoliation of the monasteries by Reformation landowners. Through this association of thought the "sweet birds" become not only the songbirds which have migrated south for the winter, but the choir singers who once sang in the now-ruined monastery churches. The image of desolation is thus intensified. In the second quatrain, "black night," because of its association with sleep, is called "Death's second self"—a kind of twin or surrogate of Death "that seals up all in rest." In the third quatrain, the ashes of the fire become the deathbed on which the fire's personified youth is expiring, paradoxically "consumed" (in a third metaphor) by the food which once "nourished" it.

Against the three quatrains with their metaphorical statements of declining life and approaching death, the speaker opposes a concluding counterstatement concerning love. He throws human love, as it were, into the teeth of death. That the couplet is a counterstatement is metrically signaled by the inversion of stress in the opening foot . It begins, however, as a summarizing statement—"This thou perceivest"—where "This" refers for its antecedent to all of the images in the preceding quatrains (that is, to the grammatical objects of the verbs indicating seeing or beholding). The speaker then asserts his belief that the friend addressed throughout the sonnet loves the speaker all the more intensely because of the friend's realization that the speaker must soon die. The friend's increased love compensates for the speaker's impending death. Death's negative is countered by an affirmation of love.

Or so it would seem, on a first reading. On a second reading, we may be less sure of the strength of the affirmation. The speaker, we notice, is a person who needs to be loved. He does not conclude:

> This thou perceivest, which makes my love more strong,
> To love that well which I must leave ere long.

That is, he is not primarily concerned with giving love but with receiving it. We may then ask what evidence he has for his final assertion and perhaps question whether he is asserting a belief, expressing a hope, or making a plea. We may also begin to wonder whether he is actually as old as the metaphors in the quatrains suggest, or whether he does not mix considerable overstatement with these metaphors, perhaps as a play for the beloved's sympathy. The poem, seemingly simple on the surface, becomes increasingly complex and ambiguous as we delve into it. Some readers will read it for moral profundity; others will find it more notable for psychological profundity. [The questions raised here are more likely to rise in the mind of a reader who has read more of Shakespeare's sonnets than in that of a beginning student who reads the sonnet out of context. Such a student, however, may be asked to recall Sonnet 138—"When my love swears that she is made of truth" (page 35), where the speaker, surely not far past thirty, also refers to himself as "old" and quite clearly feels insecure in his relationship with a younger beloved.] LP

EXERCISE 2 (page 212)

We first notice that all four of these poems have 19 lines divided into five stanzas of three lines and a final stanza of four. We notice next that they employ only two rime-sounds, and deploy them in accordance to a fixed system. If we take "Do Not Go Gentle" (page 300) as the "purest" (using "purest" as a descriptive, not an evaluative, term) we see also that there is a pattern of refrain lines entwined with the riming pattern. We can express the pattern thus: $A^1bA^2abA^1abA^2abA^1abA^2abA^1A^2$. In brief, lines 1 and 3 of the first stanza become refrains which are used alternately to end stanzas 2, 3, and 4, and then together in the concluding quatrain, becoming the last two lines of the poem.

The other three poems take minor liberties with this traditional pattern. In "The Waking" (page 294) Roethke uses approximate rimes as well as perfect ones (*go, you, how*; and *fear, there*). He also varies the wording in the second refrain (but each contains the phrases "learn by going" and "to go").

In "One Art" (page 258) Bishop slightly varies her first refrain in the concluding quatrain, but the only remnant of the second refrain is the terminal word *disaster*. She also uses approximate rimes (*master, fluster, gesture*).

In "The Story We Know" (page 218) Collins has obviously sought for variety rather than uniformity in her refrain lines. No two are alike. Lines 1 and 12 contain the same words in the same order but with different punctuation and syntax. Her first refrain lines, however, all contain the words *way, begin,* and *Hello.* Her second refrain lines all contain the words *Good-bye* and *end,* and the phrase "story we know." LP

160. *By various hands* **A HANDFUL OF LIMERICKS** (page 212)

The limerick can be useful for giving students personal experience with versification. Give them a first line ("A freshman who snored in his sleep") or part of a first line ("There was a young man from _____") and offer a prize for the best completion, taking into consideration both successful handling of the form and cleverness of the punch line. (Be sure, if you give them the first line, to provide one with ample riming opportunities.) Note that, though the basic meter is anapestic, iambs may be freely substituted in the first foot (but only in the first foot) in any line. Rarely, if ever, are the first feet in a limerick all anapests; but often (as in "There was a young lady of Lynn") they are all iambs. LP

161. *Dylan Thomas* **POEM IN OCTOBER** (page 214)

In tone this poem is rhapsodic. It begins on a note of delight and anticipation, climbs steadily to joy, leaps into an exalted state of visionary experience and recollection, then lapses slightly back into joy and hope. There are contrasts of tone in the poem, but they are not sharp contrasts. The whole poem is pitched at a high level of exultation. This exultation comes from the poet's relationship with nature, not only its beauty, but a sacredness he senses in it, akin to what Wordsworth found in it a century and a half earlier.

The poet celebrates his birthday by rising early in the morning (he hears the morning beckon him to set forth) and walking beyond the gates of the town and up the mountain that lies behind it. He climbs so high that he gets above the weather. The month is October, and it had been raining in the town, but high on the mountainside the sun is "Summery," birds are singing, and he hears only "the rain wringing / wind blow cold" in the woods "faraway" under him. From this height the town church seems small as a snail with its "horns" (its two towers) rising through mist. Where he stands, however, "all the gardens / Of spring and summer" seem to be blooming, and it is a fit spot to "marvel" his birthday away—"but the weather turned around." We must be careful not to put too much emphasis on that "but" or to read the following clause literally. The weather does not turn from rainy to sunny or from fall to summery: these changes had already occurred as he climbed the mountainside. The weather metaphorically and psychologically turns "around" in that the poet's mind is carried in vision and in time away from the "blithe" summery scene presently before him where he could "marvel" his birthday away, back to his childhood days when he felt an even intenser and completer identification with the "wonder of summer." He remembers the forgotten mornings when "He walked with his mother / Through the parables / Of sun light / And the legends of the green chapels" (the woods), and "the mystery / Sang alive / Still in the water and singing-birds." In the final stanza the first three lines are a recapitulation of lines 38-40, not a new turning; nevertheless, this final stanza brings him slowly back to the reality of the present with its full recognition that the "true / Joy" of his visionary experience had been that of a "long dead child," that it is now his "thirtieth / Year to heaven" (a recapitulation of the opening line), and that the town below him is wearing its autumn foliage. The poem ends with the poet's prayer that on his next birthday he may still be capable of such visionary experience.

Though less explicitly philosophical, "Poem in October" in several ways resembles Wordsworth's "Tintern Abbey." The adult poet is a lover of nature, responsive to its beauty, and a believer that it somehow embraces the divine (as shown by Thomas's use throughout the poem of "sacramental imagery" and language: "thirtieth year to heaven," "heron / Priested shore," "water praying," "the blue altered sky"—with its concealed pun, "parables / Of sun light," "legends of the green chapels," "mystery"). Yet the poet regrets the loss of the even intenser involvement with nature that he enjoyed as a child when he felt the divinity of nature (his "true / Joy") less consciously in the intellect but more fully through his whole being.

A minor difficulty in this poem is caused by Thomas's omission of the hyphen from such compound adjectives as *mussel-pooled, heron-priested, net-webbed, rain-wringing, lark-full,* and *blue-altered.* The involved syntax of the first stanza has also caused difficulty. Its skeleton is "It was my thirtieth year to heaven [that] woke to my hearing the morning beckon myself to set foot in the town and set forth." Thomas has omitted the relative pronoun between lines 1 and 2. "Woke" is an intransitive verb modified by the prepositional phrase beginning with "to"; the object of the preposition is the long gerund phrase "my hearing the water beckon . . . etc." The object of the gerund is an infinitive phrase with "the morning" as its subject and "[to] beckon" as its verb. For fuller discussion, see *The Explicator,* 27 (Feb. 1969), item 43. LP

162. *Matsuo Bashō / Moritake* TWO JAPANESE HAIKU (page 216)

Just as the limerick is a useful form for giving students experience with versification, the haiku is a useful form for initiating them into original *poetic* composition (experiential rather than merely clever). The brevity of the form forces them to practice verbal economy; its nature, by delivering them from the hampering notion that meter and rime are essential to poetry, frees them to concentrate on other dimensions—particularly imagery. The essence of haiku poetry is that it suggests rather than states. It strives to give the reader some unique perception of nature, or some immediate insight into the nature of things, without intervention of the abstracting intellect. It accomplishes this, most frequently, either by presenting a single sharply observed image, or by juxtaposing two images which parallel or contrast with each other in significant and suggestive ways. So essential to the form is brevity that many writers of haiku in English have abandoned the traditional 5-7-5 syllabic pattern and written poems even briefer. The haiku composition assignment may therefore be made in various ways. If you wish to give your students the discipline of working within a prescribed form, insist on their adherence to the 5-7-5 pattern. If you wish to free them from all constraints of form, ask for a poem of not more than three lines. If you want to stress chiefly verbal economy, let them write a poem of any number or arrangement of lines but containing no more than seventeen syllables. The important stipulation should be that the poem purvey its perception through imagery rather than through abstract statement. LP

163. *William Shakespeare* From ***ROMEO AND JULIET*** (page 216)

Since *Romeo and Juliet*, except for a few brief prose passages, is written throughout in iambic pentameter, and since much of it also rimes, the lines riming sometimes alternately and sometimes in pairs, it is not surprising that 14 lines, from a total of almost 3,000 should fall into the rime pattern of an English sonnet. That this excerpt does so from design, rather than from coincidence, can, however, be definitively demonstrated.

1. The passage has four kinds of unity: grammatical, situational, metaphorical, and tonal. First, the passage begins at the beginning of a sentence and ends at the end of a sentence. It is grammatically self-contained. Second, the passage covers a self-contained episode or situation: it begins with the first words of Romeo and Juliet and ends with their first kiss. Third, the passage is unified by a single extended metaphor, one in which a pilgrim, or palmer, is worshiping at the shrine of a saint. Fourth, the religious nature of this metaphor—employing words like *profane, holy, shrine, sin, pilgrims, devotion, saints, palmers, prayer,* and *faith*—combines with the delicious punning wit of the dialogue to give the passage unity of tone: a tone of earnest delicacy and delightfully charming gravity which forces us to take seriously an episode we might otherwise take cynically. Romeo, we feel, is not simply a fresh young man on the make and Juliet an easy mark: this is genuine love at first sight. "Dear saint, let lips do what hands do" is tonally a great deal different from "Gimme a little kiss, honey, won'cha?"

2. In structure as in form, the excerpt is organized into three quatrains and a final couplet. In the first quatrain Romeo, initiating the basic metaphor, apologizes for taking Juliet's "holy" hand in his unworthy one, but humbly offers to make up for the offense by giving the hand a gentle kiss. In the second quatrain Juliet reassures Romeo, telling him that he has done no wrong but shows mannerly devotion in taking her hand, for pilgrims quite properly touch saints' hands, and pilgrims "kiss" by clasping hands. She thus simultaneously encourages Romeo to hold her hand but with maidenly delicacy indicates that there is no need for him to kiss it. In the third quatrain, however, emboldened by this reassurance, Romeo decides to play the long shot and ask for a kiss on the lips. But he puts the request delicately and charmingly. Do not pilgrims and saints have lips as well as hands? he asks. Translated, this means, why should we not kiss with our lips instead of merely with

our hands? Juliet, still modest, yet keeping to the metaphor, replies that pilgrims' lips are for praying with. Then Romeo brilliantly seizes his opening: "Let lips do what hands do." The line has two meanings. Hands not only kiss, they also pray. Lips not only pray, they also kiss. So Romeo, shaping his hands into the attitude of prayer, prays also with his lips; but what he prays for is a kiss. In the final couplet Juliet, not unwillingly defeated in this contest of wit (for what can a saint do when a faithful pilgrim prays to her?) gracefully surrenders: she grants the kiss, thus answering Romeo's prayer. The first quatrain is Romeo's apology; the second is Juliet's reassurance; the third is the plea; and the couplet is the plea granted. Structure follows form.

3. In Shakespeare's time the sonnet form was used primarily for the treatment of love. His play concerns a pair of "star-crossed lovers." The episode in the excerpt concerns their first meeting and their first kiss. What more appropriate than that Shakespeare should deliberately cast the episode into the form of an English sonnet?* LP

*This discussion is abridged from the essay "When Form and Content Kiss, / Intention Made the Bliss," in Laurence Perrine, *The Art of Total Relevance: Papers on Poetry* (Rowley, Mass.: Newbury House, 1976), pp. 75-77.

164. *John Donne* DEATH, BE NOT PROUD (page 217)

This tightly constructed sonnet matches structure to form while producing some surprises for those acquainted with both the English and Italian sonnet forms. There are three quatrains and a couplet (as in the English sonnet), but the riming pattern is not *abab cdcd* etc., but *abba abba cddc aa*: the Italian quatrain is used in the English rhetorical structure, and the English closing couplet returns to the *a*-rime, thus implying circularity.

These formal elements are in harmony with the structure of thought. The sonnet, an extended apostrophe, consists of these rhetorical units: an opening quatrain which makes an assertion (based on faith) denying that death is either mighty or dreadful; a second quatrain offering "proof" that death is not dreadful; a third offering "proof" that it is not mighty; and a couplet which returns to faith and faith alone as a support, and to the riming sound of the opening line. While the speaker attempts to use reason and logical proof to shore up his opening remark, he unwittingly reveals the weakness of his reasoning, the falseness of his premise, and the desperation that would lead a man to such an undertaking: he reveals a man stating a deep wish as if it were easily demonstrable truth.

The opening quatrain, in a tone of forced bravado, uses only two techniques of argument, neither logically admissible: the simple insistence that what "some" have said is not true, and the condescending tone of "poor death." If it is a *fact* that people overthrown by death "die not," then the final phrase of the quatrain is valid, for the syllogism is clear: death cannot kill men; I am a man; therefore, death cannot kill me. What is not established here, of course, is the universality of immortality, so the syllogism though valid has been based on an unproved major premise.

It is important to bring formal logic into the discussion of this poem, for the patent illogicality of the speaker is what makes the poem so moving. In his desperate need to reassure himself, the speaker is nevertheless the butt of dramatic irony, an example of the futility of attempting to prove an article of faith by means of reason—and so intensely in need of such proof that he argues fraudulently.

The second quatrain attempts to prove that death is not to be feared. But the two "proofs" are fallacious: lines 5-6 argue by analogy (death is like sleep; sleep gives pleasure; therefore death gives pleasure), while line 7 employs the favorite device of advertisers, the "endorsement" of "our best men." The third quatrain, intended to prove that death is not powerful, opens with two illogical devices: name-calling ("slave," because death is caused by other agents) and the aspersion of dwelling with evil neighbors. It returns to argument by analogy, insisting that drugs or spells induce a better sleep than death does, and then closes with another belittling condescension.

The concluding couplet, in a tone of triumph, asserts that the case has been proved and that eternal life is our universal destiny. It does so in paradox, the death of death, which requires the only possible resolution, the faith of a believer in Christian salvation.

The key to further meaning in the poem may be found in the speaker's apparent unawareness of what he is additionally revealing about himself and his feelings about death. When in the second quatrain he attempts to disprove death's dreadfulness, he inadvertently uses death's might as his evidence: death is *more* powerful than "rest and sleep," and it has the power to deliver the soul from the captivity of the body. When in the third he attempts to disprove death's power, he calls to witness its dreadfulness: in line 9, the frailty of human life makes us subject to a frightening array of powerful killers, and in line 10 the neighbors of death are a catalogue of dread. Perhaps even more telling is the speaker's ambiguity about "sleep," death's analogue. In the second quatrain, rest and sleep are the sources of "much pleasure," though not so much as death can give. Yet in the third, the sleep induced by drugs or charms is "better" than the sleep of death—and in the couplet, what is most desired is eternal wakefulness, not rest or sleep. The great victory is that both sleep and death "shall be no more."

The speaker knows what he wants—the eternal bliss of salvation—but he is vainly trying to prove through logical argument that he can receive it. That attempt is doomed, as theologians and philosophers have long demonstrated, and the speaker's own desperation is vividly shown by his failure. Finally, he rests where he began— and where according to the scriptures he can find his much-desired certitude. He accepts and triumphs in the paradoxes of his faith, which defy logical or rational analysis, but which assure him that "the last enemy that shall be destroyed is death"

(1 Cor. 15:26), that "death is swallowed up in victory" (1 Cor. 15:54), and that "death and hell [will be] cast into the lake of fire" (Rev. 20:14). TRA

165. *Martha Collins* THE STORY WE KNOW (page 218)

The poem departs from the strictness of its chosen form by varying the two refrain lines, which should be identical in language (if not in syntactical function or meaning). Its maintenance of the proper rime scheme for a villanelle is emphasized by the high incidence of monosyllables as rime words, seeming to insist that we notice the perfect riming. That kind of self-consciousness about form and its fitness to subject (which is often the tone adopted in lighter verse) is parodied in line 2, which presents a bouncing iambic regularity in the monosyllables of an empty social encounter, mimicking the shallowness of the occasion in the monotony of rhythm. Line 2 is also one of only three perfectly iambic pentameter lines, and is the only one of them to punctuate pauses precisely between all of its feet, to reinforce its sense of empty repetition (the other two, lines 4 and 16, vary the rhythm to avoid such regularity).

The metrical norm in the poem, however, is anapestic pentameter, as determined by the relative frequency of the triple foot, and particularly by the meter of the two refrain lines:

the WAY / to be- GIN / is AL- / ways the SAME. / hel- LO, /

and good- BYE / at the END. / that's EV- / er-y STO- / ry we KNOW. /

This meter is well suited to such society verse as the villanelle, and Collins plays ironically with the expectations aroused by this traditionally light, polite form. In fact, part of the poem's force comes from setting up a shallow, blasé expectation in both reader and speaker, for if we are conditioned to the superficial pleasantries of social verse, so the speaker in her ennui seems to have conditioned herself to expect only superficiality in her relations with other people. She "knows" how all relations begin and end: a social "hello," "and Good-bye at the end," a pattern of uninvolved pairing with all the expected accoutrements of love affairs without love— external things that take the place of feelings. It is, as she says, a boring sequence, "a story we know so well / we don't turn the page." But on this occasion, something more meaningful takes place, not only a mutual dependency but a shared fear of death. The social routine of hello/goodbye comes to symbolize the physical reality of mortal life, "the way we all begin and end" signalled to the speaker by the "cold white sign" of snow obliterating both the air and the pine.

Blasé sophistication, so aptly captured in the form of light verse, turns out to have a darker implication, as the speaker learns that the pattern of her personal, social life, full of empty beginnings and endings, is also the pattern of mortal existtence. TRA

166. *Randolph Stow* **AS HE LAY DYING** (page 219)

As with "the greedy the people" (page 207), students might be asked to diagram the constants in this poem. The result would look something like this:

```
As he lay dying, two . . .
        . . . . . . . . . . . . . . . . . . . . . . [rime]
     And one . . . . . . . . . to the other:
        "Brother,
        . . . . . . . . . . . . . . . . . . . . [rime].
```

Each stanza has five lines, with exact refrains occupying the first half of the first line, the beginning and end of the third line, and all of the fourth line. The refrains in lines 3 and 4 rime with each other, and lines 2 and 5 have end rime. In addition, each first line introduces a bird of prey, and each of the fifth lines deals with a division of the prey. So the corresponding lines in each stanza are parallel in structure as well as in form. Finally, the initial refrain of the three stanzas is repeated at the end of the last stanza and is also used as the title (a true title, used by the author, not just the first line used by the editor in lieu of a title). This gives the phrase "As he lay dying" tremendous importance.

The theme of the poem? Perhaps that all life forms feed on other life forms? The crows will feed on the flesh of the man, the hawks will feed on the crows, and the eagles will feed on the hawks. And the man—there is something mysterious here, for we are not told who *he* is or *why* he is dying. Perhaps we should leave the mystery untouched; but, in absence of contrary evidence, we tend to identify him with the parallel creatures in the poem. He too is part of the food chain. Perhaps he was hurt in a hunting accident, or perhaps he overstuffed himself eating Thanksgiving turkey. This is facetious speculation, of course, but the poem does not suggest that he is different from other creatures. All life sustains itself by destroying other life. This is the cruel fact that even man cannot escape from.

The poem both in form and content has the flavor of the medieval folk ballads, especially "Edward" (page 219) and the "The Twa Corbies" (not in this edition). LP

167. *Anonymous* **EDWARD** (page 219)

The story told in "Edward"—a dark domestic tragedy of greed, guile, murder, and remorse—is unfolded gradually through dialogue, question, and answer. Not until the third stanza do we learn what Edward has done. Not until the last do we learn why he has done it. The tension of the poem mounts steadily through the first climax to the last.

A man of noble birth and heir to his father's estate, Edward has killed his father because of the "counsels" of his mother, who had hoped to get control of these properties into her own hands. To accomplish this end, she has been willing to subvert her own son. Crafty, manipulative, greedy, and entirely lacking in natural affections, she has somehow worked on her son's feelings through hint, suggestion, and insinuation, until he has felt it his duty or his interest to kill his father. But the psychological dimensions of the story exist largely between the lines.

Why does the mother, if she put him up to it, have to ask why Edward's sword drips with blood? She is perhaps surprised to see Edward "sad" rather than rejoicing, and needs to confirm her hopes. Why does Edward lie about what he has done? Since doing the deed, he has undergone a revulsion of horror and remorse, and is lying more to himself than to his mother. He cannot admit to himself what he has done. The mother calls his bluff, presses her question; Edward lies again, and is again detected; but the mother reveals something about herself. One steed is the same as another to her, and she does not understand that a man might have a peculiar affection for a particular steed, especially an old one (like his father). When Edward finally admits the truth, the mother shows no emotion; it is what she had secretly known and hoped for. In her question about what penance Edward will do for his deed, she cunningly washes her hands of any share in the guilt. Edward, overcome with guilt, sees exile from home and family and all he has loved as the only possible penance. The next question—what will Edward do with his towers and hall?—brings us to the center of the mother's interests. But Edward cares not a whit for the towers and hall: they are the witnesses of his dreadful crime. Failing of the answer she wanted, the mother shrewdly digresses in her next question, disguising her main concern. Edward's reply to what he will leave his wife and children does not indicate that he is uncaring, but only that he is so emotionally overwrought that he feels any provision made for them can only contaminate them with his own guilt. In her final question the mother returns to her main concern: "And what wul ye leive to your ain mither deir?" In that final phrase we glimpse the mother's manipulative method. Twice in the poem she has addressed Edward as her dear son (12, 28); now she reminds him that she is his own dear mother. But she is totally unprepared for the switch in parental allegiance that Edward has undergone since the killing. Edward uses the word "dear" in the poem only in speaking of his dead father (21, 23).

Edward's final outburst comes with a shock to the reader as to the mother. For the reader it is a double shock—that of hearing a son deliver the curse of hell on his mother and of learning that he killed his father at his mother's suggestion. Yet the reader is left, most likely, with a feeling of pity for Edward and of horror for the mother. The emotional Edward suffers torments of horror, guilt, and remorse for what he has done; the crafty and unnatural mother feels nothing but greed.

The narrative kernel of each stanza (lines 1, 4, 5, 8) is in ballad stanza. The two refrains ("Edward, Edward" and "Mither, mither") keep the crucial family relationship constantly before us. The repeated lines prolong the suspense and add immensely to the emotional power.   LP

168. *Maxine Kumin* 400-METER FREESTYLE (page 221)

Although the poem pays tribute to stamina and "heart," it primarily celebrates a mastery of form achieved by discipline and hard training: "Thrift is his wonderful secret; he has schooled out all extravagance." The economy of motion that eliminates any wasted movement is "schooled." The swimmer's feet "know the lesson" of steady cadence, and the lungs "know" not to list for air.

Thrift is the poet's virtue too, and this poem drives steadily forward from "The Gun" which starts the race to the announcement of the winner's "TIME: 4:25.9." There is minimal punctuation, and there are no wasted words.

The sixteen horizontal lines of the poem match the sixteen lengths of a Junior Olympic-size (25-meter) pool that have to be swum in a 400-meter race. The three-letter vertical arcs connecting the lines imitate the flip-turn used in modern competitive swimming. As the swimmer approaches the end of the pool, he ducks his head under, and in one continuous movement he brings his legs out of the water, knees bent, slaps the soles of his feet against the end of the pool while executing a half twist, pushes off hard, and glides underwater (as the spectators watch "for signs") before resurfacing and resuming his stroke.

For about one month in 1958, 4 min. 25.9 seconds was the world's record (men's) for this event. The poem was published in 1961. Maxine Kumin has herself been a competitive swimmer. LP

169. *William Burford* A CHRISTMAS TREE (page 223)

The pattern of this poem is metrical as well as typographical. The lines have respectively one, two, three, four, five, one, and two feet. The poem's meaning is reinforced visually not only in the Christmas-tree shape but also in the word "huddld," where the omission of the letter *e* huddles four tall-stemmed letters together. The rime scheme is *aabcxb*, the *b* rimes being approximate. LP

EXERCISE (page 223)

1. The Mill (Robinson, page 30)   rime
2. To a Waterfowl (page 133)   meter
3. With rue my heart is laden (page 161)   rime & meter
4. To His Coy Mistress (page 74)   structure
5. Poem in October (page 214)   syllable count

POEMS FOR FURTHER READING

Poems 194, 207, 226, 234, 237, 239, 240, 246, 258, and 261 from Part Two provide additional illustrations of topics presented in this chapter.

Chapter fifteen
Bad Poetry and Good

170. *Anonymous* GOD'S WILL FOR YOU AND ME (page 229)

171. *Gerard Manley Hopkins* PIED BEAUTY (page 230)

The poetic deficiencies of "God's Will for You and Me" are not far to seek. Its literal language is trite ("when things go wrong," "God knows best"). Its figurative language is trite ("willing feet," "our daily key"). Its remaining imagery is feeble ("song," "dark or bright," "child"). Fourteen of the poem's sixteen lines repeat the phrase "Just to," ten times followed by "be." These three words constitute almost 40 percent of the poem. The rest is mostly a string of abstract adjectives—"tender," "true," "glad," "merciful," "mild," "trustful," "gentle," "kind," "sweet," "helpful," "cheery," "loyal"—strung togehter in no particular order, and often duplicative or overlapping in meaning (*kind-helpful, glad-cheery, gentle-tender-mild*). Worst of all, the poem's tripping triple meter and childish repetition of "Just to be" make God's will for you and me seem simple, undemanding, and easy to carry out. In truth, no man could do it successfully for one whole day. The poem not only fails to create experience; it falsifies it.

Though both poems concern God, their themes are quite different. "God's Will" is didactic verse instructing us how God wishes us to live our lives; "Pied Beauty" is, first, a hymn of praise to God for the variegated, changing beauty of the natural and human worlds, and, second, a contrast between this variegated, changing beauty of the created world and the uniform, unchanging beauty of the Creator. (The theme has its Biblical base in James 1: 17: "Every good gift and every perfect gift is from above, and cometh down from the Father of lights, with whom is no variableness, neither shadow of turning.")

The first theme is stated in the title and first line of the poem and is developed and exemplified in the next eight. "Glory be to God," the poet exclaims, for the beauty of things that are pied, dappled, couple-colored, brinded, stippled, plotted and pieced, fickle, or freckled. With one exception these terms all apply to things that are of more than one color. The exception, "fickle," referring to variation in time rather than space, ties in with "swift, slow" and reminds us that this various beauty is in constant motion and is constantly changing. The white clouds move and change in shape across a brightening or darkening blue sky; the decoratively rose-mole-stippled trout swim in a changing current. In line 5, which introduces human activities into the poem, farmers alter the landscape by laying it out in plots of grazing, fallow, and plowed land.

The concluding two lines of the poem summarize the first theme and introduce the second. The praise for this diverse, changing beauty is due to a Creator whose beauty is "past [beyond] change." The poem thus brings into contrast multiplicity and unity, constant change and changelessness, plenitude and amplitude, with the implication that the latter are greater. If the wonders of the created world (which varies "who knows how?") pass understanding, how much more so must the beauty of their Creator!

The achievement of the poem lies, first, in its packed, vivid imagery. Line 4, for instance, in six words introduces three separate vivid images (two literal, one figurative). There are "finches' wings" (black and gold) and "chestnut falls" (fallen chestnuts beneath a tree, glowing in mahogany browns), these latter compared by a compound adjective to fresh firecoals glowing golden and umber in a grate. Though the imagery of the poem is chiefly visual, the opposition of "sweet, sour" reminds us that the world is variegated in its appeal to the other senses as well. Second, the poem is remarkable for its rich use of sound: patterned end-rime; paired alliterations linking words parallel or opposed in meaning ("swift, slow"; "sweet, sour"; "adazzle, dim"), or simply the complex orchestration of such a line as 4 (with the alliteration of *Fresh-fire-falls-finches*; the assonance of *fresh-chestnut* and *finches' wings*; the *l*-consonance of *coal-falls*). Third, the poem is remarkable for its concentration. In line 4 every word is image-bearing; in line 9 all words but the initial "With" carry a full freight of meaning (contrast such lines with the slackness of "Just to be tender, just to be true"). Finally, "Pied Beauty" is notable for its freshness of diction. The four adjectives in line 7 are all apposite yet unexpected; the adjectives in "God's Will for You and Me" are as predictable as those in the Boy Scout oath. LP

172. *Robert Francis* **PITCHER** (page 229)

173. *George E. Phair* **THE OLD-FASHIONED PITCHER** (page 230)

The first poem celebrates pitching as an art, the second as a feat of endurance. This is their difference of intention at the literal level, but the second poem has only a literal level.

"The Old-Fashioned Pitcher" is a familiar exercise in sentimental nostalgia for "the good old days." Its one cleverness lies in its imitation of a more famous poem of the same sort, "The Bucket" by Samuel Woodworth (1785-1842). Woodworth's first stanza begins "How dear to my heart are the scenes of my childhood" and ends by referring to "The old oaken bucket, the iron-bound bucket, / The moss-covered bucket which hung in the well." Comparison of their stanzaic pattern, and of their opening and concluding lines, shows that Phair's poem is a conscious allusion to Woodworth's. Aside from this element of parody, "The Old-Fashioned Pitcher" has little to recommend it. The adjective "old" before "village green" (2) is an obvious sentimentalism designed to elicit a stock response of warm affection for former times. The phrase "ducks from the scene" (4) is trite and slangy. Line 7 is a blatant example of "padding" (the use of unnecessary words to fill out the metrical requirements of the line): "That is the reason" could be reduced to "that's why" or therefore"; "hanker and long for" uses two verbs where one would suffice. The nouns "hurler" and "twirler" are used so often in sports pages simply as variations for "pitcher" that it is difficult to know whether the poet here intended to differentiate them. They can be differentiated, of course. A "hurler" relies upon strength and speed simply to "fire" the ball past the batter. A "twirler" puts a spin or twist on the ball, causing it to curve or break in a manner deceptive to the batter. The former relies upon strength, the latter on skill. Since throwing curve balls puts a greater strain on the muscles than throwing fast balls, the "twirler" suffers more often from a sore arm than the "hurler." Does the poet recognize this distinction? Does he mean to confess "I prefer strength to skill—Goliath to David"? Or is he not rather saying simply that "men aren't what they used to be"? Evidence favors the latter surmise. If the old-fashioned pitcher was "iron-armed," what need had he to be "stout-hearted"? It seems unlikely that this poet was thinking about such distinctions. Sentimental gush and critical thought are seldom bedfellows.

"Pitcher" celebrates the skill and subtlety of the good pitcher. His "art" is to be off-center. His "aim is how not to hit the mark he seems to aim at"—the batter's bat, or the dead center of the strike zone (directly over the center of the plate and halfway between the batter's knees and shoulders). (Notice how the two "aim's" vary slightly in meaning.) He must "avoid the obvious"—the pitch that goes exactly where it seems to be going—but he must "vary the avoidance" lest the batter learn what to expect. The other players on the team—infielders and outfielders—throw to be understood (the shortstop throwing to first base does not want to fool the first baseman); but the pitcher throws "to be a moment misunderstood" by the batter (so that the batter will swing too low or too high, or too soon or too late, hitting an easy pop-fly or an easy grounder or missing the ball altogether). Yet "not too much. Not errant, arrant, wild"—the three adjectives are not redundant (like "hanker and long for") but are skillful variations of meaning; no good pitch is "errant" (wandering or deviating from his intention), "arrant" (flagrantly and shamelessly wide of the mark), or "wild" (out of control). The pitcher does not want to walk the batter, cause his catcher to drop his pitch, or throw so wide of the plate that the catcher can't reach it (allowing baserunners, if any, to advance). Rather "every seeming aberration" is "willed" (intended, under perfect control). He wants "Not to ... communicate" (not to hit the batter's bat squarely) yet (here is the paradox) he *wants* "to communicate": he wishes the batter to understand his intention but "too late" to make a base hit.

The poet exemplifies in his own verse the subtle skill he celebrates. He "varies the avoidance" of the obvious, not only in his choice of words ("errant, arrant, wild") but in the very form of his poem. It consists of five pentameter couplets, each different in its "riming." The first pairs "aim" with "aim at." The second couples two three-syllable words with only the hissing of a final sibilant to connect them in sound. The third pairs two four-syllable participles ending in -*d*, but throws things off a bit by shoving the subject of the second of the two parallel sentences up to the end of the first line. The fourth pairs "willed" and "wild" (alliteration and consonance). The fifth has perfect rime.

So—at the literal level alone—the first poem is clearly superior. But obviously (however, in this context, it won't be obvious at all to many students) the first poem is symbolical. The poet is speaking not only about pitcher and batter but about poet and reader. (The clues are words like "art," "passion," "technique," "comprehended," "communicate," and "understand"—words more often found in discussions of poetry than of baseball.) The poet wants to be understood by his reader—but not too easily. If he is too obvious (literal, or trite), the reader will find his work dull and uninteresting; if he is not, sometimes, "a moment misunderstood," the reader will not return for a second reading. The poet, after all, is not writing directions for how to assemble a piece of furniture. He wants to communicate with the whole reader. To do this he must throw a few slides and curve balls—must use figurative language (like paradox and symbol) and other devices of indirection. As Emerson says of the poet, he "must mount to paradise / By the stairway of surprise." LP

174. *Walt Whitman* **COME UP FROM THE FIELDS FATHER** (page 230)

175. *J. H. McNaughton* **THE FADED COAT OF BLUE** (page 231)

"Come Up from the Fields Father" and "The Faded Coat of Blue" both concern the bereavement of a family by a soldier-son who has met death on a Civil War battlefield. The first poem treats this subject honestly and with insight, bringing out its inherent pathos and communicating genuine emotion. The second poem, attempting to wring every possible drop of emotion out of the situation, sacrifices truth to sentimentality.

Before endeavoring to justify this judgment, however, let us note a technical difference between the two poems which, though not an evaluative difference in itself, will be necessary to the discussion of evaluative features. This has to do with point of view, or how the story gets told. "The Faded Coat of Blue" uses the first person viewpoint in which the speaker is the dead soldier's mother. *Where* she is is not made clear,* but *who* she is is established. "Come Up from the Fields Father" uses an omniscient narrator who may be identified with the poet himself. This narrator enters at will the mind of any character, and can tell us what none of the characters themselves yet know: that the son is already dead.

---

*If she is wandering over the battlefield trying to find her son's unmarked grave (as is faintly suggested in lines 17-18), she is bound on a futile mission, for she could not find it without digging up each unmarked grave until she found her son's corpse.

The use of the mother as first-person narrator in "The Faded Coat of Blue" causes considerable confusion. The narrator says plainly (line 25) that no one was near her son when he died, especially no "gentle one" like herself or his sister. Yet in stanzas 2 and 4 she pictures his death in detail, even quoting the exact words he is supposed to have said on the occasion. She quotes him, moreover, as speaking to his "dear comrades," requesting that they mark his grave for his mother. But, in the first stanza, we are told that he is buried "sad and lonely" in "a lonely grave unknown." In the face of these contradictions we might be led to ask whether this poem is not a study of a psychopathic woman demented by grief. But the tone of the poem nowhere suggests the presence of dramatic irony. Rather it suggests a sentimental poet trying to overwhelm us with grief.

"The Faded Coat of Blue" heightens every color, exaggerates every sentiment, and spares no detail in the attempt to make its protagonist pathetic. The soldier dies "faint and hungry" and "weary" and also "sad and lonely." His uniform is "faded." No "gentle one" was near him "to close his sweet eyes." "No stone marks the sod" over his grave, which is "lonely" and "unknown." The soldier himself is a compendium of all the virtues. He is "brave," "sweet," "noble," "good," and "true," and he dies with his mother's name on his lips—and his sister's too. His destination is heaven, as he himself (or his mother) tells us. Where else could one so sweet and noble possibly go? There he will rejoin his mother and sister, for they too are sweet, gentle, good, and true. Life, in this family was apparently a perpetual love bath. But is this sweet soldier lad a counterpart of a later war's G.I. Joe—or is he only Little Boy Blue grown up? Hark to his final words:

". . . you'll mark my grave for mother, she'll find it when she comes;
I fear she'll not know me among the good and true,
When I meet her up in Heaven in my faded coat of blue."

Can we believe that these words were spoken by a man who had begun to shave? That he died on the battlefield referring to his poor little "faded coat of blue" and his future "robe of white"? And are there pancakes beneath all this syrup?

No—the author has poured the syrup on so thick that he has hid from himself the fact that his poem is an uncooked batter of trite phrases ("heart that beat so true," "sad and lonely," "nameless grave," "the good and true," "no stone marks the sod"). Moreover, the poet gives no evidence to substantiate the virtues ascribed to the characters; he merely asserts them, repeating the same adjectives over and over. The amount of repetition in the poem is astounding. There is not only a four-line refrain stanza after each four-line narrative stanza, but the words used in the refrain stanzas largely repeat words in the narrative stanzas. The phrase "faded coat of blue" is used as a refrain both in the narrative stanzas and in the refrain stanzas, and thus is used eight times in the poem (not counting the title). Well over half of the poem, therefore, consists of repetition. In addition, the phrase "good and true" occurs seven times, not counting one "brave and true" or two solo appearances of "brave" and one solo appearance of "good," making a grand total of eight times for "true" and seven times for "good." In addition the adjectives "brave," "sweet," and "lonely" each occur three times. The noun "grave" appears eight times.

To turn from "The Faded Coat of Blue" to "Come Up from the Fields Father" is to take a refreshing drink of pure spring water after a surfeit of syrup. This poet, by treating his subject honestly, gives the natural emotion in it a chance to come out; he does not have to use artificial sweetening. To begin with, he has based his poem on an authentic insight: that the real tragedies of war are often to be found back home rather than up at the front; death may be hardest for those left behind. The poem begins with the arrival of the letter which is to be its focus. During wartime, a letter from the soldier-son is the big event in the day for any family. Short of catastrophe, only this would call the father up from the fields before supper and bring the whole family together at the front door. But while the family is congregating, the omniscient narrator pauses to paint the scene: the autumn trees in yellow and red, the ripe apples in the orchard, the grapes on the vine, the buckwheat in the fields, the rain-washed sky, the wind in the leaves, the prosperous farm. In a few lines the narrator puts the scene clearly before us and appeals to all our senses in doing so. This descriptive passage not only serves to give the action of the poem a clearly defined setting; it also plays an important role in the structure of the poem. The poem is built on a contrast between the "teeming" life of the farm where everything "prospers well" and the deprivation of the mother through the loss of a single son. In the serene weather of early autumn the trees are "deeper green, yellower and redder"; at the end of the poem the bereaved is dressed all in black. In the fields all is calm, "vital and beautiful," but the mother wishes she could die. By so much does a human life outweigh the vitality of teeming nature. But now the mother comes hurrying quickly to the door, worried, not stopping to adjust her hair or her cap as usual, for a letter during wartime may bring bad news, and indeed she feels a premonition. The envelope is quickly opened; the mother's heart sinks as she sees that the writing is in someone else's hand. The letters swim before her eyes, but she skims it quickly, anxious to learn the worst, picking out disconnected phrases that tell the terrible news. The son is badly wounded. The oldest daughter, feeling her responsibility through her tears, is the one who tries to comfort the mother. She seizes eagerly on the one sentence of the letter that holds out hope. But the mother cannot be comforted: her son is in the hospital. She feels faint and sick, and leans against the doorpost, her head a-throb. The younger sisters huddle around dismayed, not knowing what to do or say. The whole picture is filled with psychological truth, and there is no talk of faded coats of blue or heavenly robes of white. But, the omniscient narrator tells us, the boy is already dead. He was a brave and a "simple soul" (contrast the four-times repeated "noble spirit" of the other poem), not a paragon. Presently we see the mother, who by now has received confirmation of the death, dressed in mourning clothes, fretful, unable to eat or sleep well, wishing she could slip away from life and be with her dead son—not up in Heaven "among the good and true"—but just with him. Her reaction is real, not exaggerated. And thus the meaning and tragedy of war are borne home to the reader by a scene from life truly presented—presented freshly and through the senses and without trite phrases or the endlessly repeated insistence that the dead boy and all his family were noble, sweet, gentle, good, brave, and true. The contrast between the phrase "simple soul" used to describe the dead soldier in this poem, and "noble spirit," used for the same purpose in the other, perhaps epitomizes the differences between the two poems. The first phrase seems just, the other exaggerated. We might also describe the first poem as "image-making," the second as "tear-jerking." LP

176. *William Blake* **A POISON TREE** (page 233)

177. *Granfield Kleiser* **THE MOST VITAL THING IN LIFE** (page 233)

One might almost judge these poems from their titles alone. The first title presents an image; the second is an abstract phrase, more suitable for an essay or sermon than for a poem.

The second poem is abstract from beginning to end. It has no dramatic situation. The poet addresses the reader directly. His message—that the most vital thing in life is to control one's feelings—is stated baldly and repeated over and over. The reader is told to "curb resentment," to "maintain a mental peace," to "learn to keep strict silence," to "keep [his] mental balance." The tone is preachy and didactic. There is no development: the good advice simply comes out in a string of platitudes. The poem is without imagery. Its one metaphor is the utterly trite one of a "battle" (13). The poet mixes formal diction ("defrauded") and colloquial diction ("peeved") without purpose and without any sense of impropriety. His meter (iambic-anapestic trimeter, with feminine endings in the odd-numbered lines) is much too swift and bouncy for so serious a theme. A number of words seem included simply to sustain the meter: "quite" (4), "mental" (6), "all" and "simply" (8), "Be assured" (23). This is didactic verse, not poetry; it conveys advice, not experience.

"A Poison Tree" also has a message, but it is conveyed through a parable or extended metaphor rather than explicitly stated. The poem has a beginning, middle, and end, and could not be rearranged in its presentation as could "The Most Vital Thing in Life."

The speaker (who is not the poet) sets up the basic contrast and theme of the poem in the first stanza. To tell one's wrath is to end it. To conceal one's wrath is to cause it to grow and become destructive. The speaker presents two episodes from his life: one in which he was open and candid about his feelings, the other in which he suppressed his feelings. The first episode is presented briefly, for it ended quickly. The second occupies the rest of the poem, for it is of slow development. It is related in a sustained metaphor, which begins in the last phrase of the stanza. The speaker has buried his wrath like a seed, and like a seed it begins to "grow." In the second stanza the speaker nurses his anger. He waters it with fears of his foe and with tears of rage and frustration. He suns it with hypocritical, deceiving smiles. The seed has sprouted. In the third stanza the seed-become-tree bears an apple, poisonous because it is the fruit of wrath, but bright and shiny on the outside because the wrath has been concealed. The speaker's "foe" sees and covets it, and in the final stanza steals and eats it. The speaker finds his foe dead beneath the tree, and is "glad." Thus the consequences of concealed wrath are shown to be horrifyingly destructive, for they include not only the death of the "foe" but the moral perversion of the speaker. The most chilling aspect of the conclusion is released by the word "glad." It touches emotional centers never approached in "The Most Vital Thing in Life." The speaker has destroyed not only his "foe" but himself. (It is here we see that the speaker is not the poet. Where the speaker is "glad" for the death of his foe, the poet is appalled, and makes us feel appalled. Dramatic irony is at work.)

Note the simplicity and economy with which this tale is told. The seed-sprout-sapling-tree development does not need stating; it is implied in the verbs of the poem. The facts that the apple is poison (stanza 3) and that the foe has been killed by eating it (stanza 4) also need no statement; they are implied by the title and the sequence of events.

Blake's message has been embodied in a simple but powerful and moving poem; Kleiser's message remains a versified message.

And what about the messages themselves? Blake's poem advocates expressing one's wrath. Kleiser's recommends suppressing it. Which advice is more valid? One may wish to hedge a little here and to suggest that it depends on circumstances (the occasion for the anger, its intensity, and one's relationship to the person causing it). One can agree with Kleiser that it is unwise to express irritation over every petty annoyance or to tell every stranger exactly what one thinks of him. But Blake is talking about "wrath" and about wrath felt toward persons with whom one is in daily association. Kleiser's maxims are tepid, conventional, and often questionable. (Is controlling one's temper really "the most vital thing in life"? More important than love? More important than standing up for justice? Is it really true that "to win a worthwhile battle / Over selfishness and spite, / You must learn to keep strict silence / Though you know you're in the right?") Blake's advice is bold and unconventional and in fact anticipates by over a century some of the insights of Sigmund Freud. In short Blake's poem presents a poet who is both feeling and thinking deeply; Kleiser's presents a poet who is doing neither.

A further question remains about the interpretation of Blake's poem. Does the speaker *plan* the death of his "foe," or is he merely pleased when it occurs? Is this poem about revenge? The answer, certainly, is that the speaker does not plan the death from the beginning. The central issue of the poem is not between forgiveness and revenge but between the expression and concealment of anger. Suppressed anger, the poet believes, festers and turns poisonous. At some point it turns into hate and the hate *possibly* into planned revenge. The question cannot be answered with certainty and is ultimately unimportant. The speaker's gladness at his foe's death fully reveals his moral perversion whether the death has been plotted or not. A good case can be made, indeed, for the contention that the speaker's "foe" is his foe *because* the speaker conceals his anger from him, rather than vice versa. If "friend" and "foe" were interchanged in the first stanza, would not the "foe" become a friend and the "friend" turn into a foe?   LP

178. *Richard Middleton*   ON A DEAD CHILD   (page 234)

179. *John Crowe Ransom*   BELLS FOR JOHN WHITESIDE'S DAUGHTER   (page 234)

A child's death is a dangerous subject for a poet. It invites sentimentality. Though the occasion is one for genuine grief, there is always a temptation to "hoke" it up a bit, to sweeten it, to picture the child as a little angel and to soften the harsher contours.

In both poems considered here, the speaker is an adult attending the funeral of a child, and in both the speaker finds it difficult to believe that the child is dead. In the first the speaker is possibly an older relative of the child or a close friend of the child's parents. In the second he is specifically a friend and neighbor of the child's father, named in the title. This title has a double meaning. The "Bells" refer to the church bells which ring for the funeral in the final stanza; they also suggest that the poem itself is a tribute, a chiming of rimes, composed in the dead girl's memory.

"On a Dead Child" suffers from lack of specificity. All we learn about the dead child is that he?/she? was "a little rose" and liked to play games. But in the poem it is the adult, not the child, who is playing a game. As if he did not know why he had come, he "wander[s]" up to the child's casket, pretending that the child is "no more dead" than the roses strewn about the grave. He tells himself that the child lies motionless only because it is "tired" from too much "straying" (suggesting a gentle kind of play). And though the child does not greet him, the adult pretends to believe that it is not dead: "Yet still I knew that you were only playing– / Playing at being dead." In stanza 3 the adult confesses that the child lay so still, its eyelids so quiet, that he "might have thought" it really dead; but he rejects this thought immediately, assuring himself that the child was "peeping" through its closed eyelids; and so he does not cry. Instead, he smiles, gently calls the child by name, adds his own rose to the "sweet heap of roses" around the grave, and leaves the child to its "game."

The first and last stanzas of the poem allude to a passage from the fifteenth-century work *Imitation of Christ* by Thomas à Kempis (written originally in Latin but translated into many languages): "Man proposes, but God disposes"—meaning roughly that, whatever plans a good man makes, God has the final disposition in human affairs. In the poem it is an additional method used by the adult to soften the reality of the child's death. "Though God's ways are mysterious, He does nothing without good reason, and the reason is always for the best" might be a modern version.

"On a Dead Child" is a sentimental poem. It chooses its vocabulary from words designed to educe tender feeling: "God" (twice); "little" (twice); "roses" (four times); "childish feet"; "smiled"; "gently"; "sweet"; it avoids words of opposite feeling.* It never persuades us that the child—"A little rose among the roses"—is a real child; more seriously, it does not persuade us that the adult is a real adult. The adult is the childish figure in the poem. By pretending that the child is only pretending to be dead, he avoids confrontation with the harsh fact of death; yet the poem presents this avoidance not as a form of neurotic escapism but as acceptable adult behavior.

The poet-speaker in "Bells for John Whiteside's Daughter" also finds it difficult to believe that the child he knew is dead. She was so rapid in her movements, so fleet of foot, so loud and boisterous in her play, that her stillness now is almost beyond belief. Rather than pretend that she is merely playing, however, he speaks of her as being in a "brown study" (a state of somber, abstracted brooding). But such a state is so uncharacteristic of the child that it "astonishes" the speaker and the other adults gathered for her funeral.

The child in this poem is clearly not a "little rose" but a real child—active, noisy, and often vexatious in her play. Indeed, her games are metaphorically described as "wars," whose clamor reached the adults in their "high window," and whose tyrannies disturbed the geese whom she woke from their "noon apple-dreams" and "harried" into the pond. The term "little lady" applied to her is ironical rather than sentimental in intention and effect (her "rod" is both scepter and prod). The one long sentence comprising the three central stanzas has a freshness of imagery and imagination unmatched in the other poem and gives us a vivid impression of the child at her play. The geese—lazy, sleepy, proud—serve both as victims of the child's

---

*Except in the title, the poet carefully avoids using words like *casket, coffin,* or *grave,* because these would clash with the speaker's fantasy that the child is only playing dead. For the casket or coffin he substitutes the metaphor "bed" (6), which is momentarily confusing because it also suggests a garden bed and a deathbed—until we realize that strewing a bed of roses with cut roses would be senseless and that a deathbed would not be on display at a funeral. The metaphorical use of "sleeping" (9) for death also confuses the meaning. That it is meant metaphorically is shown by paraphrase:

Though I knew that you were only playing at being dead, you lay so still I might have thought you were really dead; however, you were surely peeping between those eylids, and so I did not cry. [It would not make sense to say: When I saw you peeping, I knew that you were not really asleep, and so I did not cry.]

This avoidance of funereal terms also confuses the setting. It seems clearly outdoors, as the child's eyelids lie quiet "to the sky"; yet the casket is open, for the speaker can see the child's face. But at most funerals the casket is open only at the church and is closed when brought to the graveside. One is at first tempted to read "bed" as referring to the grave rather than to the casket; but surely the body would not be lying uncoffined in an open grave.

play and as a character-contrast to the child herself; yet the poet's whimsy of having them speak "in goose" is appropriate to the kind of imaginative play that a child might engage in.

In the last stanza, however, the speaker is brought back to the present reality. The bells ring for the funeral service, and the adults who have been "sternly stopped" by the child's death are "vexed at her brown study, / Lying so primly propped." If they had been sometimes "vexed" by her play in life, they are more "vexed" to see her here, lying so "prim" (who was never prim in life), "propped" rigidly in her coffin (who had such "speed" in her body and such a "tireless heart" in life). "Vexed" is an inspired word here; while pointing up ironical contrasts, it expresses genuine grief through understatement. For additional comment on Ransom's poem, see Robert Heilman, in *The Pacific Spectator*, 5 (Aut. 1951), 458-60; Thornton H. Parsons, *John Crowe Ransom* (New York: Twayne, 1969), pp. 53-55; and Robert Penn Warren, "Pure and Impure Poetry," *Kenyon Review*, 5 (Spr. 1943), 237-40. LP

180. *Emily Dickinson* **SOME KEEP THE SABBATH GOING TO CHURCH** (page 235)

181. *Anonymous* **MY CHURCH** (page 235)

In these poems of identical length, identical rime scheme, and similar meter,* both poets take nature for their church.

The difference between the poems is largely one of tone. In "My Church" the tone is earnest, solemn; the language and imagery tend toward the grandiloquent. The poet is making a universal pronouncement of his religious belief. His religion has just one temple, which, being wide as the world, set with stars, and without roof or walls or floors ("save the beautiful sod") is obviously the whole natural world. The poet's religion has no narrow creeds restricting membership by requiring acquiescence in abstruse the theological doctrines. Its one article of faith is belief in a loving and illimitable God. The thought is noble, but the expression is not memorable. The poem is not notably bad; but neither is it notably good. It lacks freshness, particularized imagery, sense of occasion, striking originality.

The tone of "Some keep the Sabbath . . ." is playful, fanciful, and though not unserious, not at all solemn. The reader senses a specific occasion: the poet is at

---

*The first poem alternates tetrameter with trimeter lines; the second is trimeter throughout. In both the iambic foot is prevalent; but the first mixes it freely with anapests (in accord with its more playful tone); the second uses anapests sparingly (in accord with its more solemn tone). Both poems introduce metrical unorthodoxies. In line 5 Dickinson omits the fourth stress in a tetrameter line—or perhaps we can explain it by saying she substitutes a metrical pause (in any case, this practice is customary in her metrics). In the second poem the last line ends with two four-syllable feet: the LOVE / of the il- LIM- / it- a- ble GOD. / A conventional prosodist would dismiss this as "incorrect." A more charitable interpretation might be that it graphically illustrates the impossibility of confining this God within limits.

home (as is her wont) on a beautiful Sunday morning while her family and friends are all at church. The poet makes a personal rather than a universal statement. While other people keep the Sabbath by going to formal services, she keeps hers by staying home. Her church also is nature, but instead of being "wide as the world" it is confined to the area around her house and has "an orchard for a dome." Her church has a bobolink for chorister and God for a preacher, and God's sermon "is never long"—never boring or uncomfortable to sit through. The "sexton"—who sings instead of tolling a bell—is presumably another small bird. Two of the metaphors are open-ended. The poet, instead of dressing in surplice, "just puts on her wings" (a joyful spirit? readiness for imaginative flight? angelic behavior?—any or all of these perhaps). God's sermon, likewise, may be any of a number of things— the joy He communicates through the beauty of nature, the sunshine streaming through the orchard branches—it would be unwise to be too specific. Whatever it is, it is pleasurable and gives a lift to the spirit. So also does the quiet humor of the poet's comparison (combining metaphor, metonymy, and understatement) of God to "a noted clergyman." Underlying all is possibly a more appropriate way of worship than attending formal services. Others attend formal services every Sunday out of duty and are sometimes bored. The poet attends her "church" out of pleasure and is never disappointed. The others hope to be rewarded for their dedicated worship by going to heaven "at last" (when they die). The poet is going to heaven "all along" (samples its pleasures every Sabbath).

"Some keep the Sabbath . . ." is the superior poem because of its continuous play of fancy, its humor, the originality of its metaphors, and its particularizing imagery. As a touchstone of the difference between the two poems, we might compare the two lines in them most nearly parallel in meaning—line 4 ("And an orchard for a dome") from the first, and line 10 ("Nor floors save the beautiful sod") from the second. In the first poem we might have expected (would have got from a more conventional poet) a substitution of "the heavens" or "blue skies" for the "dome" of her church; instead we are given "an orchard." Because it is unexpected, it comes with a small shock of surprise; at the same time it is seen to be appropriate, for it domesticates the poet's church (which she attends by staying at home), makes it more personal, and reduces it to manageable size (conformable with the bobolink and the "little sexton"). In the second poem, to substitute for the "floors" of the church we are given the "beautiful sod." The two words join with a "clunk" as in the coupling of boxcars. The adjective is abstract and overused in poetry (the first poem creates a sense of beauty without using the word); the noun seems to have been chosen largely to rime with "God," for its connotations do not go well with "beautiful." LP

182. *Malcolm Cowley* THE LONG VOYAGE (page 236)

183. *Sir Walter Scott* BREATHES THERE THE MAN (page 236)

"The Long Voyage" arises from a specific situation. The poet, or speaker, is on a ship rapidly taking him away from his native country. As is natural in such a situation, a powerful feeling of nostalgia, even of homesickness, arises in him for the land he loves and is leaving. The emotion is convincing, first, because it is expressed through images, concretely—hills, trees, birds, seasons—not abstractly; second, because it is uttered in a quiet voice—the poet does not rant about the emptiness in his heart, the tears in his eyes, the anguish in his soul; third, because he doesn't make exaggerated claims about his country, which is like "almost any country": its pines are no darker, its dogwood no brighter, its birds no swifter. Nevertheless, this is *his* country, and that makes the difference. He knows "its face, its speech." The very water folding back against the prow reminds him of his country's earth breaking against the plow—an excellent simile—and the foam on the water reminds him of his country's dogwood. The emotion is not strained or exaggerated; the poem expresses a universal feeling arising from a specific situation.

"Breathes there the man" does not arise from a specific situation. It talks about no specific man. The poet is expressing not his own feeling for his country but scorn for some other (hypothetical) man who has no such feeling. There are no images in the poem—no sharply defined pictures, sounds, or smells. The language is abstract. It is spoken not quietly but shrilly, at the top of the poet's voice. The tone is oratorical, as established by the diction and the construction of the sentences ("Breathes there the man . . . ." "Go, mark him well," "High though his titles . . . ," "foreign strands" [for "shores"], "power and pelf" [for "money"], "fair renown," and so forth). The poet climbs up the ladder of his own eloquence till he calls his hypothetical victim "a wretch, concentred all in self" who "doubly dying" shall go down to "vile dust." The poet has lashed himself into a frenzy of virtuous indignation, and the sentiment is strained and exaggerated. Surely, if a person lacks a love of country, it is more his misfortune than his crime; he deserves compassion, not consignment to the "vile dust." Love cannot be compelled. Moreover, such a person is not necessarily "a wretch, concentred all in self." Surely men who have voluntarily left the country of their birth and found other places to live that they liked better—whose hearts have not "burned" when they returned to the original country—have lived decent lives, loved their families, been kind to babies, enjoyed life, and been mourned by friends when they died. The poet has exaggerated and oversimplified the facts of life, has whipped himself up by means of words to an artificial state of feeling. The emotion does not well up naturally. The poem rings resoundingly, but it also rings hollowly, like a drum.

Sir Walter Scott was a good man who wrote good novels and some good poetry, but this poem is "rhetorical." It is taken from the opening of Canto VI of *The Lay of the Last Minstrel*, in which it is sung by the ancient minstrel who tells the story.

In context it has a certain dramatic propriety, but it is not clearly distinguished from an utterance that might not be Scott's own—that is, there is no detectable dramatic irony. It is, of course, usually reprinted out of context as a patriotic set piece. LP

184. *Eugene Field* **LITTLE BOY BLUE** (page 237)

185. *Coventry Patmore* **THE TOYS** (page 238)

"Little Boy Blue" is an appealing poem. Its melody is pleasing, and so are its rimes. The word order is natural and unforced, and so are the words themselves. The poem makes effective use of alliteration and other musical devices. The picture it presents of the loyal toy soldier and dog awaiting the return of their Little Boy Blue is touching. The poem is skillfully done, and it has been much beloved by the American public. It is nevertheless a sentimental poem, manipulating its materials to draw tears from the reader, subtly falsifying life by dimming the darker colors and brightening up the warmer ones. It aims at being sweetly sad.

Its title is sweet. The boy who dies is not Bobby, or Peter, or Donald; he is "Little Boy Blue"—the name has nursery rime associations. And he has not only a sweet name but a sweet disposition. He played nicely with his toys on the evening of the night he died (though he must have been sick, and most children are short-tempered and hard to manage when sick), and then he toddled sweetly off to bed at the appointed time, without a single protest, quite contrary to ordinary boy-nature. If Boy Blue ever had fits of ill temper or disobedience, they are not mentioned; only his pretty actions, such as kissing his toys, are mentioned. In describing Boy Blue and his possessions, the poet uses the adjective "little" eleven times in twenty-four lines. Not only is Boy Blue "little," his hands are "little," his face is "little," his chair is "little," his toys are "little." Most of these "little's" are quite superfluous; the word is being used only to manipulate the reader's sympathies, to evoke a stock response. Also, instead of telling us that Little Boy Blue *died*, the poet says that he was "awakened by an angel song." It is a sweet way of describing death; the uglier features are avoided, and death becomes a gentle and sweetly sad experience, like a song. (Some students will have difficulty with the "angel song" metaphor and think that Little Boy Blue grew up—apparently rather suddenly—leaving his childish toys behind.) This death occurred many years ago, but the little toys are still true.

But now, three questions. First, how does the poet know that Little Boy Blue "dreamt of the pretty toys" if he died in his sleep? Second, in what sense are the toys "true"? Do they really wonder what has happened to Little Boy Blue "since he kissed them and put them there"? Or is this not an example of what Ruskin called "the pathetic fallacy"—the fallacy of attributing human emotions to inanimate objects? That is, has not the author sentimentalized not only the little boy but also even his toys? And third, why, after all these years, are the toys still where

Little Boy Blue left them? (Here is a question which the poet did not intend us to ask. If the toys are still in the chair where Boy Blue left them, his parents must have closed up his room when he died and resolved to leave everything just as he left it. People occasionally do such things, to be sure, but only very rarely; and we usually feel that such a reaction to death is excessively sentimental or even morbid, not healthy. Quite understandably, the poet glosses over this aspect of the situation and concentrates our attention instead on the supposed fidelity of the toy dog and the toy soldier, as though this quality was what really kept them there.) In short, the author is not treating death seriously; instead he is playing with us and with our emotions.

"The Toys," at first view, may seem a slightly crude poem beside "Little Boy Blue." The meter is not so lilting, the rime is not so regular, there is no stanza pattern, and even the syntax may at times seem slightly strained.* But the meter is such as to keep our attention focused constantly on the content; it does not set up a separate tune or by a pretty lilt soften and sweeten a pathetic subject matter. Moreover, the treatment of the subject matter is honest. Having once described his son as "little," the poet drops the adjective and does not use it as a spurious means of attaching sympathy to his subject. He does not idealize the behavior of little boys. Though his son is grave, quiet, and thoughtful, he is also, like most boys, sometimes willful and disobedient. The father's behavior, as contrasted with that of the parents of Little Boy Blue, is normally human. He loses his temper, strikes the boy and scolds him, then later feels remorse and worries about what he has done. But the boy, though he has been sobbing, is not so grief-stricken that he cannot sleep, as a sentimentalist might have made him. He is deep in slumber, and beside his bed, to console himself, he has arranged his treasured collection of toys. These toys are enumerated and described: they include "a red-veined stone," "a piece of glass abraded by the beach," and "two French copper coins." The imagery is fresh and precise. We are not told, moreover, that the boy kissed these toys before going to sleep, or that he is dreaming of them, or that they, on their part, are faithfully waiting for him to wake up. The incident is moving because it has been honestly treated. Moreover, the poet has effectively used the incident to communicate, by analogy, a larger truth about life. We are all children, ultimately, and have our childish ways. We grown-up children have our grown-up toys no less foolish really than the contents of a child's pocket. And we too disobey the Commandments of Our Father and stand equally in need of forgiveness.

In referring to his son's having disobeyed "the seventh time" (3), the poet enriches his meaning by a Biblical allusion to Matthew 18: 21-22. When Peter asked Jesus how often he should forgive his brother's sinning against him, Jesus answered, Not seven times, but "seventy times seven."**

---

*Actually, the syntax in lines 3-6 is skillfully arranged so that "dismissed" may take either "him" or "His Mother" as its object, both meanings being appropriate. By one construction "His Mother" is the subject of an absolute phrase; by the other it is the object of the verb.

**This discussion is abridged from the essay "Are Tears Made of Sugar or of Salt" in Laurence Perrine, *The Art of Total Relevance: Papers on Poetry* (Rowley, Mass.: Newbury House, 1976), pp. 125-29.

Chapter sixteen
Good Poetry and Great

186. *John Donne* THE CANONIZATION (page 241)

Useful discussions of this poem may be found in Cleanth Brooks, *The Well Wrought Urn* (New York: Reynal & Hitchcock, 1947), pp. 10-17; Clay Hunt *Donne's Poetry* (New Haven: Yale Univ. Press, 1954), pp. 72-93; Doniphan Louthan, *The Poetry of John Donne* (New York: Bookman Associates, 1951), pp. 110-18; Patricia Garland Pinka, *This Dialogue of One* (University, AL: Univ. of Alabama Press, 1982), pp. 126-32. LP

187. *Robert Frost* HOME BURIAL (page 243)

The three critics paraphrased in question 8 are (A) John F. Lynen, *The Pastoral Art of Robert Frost* (New Haven: Yale Univ. Press, 1960), p. 114; (B) George W. Nitchie, *Human Values in the Poetry of Robert Frost* (Durham, N.C.: Duke Univ. Press, 1960), 129-30, 166-67, 223; and (C) John C. Kemp, *Robert Frost and New England* (Princeton, N.J.: Princeton Univ. Press, 1979), pp. 118-19, 155-56. Of these, Lynen seems to me furthest from the truth. Against Nitchie it may be argued that on a previous occasion of emotional conflict between them, she *had* left him (39), and had either come back to him voluntarily or been persuaded by him to come back, and that her last action in the poem is to open the door wider. The husband accepts the fact that she is leaving ("Where do you mean to go?"), and threatens that *this* time he will bring her home "by force."

The most remarkable critical discussion of this poem is Randall Jarrell's illuminating line-by-line analysis, "Robert Frost's 'Home Burial,'" *The Third Book of Criticism* (New York: Farrar, Straus & Giroux, 1969), pp. 191-231; also in *The Moment of Poetry*, ed. Don Cameron Allen (Baltimore: Johns Hopkins Univ. Press, 1962), pp. 99-132. If, after reading Jarrell, you want to read more, the following may be worth your perusal: Elaine Barry, *Robert Frost* (New York: Frederick Ungar, 1973), pp. 75-78; Frank Lentricchia, *Robert Frost: Modern Poetries and the Landscapes of Self* (Durham, N.C.: Duke Univ. Press, 1975), pp. 62-65, 71; and Richard Poirier, *Robert Frost: The Work of Knowing* (New York: Oxford Univ. Press, 1977), pp. 124-35. LP

188. *T. S. Eliot* **THE LOVE SONG OF J. ALFRED PRUFROCK** (page 246)

"Prufrock" is one of the most discussed poems of the twentieth century. Of the mass of commentary that has accumulated concerning it, some of the following may be particularly helpful: Roy P. Basler, *Sex, Symbolism, and Psychology in Literature* (New Brunswick, N. J.: Rutgers Univ. Press, 1948), pp. 203-21; Cleanth Brooks and Robert Penn Warren, *Understanding Poetry*, 3d ed. (New York: Holt, 1960), pp. 386-99 (also in earlier editions); Elizabeth Drew, *T. S. Eliot, The Design of His Poetry* (New York: Charles Scribner's, 1949), pp. 34-36; Paul Engle and Warren Carrier, *Reading Modern Poetry*, rev. ed. (Glenview, IL: Scott, Foresman, 1968), pp. 148-55; Laurence Perrine and James M. Reid *100 American Poems of the Twentieth Century* (New York: Harcourt Brace Jovanovich, 1966), pp. 110-12; Grover Smith, *T. S. Eliot's Poetry and Plays* (Chicago: Univ. of Chicago Press, 1956), pp. 15-20 *et passim*; and Morris Weitz, *Philosophy of the Arts* (Cambridge: Harvard Univ. Press, 1950), pp. 94-107, 145. LP

POEMS FOR FURTHER READING

Poems 191, 218, and 219 from Part Two provide additional illustrations of topics presented in this chapter.

part 2
POEMS FOR FURTHER READING

189. *Joan Aleshire* **SLIPPING** (page 255)

The subject of this poem—seeing and reacting to the physical deterioration of one's father—is rife with sentimental possibilities. Aleshire explores these through the speaker's original indulgence in pity (and some self-pity) through the first two verse paragraphs, cataloguing the "slow slipping" of increasing lameness and the growth of a cataract, and generously accommodating her gait to his slowing pace. These physical failings she presents in metaphor and simile ("curtain of mist," "like pickpockets," "like a raft on a river," "like a child who keeps pulling on your hand," lines 3, 4-5, 8, 13-14), as if such infirmities are best handled emotionally as the stuff of poetic comparison. In this presentation, there are both emotional distancing and self-gratification, masking pain and pity with slight cleverness—but most of all, avoiding sentiment.

What the poem is revealing with some dramatic irony is a speaker who has inherited the trait defined by the mother—a reluctance or inability "to talk about feelings" (11). So she resorts to the indirection of poetic statement. She has learned to identify talking "about feelings" with sentimentality, and so at the outset seems incapable of speaking a truly felt sentiment.

She realizes this flaw, and overcomes it, in lines 24-30. The "slipping" away of her father's physical strength has broken down his "reserve"—and in response to his new, direct statement of feeling, she senses her own reserve slipping. So his feeling is exposed "like a screen suddenly falling" (the last figure in the poem) from a patient in his examining room, revealing himself as a person who feels, and revealing to his daughter the honest, nonpoetic reality of his aging flesh. The reserve of trying to avoid sentimentality can prevent the expression of honest sentiment. TRA

190. *A. R. Ammons* **PROVIDENCE** (page 255)

This example of "minimal" poetry, in brief free verse lines, without any images, is an echo-response to Frost's "Nothing Gold Can Stay" (No. 131). The only figurative language is found in the word "bright" (2), which metaphorically compares visual brilliance to a sense of newness and excitement—not a *very* striking metaphor. Essentially, Ammons's theme is simple and romantic: excitement, novelty, beauty, and the freshness of apparent spontaneity all are predicated upon transience and mortality. Permanence is the opposite of brilliance, and dullness and ennui its results. Whereas Frost makes of this observation a wistful regret, a desire that the beautiful could also be the permanent, Ammons (through his title) declares this condition to be what God ordains in our best interests.

The poem is formally quite regular, for free verse: the first four lines are disyllabic, the last three trisyllabic; each line contains only two words; and the three concluding lines almost establish a metrical norm—EARTH re- QUIRES / ON- ly THAT / NOTH- ing STAY—two stresses surrounding an unstressed syllable. The syntactical arrangement of the single sentence (ungrammatical in the omission of a period at the end of the poem and of a comma at the end of line 4) contains surprises. The phrase *bright as* momentarily seems to be introducing a simple comparison ("bright as a penny," "bright as the sun"), but in fact the *as* is instead part of a simile, *as if*, creating a negative contrast (comparing unlike things, as similes always do): the earth of course is not fresh and new, though one would like to feel as if it were. Similarly, *as if just* momentarily implies a standard of justice, perhaps even divine justice because of the title; but *just* turns out not to be an adjective but an adverb in the phrase *just thought of*, colloquially informal and leading to the omission of the comma. TRA

191. *Matthew Arnold* **DOVER BEACH** (page 256)

"Dover Beach" is Arnold's lament over the decline of religious faith in his time. "The Sea of Faith," he tells us, was once "at the full," but now he only hears "its melancholy, long, withdrawing roar," like the roar of waves receding or of the tide going out. Certainly, the mid-nineteenth century was a time of religious crisis—a time when vast numbers of thinking people were losing the simple Christian faith of their childhood teaching before the advance of scientific and rationalistic thought. The conflict and the agony are recorded in work after work of literature. Arnold's poem, first published in 1867 but possibly composed some ten or twelve years earlier, is surely one of the most eloquent expressions of despair ever written, combining profound pessimism with imperishable beauty.

The speaker is in a room overlooking the cliffs of Dover. He is so situated—where the cliffs curve—that not only can he look out over the English Channel and occasionally glimpse the coast of France (twenty-two miles away at this point) as it catches a gleam of moonlight, but he can also see, across the bay, the face of the cliffs themselves and the waves breaking on the shingle at their foot. In the room with him is a beloved woman (wife or sweetheart) to whom he unburdens his despair—not over any personal misfortune but about the state of the world.

The poem turns on a series of contrasts, of which the two most important are those (a) between the physical beauty of the world he sees outside his window and its actual spiritual darkness, and (b) between the full tide he sees outside the window and the ebbing "tide" of faith which he feels is responsible for the world's spiritual darkness.

Looking from his window, the speaker is first impressed by the beauty of the moonlit scene before him, and he summons his companion to the window to share its beauty with him. But then he becomes aware of the sound of the breakers crashing on the shingle, and this sound is a sad one. Being a person of broad intellectual culture, he is reminded by the sound of a passage in a Greek drama by Sophocles, who compared the ebb and flow of the sea to the ebb and flow of human misery. Then he thinks of his own time, and he is reminded by the sound of the ebbing of religious faith. This thought is so melancholy to him that he cries out to his beloved, "Ah, love, let us be true to one another!" for a loving human relationship seems the only value left in a world which has lost every other source of meaning—a world which, despite its illusory physical beauty, has "really neither joy, nor love, nor light, / Nor certitude, nor peace, nor help for pain"—surely two of the most pessimistic lines in English poetry. The simile ending the poem gives concrete embodiment to this abstract statement and is deservedly one of the most famous in English poetry. As an image for complete meaninglessness in human life, it can hardly be surpassed. Words of negative connotation pile up—*darkling, confused, alarms, struggle, flight, ignorant, clash, night*—to give a picture of utter confusion, blindness, cross-purposes, and uncertainty, in which warring armies cannot tell friend from foe and strike at both alike in the darkness. This uncertainty embodies the lack of "certitude" mentioned in line 34, which in turn stems from the ebbing Sea of Faith. The one remaining consolation—the possibility of a loyal personal relationship between two lovers, because of its positioning, seems a very frail one indeed. Instead of one person lost on a tiny raft at night in midocean, we are left with two people on the raft clinging to each other out of desperation. The poem begins with light and ends in darkness.

Students must be made to see that the image in the last three lines is the figurative, not the literal, term in a simile. This poem is not about war, nor was it written during time of war—it is a poem about the loss of a common religious faith that once linked men together in a belief, hope, and some degree of brotherhood or community—a loss that has resulted in a world where men work only for self-advancement and at cross-purposes with each other.

It is also important to note that the poem was written, not by a believer blaming the rest of the world for its lack of belief, but by a poet who himself can no longer accept the stories and assumptions on which the old faith was based, and who regards its consolations and certainties no longer possible for thinking men. If he had been himself a believer, he would have cried out, "O Lord! bring these people back to a belief in your eternal truth and loving overlordship!" Instead, his cry is to a human companion, "Ah, love, let us be true / To one another!"

The syntax in lines 7-14 is somewhat involved. The noun "roar" (9) is not the direct object of "hear" but the subject of the infinitives [To] "Begin," "cease," "begin," and "bring" (12-13). The direct object of "hear" is the whole infinitive phrase of which "roar" is the subject. In reading the poem one must reject the temptation to drop one's voice at the end of line 11. LP

192. W. H. Auden MUSÉE DES BEAUX ARTS (page 257)

The poem descriptively alludes to three paintings by Pieter Brueghel the Elder (which might be shown to students): lines 5-8, *The Census* (or *The Numbering at Bethlehem*); lines 10-13, *The Massacre of the Innocents*; and lines 14-21, *Landscape with the Fall of Icarus*. The title of the poem may be derived from the name of the museum in Brussels where the Icarus painting hangs, the Musées Royaux des Beaux Arts, though it simply means "Fine Arts Museum," a title general enough to include all three "Old Master" paintings.

The poem is in free verse and has an irregular rime scheme. In the opening verse paragraph the following lines rime: 1/4, 2/8, 5/7, 6/13, 9/11, 10/12, and there is no rime for line 3. The concluding paragraph, while not regular, tightens up the rimes somewhat, in keeping with the single focus of the subject: 14/15, 16/20, 17/21, 18/19. The two sets of rimed couplets begin to suggest some more explicit closure of meaning for the poem, but the last two lines return to the more random pattern, reinforcing the understated meaning—that something as momentous as a boy falling out of the sky does not signal a definitive event, but only a momentary amazement to the men who continue on about their business. The apparently irrelevant or random riming may thus be seen as a reinforcement of the theme, that great events seem irrelevant or not personally significant to the mass of self-involved people.

The sequence of the pictured events may also be seen as reinforcing the theme: from the birth of Christ, to the slaughter by Herod of the first-born sons, to the mythical story of Icarus—events that would seem to the modern picture-viewer of decreasing personal significance, even if the last of them did originally symbolize a very human problem, the danger of rashly pursuing a superhuman aspiration. TRA

193. D. C. Berry ON READING POEMS TO A SENIOR CLASS AT SOUTH HIGH (page 257)

The poet begins by assuming, from their orderly appearance in rows of chairs, that the students are "frozen" and incapable of a living response to his poetry. But as he reads, planning "to drown them" with his words, the power of poetry floods the room, and the surprised poet and the class metaphorically swim together until the ringing of the school bell, which breaks the enchantment. All of them, students and poet, then go on to other more normal pursuits, back to their ordinary lives. The experience, however, has transported the poet beyond himself, and it takes his domesticated, imaginatively named cat to bring *him* back to normal.

The poet's defensive condescension—his prejudice that these students are cold to poetry, his fear that his poetry may not move them—is washed away by the mutual experience, to the extent that he himself must be restored to his human form. The poem wittily converts the pejorative image of "frozen fish" into the vital image of "thirty tails whacking words," and his plan of drowning his audience converts into the water in which, for the time, the poet and students have a medium they can share. Both "frozen fish" and "drown" are used metaphorically, apparently as the poet's self-conscious device for asserting his superiority, but both come so vitally to life that even after the experience the poet feels fins at the end of his arms. Ironically it is his cat who restores him from his fishy condition. TRA

194. *Elizabeth Bishop* ONE ART (page 258)

With a forced tone of nonchalance, the speaker in this modified villanelle insists that all losses can be faced stoically. She begins with insignificant losses—keys, a little time, memories of places and names—and proceeds to those of greater emotional value—a prized keepsake, loved houses. Hyperbolically, she reports the loss of realms, rivers, and a continent. The climax of the poem occurs in the final stanza, the loss of a beloved person, which too can be mastered—almost. The last line, with its parenthetic command to herself, reveals that the mastery of this loss requires a great exertion of will, if indeed it can be mastered at all.

Whimsically, the poem is presented as a lesson to the reader: "Lose something every day," until practice in mastering the sense of loss will render future losses less disastrous in their effects. The first three stanzas, in the second person, present the lesson; in the last three the speaker offers her own experience as supporting evidence. But with the increasing sense of regret and even pain, the ironic stance of the speaker is made clear: mastering the sense of loss is not "one art" that can be learned through coping with lesser losses.

The word "loss" is used both metaphorically and literally, undercutting the statement that all losses are equal. The inequalities are manifest when one questions whether or not the references to losing keys, losing time, and losing a beloved person employ the term "loss" in the same sense. What the poet achieves, in seeming to believe that the word is single in its meaning, is the statement that not all loss can be mastered. TRA

195. *William Blake* THE GARDEN OF LOVE (page 259)

The important words and images in this poem may be ranged in two columns. On one side are the Garden of Love (1, 7), play (4), the green (4), flowers (8, 10), joys and desires (12). On the other side are the Chapel (3, 5) shut gates (5), "Thou shalt not" (6), graves (9), tombstones (10), Priests in black gowns (11), binding with briars (12). The words and images in the first series have positive connotations: they represent the natural and are associated with joy. Those in the second series have mainly negative connotations: they represent institutionalized religion and are associated with death.

Blake was a deeply religious poet who had his own highly unorthodox version of Christianity. He believed strongly in individual liberty, he felt that man's natural impulses are good, and he despised the institutions of church and state for attempting to control man's behavior with repressive rules and laws. In this brief allegorical lyric the speaker relates what the institutionalized church has done to the natural state of man. It has replaced the green where the speaker used to play as a boy with a chapel, its gates shut, and "Thou shalt not" writ over the door. The garden beds around the chapel, where sweet flowers used to grow and ought to be growing now, are filled with graves. Black-gowned priests, following prescribed rounds, are binding the speaker's joys and desires with briars. Clearly "desires" and the "sweet flowers" in the "Garden of Love" are linked with the joys of what the speaker regards as an innocent sexuality, which the Church has forbidden or restricted by threats of punishment ("briars") and death ("tombstones") under a repressive and negative moral code ("Thou shalt not" . . . pick the flowers, fornicate, commit adultery, engage in natural pleasures). As is evident from "Soft Snow" (page 97), Blake believed in free love, just as he believed in political and religious freedom. (Ideas and opinions expressed on this program are not necessarily those of the management.) LP

196. *William Blake* **THE LAMB** (page 259)

197. *William Blake* **THE TIGER** (page 260)

"The Lamb" was first published in *Songs of Innocence* (1789) and "The Tiger" in *Songs of Experience* (1794). Blake described the two volumes as "Showing Contrary States of the Human Soul." Though the poems in *Songs of Experience* are generally darker in tone than those in the earlier book, Blake is not necessarily suggesting that innocence is better than experience. Rather, each state shows the incompleteness or the inadequacy of the other.

In the "Introduction" to *Songs of Innocence* (page 180), Blake was bid by his muse to "Pipe a song about a Lamb." This is it. The central question asked in this poem is "Little Lamb, who made thee?" The central question asked in "The Tiger" is "Did he who made the Lamb make thee?" "The Tiger" was obviously written to complement "The Lamb." Together the two poems make a poetic diptych.

In "The Lamb" the speaker is a child, and the chief effect of the poem is a childlike simplicity, produced by the use of a simple vocabulary—mostly monosyllabic, end-stopped lines—one statement to a line, a song-like meter (six four-beat lines in each stanza, framed at beginning and end by a pair of three-beat lines), paired rimes, and frequent repetitions. The situation and content of the poem also express this childlike simplicity. The child talks to a lamb, asks it a question and answers the question himself, and in his answer shows his trustful unquestioning acceptance of the Christian story he has been taught. The lamb was created by Christ, who in the New Testament is called "the Lamb of God," and who through his incarnation became "a little child." The child and the lamb are thus one with Christ in name as well as in gentleness and love, and the poem appropriately ends, "Little Lamb, God bless thee."

In "The Tiger" the speaker is an adult, possibly the poet; he does not literally speak to the tiger, he apostrophizes it; and the central question of the poem is left uanswered.

The image in the first two lines is one of the most vivid in English poetry. Primarily we are meant to see two eyes glaring in the dark (see line 6); but if we think of the orange and black stripes of the tiger's body, we also have a flame-like image. The tiger is associated with images of fire throughout the poem. He is imagined to have been made in a cosmic smithy ("forged," "hammer," "chain," "furnace," "anvil"), and his creator is personified as a powerful smith. But is this smithy in "distant deeps or skies"—hell or heaven? And was the smith Satan or God? And, having created the tiger, did the smith "smile" to see what he had made? These are the questions urged on the reader, insistently, like the blows of a hammer on an anvil (the interrogative "what" is used thirteen times during the poem), and in a meter whose accents fall also with the force and regularity of hammer blows. The tiger is described as awesome—that is, as arousing both fear and admiration in the beholder. Its "fearful symmetry," the burning brightness of its eyes, its twisted sinewy heart, the "deadly terrors" of its brain—these qualities suggest beauty, strength, fierceness, and violence. But if the tiger is awesome, its creator is even more so. He is "immortal" (3, 23), daring (7, 8, 24) winged (7), strong (9-10), "dread" (12, 15), and an artist (9).

The difficult lines 17-18 have been explained in too many ways to go into here— in terms of astrology, as metaphor for dawn and dewfall, as symbolic of love and pity, as an allusion to the war in heaven between the good and the rebel angels depicted in Milton's *Paradise Lost*, as an allusion to symbols in Blake's private mythology, as an image for showers of sparks sent out from the cosmic forge and of the water used to temper the glowing metal, etc. Perhaps, in their broadest and simplest sense, they can be taken to suggest, "When even the stars wept, did the creator of the tiger smile?"

No answer to its central question is stated in the poem. Is one implied? A survey of Blake criticism produces no consensus. About half of the critics say that the question is rhetorical, intended by Blake to be answered Yes. The creator of the Lamb was also the creator of the Tiger, and He looked on his work and found it "good." The power of the poem is the power with which it expresses this mysterious paradox in the nature of God, creator of both the rainbow and the whirlwind. But another half say that the question is unanswerable, and was not intended by Blake to be answered one way or the other—that Blake's poem is about the mystery and ambiguity of the universe, which is ultimately beyond man's understanding. [And one lonely voice—Kathleen Raine, in *Encounter*, II (1935), 48—declares boldly: "The answer is beyond all possible doubt, 'No'; God, who created the lamb, did not create the tiger."]

A greater variety of answers is produced by the question, What do the lamb and the tiger symbolize? But here we welcome a variety of answers, for the symbolism is rich and permits a range of meanings. (The poems obviously call for symbolical reading. We are being asked much more than whether the same god created the aardvark and the camel.) Among the answers suggested are good and evil, God's love and God's wrath, gentle meekness and powerful energy, innocent purity and strong sexuality, peace and war, mercy and justice, pardon and punishment.

Textual note: The text of "The Tiger" used here differs in line 12 from that published by Blake in *Songs of Experience* ("What dread hand? And what dread feet?"). In the original manuscript this line is followed by a discarded stanza of which the first line is "Could fetch it from the furnace deep?" The cancellation of the stanza left line 12 syntactically incomplete, and Blake seems to have been dissatisfied with it, for in a copy later given to a friend he altered the line in ink to "What dread hand formed thy dread feet," and another friend, perhaps on Blake's authority, printed the poem in a book of memoirs with "forged" in the place of "formed." I have used the version which seems to me best, and which may have represented Blake's final intention. LP

198. *Lucille Clifton* **GOOD TIMES** (page 260)

Occasions for joy in the lives of the poor are few and far between, but when they come they are likely to be jollier, more spontaneous, and more festive than the pleasures of the well-to-do. The joyousness of the occasion is in direct proportion to its rarity. Lucille Clifton, a black poet, here presents just such an occasion in the lives of a poor black family. The first stanza states the causes for celebration, the second stanza presents the celebration itself. For once the rent, the insurance premiums, and the electric bill have all been paid, and uncle Brud has "hit / for one dollar straight"—that is, his one-dollar ticket in a lottery or numbers game has won the whole prize: it does not have to be divided among several winners. The result is that the mother has made home-made bread, Grampaw has come to visit, and there is spontaneous dancing and singing in the kitchen, with a bottle to add to the gaiety.

The speaker is one of the children in the family, possibly the oldest one. She is so deeply impressed by the "good times," which are in such contrast with their usual life of debt and privation, that she ends each stanza with three lines devoted to proclaiming them, and then adds a two-line coda in which she instructs her younger sisters and brothers to "think about the / good times." Lay them up in your memory, for you may not experience many more.

The irony in the poem is that the "good times" being celebrated in this poem are what a middle-class observer would call hard times. LP

199. *Samuel Taylor Coleridge* **KUBLA KHAN** (page 261)

The first publication of this poem included a lengthy note by Coleridge attributing its inspiration to a combination of having taken a prescribed dose of opium, for an illness he was suffering, and then reading a seventeenth-century travel book about the Chinese ruler; he claims that in his "reverie" he had composed between two and three hundred lines of verse, but as he was beginning to write them down he was interrupted by a visitor, and returning to his work discovered that he had forgotten the rest. (The account is available in any collection of Coleridge's works, and need not be quoted here.) Whether this was literally true is less important than the effect Coleridge had in mind in reporting it; the account was written some fifteen years after the poem, and seems to have as its purpose emphasizing the air of magic and mystery of the poem itself, as well as promoting the Romantic ideal of poetry as spontaneous, impulsive, and free of narrowly rational thought.

But as many commentators have shown, the poem itself is highly crafted, not likely the product even of a practiced poet unless he is paying close attention to his effects. Elisabeth Schneider analyzes at length the assonance, consonance, alliteration, and internal and end rimes of just the first five lines, demonstrating the "half-caught echoes, correspondences of sound felt but too complex to be anticipated or to remain tabulated in the mind even after they have been analyzed."

Through line 36 the poet describes the site of Kubla Khan's pleasure-dome: a landscape of contrasts and opposites, with a river bursting forth with great force from a fountain in a "romantic chasm," meandering through a pleasant valley, then sinking once again into a cavern leading to the "sunless sea." The dome itself is built over "caves of ice," and the dome is surrounded by gardens and forests, bounded by walls and towers. The scene combines wildness with gentleness, heights with depths, explosive creative force with calm obliteration, warmth with coldness, holiness with demonism, tumult with lifelessness, artifice with nature, the momentary present with an ancestral past, light with dark, a peaceful scene with prophecies of war. It is, says Harold Bloom, a "vision of creation and destruction, each complete." It presents "the balance of reconciliation of opposites" which for Coleridge was "the mark of the creative imagination."

At line 37 the poem turns to a different scene, a "vision" the poet once had of another distant and exotic moment, of a singing maiden playing on an antique instrument whose song seems to him to have corresponded to Kubla Khan's pleasure-dome. If he could revive within himself the feelings aroused by this vision, he too would be able to create "in air" what Kubla did on earth—and his creation would mark him off from the multitudes who would see in him a holy man of magical powers.

His desire is to create poetically the totality that was expressed in Kubla Khan's achievement; as he phrases it, however, this is only a wish, something beyond his powers. Yet as Bloom points out, what the poem "Kubla Khan" does is precisely that.

This intriguing poem has excited much commentary, among the best of it the following: Walter Jackson Bate, *Coleridge* (New York: Macmillan, 1968), pp. 75-84; Harold Bloom, *The Visionary Company* (Garden City, N.Y.: Anchor/Doubleday, 1963), pp. 229-33; G. Wilson Knight, *The Starlit Dome* (London: Methuen, 1968), pp. 90-97; Elisabeth Schneider, "Kubla Khan," from *Coleridge, Opium and Kubla Khan*, reprinted in *Coleridge: A Collection of Critical Essays*, ed. Kathleen Coburn (Englewood Cliffs, N.J.: Prentice-Hall, 1967), pp. 88-93. TRA

200. *Emily Dickinson*   BECAUSE I COULD NOT STOP FOR DEATH (page 262)

Beyond doubt, this is the most discussed of Emily Dickinson's poems, and it has excited a wide array of interpretations. The literal content seems to offer few difficulties: a woman so busy with her life is called away from it by a kindly gentleman (Death), who takes her for a carriage ride past the living, pauses at what must be her grave, and proceeds through centuries toward the destination "eternity." There are many fine details characterizing the stages of life in stanza 3; stanza 4 emphasizes both the femininity of the speaker and the chilliness of her ride; stanza 5 mysteriously understates her burial; and the last stanza perpetuates the ride in Death's carriage beyond the human comprehension of time (the concept of eternity, as Keats says in the last stanza of "Ode on a Grecian Urn," teases us "out of thought").

There is little quarrel among the critics about these literal matters. The continuing question is what this little allegory *means*. Does it link death with sexuality (the gentleman come courting)? Does it pretend to render a judgment on posthumous experience? Does it define the values of life as they are discovered in the moment of dying? Does it celebrate the soul's entry into heaven? These suggestions, and several others, have been made by eminent critics and scholars. Furthermore, there is little agreement about the tone of the poem—is it confident? whimsical? terrified? triumphant? uninvolved?

What follows, then, is *one* interpretation which is both plausible and consistent with the poet's ideas. The teacher may wish to use this poem, and the references below, as an introduction to discriminating between critical approaches and interpretations.

Death is remarkably, and surprisingly, characterized in this personification as "kindly," a word which so violates normal expectations as to signal the need for interpretation. Death has traditionally been thought of as "kind" to the extent that it releases a person from a life of suffering or from the limitations imposed by mortality. Such a meaning might be implied by the fact that "Immortality" is included as a personified fellow-passenger in the carriage, but the images of life in the poem do not suggest a life of pain—it contains both labor and leisure, nonchalantly linked by alliteration, which are as easily put away as a basket of sewing; and it is represented by the playing children and the maturing grain. In fact, life and death seem equally attractive, and the speaker, pleased with Death's "civility," apparently accepts his invitation with pleasure. The poem presents Death's visit not as an inevitable and unavoidable event, but as a polite invitation which the speaker finds attractive—an interpretation which divides the speaker from ordinary people.

The tone of the poem is governed by the speaker's willingness to accept Death's kind offer, and the key to the speaker's choice lies in the final stanza. Until then, the poem has been a retrospective recollection of events, reported from the speaker's present situation and colored by her perceptions and attitudes "centuries" later. Although in real terms (calendar terms, sun terms) hundreds of years have passed since the beginning of the ride with Death, to the speaker this whole span of time "*Feels* shorter than the day" she died. Now being dead, the speaker no longer shares the feelings or the ideas of the living. The word "surmised" (line 23) underscores this, for in mid-nineteenth century America, and in several other poems by Emily Dickinson, the word had decidedly negative connotations; it meant to guess in error, or to guess without personal experience as a basis. The speaker guessed at the destination of her ride—eternity—but has not reached what the living suppose that implies, heaven. Instead, what she is now experiencing is an endless, cool, and detached journey toward an unknown destination. The speaker retains the power to remember her life, and retains her consciousness, but her present situation is undefinable. In this interpretation, the poem presents an allegorical dramatization of posthumous experience: it is neither hellish nor blissful, but only eternally conscious and emotionless.

Among the important critical readings of the poem, the following offer much variety: Richard Chase, *Emily Dickinson* (New York: William Sloane Assoc., 1951), pp. 249-51; Theodore C. Hoepfner, "'Because I Could Not Stop for Death,'" *American Literature*, XXIX (1957), 96; Charles R. Anderson, *Emily Dickinson's Poetry: Stairway of Surprise* (New York: Holt, 1960), pp. 241-46; Clark Griffith, *The Long Shadow: Emily Dickinson's Tragic Poetry* (Princeton, N.J.: Princeton Univ. Press, 1964), pp. 127-34; Richard B. Sewall, *The Life of Emily Dickinson* (New York: Farrar, Straus, 1974), pp. 571-72, 717; Robert Weisbuch, *Emily Dickinson's Poetry* (Chicago: Univ. of Chicago Press, 1975), pp. 113-17. TRA

201. *Emily Dickinson*   I TASTE A LIQUOR NEVER BREWED (page 263)

The poet's delight in nature is expressed through an extended metaphor in which ecstasy is likened to intoxication. The liquor on which the poet gets drunk is air and dew and all the beauty of summer. This liquor is natural: it has not been brewed; and "not all the vats upon the Rhine" (famous for its breweries) yield a comparable liquor. She drinks it from "tankards scooped in pearl" (cumulus clouds in summer skies by my interpretation, but other interpretations are possible). The "inns of molten blue" are summer skies, and "endless" is an overstatement modifying "days" or "summer" or both. Bees and butterflies (both of which take nectar from flowers) are her drinking companions, but the poet declares she will outdrink both—drink them under the table! Indeed she will make such a spectacle of herself and raise such a hullabaloo that seraphs and saints will run to the windows of heaven to investigate, and, looking out, will see the poet leaning drunkenly against the celestial lamppost!

The fancifulness of the poem's metaphors keeps the poem bubbling with high-spirited fun. The alliteration of "debauchee of dew" (6) follows the vowel-alliteration of line 5 (all vowels alliterate with each other), in which *every* syllable except one (*-bri-*) begins with a vowel, so that reading it is like taking continuous small sips of air. The trochaic substitution in the first foot of line 7 not only emphasizes the word "Reeling" but introduces a reeling movement into the line. (The basic metrical and rime pattern is iambic $x^4a^3x^4a^3$, but in line 15 a metrical pause replaces the last beat, giving emphasis to the delightful assonantal phrase "little tippler" by which the poet characterizes herself.) LP

202. *Emily Dickinson* **IN WINTER IN MY ROOM** (page 264)

See No. 230 (Sharon Olds).

203. *John Donne* **THE GOOD-MORROW** (page 265)

As the title announces, this poem is a morning greeting addressed by the speaker to his love. The questions in the opening lines colloquially declare a parallel between this morning's awakening and an awakening to life that took place when they began to love. All time before then was like infancy, or like a miraculous two-century sleep. The conversational quality of these lines continues throughout the poem, producing the kind of syntactical and elliptical problems found in line 5: "but this, all pleasures fancies be" means "with the exception of this (our love), all pleasures are merely imagined ones." The mock innocence of the first three lines is elaborated on in lines 6-7: the speaker has in the past had his share of sexual experiences, but to his innocent sleeping soul they were only prophetic dreams of the love he now shares.

Pursuing his reference to other love exploits, the speaker assures his lady that there can be no cause of jealousy between them. He puns on the words "watch" and "wake," synonyms in Donne's time, to insist that the alertness to each other which this morning has brought is not for fear of loss, because (he logically says) our mutual love rules out the possibility of loving others. Each of them is the whole of the other's society, just as the room they share is equivalent to all other places. The elliptical syntax of lines 11-12 extends this spatial reference. "Let" in these lines means both "let us concede" and "let us ignore." For other people whose sense of the spaciousness of the world derives from traveling, explorers and mapmakers are necessary; but these two lovers in themselves contain all worlds. (Line 14 alludes to the Renaissance theory that each individual human being is a microcosm, a little world that parallels the greater universe and contains all its elements. Each of the lovers is thus a world, and being joined by their love, each *has* a world.)

The third stanza further extends the geographical metaphor, but it begins with a Renaissance commonplace, that the face of the lover is mutually mirrored in the eye of the partner, both of them being simultaneously a mirror and the image in the other's mirror. Line 16 momentarily returns to the theme of jealousy, as the speaker assures his love that their mirrored faces reveal the honesty in their hearts. They are themselves like the hemispheres of the newly explored and mapped earth—but better, since they do not have the sharp coldness of the north, nor the sinking sunset of the west. Lines 19-21 employ another Renaissance notion, that mortality and decay are the result of the mixture of unequal or dissimilar elements in the body. Donne concludes that since the two of them are not dissimilar (being "one" in their love), or, at least, since they are completely "alike" in the intensity of their feelings, they need not fear death.

The rich allusiveness of the poem, with its hyperbolic declarations balanced against recurrent denials of any need for jealousy or the fear of infidelity, make this a more complicated poem than its declarative statements suggest. The speaker insists on the perfection and permanence of their mutual love, but this idealism is presented in a context that acknowledges the probability of change. The references to new geographical discoveries attest to the temporal nature of human knowledge, just as the opening stanza shows that individual human beings develop and change. Despite the insistence in the last three lines, death is a certainty for these perfect lovers; and if the real hemispheres of the earth contain "sharp north" and "declining west," the microcosm of the lovers' united being will ultimately be subjected to the same vicissitudes. At the same time that the poem declares the permanence of this love, it alludes to the actual impossibility of it.

The fullest analysis of this poem is by Clay Hunt, in *Donne's Poetry: Essays in Literary Analysis* (Hamden, Conn.: Archon Books, 1969), pp. 53-69, a reprint of the Yale University Press edition, 1954. Other valuable comments may be found in Wilbur Sanders, *John Donne's Poetry* (Cambridge: Cambridge Univ. Press, 1971), pp. 64-68, and Judah Stampfer, *John Donne and the Metaphysical Gesture* (New York: Simon and Schuster, 1970), pp. 142-46. TRA

204. *John Donne*   SONG: GO AND CATCH A FALLING STAR (page 266)

In content this poem expresses an extremely disillusioned and cynical view of human life and particularly of feminine virtue. The speaker, addressing an unidentified interlocutor, bids him in the first six lines to perform a series of tasks which have the common characteristic of being impossible. The implication is that the task he commands in the last three lines of the stanza is equally impossible: to find any condition of life that favors the advancement of "an honest mind." (In modern idiom, "Nice guys finish last.")

In the second stanza the speaker zeroes in on his true target—feminine virtue. If, he tells his companion, you are a person with a gift for seeing miraculous events or things invisible to the ordinary eye, go on a journey, ride "ten thousand days and nights," do not return until you are old; no matter how wide or long your search, even with your gift for seeing wondrous things, you will be unable to find a woman who is both beautiful and faithful in love. (He may perhaps find some faithful ugly ones, but those women with opportunities to be unfaithful will take them.)

In the third stanza the speaker seemingly retreats half a step from this extreme conclusion. *If* you find one, he tells his companion, let me know, for it would be sweet to make a "pilgrimage" to see such a saint. But then he retracts this injunction, showing that he has not really retreated at all. Do not tell me, he says, for even were she still true when I received your letter, still, by the time I could complete my journey, were it only next door, she would have proved unfaithful to two or three lovers. His "pilgrimage," he is convinced, would turn out to be a fool's errand. It is as impossible to find a woman both "true and fair" as to catch a falling star.

How seriously are we to take this poem? Should we imagine the speaker or poet as a man extremely embittered from a series of personal betrayals? Possibly. But it is called a "Song," and was indeed written to an "air" already in existence. Its meter is songlike (tetrameter, except for two monometer lines in each stanza). Its riming is copious (alternating in the first four lines, then a couplet of feminine rimes, then three rimes on one sound). Moreover, its images and overstatements are so extreme, or so witty and charming, and its progress so amusing, that it is hard to take the poem gravely. It seems more playful than disenchanted, more entertaining than sad. The poet, one feels, has adopted a fashionably cynical pose and tried to see how ingeniously and entertainingly he could deal with it. In short, the poem—and its speaker—are too lively to be lugubrious. LP

205. *Keith Douglas* **VERGISSMEINNICHT** (page 266)

The setting is probably the North African desert where British forces under General Montgomery fought a prolonged and bitter campaign against German forces under General Rommel ("The Desert Fox") during World War II. The speaker, a British soldier, accompanied by one or more fellow-soldiers, has returned, three weeks afterwards, to the site of a particularly fierce engagement. They find, still sprawled under the barrel of his antitank gun, the body of a German soldier who had made a direct hit on the speaker's tank before being killed. In the gunpit spoil the speaker finds a photograph of the dead German's sweetheart, signed with her name and the German word for "Forget me not." The poem is based on a series of ironies: the inscription "Forget me not" addressed to a soldier incapable now of memory; the fact that the dead soldier's war equipment is still "hard and good" while its user is "decayed"; the horrible contrast between the living man loved by the girl and the corpse with its burst stomach and dusty eyes; the dual nature of man which makes him capable of both love and killing; the fact that the shot aimed at the soldier "has done the lover mortal hurt" (an ironic understatement). What the speaker discovers in the dead German is a man once much like himself. His tone expresses neither enmity, hate, nor triumph, but only pity and shared humanity. The poem may be usefully compared with Hardy's "The Man He Killed" (page 19). LP

206. *Carolyn Forché* **THE COLONEL** (page 267)

The country is El Salvador, as we know from the context in which it appears—Forché's book *The Country Between Us* (New York: Harper & Row, 1981) in which perhaps a third of the poems stem from visits to El Salvador made over a two-year period. Since the students do not have that context, perhaps they should be told beforehand what country is referred to. On the other hand, there may be value in asking them to identify as nearly as possible the locale of the poem. There are sufficient clues to identify the locale as a small Latin American country dominated by American culture and governed by a military regime, against which there is considerable opposition.

The precise date appended at the end suggests that the poem is based on an actual incident. Does this mean that the poem is factual, not fictional? It is written in prose, not verse. How does it differ, then, from a reportorial account? In many ways. No names are named, either of persons or places. The poem is addressed to a particular reader (a "you"), not to a general reader. The poem uses images that would not ordinarily be found in a newspaper account: "The moon swung bare on its black cord over the house." Perhaps most importantly, the last two sentences are surrealistic. They take us into a fantasy world. How distant they are from the first two!

The first two sentences reveal that the poem is a reply to a friend back home. The friend has asked her some such question as "Is it true, as I heard on a news report, that you have been to Colonel _____'s home?" The speaker replies, "I was in his house." The failure to give the "his" an antecedent in the poem, plus the fact that the friend knows his name, suggests that the colonel is well known outside his country and is important within it. His name has appeared in the newspapers. He may be the military dictator; he is at least a member of the ruling military junta. What does he mean when he talks of "how difficult it had become to govern"? What would he consider the signs and purposes of good government?

The central point in this poem lies in the shocking contrast between the civility and the brutality implied by the colonel's life style. The tray of coffee and sugar, the daily papers, the pet dogs, the TV set, the good dinner—all suggest a style of civilized and gracious living such as many in our country enjoy. But the pistol on the cushion, the broken bottles embedded in the walls, the bag of human ears, and the colonel's angry outburst against "rights"—all suggest something quite different. LP

207. Robert Frost ACQUAINTED WITH THE NIGHT (page 268)

At a purely literal level this poem says merely that the poet has taken many walks at night through the city and is thoroughly familiar with its nighttime aspects. But clearly the poem is meant to be read symbolically. The chief symbol is the night, which suggests the darker aspects of existence. But to grasp anything like its full significance, we must examine the details of the poem. The following discussion does not pretend to exhaust their implications.

That the poet has walked out and back in rain indicates that he has endured physical discomfort. That he has walked beyond the furthest city light—beyond the city limits—may suggest that he has "transgressed"—gone beyond legal or moral limits. His having looked down "the saddest city lane" indicates that he has seen the poverty and misery of the city's slum areas. His unwillingness to explain to the watchman what he is doing out so late at night suggests feelings of guilt or embarrassment. The "interrupted cry" across houses from another street—possibly a scream of terror cut short by strangulation—suggests violence and evil. That the cry is not directed toward him suggests his loneliness. The illuminated clock which seems detached from the earth and at "an unearthly height" (because its tower is blotted out by darkness) may at first seem like something supernatural, but is really only a manmade instrument which can "proclaim the time" but cannot judge it. It thus suggests a universe without moral or divine oversight—a universe indifferent to man.

The night in Frost's poem is thus a remarkably subtle and evocative symbol for hardship, guilt, sorrow, loneliness, evil, desolation, and isolation at the personal, social, and cosmic levels. The clock against the sky, man-made but "at an unearthly height," strikingly proclaims the absence of authoritative moral direction, human or superhuman, in an indifferent universe.

And how does the poet respond to this dark perception of the universe? The calm, matter-of-fact tone of voice in the first and final lines counters the dark experience of the intervening lines with a quiet refusal to be daunted. The final line is indeed an understatement. The poet has been more than "acquainted" with the night—he has explored it thoroughly; but his tone of voice says, in effect, "I can take it."

Though the poem resembles a sonnet in containing fourteen lines of iambic pentameter, its rime schemes is that of *terza rima*, made famous by Dante's use of it in *The Divine Comedy*, of which the "Inferno" is the best-known section.

Some critics have read the "luminary clock" as a metaphor for the moon. But (a) one cannot easily tell time by the moon as one can by the sun; it rises at a different hour every day and is often observable in full daylight; (b) this is a city poem, and its imagery is city imagery; (c) if the clock *were* the moon, then the phrase "at an unearthly height" would be literal, obvious, and uninteresting; (d) Frost has himself identified the clock as a tower clock in Ann Arbor [see *Frost: Centennial Essays* (Jackson: Univ. Press of Missippi, 1974), p. 521; and *Frost: Centennial Essays III* (1978), p. 296].

There are excellent discussions of this poem in Reginald L. Cook, *The Dimensions of Robert Frost* (New York: Rinehart, 1958), pp. 107-08; and in Reuben A. Brower, *The Poetry of Robert Frost* (New York: Oxford Univ. Press, 1963), pp. 126-29. LP

208. *Robert Frost* **MENDING WALL** (page 268)

At first reading this poem will seem to be about walls and about two New England farmers who have opposite philosophies concerning them. Each philosophy is stated twice: the speaker's in the first line and in line 35: "Something there is that doesn't love a wall"; the neighboring farmer's in line 27 and in the final line: "Good fences make good neighbors." But as we dig into the poem a little deeper we may conclude that the poem is less about walls and opposed philosophies concerning them than it is about opposed kinds of mental habit. The neighboring farmer's philosophy is clear and definite, and we know exactly where he got it. He got it from his father, who got it from his father, who got it . . . In short, it is a traditional piece of folk wisdom, a proverbial saying which he has accepted as dogma without questioning its meaning or validity. The speaker, on the other hand, states his philosophy more tentatively: "*Something there is* that doesn't love a wall." He seems not quite certain what that "Something" is, though, as a matter of fact, he knows exactly what "spills the upper boulders in the sun" over the winter months. It is "the frozen-ground-swell" underneath the wall: the expansion of the earth caused by the freezing of the moisture always present in the ground. Nature causes the wall to crumble. But he inclines to think there may be more to it than that: not just nature but something *in* nature or in the-nature-of-things "doesn't love" a wall. He hasn't put a label on it. But not only is he more tentative in his thinking than his neighbor, he is also more reflective, thoughtful, and flexible. He has a questioning habit of mind. Of his neighbor's proverbial saying he asks, "*Why* do they make good neighbors? Isn't it / Where there are cows?" ("*Why*" is the kind of question his neighbor has never asked.) But in asking this question, or rather these two questions, he confesses that there is some truth in his neighbor's position, and he identifies exactly the source of that truth. When one or both neighbors own livestock, the wall prevents contention between them by keeping the livestock in their proper fields and keeping one farmer's cows from eating the other's crops. (A "good neighbor," as defined by the proverb, is one whom you can live next to without friction.) The neighbor's attitude toward walls, like most proverbial wisdom, contains a half-truth. ("Look before you leap" and "He who hesitates is lost," though contradictory, both state half-truths; that is, each is true in some situations, neither is true in all situations.) It is now apparent that the speaker's attitude toward walls is not so diametrically opposed to his neighbor's as at first appeared. He recognizes the necessity, the desirability, of *some* walls. Indeed he has all by himself on occasion gone out and "made repair" after hunters have completely torn down part of a wall. Still, the desirability of a wall depends upon the situation, and "here there are no cows." Before *he* built a wall he'd ask what he "was walling in or walling out." He continues to think that there is "Something" that "doesn't love a wall, / That wants it down," but he is not himself opposed to all walls, just unnecessary ones, and especially those that wall in or wall out something that ought not to be walled in or out. However, he is flexible. *He* is the one who contacts his neighbor "at spring mending-time" to let him know when he is available. He knows what his neighbor's attitude toward walls is, and he knows that to stay on neighborly terms with him, he must honor that attitude even while trying to argue him out of it.

But there is much more to the contrast between these two farmers than simply their attitudes toward walls. The speaker is observant: he can tell the difference between the gaps made by the frozen-ground-swell in winter and those made by hunters in other seasons. He knows how handling rocks all day can wear one's fingers "rough." He has imagination, a playful, whimsical turn of mind, and a sense of humor. Some boulders, he observes, are so round that they "have to use a spell to make them balance: / 'Stay where you are until our backs are turned.'" He compares the process of mending wall to "just another game, / One on a side." He anticipates his point about the cows by saying: "My apple trees will never get across / And eat the cones under [your] pines." His perceptiveness is apparent when he thinks about how to explain what the "Something" is that doesn't love a wall. Whatever it is (Love perhaps? Some principle of community or brotherhood?), the speaker knows that, to reach his neighbor's understanding, he must communicate the idea in concrete terms, not in abstractions. He fleetingly thinks of "elves" because his fancy has a fondness for elves and because elves (if one actually believes in them, as the speaker almost surely doesn't) are a physical agency which the neighbor's mind could grasp—and might accept if he were an Irish peasant rather than a New England farmer. But the speaker immediately realizes the absurdity of this explanation and casts it aside, for "it's not elves exactly, and I'd rather / He said it for himself." This last remark shows the speaker's grasp of an important principle of education: that the learner will be much more likely to grasp and accept a concept that he has figured out for himself than one he has merely had *explained* to him (if you want a fancy name for this method of teaching, it's *heuristic*). Thus we find in the speaker a mind that is probing, perceptive, and critical, but also imaginative, whimsical, and playful, though possibly a little indefinite in its inability to define that "Something" even to itself. In the neighbor we see a matter-of-fact, uncritical mind which accepts traditional wisdom unquestioningly and holds on to it dogmatically. It is this contrast of minds that provides the central interest of the poem. In the speaker's perception his neighbor "moves in darkness"—the darkness of ignorance and uncritical acceptance. He sees his neighbor there, "Bringing a stone grasped firmly by the top / In each hand, like an old-stone savage armed." The implications of the simile are two: first, that an unquestioning habit of mind is primitive, like that of paleolithic man; second, that there is something potentially menacing about such a habit of mind. No doubt the speaker and his neighbor will continue to get on amicably enough, and not start throwing rocks at each other: the neighbor is conscientious and hard-working, and both men want to be "good neighbors" in some sense of the term. Nevertheless, it is people shouting slogans, clinging to half-truths dogmatically, who rush into wars against each other and go on "holy crusades." It is this kind of mental set that creates unnecessary "walls" between men, and which "Something" (Love? Reason? Brotherhood?) "wants down."

Such, at least, is my reading (a fairly old-fashioned one) of what has become one of Frost's most controversial poems. On one axis, the range of opinion goes from Robert Graves's statement "If anyone asks: 'But what *is* the something that doesn't love a wall?" the answer is, of course, 'frost'—also its open-hearted namesake, Robert Frost," to Elizabeth Jennings's assertion that "Good fences make good neighbors" is the moral of the poem. On another axis, opinion ranges from Carson Gibbs's assessment of the speaker as "witty, tolerant, and reasonable" to Donald Cunningham's that he is "hollow, vain, and foolish." For varying viewpoints, see Elaine Barry, *Robert Frost* (New York: Ungar, 1973), pp. 109-12; Marie Boroff, *Language and the Poet* (Chicago: Univ. of Chicago Press, 1979), pp. 24-30; Donald Cunningham, "Mending a Wall," in *Gone Into If Not Explained*, ed. Greg Kuzma (Crete, Nebraska: Best Cellar Press, 1976), pp. 65-73; Carson Gibbs, "Mending Wall," *The Explicator*, 20 (Feb. 1962), item 48; Robert Graves, "Introduction," *Selected Poems of Robert Frost* (New York: Holt, 1963), p. xiii; Elizabeth Jennings, *Frost* (New York: Barnes & Noble, 1966), p. 24; John C. Kemp, *Robert Frost and New England* (Princeton, N.J.: Princeton Univ. Press, 1979), pp. 13-26; Frank Lentricchia, *Robert Frost* (Durham, N.C.: Duke Univ. Press, 1973), pp. 104-07; John F. Lynen, *The Pastoral Art of Robert Frost* (New Haven: Yale Univ. Press, 1960), pp. 27-31; Marion Montgomery, "Robert Frost and His Use of Barriers," *South Atlantic Quarterly*, 57 (Sum. 1958), 349-50; Richard Poirier, *Robert Frost* (New York: Oxford Univ. Press, 1977), pp. 104-06; Charles N. Watson, Jr., "Frost's Wall: The View from the Other Side," *New England Quarterly*, 44 (Dec. 1971), 653-56. LP

The other editor speaks

"Good fences make good neighbors" may be the most famous phrase in all of Frost's poetry. Like many famous quotations, it is misleading when quoted out of context or when it is offered as Frost's "philosophy."

The poem is a narrative, restricting itself to the speaker's attitudes. It poses the narrator against his neighbor, as men of two opposing philosophies, and as can be the case when we report our experiences, the narrator is given the privilege of considering his position the correct one. The neighbor is only permitted to speak his famous line, twice; what *he* thinks of the speaker is altogether missing from the poem. It can be instructive to ask a class to imagine exactly what the neighbor might be thinking about the speaker—what a man who "will not go behind his father's saying" (or so the speaker claims) thinks about a man who first informs him it is time to mend the wall, and then wants to ask what walls are for, and who seems to believe in some vague "something . . . that doesn't love a wall."

A proper reading of the poem requires taking into account the limitation and the implicit prejudice that results from one participant's report of a debate, and which naturally renders the resolution suspect: the speaker clearly thinks he has "won" because he is a thinking man who wants "to go behind" rural lore, while his neighbor "moves in darkness" of the mind. The reader also needs to understand the dialectic opposition of the two points of view. The speaker is a man who wants to know the reasons for his actions, who investigates and meditates, who likes to believe (probably thinking himself only whimsical) in the vague "something," in using spells to balance the stones, even—almost—in elves. That is, he is a compound of rationality and a desire to find something beyond rationality. He is also a man of apple orchards, of domestication, of playing games according to equitable rules, who takes pride in being civil and civilized.

Stripped of the prejudiced reporting of the speaker, the neighbor is a man who accepts traditional teachings, who shares in the responsibility of maintaining private property, and whose land is in its natural state, a pine forest. He also believes in neighborliness and the soundness of workmanship. What the speaker's attitude contributes to the portrait of the neighbor reveals more about the speaker than about his opponent in the game of wall-mending. Because of the neighbor's taciturnity, the speaker thinks him shallow-minded, ignorant, primitive, unable to think or investigate. That is, he interprets the neighbor's attitude as further evidence of his own superiority. The man who is different from him is the man who is inferior to him. Does the neighbor go so far in interpreting the speaker's difference?

John F. Lynen points out that the poem presents an unresolved question: "Should man tear down the barriers which isolate individuals from one another, or should he recognize that distinctions and limitations are necessary to human life?" Attempting to answer this question, many readers have tried to pin the poem down to a simple set of paired opposites—liberal and conservative, rational and instinctive, civilized and primitive, and many more. But although the terms of the poem teasingly invite the search for an easy symbolic reading, and also tease the reader into supposing that the speaker is "right," no easy symbols or easy solutions are available. The poem is memorable for the irresolution that keeps us searching.   TRA

209. *Isabella Gardner* **GIMBOLING** (page 269)

For anyone familiar with Lewis Carroll's two *Alice* books, the title of this piece will call to memory that delightful piece of nonsense verse "Jabberwocky," at the end of the first chapter of *Through the Looking-Glass*. It begins, "'Twas brillig, and the slithy toves / Did gyre and gimble in the wabe." In a later chapter, Humpty-Dumpty "explains" the poem to Alice. *Brillig* means "four o'clock in the afternoon—the time you begin *broiling* things for dinner." *Slithy* means "lithe and slimy." It is "like a portmanteau"—it has "two meanings packed up into one word." *Toves* are "something like badgers—something like lizards—and . . . something like corkscrews" and "they make their nests under sun-dials." To *gyre* is to "go round and round like a gyroscope," and to *gimble* is "to make holes like a gimlet." The *wabe* is "the grass-plot round a sun-dial," so-called "because it goes a long way before it, and a long way behind it—and a long way beyond it on each side."

Does this allusion to "Jabberwocky" help us in understanding "Gimboling"? Perhaps in part. Both poems have the power of seeming to be nonsense and at the same time to be making some strange kind of sense if we could only just grasp it. But there are differences as well. The chief difficulty in "Jabberwocky" is produced by the strange words used—nonsensical words, not found in the dictionary. In "Gimboling" the difficulty lies mainly in the grammar—what do all those adjectives (*Nimble, sleek, supple, compliant, folding* and *unfolding*) modify? The words themselves are all straightforward except for *gimble* and *gimboling*. But in them too we face a puzzle. The present participle of *gimble* would be *gimbling*, not *gimboling*. Why does Gardner make this change? Perhaps she is making her own portmanteau word, combining *gimble* with *gamboling*, meaning frolicsome play. And indeed, gamboling seems to be the chief activity of the poem. The poet is gamboling with the sounds of words, and the whatever-it-is or the whatever-they-are are gamboling with each other in the water.

And here is another difference. The activities in Gardner's poem take place in an underwater world, not in front of a sun-dial. Perhaps *wabe* made Gardner think of wave? In any event these activities are playful and erotic yet innocent. No moral judgments apply. The last two lines perhaps explain why. They speak of "the sweet waking / the floating ashore into sleep and to morning." Perhaps this underwater world is a dream world, and its entire content is a dreaming? That would account for its vagueness, its suggestiveness, and its lack of logical connections.

In discussing this poem I have used many *perhapses*. But of one thing we may be certain. The poet is gamboling or gimboling with the music of words. Perhaps we should just sit back and enjoy it. LP

210. *Christopher Gilbert* **PUSHING** (page 270)

Lines 21-22 generalize the central idea of the poem, though with enough vagueness of specificity to invite a symbolic interpretation. They define two kinds of motive—desire and rebellion against limits or restrictions. The title refers to the second of these, and is exemplified by two of the three events in the poem—the boys' "pushing" beyond the limits of the shop-owner's restrictions (returning to "try his nerve again") and their throwing snowballs at the sun. The shop-owner too pushes, not as a means of going beyond limits but in order to establish them: "'buy something or else you got to leave.'" The narrator, being pressed by his young brother to explain why they push against the restriction (knowing as they both do that what they "want" is to be warmed), finally comes up with his "guess" about the second kind of motive.

The things that the boys "can't" do include both the naturally and the artificially prohibited: they cannot own the cars they name nor escape the restrictions imposed by the store owner, both examples of limits placed by social and economic forces; nor can they alter the cold weather or hit the sun with their snowballs. The word "can't" nicely represents the two kinds of limit: strictly defined, it refers to absolute impossibility—if you cannot, you cannot; but its colloquial usage, as a substitute for "may not," refers to the prohibitions of social order. What the older boy is learning (and teaching) is that the apparent impossibility of a task should provoke you to try to do it, rather than to accept inability. "Pushing" is an appropriate title, for it does not offer any false promise of achievement, only an attitude toward restriction.

One may infer from line 9 ("a decent White man") that the speaker, like the poet, is black, and that the restrictions presented in the poem symbolize conditions beyond the rules shop-owners make to protect themselves from "big-eyed" boys and what they are "up to" in loitering in the aisles.   TRA

211. *Robert Graves*   **DOWN, WANTON, DOWN** (page 270)

See No. 230 (Sharon Olds)

212. *Thomas Hardy*   **CHANNEL FIRING** (page 271)

Hardy's dating of this poem may make it seem prophetic, since World War I broke out in August, 1914; but it was a prophecy almost anyone could have made, for the event referred to in line 1 was well known: the Royal Navy was conducting gunnery practice in the English Channel, and the guns could be heard many miles inland. (Hardy is reported to have been surprised, in fact, that the war began only a few months afterward.)

The speaker in the poem is one of the dead, presumably a clergyman buried within the chancel of his church where the clergy were usually interred; he is familiar with the altar, chancel windows, and "glebe cow," and seems to be in the habit of having chats with others buried nearby, including "Parson Thirdly." The folklike simplicity of the poem, achieved through its tetrameter quatrains and simple diction, makes the whole experience seem rustic and unsophisticated, the material of a ballad. The dead have been awakened by the great guns ("loud enough to wake the dead," we might say), and at first they suppose that "Judgment-day" has come. The noise has even terrified the hounds, the churchmouse, the worms, and the cow —not because they anticipate the apocalypse, of course, but because they instinctively fear loud sounds.

God, however, sardonic but comforting, tells the dead to return to their sleep: it's only men threatening men, not a divine event. Although many men *deserve* to go to hell, God has not destroyed the world, nor does he seem to want to anytime soon, for he takes pity on mankind's need for "rest eternal."

Parson Thirdly's reaction to this news in the penultimate stanza is pragmatic: if God is not going to separate the sheep from the goats, it might have been more pleasant to have "stuck to pipes and beer" instead of depriving himself for the sake of piety.

The tone of the poem shifts markedly in the last stanza. Instead of the folk narrative of the speaker and the paternal chattiness of God, the last stanza turns to brooding lyricism. Alliteration, consonance, and assonance (*r*oaring/*r*eadiness; aga*in*/gu*ns*; hou*r*/*r*oaring; *r*e*a*diness/*a*venge) pack the first two lines. The last two abound in *st* and *t* sounds: *St*our*t*on *T*ower, Camelo*t*, *st*arli*t St*onehenge; and the last two feet in this iambic poem are trochees, mysteriously trailing off in the mournful music that the theme demands. The bulk of the poem has been whimsical, folksy, and not particularly alarming—ironically, since the subjects have included naval bombardment, skeletons, damnation and piety, and God's potential wrath; but the theme is the persistence among men of aggression, violence, and the recurrence of military conquest to establish and maintain civilization. God (who tends to speak in clichés, the rustic father of his rustic flock) puts it directly: "The world is as it used to be."

A "glebe cow" is pastured in the parcel of land allotted to a clergyman as part of his benefice; like the land and the parsonage, it is provided for his use but is not his private property. The name "Parson Thirdly" may allude to the Holy Trinity; a Parson Thirdly is a character in Hardy's novel *Far from the Madding Crowd*. The spelling "Christès" (line 15) is archaic, in keeping with the ballad style and the time references implicit in the last stanza.

For further discussion see: Babette Deutsch, *Poetry in Our Time* (Garden City, N.Y.: Anchor/Doubleday, 1963), pp. 9-10; John Crowe Ransom, "Introduction" to *Selected Poems of Thomas Hardy* (New York: Macmillan, 1961), pp. x-xii; Cleanth Brooks and Robert Penn Warren, *Understanding Poetry* (New York: Holt, 1976), pp. 45-48; J. O. Bailey, *The Poetry of Thomas Hardy: A Handbook and Commentary* (Chapel Hill, N.C.: Univ. of North Carolina Press, 1970), pp. 262-64.
TRA

213. *A. E. Housman* BREDON HILL (page 272)

The poem is dominated by the imagery of bells, their chiming partly conveyed by the three rimes in each stanza. But the bells have a different meaning for the speaker at different times in the poem, and in this difference the drama of the poem lies.

In stanzas 1-4 the speaker recalls summer Sunday mornings spent with his sweetheart on Bredon Hill. They heard the bells ringing for church service in "steeples far and near." Though heedless of the summons, they found the ringing a "happy noise," for it formed a background to their delight in each other. That she preferred his company over going to church probably made the bells even sweeter to the speaker, and he would call back to them, "Oh, peal upon our wedding" and we will come "in time."

In stanzas 5-6, however, we learn that the girl went to church that winter, not for a wedding but for a funeral service—her own. "Unbeknown" to her lover, she had died and gone to church (was carried there in her coffin) without him. Only one bell was tolled—a bell in only one church, and only one bell of its set of bells—the funeral bell.

In the final stanza the lover again hears the bells ringing on Bredon as he had that summer. But they no longer make a "happy noise"; they only remind him more keenly of his lost happiness. In accents of extreme bitterness he cries out (futilely) to bid them "Be dumb," and with almost surly resignation adds, "I hear you, I will come." He will come when he is ready, either to mourn at his sweetheart's grave or to be buried himself.

Bredon Hill is in Worcestershire close to the Shropshire border: these are the two shires mentioned in line 3. From the top of Bredon on a clear day one can see three additional counties—Herefordshire, Warwickshire, and Gloucestershire. The image of "colored counties" (8) conflates that of farmland laid out in plots of different colored crops with a map showing the counties in different colors. LP

214. *A. E. Housman* TO AN ATHLETE DYING YOUNG (page 273)

The speaker is a fellow townsman of the dead athlete, possibly (though not necessarily) one of the pallbearers carrying his coffin to the cemetery for burial. The athlete had died within months of winning the annual race for his town. The poem is an extended apostrophe addressed by the speaker to the athlete.

The parallelism of action and language between the first two stanzas beautifully underscores the ironic contrast in situation. After his victory in the race, the townspeople had "chaired" him (borne him in triumph on their shoulders) through the market-place to his home. Now, less than a year later, they bring him "home" again, again "shoulder-high." But the meaning of "home" has changed between the two stanzas. In the second it is a metaphor for the grave. The "road all runners come" is death, and the youth is being borne "shoulder-high" in his coffin. The "town" to which he now belongs ("stiller"—an understatement—than that which noisily "cheered" just a few months ago) is the cemetery or necropolis (*city of the dead*).

The chief ironic shock of the poem, however, comes in the third stanza. Most people would consider the death of a young athlete at the peak of his ability an occasion for lamentation; the speaker considers it one for congratulation. "Smart lad," he says (not *Poor lad*), and proceeds to praise the young athlete for dying "betimes." Except for his hyperbolic use of the word "Smart" when he literally means *fortunate* (the athlete did not commit suicide), the speaker is perfectly serious, and speaks for the poet; that is, the irony involved here is neither verbal nor dramatic but situational. Both speaker and poet regard the athlete as fortunate; the irony lies in the discrepancy between our expectation (initiated by the title and sustained through the first two stanzas) that the athlete's death will be regarded by the poet as pathetic or "tragic" and our discovery that it is regarded quite otherwise.

In the rest of the poem the speaker supports this attitude and is not undercut by the poet. The athlete has "slipped away" from "fields where glory does not stay." It is better, the speaker feels, to die when everyone is singing your praises than to die in obscurity years later (as so many once-celebrated athletes do). The "fields where glory does not stay" are literally athletic fields, symbolically earth or life in general; the "glory" is fame and the pride of triumph. The "laurel" is the symbol, not just of victory (the ancient Greeks awarded a laurel wreath or "crown" to victors in the Pythian games) but of fame. The "rose" is traditionally a symbol for a girl's beauty. Though athletic fame is won by young men at an early age, the speaker declares, its duration is even shorter than a young woman's beauty. This runner, who set a new record for the course he ran, will not be alive to see his record broken; the silence that would have greeted his future athletic decline will sound "no worse than cheers" (an ironical understatement: he will be aware of neither) now that he is dead. In stanza 5 the speaker praises the athlete for having won (metaphorically) one more race: he has raced his fame to the grave and has arrived there first (has died while his name is still unforgotten). In stanza 6 the speaker again speaks to the athlete as if he had some choice in the matter, and urges him to set his "fleet foot on the sill of shade / And hold to the low lintel up / The still-defended challenge-cup." The "sill of shade" is the threshold of the door to the tomb, the "low lintel" is the crosspiece over it. The "still-defended challenge cup" (his trophy) is the kind that has the winner's name inscribed on it each year and which the winner is allowed to keep until he is defeated, when it passes into the hands of the new winner. This athlete has died with the challenge-cup still in his possession.

The last stanza contains a sophisticated literary allusion that supports some identification of the speaker with the poet (Housman was a celebrated classical scholar). In Book XI of the *Odyssey*, when Odysseus visits the Greek underworld (Hades), he is surrounded by shades of the "strengthless" dead. Since these shades are depicted as peculiarly impotent—strengthless and senseless—Housman is not predicting here some kind of immortality for the dead athlete, but simply making one more contrast between what he was in life and what he will become in death, "strengthless" and senseless. Nevertheless, these shades will find "unwithered" on his head the laurel garland (fame) "briefer than a girl's" rose garland (beauty). The last two lines of the poem allude to the symbols of stanza 3.

Housman in this poem dwells on the transience of youth, fame, and beauty, and on the desirability of dying while one still has them rather than after they are lost. It is a theme that appears elsewhere in his poetry (see especially *A Shropshire Lad*, XXIII and XLIV—"The lads in their hundreds" and "Shot? so quick, so clean an ending?"). It reflects one part of Housman's mind but not the whole of it, as can be seen from "Terence, this is stupid stuff" (page 14) and "Loveliest of trees" (page 76). LP

215. *Randall Jarrell* **THE DEATH OF THE BALL TURRET GUNNER** (page 274)

The poem captures both the terror and the ironic humor of its subject in the phrase "washed me out," which takes literally the euphemism for the failure to qualify for military duty. Rather than failing to measure up to training standards, the speaker has been so mutilated that his body must be flushed from his turret by a water hose.

The poem refers explicitly to the U.S. Army Air Corps in World War II. The B-17 "Flying Fortress" bombers had a gunner's glass turret on the belly of the fuselage, and airmen wore fur-lined leather jackets; anti-aircraft shells were called "flak" as an acronym for the German word "Fliegerabwehrkanone," though the shorter word sounds like an onomatopoetic imitation of the noise of the explosion; and the bombers were attacked by squadrons of fighter planes.

The first three lines of the poem abound with musical devices, chiefly alliteration (*sleep, state; loosed, life; fell, fur, froze*) and assonance (*mother's, hunched; fell, belly, wet; sleep, dream*). These culminate in the internal rime "black flak," whose flat *a* and harsh *k* sharply bring to a halt such devices. After this rime, the only musical device is the concluding and horrifying rime "froze / hose." This pattern of sounds reinforces the irony of the poem's conclusion.

The metaphors of the first two lines create a parallel between the position of the unborn child in his mother's womb and the man's position in the "belly" of the bomber. The movement from one to the other is ominously referred to as falling, and the animal processes of generation and birth are obliquely implied in "my wet fur." The speaker seems to pass directly from the moment of birth to his place in the gun turret, and his existence is governed by the dreams of his mother (for her child's success, happiness, and safety) and the subsequent dream of the "State" (for its own safety and its national ideals). These dreams are both shattered when, flying above 30,000 feet, he is shocked by the shells of anti-aircraft guns to the opposite kind of dream, the nightmare of attacking fighter planes. He awakens from idealistic dreams to discover that reality is a nightmare, but his wakefulness lasts only a moment. TRA

216. *Ellen Kay* **PATHEDY OF MANNERS** (page 274)

Though it wittily satirizes certain modes of social behavior, this poem does not quite fit the literary category of "comedy of manners," for it has no happy ending; nor does it fit the category of "tragedy," for it does not dramatize the sudden "fall" from high to low estate of a protagonist of heroic stature. It is accurately labeled a "Pathedy of Manners," for it concerns the pathetic waste of life and talent by a woman whose false values made her prefer appearance to substance and choose manners over merit. Inasmuch as her false values are also those of a class, the poem presents a form of social pathology.

Brilliant, beautiful, and wealthy, the woman of the poem wasted her gifts on inauthentic goals. She might have made some great and useful contribution to humanity; instead she chose to shine in fashionable society, and expended herself in acquiring the superficial graces to make her successful there. She learned to distinguish authentic pearls from paste (in necklaces or cufflinks) and to tell real Wedgwood from a fraud, but she let fashionable opinion ("cultured jargon") govern her artistic tastes rather than a truly formed and independent judgment. Back home from the obligatory trip abroad, she made an "ideal" marriage (that is, she married a man with impeccable social credentials) and had "ideal" (well-behaved, well-dressed, clean) but lonely children, in an "ideal" (fashionably situated and well-appointed) house. (The thrice-repeated adjective exemplifies verbal irony.)

Now at forty-three, her husband dead and her children grown, she is going through a middle-age crisis, reevaluating her life and regretting that it has not been more meaningful. She "toys" with the idea of taking a new direction, but it is too late. The phrase "kill time" (19) has a double meaning. She would like to destroy the time lost since her college years, but she can only waste time by dreaming of doing so. Her dreams of taking up that lost opportunity are only an illusion; and she can only "re-wed" (another double meaning) these illusions. Unable to pursue an independent course of action, she can only fend off "doubts" (about the value of her present life) with "nimble talk." Though a hundred socially elite acquaintances call her, she is without a single intimate friend. The poem ends with a brilliant combination of pun and paradox. "Her meanings lost in manners, she will walk / Alone in brilliant circles to the end." In terms of true intimacy she will be alone, although she will move in brilliant social circles to the end of her life; in terms of meaningful living she will walk in circles till the end of her life, not advance along a line of significant purpose.

The speaker is probably a college classmate of the protagonist, who has seen her the day before, roughly a quarter-century after their first acquaintance. This meeting has caused the narrator to reflect on the protagonist's life. LP

217. *John Keats* **LA BELLE DAME SANS MERCI** (page 275)

Vocabulary: *sedge* (3), *haggard* (6), *meads* (13), *zone* (18), *manna* (26), *grot* (29), *thrall* (40), *starved* (41), *gloam* (41).

Even with full explication, this literary ballad retains its air of melancholy mystery, because the meaning of the encounter between the knight and the faery lady is never made explicit. This sense of an unresolved riddle is characteristic of many folk ballads, and it may be that Keats was after no more in the poem than a narration of fairyland and dream omens. When the knight concludes "this is why I sojourn here," the reader might very well reiterate the narrator's opening question, for the events reported by the knight don't seem to account for his despair, his physical debility and suffering, which are what the narrator has asked about.

The three opening stanzas ask the question—"what can ail thee?"—and describe the landscape and the knight. Both are incongruous, the speaker reports: knights should be hearty, purposeful, strong, not pale and feverish; they should be in quest of adventure, not "loitering" beside the dried marsh grass at a lakeside; it is early winter, and the natural creatures have withdrawn either to more congenial climates or to their stored-up winter hoards. This is no place for a knight, nor despite his armor does this man seem heroic.

The tale of the knight's encounter with the faery connects her with the fullness of nature: like an animal, light-footed and wild-eyed, she is met in a meadow, and the knight bedecks her with nature's flowers, and as if rescuing a lost maiden sets her on his horse, rapt with her beauty and her song. (But lines 19-20 ambiguously report her initial response to him: does "as" mean "while," or does it mean "as if"?) Like a goddess of nature, the lady repays his adoration with nature's plenty, and speaks to him an unknown language; surely, he supposes, she is saying she loves him. Strangely, once she has taken him to her cave, her "sweet moan" becomes weeping and sighing, and he must tame her by kissing her "wild wild eyes"; again, as if in repayment, she lulls him to sleep, but that sleep turns to nightmare with a dream that began in the cave and continues to be repeated here on the "cold hill side" where he awakens and the narrator finds him. The dream is apparently of his precursors, vigorous kings, princes and knights, now in the paleness of death as he will be, warning him that he has been enslaved by "La Belle Dame sans Merci."

Obviously, what a reader wants to know is "who *is* this beautiful woman without pity, and why has she done this to the man?" Does what happened to the knight have any relevance to our lives? Does the poem do more than warn us against sexual indulgence? One plausible (but by no means the only or inevitable) interpretation links the poem with the processes of nature and human attitudes toward them. The first three stanzas establish a sense of appropriate behavior as the seasons change, and of appropriate actions for people: in winter, squirrels, birds, even grasses retreat before the coldness and dryness, and wandering knights with their manly strength should be leading their active lives where they can perform their heroic deeds. But this man has fallen in love with the beauty and wildness of nature, and supposes that she loves him, and that he can tame her and live with her. What his horrid dream discloses is that this is illusion, and that by loving her he has become her thrall. His fate is the fate of all men—death—but he must also languish in despair because he has set his heart on what must always be changing. TRA

218. *John Keats* ODE ON A GRECIAN URN (page 277)

Like other poems by Keats (e.g., "Ode to a Nightingale"), this ode explores the human desire to escape the inevitable effects of living in a temporal world, expressing this desire in response to the permanence of an art object. The poem is a meditation on the continuing beauty of a painted vase from classical Greece and what it seems to communicate to a man who knows his time on earth is brief by comparison. The structure is a dramatic enactment of the stages of the speaker's emotion and imaginative projection.

The poem opens with the speaker praising the urn's calm stillness and its freedom from the ravages of time. Punning on the word "still," Keats encapsulates his attitude: the urn is both silent and unmoving, and it still exists in time. Like the maidens painted on its surface, it has retained its virginal beauty as well as the freshness of a bride. In the paintings on the vase he sees a similarly tantalizing doubleness: they seem to have narrative meaning, displaying figures (human or divine) in a state of motion, yet as paintings they cannot move. He asks, in the last six lines of the first stanza, a sequence of increasingly insistent questions: to what narrative events do the paintings refer?

In the second stanza, however, he changes his attitude, presumably in the light of his not receiving answers to his questions. (In Keats's odes there is a skillful manipulation of psychological transitions that occur *between* the stanzas, where changes of thought and feeling are only implied by what precedes and follows the break.) The speaker moves from the excited forcefulness of his questions to a calm denial of the validity of answers. He now prefers *not* to hear the narrative facts that the urn will not reveal, and relishes instead the "unheard melodies" of feelings without explicit meanings. In lines 15-20, he turns to one of the scenes on the urn: a pastoral scene in which one youth makes music, a tune played on pipes, while another, a "bold lover," is about to capture a maiden he pursues. The speaker celebrates the fact that this amorous pursuit will never end—neither in "winning" the woman nor in losing her. Since they are permanently frozen in a painting, the youth will continue to exist in his state of anticipation just as her beauty will never fade.

The third stanza extends the speaker's delight in the image of time stopped at the height of anticipated bliss: the pictured trees will never be subject to seasonal change, the piper will never tire of playing, and the unfulfilled lover will be forever young and forever in the excitement of desire. This is contrasted with the state of "breathing human passion," which is subject not only to the debility of time but also, more emphatically, to the certainty that continued intensity of feeling would finally exhaust and sicken a mortal human being. Human passion such as the speaker is capable of feeling would ultimately become cloying or feverish, a fact previously implied in the excessiveness of the line the speaker devised to describe the permanence of bliss: "More happy love! more happy, happy love!"

Perhaps because he has exhausted his own capacity to respond to the scene of the piper and the lover, or perhaps because he recognizes that his ecstatic description has become "cloyed," or perhaps because his celebration of the lover's happiness has led him to think of the reality of the human condition—that is, for a number of psychological reasons implied between the stanzas—the speaker in stanza four turns to a second scene, on the other side of the urn. A priest ("mysterious," because he is an initiate in secret rituals, and because he is himself a mystery to the speaker) is leading a heifer bedecked for ritual sacrifice, and a crowd of worshippers follows. Like the end of the first stanza, the beginning of the fourth presents the speaker asking for information: who are the people? what or where is the altar? The priest's mystery extends beyond his religious rites to envelop the whole scene. Imaginatively stepping beyond the pictured scene, the speaker asks further: if these people are here, what has happened to the place they have come from? Line 38 is a turning point in the poem, for the speaker for the first time projects his imagination to a place not actually portrayed on the urn—he tries to create an image to answer his question, the image of an empty, abandoned town.

The psychological space between the fourth and fifth stanzas is the most striking in the poem. In his desire to penetrate beyond the pictured events, the speaker had created an image of desolation, an emotional contrast to the permanent anticipation of the lover or of the priest and worshippers. He discovers that such permanence as he has been praising implies other "still" moments of opposite emotional meanings. While some people are frozen in their state of desire (both lover and worshipper), he can imagine other scenes of permanent desolation.

In the fifth stanza the speaker recoils from what his imagination has produced. The urn is no longer a "sylvan historian," a source of feeling and meaning—it is now, as he willfully distances himself from his projected feelings, a "shape" covered with "marble men and maidens," a "silent form." It has tantalized him into expressing his own desires for permanence (ideas that "thought" could not support, any more than thought can encompass "eternity"). He has been tempted in the course of his meditation to celebrate a pastoral would of idealized love and perfection, but he now recognizes that it is not the warm, sunny world he wanted, but a world gone cold with the realization that the stoppage of time necessary for its perfection implies the permanence not only of love's anticipation but also of loneliness and desolation.

The last five lines, with their famous simplifying tautology that "beauty is truth, truth beauty," comment ironically on the value of the urn as a source of wisdom or feeling. It will outlive the generations of man, and will retain its beauty while human beauty fades. Though its beauty makes it seem friendly, its philosophical advice can never satisfy someone in quest of the meaning of change and transience. The urn can only say "is," not "will be," and thus though it will outlast the life of a human being, it cannot give any information that will make his passage through a lifetime any more meaningful. The urn beautifully exists beyond time (as the speaker had said in the first stanza), and cannot teach the meaning of living *in* time.
TRA

219. *John Keats* ODE TO A NIGHTINGALE (page 278)

The thematic elements of this great poem are at the heart of Keats's work: poetry, human misery, time and change, and the power of sensations. The speaker, moved by the beauty of a nightingale singing, wishes he could join with the bird and escape "the weariness, the fever, and the fret" of human existence. At first he supposes that wine might be the vehicle, but then decides that the poetic imagination will serve him better; and no sooner has he said so than he feels himself transported on "viewless wings of Poesy" to be with the bird. Unable to see in the darkness, he can only guess by scent at the richness of nature, all of it partaking of the "fast fading" intensity of growth and decay. Still listening in the dark, he recalls his repeated wish to escape the world through death, and that desire seems even more intense as he is ravished by the beauty of the bird's song.

But the nightingale is a bird of life, not of death—it is immortal in the sense that nightingales have flourished in ancient days, in biblical days, and even in legends and fairy tales. Yet through all the past and in fiction, the word "forlorn" has existed, as the speaker discovers to his chagrin when his imagination leads him to re-create an image out of fairy land. He discovers as well that though the imagination can cheat us out of our grasp of reality for a time, the power to think and understand will once again intrude. To use the word "forlorn" in imagining a fairy world is to invite the analytic mind to see that one is not in fact "with" the bird, but alone, a "sole self." Returning to one's own reality also leads to the recognition that the song of a nightingale is the creation of a living thing, and it too will fade, move away, and finally die away, "buried deep" in another valley.

The poem ends in a state of puzzlement: was the experience a "vision" (revealing a supernatural reality) or a "waking dream" of what can never be? Without the actual stimulus of the singing bird, without its music, the speaker is left to ask which is the true state of awareness—this present, grasping the literal reality of existence, or that moment of poetic transport?

This brief outline of the poem does not pretend to exhaust its richness, nor even to touch upon all its complex concerns. Many valuable comments have been written, of which the following are recommended. The most helpful single volume for study of this poem is *Twentieth Century Interpretation of Keats's Odes*, ed. Jack Stillinger (Englewood Cliffs, N.J.: Prentice Hall, 1968). Besides Stillinger's excellent introductory essay, it contains the essays by Brooks and Fogle separately listed below and a note by Anthony Hecht. Additional useful references include Harold Bloom, *The Visionary Company* (New York: Doubleday Anchor, 1961), pp. 427-32; Cleanth Brooks, *Understanding Poetry*, 3rd ed. (New York: Holt, 1960), pp. 44-47; Douglas Bush, *John Keats: His Life and Writing* (New York: Macmillan, 1966), pp. 132-38; Morris Dickstein, *Keats and His Poetry* (Chicago: Univ. of Chicago Press, 1971), pp. 205-21; Richard Harter Fogle, "Keats's Ode to a Nightingale," *PMLA*, 68 (1953), 211-22; F. R. Leavis, *Revaluation* (New York: Norton, 1963), pp. 244-52; H. M. McLuhan, "Aesthetic Pattern in Keats's Odes," *University of Toronto Quarterly*, 12 (Jan. 1943), 175-79; David Perkins, "The Ode to a Nightingale," in *Keats: A Collection of Critical Essays*, ed. Walter Jackson Bate (Englewood Cliffs, N.J.: Prentice-Hall, 1964), pp. 103-11, reprinted from David Perkins, *The Quest for Permanence* (Cambridge, MA: Harvard Univ. Press, 1959), pp. 244-57; Stuart M. Sperry, *Keats the Poet* (Princeton, N.J.: Princeton Univ. Press, 1973), pp. 262-67; and Helen Vendler, *The Odes of John Keats* (Cambridge, MA: Harvard Univ. Press, 1983), pp. 77-109. TRA

220. *Galway Kinnell* **BLACKBERRY EATING** (page 280)

In this brief poem Galway Kinnell uses gustatory imagery with gusto. The taste of those "fat, overripe, icy, black blackberries" is conveyed from the speaker's tongue to the reader's imagination so vividly as almost to make the reader's mouth water. The vivid gustatory image is compounded with visual imagery ("fat," "black") and tactile imagery ("icy"). There is tactile imagery also in "the stalks very prickly" where the repeated k-sound (which also picks up the k's in "black" and "breakfast" of the preceding line) reinforces the prickliness. Then, since the speaker is a poet as well as a blackberry-eater, he notes that the "ripest" berries "fall almost unbidden to [his] tongue, / as words sometimes do." The poet slyly uses the word "tongue" in two senses here, first as an organ of taste and then as an articulator of speech. Notice that blackberries (like raspberries, dewberries, and loganberries; unlike blueberries, cherries, and grapes) are composed of many smaller parts (called drupelets). The words that he especially loves, like the blackberries, come in "fat" little lumps: they are "one-syllabled" but "many-lettered." The words "strengths" and "squinched," both containing nine letters, are according to authorities the longest monosyllabic words in the language (*squinch*, to be found only in an unabridged dictionary, is a dialect word meaning to twist). But notice that the speaker demonstrates his love for such words not only by his two examples but by choosing three seven-lettered monosyllabic words ("squeeze," "squinch," and "splurge") for his verbs in the final clause of the poem.

The speaker's favorite word in this poem, however, is "black." It occurs three times by itself and four more times as part of "blackberries." We may profitably examine its three solo appearances. In its initial use, "black blackberries" (2), it may at first seem a redundant, but it is not, for unripe blackberries are green, and the speaker is emphasizing that these berries are ripe or overripe. The poet must have chuckled to himself when the next phrase fell "almost unbidden" to his tongue. He was so charmed that he invented a whimsical myth to go with it. The blackberry stalks were given their prickles as a penalty for knowing "the black art" (5) of blackberry-making! This myth obviously lacks the magnitude of the myth of Adam and Eve in the garden, which inspired Milton to write *Paradise Lost* (the prickles are a "penalty," not a punishment), but it is perfectly sized for the brief poem Kinnell puts it in, and is a delightful spin-off from the phrase "the black art." The black arts are ordinarily the arts practiced by witches and conjurors for unauthorized and wicked purposes, but in Kinnell's poem the phrase is stripped of all of its negative implications. The art of making blackberries is a black art only in that it produces black berries; the word is placed in a context where it means only good, not bad. Finally, in its last two lines, the poem gives us a "black language" of "blackberry-eating," thus completing the metaphorical comparison between blackberries and words—both of them good. The image of "black language" may summon up for the reader the image of black words printed on white paper; but in any form it calls up an experience of pleasure and delight. LP

221. *Etheridge Knight* THE WARDEN SAID TO ME (page 281)

As an example of verbal irony, this poem requires the reader to recognize the distance between the speaker's expressed attitude and his real intention. The repeated parenthetical phrase "(innocently, I think)" has two distinct meanings. In line 2, it pretends to allow the possibility that the warden's bigotry is merely ignorant and therefore excusable; in line 6, it indicates that the speaker intends to seem obsequious and ignorant, to please the warden. These phrases are verbally ironic, since the speaker does not accept the warden's mock ignorance as a sufficient excuse for his bigotry, nor is the speaker sincerely innocent in his rejoinder.

The warden's purpose in asking the question is also verbal irony used in the service of sarcasm: he does not want to know *why* his black prisoners don't attempt to escape, but rather is taunting the black speaker with the fact that they are more stupid, obedient, passive. It is that taunt which the speaker answers with stereotyped gesture and statement: "yes, sir, we cast our eyes down and scratch our heads when we have to answer hard questions, and we finally come up with the simple fact that you already know—there's no place for a black man in this world."

What the speaker means, of course, is that a society constructed on the lines approved by the warden, in which color defines attitude and ability, excludes *all* thoughtful and sensitive people. TRA

222. *George MacBeth* BEDTIME STORY (page 281)

"Bedtime Story" is science fiction in poetic form. The speaker is a parent (mother or father) telling a "bedtime story" to a child of its species; but this story is supposed to be true—a chapter from history (19), not a "fairy tale." It concerns the accidental killing of the last man, "the penultimate primate" (the ultimate primate being the monkey or ape that the man was stalking), the extinction of the human race as a species. The time of the telling of this story is, from our point of view, in a far far distant future; and the time of the incident which it concerns is, from our point of view, still a distant future; but from the teller's point of view it is in a remote past—not "Once upon a time," but "Long long ago when the world was a wild place . . . ."

The speaker is a huge ant, evolved in size and intelligence from presently existing species. Because of the Queen and the sting, students may suggest a bee. But ants too have queens and stings, and these insects "march" rather than fly through the forest; they are organized in a military fashion (in "brigades"); they forage for greenfly (a kind of aphid that some ants keep like cows and "milk"); and their jaws cut through bark. Ants, moreover, have developed a high degree of social organization and cooperation and are thought by many to be the nearest competitors to man in the struggle for existence. In the poem they have become the dominant species, are larger than men, have developed a language and a recorded history, and have an ethical sense superior to man's.

Although this "bedtime story" tells how the last man was inadvertently killed by a soldier ant, the point of the poem is that man has destroyed himself—or, since the poem is set in the future, may destroy himself. Two facts are stated about man: that he exterminates other species of animals "for pleasure," and that he kills his own kind in wars that "extinguished the cities." The poem is thus an indictment of man's passion for killing and a prediction that unless he acquires the power to govern himself by peaceable methods and becomes as "humane" to other species as the ants in the poem, he will be replaced by another form of life.

The conclusion of the poem links the fate of man with that of the dodo. Dodos are a presently extinct species with a reputation for foolishness. "Dumb as a dodo" is a familiar expression.

The poem is written in dactylic lines of four feet in the first three lines of each stanza and two feet in the last. The phrasing and run-on lines make it difficult to read trippingly, however, and it should not be read so. LP

223. *Naomi Long Madgett* MIDWAY (page 282)

Line 5 establishes the speaker of the poem as a black, and the context, especially the second stanza, shows that she is speaking not as an individual but as a representative or embodiment of her race. The "you" of the poem is obviously the white race, and the journey imagery throughout the poem ("Midway," "I've come this far," "turn back," "destination") is a metaphor for the struggle of American black people to overcome their cruel subjugation by the white race and to achieve freedom and equality (both *de jure* and *de facto*). The mountains looming ahead represent the obstacles to be surmounted before the destination is reached.

This song of determination is remarkable for its aggressive use of musical devices (alliteration in "Mighty mountains," assonance in "prayed and slaved and waited," alliteration plus consonance in "sung my song," and especially the patterned feminine end rime in lines 3-4 of each stanza, which surprisingly turns up again as internal rime in the fifth lines).

But this song of purposefulness gains its greatest force from the skillful and varied use of its swinging dipodic meter (see pp. 184-85), with regular alternation of heavier and lighter stress given to the stressed syllables, from the syncopation provided by the spondees ending lines 1, 2, and 5 of each stanza, and from the effect of runover feet at the ends of lines 3 and 4. The metrical pattern is repeated identically, so the scansion of the first stanza will illustrate:

i've *COME* / this FAR to *FREE-* / dom AND i *WON'T* / TURN *BACK.* /
i'm *CLIMB-* / -ing TO the *HIGH-* / way FROM my *OLD* / DIRT *TRACK.* /
   i'm *COM-* / ing AND i'm *GO-* / ing
   AND i'm *STRETCH-* / ing AND i'm *GROW-* / ing
AND i'll *REAP* / what I'VE been *SOW-* / ing OR my *SKIN'S* / NOT *BLACK.*

The sound of runover feet is the result of the line breaks coming in mid-foot at the ends of lines 3 and 4, which would be perfectly regular (and of course lose their emphatic rimes with lines 5) if printed thus:

   i'm *COM-* / ing AND i'm *GO-* / ing AND
   i'm *STRETCH-* / ing AND i'm *GROW-* / ing AND
i'll *REAP* / what I'VE been *SOW-* / ing OR my *SKIN'S* / NOT *BLACK.* /

These syncopated rhythms are suited to the purpose of the poem—to express an unsophisticated confidence and optimism, despite the hardships and injustices of both the past and the present. This simple, singing determination is particularly fitted to the spondaic ends of the long lines, so emphatic in their insistence on the key ideas: "I won't turn back," "I've still grown strong," "it won't be long," and so forth. LP, TRA

224. *Andrew Marvell* **A DIALOGUE BETWEEN THE SOUL AND BODY** (page 283)

One of the oldest and deepest philosophical problems is that sometimes referred to as the body/soul or the mind/matter problem. Are the body and soul two separate entities, like a paper bag and its contents? Or are they simply two aspects of a single entity, like the two sides of the sheet of paper, and thus inseparable? From this problem hang various contingent problems. How are body and soul related in life (the problem of determinism and free will)? What happens to them at death (the problem of immortality)? These problems are as legitimate a subject for poetry as for religion, science, and philosophy. In literature they especially invite allegorical treatment. (See, for instance, *Everyman*.)

In an earlier poem, "A Dialogue between the Resolved Soul and Created Pleasure," Marvell, a puritan poet, pictures the resolved Soul, armed with the shield of faith, the helmet of salvation, and the sword of spirit, as a soldier singly facing a whole army under the command of Pleasure. Pleasure, however, instead of challenging the Soul to combat, invites him to share "Nature's banquet" and therewith offers him a series of earthly temptations (the pleasures of the five senses: taste, touch, smell, sight, and hearing; plus the pleasures of love, wealth, and glory). The Resolved Soul easily rejects each of these in a victory so effortless that the reader gets no sense of conflict.

How much more interesting and complex is the allegory in "A Dialogue between the Soul and Body"! Here, though there is no combat, the conflict is real, and the poet does not betray his sympathy for either side. He even allows Body the last word, though in the earlier poem he was clearly on the side of Soul. Here each participant complains of his bondage to the other. They are not two completely separate forces armed against each other, as in the simplistic concept of the earlier poem. But neither are they one. They are two, so tangled up together that neither can get loose from the other. Their "Dialogue" is a debate, and the object is to see which can make his plight seem more burdensome and himself more oppressed by the other. Which wins? Does anyone have the audacity to judge?

But how wittily the debate is conducted! What a succession of brilliant paradoxes, stunning metaphors, and multi-dimensional words! The Soul complains of being "fettered" with "bolts of bones" (how does sound here echo sense?), "blinded with an eye" (paradox), and "deaf with the drumming of an ear" (the paradox enriched with a pun on "drumming"), "hung up in chains . . . Of nerves, and arteries, and veins" (metaphor), and being tortured in a "vain" head (useless, hollow, egotistical) and a "double heart" (two-chambered, duplicitous, an organ of the body).

The body, in turn, laments that his soul so "impales" him that he is "his own precipice" (in danger of falling off the edge of his own upright self). He concedes that his soul warms and moves him, but declares that a mere fever could do as much, and complains that his feverish soul has never let him rest.

In the third stanza the soul replies, in a series of dazzling paradoxes, that it suffers the pains of the body as well as its own. Being the more compassionate and "sensitive" partner (though without senses), it shares whatever suffering the body undergoes: "I feel, that cannot feel, the pain." Thus the soul is "Constrained not only to endure / Diseases, but, what's worse, the cure; / And ready oft the port to gain, / [Is] shipwrecked into health again." The "port" (29) in this metaphor is heaven; the "cure" (28) is entry into heaven. Thus, when the body is cured from an illness, the soul is deprived of the opportunity to reach its own desired destination and is "shipwrecked into health" again!

But, replies the body, in the final stanza, the ills visited by the soul on the body cannot be cured by any medicine. The "cramp of hope," the "palsy shakes of fear," "the pestilence of love," "hate's hidden ulcer"—all are maladies of soul that are imposed upon the body, just as those in stanza three were maladies of the body imposed on the soul.

It is evident, in this poem, that the poet believed body and soul to be two entities, not one, for both disputants are confident that they will eventually be separated and relieved of their mutual bondage. The body declares (18) that the spirit "Has made me live to let me die." And the soul complains (29-30), when the body is saved from death, that he (the soul) has been "shipwrecked into health again." But this is a minor theme in the poem; the major theme is the intricate entanglement of the soul and body during life. LP

225. *Cleopatra Mathis*   GETTING OUT (page 284)

The most striking detail of this failed marriage is "our matching eyes and hair," for it establishes the identical nature of the two people, as well as the sort of immaturity that would lead a wife and husband to share a matching hair style. But if they are such a "match," what caused their marriage to fail? The poem seems to suggest that it was their very closeness, the resemblance they had to one another. With one exception, the statements in the first two stanzas are first-person plural, relating that the stages in the break-up were mutually achieved: "we hardly slept," "we gave up . . . escaped," "we paced," "we cried," and then the final sentence, "We held on tight, and let go." The exception is in lines 12-14, when the husband "tried to pack up and go"—but failed.

The extended metaphor in the poem, begun in the title, reinforces the idea of mutuality, for they together were "like inmates" wanting to escape, "finally locked into" blaming each other as the last mutual act before the divorce. Their marriage was a prison, increasingly more restricted and confining to them both, until—*finally* —they began to find things to accuse each other of. This looks ironic, that they shared the increasing sense of imprisonment as if they together had been locked up by someone else, until they finished with what we would expect at the beginning of the process, turning against each other.

The poem embodies in the person of the lawyer the reader's proper response: bewilderment. Clearly from her tone, the speaker still loves her former husband, and his reassuring annual message implies that he cares for her. How can so much love cause a divorce? Yet it can. The concluding image expresses best the tone: love and regret. TRA

226. *Marianne Moore* NEVERTHELESS (page 285)

As the title implies, the subject of the poem is persistence and pertinacity, both physical and moral. The various examples of plant life "overcome" apparent obstacles, from which the poet derives the moral lesson for human beings: "Victory won't come to me unless I go to it . . . The weak overcomes its menace, the strong overcomes itself. What is there like fortitude!"

What looks like random diversity, mingling bizarre examples, has its order, from seed to root to tendril to fruit, an upward growth representing the cycle of vegetable nature. It commences with the "multitude of seeds" on the surface of a crushed strawberry (transformed, by its "struggle" to maintain its integrity, into the semblance of animal forms); it proceeds to the protected internal seeds of an apple, doubly enclosed in the core. Whether vulnerably superficial or protectively enclosed, these seeds are designed to reach fertile soil and give birth to new growth.

Parallels exist in the root references: there is growth both in the rigid enclosure of frozen soil and in exposed air, and some plants' roots undergo such twisting that they seem to transform themselves into the shapes of animal forms. Even the fragility of grape tendrils and the stems of cherries possess transforming potency, the frail tendril capable of binding what has supported it, the "thread" transmitting the ripening coloration of the cherry. And the poem ends its plant references where it began, with sweet fruits that carry the source of new growth.

Thus what may seem a random collection of "oddities" in nature has a direction, drawing comparisons between the seemingly disconnected examples. The whole plant world illustrates the power of life to maintain and propagate itself—and so the human world should learn to persist, employing its inner moral virtues as well as its outward physical powers. To paraphrase the moral statements: "Real bravery, and true victory, are seen not only in overcoming external dangers but also in self-control."

The poem is written in syllabic verse (only the number of syllables in a line is counted, not accents) rimed *xaa*. The form, which appears like free verse, thus echoes the meaning, since random rhythms (like bizarre subjects) are "locked in" by syllable-count and rime. TRA

227. *Ogden Nash* I DO, I WILL, I HAVE (page 286)

Ogden Nash got rave reviews
By deliberately thumbing his nose at the Muse.
The rules of his craft he consistently breaks them
Or wholly forsakes them.
He thinks verse is sweeter
Without the meter.
If students ask whether free verse can be written in rime,

The answer, for Nash, is "all of the time."
For the sake of a rime he'll commit any crime.
He'll tie his own grammar in Gordian knots,
With no resemblance to Grecian urns or well-wrought pots.
He'll twist syntax into shapes like a pretzel.
Which yet will have charm more than choice epithets'll.
He'll cast a misspell
Over guardians of the sacred well.
What's worse,
He won't acknowledge the number of his sins per verse.
So my views
For the Muse
Are "Come out of your nunnery;
Stop gNashing your teeth
And give an urned wreath
To this master of funnery punnery." LP

228. *Howard Nemerov*   GRACE TO BE SAID AT THE SUPERMARKET (page 287)

Superficially the butt of Nemerov's satire seems to be the application of technology to the presentation of food, the complaint of a man who is disturbed by standardized, hygienic market methods. But this commonplace of modern social critics is given a sharper edge when the speaker pretends to be praying not to technology, but to geometry. His target is more ancient and more universal, the very source of these modern effects: our intellectualizing tendencies that we express not merely in the uniform packaging of meats but in the packaging of ideas in language.

The diction of this seriously witty, ironic poem is highly varied, ranging from plain colloquialism to scientific and mathematical terms, from the language of religion to that of literary criticism. Such wide linguistic reference punctures the pretensions of all these mis-users of language: advertisers ("streamlined . . . for greater speed," "like a philosopher should"), casual conversationalists ("if you want to put it that way," "maybe"), literary critics ("aesthetic distance," "significant form"), philosophers ("the greatest good"), preachers and theologians ("our birthright," "the mystical body"), and—the metaphorical center of the poem—mathematicians ("cubes," "cylinder," "ellipsoid," and the rest).

All of these display what Nemerov regards as a linguistic replacement of the honest, natural expression of human nature with inflated—or deflated—terminology. The subject of the poem is the human being as a carnivore, and the variety of dodges we employ to avoid acknowledging the fact. Line 15 represents the only honest expression of it: both we and the "brutes" we consume lead "bulging and blood-swollen lives," though we would prefer to think and speak otherwise. TRA

229. *Naomi Shibab Nye* **FAMOUS** (page 287)

The word *famous* generally means someone (or some act or thing) widely known or celebrated. Alexander the Great is a famous person. Sir Walter Raleigh's throwing down his expensive cloak so that Queen Elizabeth would not soil her shoes at a muddy crossing is a famous act. The Taj Mahal in India is a famous thing. Fame is relative of course. Adolph Hitler is more famous than General Franco. Nevertheless, the scale of fame in Nye's poem takes us by surprise. She works at the opposite end of the scale. Every one and every thing is famous (important, much thought about, well known) to someone or something. Nye's poem is about the humbly famous, about things that are "famous" to limited audiences. In the first eight divisions of her poem she gives examples of this kind of fame. In the last two she tells us the kind of fame she desires for herself. She wants to be famous to the shuffling old and to the sticky young. She wants to be

> ... famous in the way a pulley is famous,
> or a buttonhole, not because it did anything spectacular,
> But because it never forgot what it could do.

The pulley and the buttonhole, both small things, the buttonhole almost nothing at all; but each one always ready to perform its function, always useful, never doing anything spectacular, but each always *there*, never forgetting or failing to perform what it can do. LP

202. *Emily Dickinson* **IN WINTER IN MY ROOM** (page 264)

211. *Robert Graves* **DOWN, WANTON, DOWN** (page 270)

230. *Sharon Olds* **THE CONNOISSEUSE OF SLUGS** (page 288)

These three poems all deal with the same subject: the manifest physical indication of sexual arousal in the human male; they treat this subject, however, with wide differences in tone. In each, the speaker may be taken, without harm, as the poet.

Emily Dickinson's speaker treats the subject with a combination of fascination and fear mounting to terror. The poem is a Freudian fable using Freudian symbols (though Dickinson would not have known them as that, for she wrote it considerably before Freud's name was known to American readers). The worm, "pink, lank, and warm," is clearly the male penis in its ordinary, untumescent state. The speaker, not quite at ease with it despite its apparent weakness, ties it with a string to something in her room. When she next looks, it has turned into a snake, mottled and "ringed with power"—the penis has become tumescent and erect. The speaker's fear is manifested by her "creeping blood" and by her shrinking from the snake. When the snake praises her beauty ("How fair you are!") she interprets the compliment, rightly or wrongly, as dangerous flattery ("propitiation's claw") designed by the snake to insinuate itself into her favor. Recognizing her fear, the snake pretends incredulity ("Afraid . . . of me?"). But the speaker hears the query as a menacing hiss, and admits (in a tremendous understatement) that she feels "no cordiality" toward it.* Then, as the snake, beginning to throb, approaches nearer, her fear turns to terror, and she flees to a distant town, many towns away from her own town.

The speaker's fear of the snake is obvious. Her fascination with it is revealed in her description of it as having "mottles rare," being "ringed with power," moving with "a rhythm *slim*," and projecting itself in "patterns."

Throughout her poetry Emily Dickinson expressed strongly ambivalent attitudes toward sexuality and male dominance. Many of her "love poems" express a desire to be swept away on a tide of passion for some man whom she will humbly serve as her "master." In others she expresses a resolute determination to maintain her self-dependence and to be her own "master."

In its explicit treatment of sexual matters, Dickinson's poem is a truly remarkable one to have been written by a nineteenth-century female, especially one who almost certainly died a virgin and who lived in a small New England town like Amherst. Partly to disguise its impropriety, she ends the poem saying, "This was a dream." The designation is perfectly appropriate for a fantasy which, if read literally, is about a worm that turns into a talking snake. But we would be badly mistaken if we thought that Dickinson did not *know* what the dream was *about*. The descriptions are too exact and their purport all too clear.

In "Down, Wanton, Down" the tone is one of comic embarrassment. Graves presents us with an extended apostrophe in which the object addressed is presented through an extended personification in which the literal term of the comparison, though never named, is easily inferred. The speaker addresses an uncontrollable part of himself which he personifies as a poor "bombard-captain," "wanton" and "witless," who constantly annoys or embarrasses the speaker by springing up, staunchly erect, at the merest thought or intimation ("whisper") of Love or Beauty. Love and Beauty are also personified, but as feminine rather than masculine. In stanza 2 the word "ravelin" refers literally to a triangular outwork in fortifications, but metaphorically to the pubic region of the female; the word "breach" has obviously both military and sexual meanings; and in the word "die" Graves uses a favorite pun of Renaissance poetry (see Donne's "The Canonization," page 241), in which "die" means not only to suffer death but also to experience a sexual climax or orgasm. The last two stanzas present a series of rhetorical questions, to all three of which the implied answer is *Never*. The humor of the poem derives in part from the speaker's predicament (never before, to my knowledge, thematically addressed

---

*An interesting comparison-contrast may also be made between this poem and "A narrow fellow in the grass" (page 52).

in a poem), from the comic yet appropriate incongruity between the literal and figurative terms of its central personification, from its puns, and from its cunning withholding of any name for its central subject. But if the poem is comic, it is serious as well, for the ability to distinguish between lust and love, between physical and spiritual attraction, is one of the most important problems of our lives.

The title of this poem is taken from Shakespeare's *King Lear*, II, iv, 121-26, where the Fool says, "Cry to it, nuncle, as the cockney did to the eels when she put 'em i' the paste alive. She knapped 'em o' the' coxcombs with a stick, and cried, 'Down, wantons, down!'"

The speaker in Sharon Olds's poem expresses neither fear nor embarrassment, but wonder and delight, at her first viewing of a male erection. In content the poem falls into two parts, the first (lines 1-16) beginning with "When" and the second (lines 16–22) with "Years later." For the title and first line she coins the word "connoisseuse," meaning a female connoisseur, and in the first part of the poem she relates the delight and wonder she felt as a girl when she would observe a garden slug unfurl, transforming itself from a shapeless gelatinous blob into a snail-like creature with mouth, antennae, and eyes. The adjectives "gold," "translucent," "glistening," "glimmering," "sensitive," "delicate," and "intimate" indicate the quality of the experience for her. In the second part of the poem, the speaker, no longer a girl but a young woman, gasps "with pleasure to see that quiet / mystery reenacted" in a naked man. Adjectives like *elegant* and *gleaming* parallel those used in earlier lines. The two parts of the poem, linked by the word "naked," are not visually separated, for both phenomena are natural processes, and the poet wishes to indicate that they are natural, not shameful. But if they are natural, they are also a "mystery" (the word has religious overtones), something to be wondered at, something finally inexplicable, but something to be accepted "with pleasure."

These three poems treat a common phenomenon with widely different tones. It may be noticed, however, that all avoid an explicitly sexual vocabulary (words like *penis, erection, pubic,* and *orgasm,* used in this discussion), and this avoidance may partly account for their success. LP

231. *P. K. Page*   THE LANDLADY (page 288)

Through line 10 this portrait generalizes the landlady's attitudes and motives, and includes the attitudes of her boarders. Although they seem "impersonal," her hovering, curious presence causes them to alter their behavior: they become secretive, punctual, and reticent to display their feelings. The second line initiates the syntactical pattern of the poem: the subject "boarders" is omitted from the two clauses of the second sentence. This device becomes the controlling pattern from line 11 ("She peers"), after which "she," or more properly the title "The Landlady," is the subject of the sentence fragments that constitute the remainder of the poem.

The portrait is of a woman whose curiosity about the lives of her boarders is obsessive. She achieves no contentment simply from knowing all there is to know about their habits, their actions, or even their health. "Like a lover," but without love, she is consumed with the details of their lives, and "must know all, all, all." Even "all" is insufficient for her hunger for knowledge, for what she seeks is the most secret meaning of their lives, "hoping the worst" will be revealed to her at last.

Without real malevolence but with an insatiable desire to know everything about them, the landlady becomes at the end of the poem a kind of monster of curiosity. But is this really the woman, or is it the speaker's invention? As the poem focuses ever more narrowly on the landlady as the speaker sees her, attributing to her an insane attachment to the lives of her boarders, a reader might legitimately wonder whether the portrait does not represent an equally obsessive hunger for privacy on the part of a boarder. TRA

232. *Linda Pastan* ETHICS (page 239)

The poem appears to present an elementary (one might say childish) problem demanding an ethical solution for a hypothetical conflict between art and life. To define it thus is to demonstrate that the poem is not in fact about ethics, for that branch of philosophy cannot mediate such a conflict, and as the final sentence of the poem indicates, no childish (or childlike) answer could suffice anyway.

Which is more valuable, an old woman or a beloved painting? Or, which is more valuable, an old painting or a beloved woman? If the woman has only a few "years left" and the painting can last more or less forever, is this a question of permanence? If the painting can give pleasure to millions over the centuries, how much pleasure can the old woman give? Can one measure the pleasure of a grandmother "in her usual kitchen"?

That is, the central purpose of this poem is not to leave readers asking "which is the *right* answer," but rather to remind them that such questions are both unanswerable and fruitless. Even if you *could* decide that a person is more valuable than a painting—or that a painting is more valuable than a person—what would you have achieved? The poem basically pits the abstract against the real, the intellectual ability to ask such dichotomizing questions against the vividness of real perceptions. This satiric dimension of the poem is reinforced by the apparent impossibility of its literal statement: how *can* that same ethics teacher have asked that same question to the same students "every fall"? How could that class "opt one year for life, the next for art"? The situation must be taken figuratively, perhaps symbolically, as an abstraction of childhood, authority, ethical quandaries.

The resolution is signaled when the speaker finds herself "in a real museum," not the "half-imagined" one that her teacher conjured for her. All that imaginary experience, and the imagined necessity of choice, are replaced by the richness of the experience of being old and seeing a Rembrandt. The hypothetical vanishes, and the paradoxes of life replace it: "woman and painting and season are almost one"— not only beyond the ethical answers a child might obediently give, but beyond the abstracting, defining, separating exercises of the intellect.

In a sense, then, one might regard the ethics class and its perpetual question as a symbolic presentation of the natural desire for simple either/or answers, to which one may respond dutifully or whimsically, and so be categorized. What will replace such simplifications can come only, if at all, through maturity and experience. TRA

233. *Dudley Randall* BALLAD OF BIRMINGHAM (page 290)

The year 1963 was the peak year for civil rights agitation in the American South. On April 2 Martin Luther King, Jr., led a freedom march, starting in Birmingham, Alabama, protesting racial segregation in the nation's schools. On May 2-7, police used dogs, and firemen used high-pressure firehoses, to break up parades. On May 11 the bombing of a black leader's home and of a desegregated motel caused President Kennedy to station federal troops in bases near Birmingham. On June 11 Governor George Wallace defied a presidential order by barring two black students from enrolling in the University of Alabama. On June 12 Medgar Evers, a black civil rights leader, was murdered by a white sniper in Jackson, Mississippi. On August 28 over 200,000 civil-rights activists converged on Washington, D.C., to protest against racial discrimination and heard Martin Luther King, Jr., deliver his famous "I Have a Dream" speech. On the morning of September 15 just as Sunday School was ending a bomb exploded in a black church in Birmingham, killing four small girls and injuring twenty others.

It was against this background, and with these materials, that Dudley Randall, a black poet, wrote "Ballad of Birmingham." Specifically Randall melded the freedom marches of May 2-7 with the church bombing of September 15 to create a powerful situational irony. A mother will not let her young daughter participate in a freedom march downtown because of the dangers involved, only to find that the church, traditionally a sanctuary, is the more dangerous place of the two.

Appropriately Randall chose the form of the medieval folk ballads to relate his story. Many of them also started out as accounts of some contemporary local violence. Randall uses the ballad stanza (four lines of alternating iambic tetrameter and trimeter with the second and fourth lines riming) used in most of the ballads. And he tells much of the story, as they do, through dialogue. Even his epithets (e.g., "night-dark") sound like those of the folk ballads. The result is a very effective rendering of contemporary events in an old, old form. LP

234. *Alberto Ríos* **NANI** (page 291)

The sestina, of which this is the only example in this book, is a highly contrived fixed form making use of the patterned repetition of six end words through six stanzas, followed by a three-line envoi in which the six words are repeated in the middles and at the ends of lines. Ríos has slightly disguised the fact that his poem is a sestina by not providing stanza breaks except between what the pattern defines as the third and fourth stanzas, and before the envoi.

But even if we do not recognize the form for what it is, the poem becomes hypnotic in the repetition of end-words which in themselves are emblematic of the poem's theme: *serves, me, her, words, more,* and *speak* (to list them in the order of the first stanza). These words display a variety of sound links, including the assonance of *serves/her/words* and *me/speak* and the alliteration of *serves/speak* and *me/more*, which increase the feeling of repetition and reinforce their significance in the poem. Essentially Ríos presents a small domestic scene in which a man is being served food by his grandmother, "the absolute *mamá*" (*nana* and *nani* are diminutive nicknames for a grandmother in the Spanish of America). Her serving, and then her smiles, and climactically her wrinkles, are her means of communication, and they speak wordlessly about her love for the speaker and for her dead husband, and finally about her children and all the ties of love. The speaker has lost two-thirds of his ability to speak or understand Spanish, so even when his grandmother speaks, it is to him as if her words dribble down her chin; but mostly she does not speak words, only gestures, looks, wrinkles, though she is so eloquent in these that when she cooks something at the stove it is as if she were doing "something with words." The "me/her" relationship is tenuous, not held by language but by a deep sense of closeness. As the "absolute *mamá*," nani speaks by serving, loves by feeding, and expresses the rich heritage of the family by the accumulated wrinkles of a long life of service and love. To the grandson who has lost the spoken language, the question is how much of this heritage he will be able to maintain: "I wonder just how much of me / will die with her, what were the words / I could have been, was." Yet the nani goes on serving, serving love. TRA

235. *Edwin Arlington Robinson* **MR. FLOOD'S PARTY** (page 292)

Few poems balance so precisely on the point between comedy and pathos, tears and laughter, as "Mr. Flood's Party." For the poet to have poised it so was a triumph in the management of tone.

The drunk has always been a figure of comedy, and Mr. Flood, as he drinks and sings with himself, "with only two moons listening," is richly comic. The similes enhance the humor. Mr. Flood with a jug at his lips and the ghost of a warrior with a horn at his lips may be visually similar, but the discrepancy between their emotional contexts makes the comparison ludicrous. Mr. Flood setting his jug down may resemble a mother laying down her sleeping child, but the incongruity between the drunk's solicitude for his jug and a mother's solicitude for her baby again is ludicrous. But the fun is not supplied entirely by the poet; it is supplied also by Mr. Flood himself. The grave solemnity, the punctilious courtesy, with which Mr. Flood goes through the social ritual of greeting himself, inviting himself to drink, welcoming himself home, and cautioning himself against a refill ("No more, sir; that will do")—all show a rich vein of humor which makes us laugh with Mr. Flood as well as at him. This is a lovable drunk—though he is not loved. With two Mr. Floods, and two moons, we are almost prepared ourselves to believe that "the whole harmonious landscape rang" (it takes two people to create harmony) until we realize that this is only the heightened sense of appreciation that every drunk has for the beauty of his own singing.

But the things that make Mr. Flood ludicrous also make him pathetic. The allusion to Roland winding his horn calls up one of the most famous and moving episodes in all literature, in *The Song of Roland*, and the comparison, though ludicrous, is also plangent and moves us with emotions more profound than comedy. Roland was sending out a call for help, and Mr. Flood needs help too; but we know that no help came for Roland in time to save him. The comparison to the mother and her sleeping child, in much the same way, reminds us of the familial relationships and gentleness and love which are missing from Mr. Flood's life. These two images, with the help of the silver moon, lay a veil of tenderness and soft emotion over the poem, which moves us to compassion as well as laughter. Mr. Flood, after all, is not a mere ne'er-do-well. He has a delightful sense of humor and an old-fashioned courtesy. He was once honored in the town below and had many friends there. He has an educated man's acquaintance with literature: in speaking of the fleetingness of time, he can quote from "The Rubáiyát of Omar Kháyám" ("The Bird of Time has but a little way / To flutter—and the Bird is on the Wing") and then use the quotation wittily and gracefully to propose a toast. The reference to *The Song of Roland*, though made by the poet, reinforces our sense of Mr. Flood as a sensitive and educated man. The song he sings—"For auld lang syne"—has added force because Mr. Flood can look only backward for better times; he can't look for them in the present or the future. Mr. Flood is old: the husky voice that wavers out, and the trembling care with which he sets down the jug are signs of age as well as of drink. His loneliness is stressed throughout the poem: he climbs the hill "alone" (line 1), there is "not a native near" (line 6), he speaks "For no man else in Tilbury Town to hear" (line 8), he must drink with himself (line 9), he stands "alone" (line 17), the moonlight makes a "silver loneliness" (line 45), he is "again alone" (line 52), he has no friends in the town below (lines 54-56). A ghost in the moonlight, Mr. Flood sends out his call for help, and is answered only by other ghosts—"A phantom salutation of the dead"—old memories.

We are not told why Mr. Flood has been cast out from the town below, why he is no longer honored, for what social sin or error he has lost his place in society. We know only that he is old, alone, friendless, dishonored, deserving of compassion but getting none. The "strangers" who would have shut their doors to him in the town below are probably many of them literal strangers, but some are former friends from whom he has been estranged. The final note of the poem is not one of laughter, but of heartbreak.* LP

*Reprinted from Laurence Perrine and James M. Reid, *100 American Poems of the Twentieth Century* (New York: Harcourt Brace Jovanovich, 1966), pp. 7-8.

236. *Theodore Roethke* I KNEW A WOMAN (page 294)

This poem is a tribute of praise and gratitude from a middle-aged poet to a younger woman whose eager sexual genius taught him in fullest measure the delights of sensual love. The verb in the title may be understood in both its ordinary and its Biblical sense. The imagery of the poem throughout emphasizes physical movement and the attractions of the body. The woman was "lovely in her bones," and "when she moved, she moved more ways than one." The "bright container" (4) is her skin. The tribute paid in lines 6-7 is both humorous and deeply meant, for "English poets who grew up on Greek" would include such favorites of Roethke's as Sir John Davies, Ben Jonson, and Andrew Marvell. In stanza 2 the terms "Turn," "Counter-turn," and "Stand" are the English equivalents of the Greek words *strophe, antistrophe*, and *epode,* indicating the movements of the chorus in Greek drama while chanting a choral ode. The metaphor in lines 12-14 compares the woman to the curving sickle that cuts the grass in harvesting and the speaker to the straight rake which gathers it up. Moving in synchronism they produce a "prodigious mowing." Although the metaphor hardly needs further explanation, it is not irrelevant that the verb "to mow," in Scottish dialect, means to have sexual intercourse, and that the noun "rake" refers not only to the harvesting tool but to a sexually oriented male. Stanza 3 continues the poem's tribute to the sexual talents of the woman. The "mobile nose" in the whimsical mixed metaphor of line 20 suggests that of a rabbit (or other animal) sniffing the air.

Stanza 4 is difficult, for the poet here turns philosophical, and his transitions are abrupt. But if the precise meanings are puzzling, the tone is not. Clearly the poet sees no contradiction between "eternity" and enjoyment of the sensual life. He swears his lady cast a "white" shadow, not a dark one. Perhaps such pleasure as she afforded him is a foretaste of eternity. If he is "martyr to a motion not his own [hers]," he has been a willing martyr, and his old bones still "live to learn her wanton ways." "To know eternity" is the important thing, "But who would count eternity in days?" The question is rhetorical; the answer is, No one but a fool; eternity may be tasted in a minute. The poet himself measures time "by how a body sways." The first line of the stanza seems to refer to the natural process of the human life-cycle from conception to death, but also to glance back at the sexual metaphor in lines 12-14. The simile "white as stone" calls up the image of a white marble gravestone, a marker separating life from eternity. The use of the past tense in the first three stanzas, and the switch to present in the fourth, may indicate that the woman is dead (and the poet himself is certainly older). But the last two lines indicate that he has not forgotten the lessons she taught him. The poem ends, as it began, as a celebration of sensual love.

For additional suggestions, see discussions in *The Explicator* by Virginia L. Peck, 22 (Apr. 1964), item 66; Helen T. Buttel, 24 (May 1966), item 78; Nat Henry, 27 (Jan. 1969), item 31; and Jenijoy La Belle, 32 (Oct. 1973), item 15. LP

237. *Theodore Roethke* **THE WAKING** (page 295)

In form "The Waking" is a villanelle. A villanelle is a nineteen-line fixed form using only two rimes and having two refrains (on the same rime) in the following arrangement (where A represents the first refrain, and *A* the second): Ab*A* abA ab*A* abA ab*A* abA*A*.

In "The Waking" the poet joyfully affirms his acceptance of a life in which the only constant is change. Though its tone is clear, the details of its meanings are not, and the following suggestions are made diffidently. Line 1: "I wake to sleep." Literally, this means, I wake in the morning only to have to sleep again at night. Symbolically it means, I am born to die—death is the inevitable concomitant of life. Nevertheless, the tone indicates a full acceptance of life on these terms. The speaker takes his waking "slow": he wishes to savor it fully. Line 2: The speaker feels his "fate" (change and death) in what he cannot fear (the life process). Line 3: He learns about life only through experiencing it. Line 4: "We think by feeling." Our deepest understandings come through intuition and emotion rather than through reasoning. Line 5: The speaker hears his being "dance from ear to ear": he is joyfully conscious of his existence. Line 7: He is conscious of other people, and wishes to know about them. Line 8: He blesses the earth, which is the "Ground" of his existence and will be his place of burial. Line 10: Life is a mystery. The ultimate secret of how sunlight nourishes the tree, of how Light illuminates the "Tree of Life," or of how spirit enters matter, cannot be intellectually known. Line 11: Life is process. The worm climbs up the evolutionary scale of being: death constantly recurs in this evolutionary life cycle. Lines 13-15: Great Nature holds death and dissolution in store for all of us, so let us enjoy each moment while we may. "Lovely" may be construed as an adjective (paralleling "lively"), as an adverb (modifying "learn"), or as a noun of direct address to the "you" of lines 7 and 14. Line 16 (the most difficult of the poem's several paradoxes): Physical decay and the speaker's knowledge of constant change (degeneration and regeneration) in life's processes keep him resolved to make the most of life and to trust the goodness of the cycle. Line 17: The present falls away from us eternally; what falls away from us is permanence. Change and death are constantly "near" to us. Line 19: Take all the above suggestions with two pinches of salt. At best (like all paraphrase) they are reductive, and some may be flat wrong. For additional discussion, see Richard A. Blessing, in the *Ball State University Forum*, 12 (Aug, 1971), 17-19, and Karl Malkoff, *Theodore Roethke* (New York: Columbia Univ. Press, 1966), pp. 121-22. LP

238. *William Shakespeare* **FEAR NO MORE** (page 295)

Both the tone of this dirge from the fourth act of *Cymbeline* and the dramatic situation which is its occasion are characteristic of the late romances of Shakespeare. This is sung or spoken by two young men who suppose their adopted stepbrother is dead; but not only is the stepbrother only in a drugged sleep, "he" is really a princess who has had to flee the tyranny of the court—and the two singers who have been raised as Welsh shepherds are in actuality her long-lost princely brothers. These plot details contribute little to interpreting this song as a poem. But they make it, in its place in the play, a reinforcement of the mysterious powers of goodness that defeat the malevolent plotting of the villains in Shakespeare's last plays. Since all does work out for the best, despite all odds, a funeral lament like this emphasizes escaping life's pains and fears, not the grief of the mourners. Their love is expressed not in joy that the dead person has gone to heavenly bliss (the play is set in pre-Christian Britain), but in the consolation that he is now safe from danger and is sharing in a universal fate.

The "fears" that beset the living are of two kinds: natural (summer heat, winter cold, lightning and thunder) and social, with the greater emphasis on the latter. Although they personally know nothing of court life, these young men describe the conditions of a capital city, where ordinary people have to work for food and clothing, and where social disparities (chimney-sweepers with their gruelling and miserable lives contrasted to "golden lads and girls") subject people to the frowns of their superiors and the cruelty of tyrants as well as to slander and rash censure. There is some "joy" in such a life, however slight: there is love, momentarily alluded to in line 17. But the preponderance of experience has been "moan," and death's release is to that extent to be welcomed.

The universality of death, encapsulated in the repeated rime "must ... come to dust," contrasts the equality of the dead to the social hierarchies and injustices that govern the living. Rich and poor, mighty and weak, learned and ignorant, all "must ... come to dust," and the inequities of society will be obliterated. Death is the great deliverer and equalizer. TRA

239. *William Shakespeare* **LET ME NOT TO THE MARRIAGE OF TRUE MINDS (Sonnet 116)** (page 296)

This sonnet makes an interesting contrast to the one which follows, "My mistress' eyes." The subject here is a union of minds, while the other is a poem about physical attraction; and this sonnet is idealistic, the other realistic. The opening sentence refers to the marriage ceremony in the Anglican *Book of Common Prayer*: ". . . if either of you do know any impediment why ye may not be lawfully joined together in matrimony . . . confess it." This reference is made emphatic by the extreme metrical irregularity of the first line, and made more vivid by the regularity of the first three feet of the second line.

The first quatrain proceeds negatively: I do not admit impediments; love is not love if it alters or bends. The second quatrain reverses the rhetoric, insisting that love is permanent and fixed; and the third returns to the negative, "Love's not Time's fool" and again, "Love alters not." In effect, the three quatrains describe what intellectual love is not, what it is, and again what it is not. (One scholar discovers in this, and in other details of the poem, that this sonnet is "protesting too much," and that it must be seen as ironic overstatement. While the poem may seem too hyperbolic when laid beside "My mistress' eyes," there really is little within this poem to suggest less than sincerity.)

The examination of the three quatrains as rhetorical parallels reveals a frequent pattern of Shakespeare's sonnets: they are repetitive, offering three different contexts to make the same statement. In the first quatrain, the context resembles a courtroom or public debate, as the echo from the marriage ceremony implies question and response. Here, the response is suitably intellectualized, a matter of defining terms which is appropriate to the subject of "minds." The diction reinforces the effect, being rational and legalistic ("let me not," "Admit impediments," "alters . . . alterations," "remover to remove").

The second quatrain develops two two-line images, the "ever-fixèd mark" of a beacon or lighthouse unshaken by storms, and the pole star by which navigators steer, both images sharing the context of nautical travel, its dangers and its safeguards. Line 8 states our inability to know the exact value of the star, even though we can make use of our instruments to steer by its steadfastness, and it contrasts the "wandering" of human life with the star's immobility. True intellectual love preserves us in danger, and guides us when we wander.

The third quatrain continues to develop single images in two-line statements linked together in a common context. "Time's fool" is the toy or plaything of personified time, having no value to him. This is "Father Time," who dispassionately destroys the "rosy lips and cheeks" of the young (this is the only reference to physical beauty in the poem—it *is* "Time's fool"). Time with his sickle is linked to the "grim reaper" who at the day of "doom" will finally destroy all life, and only then will the "marriage of true minds" be dissolved.

The couplet returns the poem to the courtroom of the opening quatrain. The poet invites disproof of his testimony, and employs as his witnesses two incontrovertible facts: since I have written (this poem proves that), and since certainly at least one man has loved, then my statements must be true. The couplet seems irrefutable, except that its conclusion is not necessarily valid: while it claims that these self-evident facts prove that the argument of his sonnet is also self-evident, there is no real connection. The "proof" is rhetorical rather than logical (and like the opening quatrain, couched in negative rhetoric).

This justly popular poem has been much analyzed. Among the most interesting commentaries are the following: Edward Hubler, *The Sense of Shakespeare's Sonnets* (Princeton, N.J.: Princeton Univ. Press, 1952), pp. 92-93: Kenneth Muir. *Shakespeare's Sonnets* (London: Allen & Unwin, 1979), pp. 107-08; Paul Ramsey, *The Fickle Glass: A Study of Shakespeare's Sonnets* (New York: AMS Press, 1979), pp. 157-58; Katharine M. Wilson, *Shakespeare's Sugared Sonnets* (London: Allen & Unwin, 1974), pp. 301-03. TRA

240. *William Shakespeare* **MY MISTRESS' EYES (Sonnet 130)** (page 296)

This witty sonnet might serve as a model of courtship, if a lady were to be won by realistic honesty. The speaker at length rejects the customary (lying) praise of hyperbolic lovers, insisting that his lady is only a woman, not a "goddess," and yet she is "as rare" as any woman who has been praised with overstated comparisons. In other words, he loves her for what she is, and does not think she wishes to be lied to about qualities she does not possess. It is a different kind of praise he offers, a high estimate of her common sense and her delight in wit.

The object of his satire is the "false compare" of the Petrarchan sonnet tradition. The formalities of the tradition required that the poet begin by praising the lady's hair (usually as fine and bright as spun golden wire), proceed to her ivory or alabaster forehead, her eyebrows arched like Cupid's bow, her pearly teeth, cherry-red lips, and so on, moving down the various parts of her body (generally rather coyly below the waist) to her delicate light feet. But Shakespeare seems realistically to present the order in which a man might look at a woman whose inner worth is also important to him, moving from eyes to lips to breasts, then to hair, cheeks, breath, voice, and gait, and at each stop he realistically claims her to be less than ideal. To the modern ear, the least complimentary word in the poem is "reeks," but the word was not used to mean "stinks" until the eighteenth century, and Shakespeare's meaning is much less offensive—it means "exhales." His tactic throughout the poem is not to substitute some other quality for the traditional overstatement, but just to say "she is not like *that*." What she *is* like is a woman, and for that he loves her. TRA

241. *Gary Soto* **SMALL TOWN WITH ONE ROAD** (page 297)

The speaker, now a man whose "easy" job is "only words" (poet? professor?), has returned to the cotton farming valley where he was raised. He is accompanied by his small daughter, and as they "suck roadside snowcones in the shade," he meditates on his beginnings. He recalls being a barefoot kid, leaping across the black asphalt highway to spend dimes for red candies, and a home life busy with dogs, cats, chickens, beans for supper: "It's a hard life where the sun looks," for "Okie or Mexican, Jew that got lost." The memories are of a life of manual labor, sweating in the hot sun, dreaming "the money dream" of relief from "shovel, hoe, broom."

And yet there is a vividly sensuous side to this reminiscence, a richness captured in images of sight, sound, feeling, taste—captured particularly well in the sixth line— "Sweetness on their tongues, red stain of laughter"—where the color of candy or snowcone is transferred to the tongue in a synesthetic mingling of taste and color, so that the pleasure of the taste is transferred to the color, and that in turn is the color of laughter. Soto intensifies what might be a prosaic description (openmouthed laughing kids reveal the candy's red dye stain on their tongues) through the concentration of metonymy and metaphor. The leaps of meaning in this phrase are like the leaping kids themselves.

The tone of the poem is thus complex: the speaker is pleased that he is no longer trapped in the "hard life," fearful that the success he has had in escaping it might disappear, and concerned for his worrying, serious daughter. Yet as he recalls himself (and then sees himself in the "brown kid" standing and then leaping as he had done), he feels nostalgia for the rich exuberance that he has lost—and probably a little regret that his daughter will not experience it for herself. TRA

242. *Wallace Stevens* **THE DEATH OF A SOLDIER** (page 298)

This poem has both a specific and a general subject, and it might best be read as a symbolic statement: it presents what the title says, but the meaning expands from the specific issue of the death of a soldier on a battlefield to encompass human death in general. The "soldier" is only an extreme example, whose death invites certain special responses not always associated with the deaths of ordinary people— chiefly, those traditional attitudes that are so easily evoked by apologists for war, by national holiday commemorators, by politicians and patriots: those who die in war "have not died in vain," but have served some national (or religious, or universal) purposes. Stevens has chosen a soldier so as to excite such stock responses, which he subjects to situational irony: a military death is apparently the most meaningful death in a secular, non-theist society—and it is no more meaningful than the changing of the seasons.

Death in this poem is part of a natural process, linked in simile twice to the change of season in autumn, just another "fall." It is not the occasion for imposing upon survivors the duty of memorials or funereal pomposity. Its apparent uniqueness—that something in particular has stopped, a singular human life—is compared to the momentary cessation of wind, a stillness which is deceptive in the larger context of climatic motion. No human life is important, no human death is important, not even those which a secular, patriotic nation celebrates.

Such nihilism is not pleasant to contemplate, yet this poem has a shapeliness and rhetorical power that make the ideas less repugnant. There is, after all, a kind of beauty in the stark, simple, and unadorned presentation of the idea: an individual human death is no more important than the change of the seasons, and the impersonal physical processes of the world will go on, "nevertheless," in the impassive reality of absolute truth. ("Nevertheless" is a marvelously evocative word, in this context, for in its double negation it emphasizes Stevens's point: mere human life or death can *never* make any *less* the reality of a world of factual truth.)

Formally, the poem reflects its reductive philosophy in its structure. The free verse stanzas have a syllabic pattern made visible by the printing. The norm is an opening line of about 10 syllables, a second line of 8, and a final line of 4 (the last stanza offers this variation: 7 in line 2, 5 in line 3). The stanzas themselves, that is, seem to dwindle down toward immobility and silence, "as in a season of autumn / When the wind stops . . ." Yet, as the stanzas repeat the pattern and thus imply continuity, the clouds (and poetry) will "go, nevertheless."

This book contains several poems on the titular subject of this poem, among them Douglas's "Vergissmeinnicht" (page 266), Owen's "Dulce et Decorum Est" (page 8) and "Anthem for Doomed Youth" (page 201), and Brooke's "The Dead" (page 89). Compared to these, Stevens's poem has neither the horrific physical detail of the first two, nor the sense of tribute and bereavement of the other two. Neither does it express ironic disgust at the injustice of death delivered on the young, as in Sassoon's "Base Details" (page 45), nor skepticism about the meaning of national enmity, as in Hardy's "The Man He Killed" (page 19). Rather, its skepticism is cosmic, as life and death themselves seem to have no meaning and the universe itself no more than mechanical processes. TRA

243. *Wallace Stevens* **THE SNOW MAN** (page 298)

The single sentence constituting this poem is ambiguously framed, either offering advice or a definition: in its barest statement, it can be paraphrased, "only a person as cold-minded as a snow man would not think such a cold place implies misery." Is the speaker advocating such emotionlessness, as appropriate to the surroundings and as a defense against despair? Or is he lamenting the inhumanity that would be necessary to escape such emotions? The last two lines provide a partial answer: the reality of the situation is that this observable landscape contains "the nothing that is," and that it has no further dimensions of meaning beyond its mere physical existence. To "think of misery" therefore is to add a false meaning, one derived not from reality but from an observer's emotional reaction.

These last two lines may echo *Hamlet*, III.iv when the Ghost appears to Hamlet in Gertrude's closet but remains invisible to her. Hamlet asks his mother, "Do you see nothing there?" and she replies "Nothing at all; yet all that is I see" (lines 131-32). Stevens's snow man is an unemotional, practical realist, unable to see anything but actuality, and able to see that the actuality implies nothing beyond itself. Neither ghosts nor implications of meaning are available to him.

The only way a person can avoid thinking of misery in such a barren place is to be, like the snow man, "nothing himself," a person without feeling. The first three stanzas create the visual scene, in details that seem quite forbidding. The trees have been subjected to wintry transformations, "crusted" and "shagged" and made "rough" in appearance by the weakness of the distant sun. Stanzas 4 and 5 add the effect of the "sound of the wind," which to an emotional observer would imply misery. The defense against such feeling is "a mind of winter," coldly unemotional and in total harmony with the surroundings.

While this is the overt statement of the poem, there remains a third alternative to either misery or emotional coldness: the visual imagery implies the possibility of perceiving beauty in the chiaroscura of shapes and textures. The three types of evergreen trees have distinctly different shapes, and the winter has given them three distinct textures. The crusted pines tower above with their foliage at the tops of their tall trunks: the shaggy junipers sprawl flat and disorderly in their low branching; and the conical Christmas-tree-shaped spruces are roughened but glittering. Although the scene is not inviting, it nevertheless possesses stark beauty. The snow man's coldly analytical philosophy is a defense against misery and a definition of reality, but it does not comprehend esthetic responses.

For two slightly different interpretations of this much-discussed poem, see A. Walton Litz, *Introspective Voyager: The Poetic Development of Wallace Stevens* (New York: Oxford, 1972), pp. 99-100, and Daniel Fuchs, *The Comic Spirit of Wallace Stevens* (Durham, N.C.: Duke, 1963), pp. 69-70. TRA

244. *May Swenson* **QUESTION** (page 298)

Like Marvell in "A Dialogue between the Soul and Body" (page 283), but some three centuries later, May Swenson is concerned with the soul/body question. Her poem, however, should probably be classed as an extended metaphor rather than as allegory, for it is neither narrative nor descriptive. It is a meditation consisting of a series of questions which the speaker asks herself but is unable to answer. The speaker—the "I" of the poem—is the soul. The body is the literal term of a metaphor which has three figurative terms, all named in the first two lines of the poem: *house, horse,* and *hound.* The linkages in sound of these three words—all monosyllables alliterating on *h*, the first two having in addition consonance on *s*, and the second two assonance on *ou*—enhance the unity of the poem, which in its structure refers to each of them three times. The first two lines of the poem explicitly announce its subject by stating its central metaphor: the body is the speaker's house, horse, and hound (metonymies for a human being's most basic needs—shelter, transportation, and a means for securing food). Lines 3 and 4 state the "question" referred to in the title: "what will I do / when you are fallen?" The past participle "fallen" goes with all three figurative terms. Lines 5-7 break the question down into three parts, line 5 referring to the house, line 6 to the horse, and line 7 to the hound. In the following lines, the three terms are referred to again but in a different order: lines 8-10 refer to the horse, lines 11-15 refer to the dog, and lines 16-19 to the house. The final two lines of the poem introduce a new metaphor. The word "shift" has a number of relevant meanings here, but the most important one is a woman's thin undergarment. If the soul has nothing but a cloud for clothing, how will it "hide"?

The poem is written in a loose iambic dimeter: the second foot in each line is usually an iamb but occasionally an anapest. The first foot is more variant, containing a number of trochaic substitutions. It has been noted that the poem consists of a series of questions: *what?* (3), *Where?* (5), *How?* (6), *What?* (7), *Where?* (8), *How?* (11), *How?* (16), *how?* (21). Each of these question-opening monosyllables occurs in a trochaic substitution in the first foot of a line, thus giving these words a metrical importance that matches their importance in the structure and meaning of the poem. Occasional riming (*hunt-mount, go-know, ahead-dead, sky-eye*) adds to the attractiveness of the poem. LP

245. *Jonathan Swift* A DESCRIPTION OF THE MORNING (page 299)

There is a long tradition, stretching back to ancient Greece, of poetic descriptions of morning, idealized and romantic treatments of the joys of the beginning of a new day. One of the most famous in English is Romeo's description of dawn in III.5:

> Look, love, what envious streaks
> Do lace the severing clouds in yonder east.
> Night's candles are burnt out, and jocund day
> Stands tiptoe on the misty mountain tops.

Swift's poem plays with the tradition in two witty ways: it is a city morning, not a rustic or natural one; and it presents details of realistic ugliness rather than idealized beauty. One critic compares the poem to a drawing by Swift's younger contemporary William Hogarth, whose "Morning" shows such social types as "the Begging Crone, the Loose Girl, the Persistent Rake, the Shivering Page, and the Old Maid" in a snowy street scene with dark buildings and a darker sky (Johnson, p. 11, cited below).

The first two lines of this poem are parodic, indicating their literary target in the "poetic" phrase "showed the ruddy morn's approach." What signals this morning, however, is not sunlight on a misty mountain top, but the beginning of urban bustle as the traffic begins to appear. Lines 3-4 lead us to anticipate a satire on sexual behavior between the upper and lower classes, as the servant girl sneaks back to her bedroom from her master's, to muss up her own bed to make it look slept in.

But Swift is not really in one of his satiric moods in this poem; the only other direct references to the injustice of social rank occur at line 13 (the nobility can live in debt, and must be pestered by bill collectors) and lines 15-16 (the prison system requires the convicts to pay for their keep, and thus they are permitted to roam the streets at night to "steal for fees").

What the poem mostly catalogues are ordinary working-class people energetically starting their daily pursuits. They are not particularly attractive, but they are not grotesques: the apprentice in his worn-out shoes cleans the grimy shop front and sprinkles water on the floor to keep down the dust; Moll (a lower-class nickname for Mary), ruddier than the morn with her flaming face (perhaps from drink), flourishes her mop ostentatiously as she prepares to scrub; the scavenger pokes in the gutters for objects to sell; the dealer in "small-coal" (either charcoal, or small lumps of coal, for domestic heating) boomingly announces his wares, while his counterpart the truly small boy who cleans chimneys chimes in with his shrill soprano voice. The town is busy, and most of the business of these people is concerned with putting the street back into some semblance of cleanliness. (The "small-coal man" is by contrast a source of grime, both from the smoky fires he supplies and from the coal dust that must coat his clothes and trail behind him as he walks.) Whatever has gone awry in the night must be put to right, the removal of dirt and of thieves, so along with the cleaners come the turnkey and the "watchful bailiffs."

The last two couplets put an end to the busy activities—the prison doors are locked up, the bailiffs stand silently, and finally (late?) some schoolboys shuffle slowly to *their* form of imprisonment. The scene subsides into a relatively calm day.

Useful analyses of the poem are F. W. Bateson, *English Poetry: A Critical Introduction* (London: Longmans, 1950), pp. 175-80, and Maurice Johnson, *The Sin of Wit: Jonathan Swift as a Poet* (Syracuse, N.Y.: Syracuse Univ. Press, 1950), pp. 10-15. TRA

246. *Dylan Thomas* **DO NOT GO GENTLE** (page 300)

In form this poem is a villanelle. Its nineteen lines utilize only two rime sounds (based on "night" and "day"); its alternating refrains rime "night" and "light." Most villanelles are charming, graceful, light poems, characteristic of society verse. Thomas here gives the villanelle a force and intensity it had never had before—though many poets have tried to match it since. ("Do not go gentle" is perhaps a turning point in the history of the villanelle.)

As shown by the concluding section, the poem is addressed to the poet's father. In some respects a fierce militant most of his life, the elder Thomas in his 80s went blind, became ill, and showed a tendency to turn soft and gentle. The son was dismayed by this change. He wanted his father to die as he had lived, to maintain his salty individuality to the last. Though the poet was something of a pantheist in his religious belief and felt that death was "good," he still considered it right and natural that men should resist death, put up a struggle against it, not die placidly. "Wise men . . . Good men . . . Wild men . . . Grave men," he tells his father in separate stanzas (punning on the word "Grave"), have all for good reasons raged against their approaching deaths. In the last section (where his tenderness toward his father is manifest), he prays his father (paradoxically) to "Curse" and "bless" him with his "fierce tears" and to "not go gentle into that good night." ("Good night" is both a metaphor for death and a pun for farewell.) LP

247. *Dylan Thomas*   FERN HILL (page 309)

"Fern Hill" is Dylan Thomas's evocation of the delight, the wonder, the long carefree rapture of boyhood summers spent on a farm in Wales. The reader is made to share his pleasure in the barns and fields and orchards, in the farmhouse itself, in the animals both wild and domestic, in afternoon and night and morning. In the fourth stanza the poet compares this boyhood experience to the experience of Adam and Eve in Eden. Like theirs, its chief characteristics were joy and innocence and a feeling of timelessness. Like theirs, his experience came at the beginning of life, and, like them, he felt it would last forever. But the theme of the poem is the transience of youthful joy and carefree innocence. All the time that he is heedless of time, he is bound by its chains, which hold him "green and dying." Just as Adam and Eve were thrust out of Eden, so the boy is to be thrust out of the garden of childhood.

The boy is the protagonist of the poem. Time is the antagonist—unseen, unfelt, and unheeded by the boy, but comprehended clearly by the mature poet looking back. The boy, "happy as the grass was green," feels that he has forever. But, inexorably, in its alternation of afternoon and night and morning, Time is carrying him out of the enchanted realm, "out of grace," toward age and death. The boy who is "prince of the apple towns" (6)—and described with such aristocratically connotative adjectives as "golden" (5), "honored" (6), "lordly" (7), and "famous" (10), who feels himself master of all he surveys—is at the same time, though unaware of it, a slave, held by Time in "chains" (54).

Thomas has a talent for refurbishing clichés and getting new or double meaning out of them, both the old and the new. "Happy as the grass was green" (2) and "Happy as the heart was long" (38) both remind us of the commoner expression "Happy as the day is long" and gather its meaning into fresher expressions. "Once below a time" (7) gathers up the meaning of "Once upon a time" and bends it to the use of the poem's theme—that the boy is really a slave of time, not master of it. In "All the sun long" (19) and "All the moon long" (25) the poet freshens the familiar phrases by substituting metonymies for the expected "day" and "night." In "Adam and maiden" (30) Thomas substitutes for "Eve" a noun which represents her in her innocence and at the same time sounds like "Eden," thus tripling its significance.

If you have to beg, borrow, or steal, get a tape or record of Thomas reading this poem and play it for your class. Thomas's voice is as "golden" as his poetry. Mary C. Davidow in the *English Journal*, 58 (Jan. 1969), 78-81, and Sister M. Laurentia, in *The Explicator*, 14 (Oct. 1955), item 1, offer further interesting and useful observations about this poem. LP

248. *Jean Toomer* REAPERS (page 302)

The plural title ambiguously captures the central contrast of this brief lyric: there are two sets of reapers, both identified as "black"—men, in the first line, and then "horses" in the fifth. The contrast is developed between the human reapers with their sense of completeness (as well as their sense of tradition—"as a thing that's done" refers both to their satisfaction with the accomplishment of a sharpened scythe, and to their sense that this is the way the job is to be done), and the machine-like horses drawing the mechanical mower, insensitive to what they destroy, cutting both "weeds and shade," and slaughtering animals in their path.

There is of course a distortion in this contrast, since it does not pit the human reapers against the human driver of the mowing machine. Instead it pretends that the inhuman horses are the voluntary force in the use of the machine. The focus moves from the observed and admired human mowers of lines 1-4 to the observed and detested effects of mechanical mowing in lines 5-8. But do not human reapers *also* cut both weeds and "shade," and do they not kill field rats? Contrasting the effect of the mechanical mower to the attitudes of the human mowers is in its way unfair, thematically, for it compares not the acts of mowing, human or machine, but the feelings of the observer. He sees in the reapers a collective humanity which nevertheless maintains its individuality—although they act in unison, and in a traditional, inherited fashion, they start "one by one" (4). On the other hand, he does not see the driver of the horses drawing the mower; in fact, he credits the horses with driving.

It is tempting to see here a racial suggestion: to the white owners of the fields, black men and black horses are synonymous. But there is the further suggestion that the sensitive observer, pitying the bleeding rat, cannot *see* the driver of the mowing machine. Is he white? Is he driving horses now, as he drove black men formerly? And is the speaker of the poem black (as the poet was)?

However we answer such questions, we must at least recognize that the poem is clear in its preference for "black reapers" over "black horses," even to the extent of glossing over the distorted comparison that results from such a preference. The sound qualities of the poem reinforce the preference: in the first quatrain, the frequent alliteration of *s* and *st*, the assonance of long *e* sounds, and the lilting repetition of "one by one" create a musicality that harmonizes with the speaker's approving tone; in the second quatrain the *s* alliteration serves to emphasize not "silent swinging" (4) but "startled . . . -stained" violence, and *b* and hard *c* alliteration lend weightiness and abruptness, while the long *e* assonance turns up in words of negative connotation: *weeds, field, squealing, bleeds.* TRA

249. *John Updike* **EX-BASKETBALL PLAYER** (page 302)

So much of this pathetic portrait is involved with realistic detail that the poem seems at first to have no purpose beyond the poignant presentation of a has-been. There is even the danger, in such precision of local detail, that the reader may fail to "see" what the imagery presents. For example, the footnote to lines 10-11 might be expanded to include what Updike remarks in the preface to his 1982 reprinting of the poem (*The Carpentered Hen*, p. xvi): students today "have never seen glass-headed pumps" and thus will not recognize the cartoon-like personification as being very nearly literal. And the imagery of lines 29-30 is also very close to being literal, depending on one's ability to visualize those particular (and now nearly forgotten) candy wrappers and boxes in the variety of shapes and colors that *might* look quite a lot like tiers of fans in the grandstands. This realistic near-literalism, now rapidly losing itself in specific references that can only be recaptured historically, is directly related to the central theme of the poem; the obscurity of reference may be seen as an analogue to the obscurity of the title character. He *was*, vividly and in living memory (22), "the best" basketball player in a small-town high school. But that reality has slipped into the past, and he is now only a gas-station attendant.

The small-town atmosphere is evoked by the proper naming—Pearl Avenue, Colonel McComsky Plaza (no doubt named for a "famous" resident), Berth's Garage, Mae's luncheonette—as if these local landmarks are totally familiar to speaker and reader. Flick played for "*the* high-school then, the Wizards," not for Central High or Jefferson High—there's only one in this town. The team name suggests how little, and how much, the magic of high school athletics may actually achieve. Flick was the best wizard among the Wizards, setting "a county record," but how big is a county? And more to the point of the poem, what is the value of such a record, whatever the size of the competitive field?

That of course is Updike's question: What is the meaning of this life that found its definition and achievement in an adolescent accomplishment, and that now lives in the nostalgia of former spectators and adorers, but is vestigially present only in "hands . . . fine and nervous on the lug wrench" (23)? The situational irony of line 24 points to the value issues of the poem: "It makes no difference to the lug wrench, though."

There are two potential difficulties in teaching this poem, depending on the student level. If taught in high school, the poem may too easily be taken for a sermon ("He never learned a trade," so we should or we'll wind up like Flick); if taught in college, it may too easily lead to smugness (we knew better than to make small-town high school and "a county record" our goals). These potential problems may of course lead to fruitful discussions: *Is* this a satire directed at young people who have too narrow a goal? Did Flick *choose* to be what he became? Was it Flick himself who defined his life, who bestowed on himself the nickname that so aptly fits a star basketball player, but now ironically seems to refer to nothing more than what he must do with his ashes as he "smokes those thin cigars"? TRA

250. David Wagoner RETURN TO THE SWAMP (page 303)

"To begin again, . . . [to] shape, again, something from nothing" (lines 1 and 18), is the speaker's direct statement of his purpose, presented in the symbolic action of returning to a swamp so as to learn "what the mergansers know" (12). The symbol is open-ended, suggesting as it does the various possibilities of instinctual truth, divine inspiration, or creative imagination. The speaker seeks certainties, wanting to penetrate the reflecting and refracting surface of the water, wanting to find some hidden clue that will make more meaning than he has been able to discover.

But the truth is presented with dramatic irony in the very description of the swamp with which he begins: "its rich decay, its calm disorder" (2), the solidity of shallows, the "upside-down redoubling" of the visible world (8). This originally frustrating condition is the paradoxical truth that has sent him "back to the swamp," to the origins represented by evolutionary development and/or divine creation, where he hopes to find something more satisfying to his need. What he finds is a redefinition of the world as he already knows it, all its beautiful and frustrating swampiness made momentarily exciting by an imaginative, artistic action. The very natural event of a "bass taking a fly" (20) is metaphorically compared both to the illusive skill of a circus ring-master and to the creative skill of a poet remaking the world in "beautiful exchanges of stress" (22). The thing most sought for, the scientific/spiritual certainty, gives way to the excitement of rediscovery "suddenly near, there, near in the water" (25) of the fairy-tale frog-prince. TRA

251. Derek Walcott THE VIRGINS (page 304)

Derek Walcott, a native Caribbean poet, is disturbed by what American commercial exploitation (the "American dream" of a better life for all achieved through abundant material goods) has done to the once simple life and unspoiled natural beauty of the American Virgin Islands. He expresses his distress through his observation of (and observations on) Frederiksted, the chief seaport of one of these islands, while walking through its streets. His observations are sharpened by his skillful use of irony and of words and phrases of double meaning.

The irony begins with the title, for clearly these islands (originally named after Elizabeth, the virgin queen) are no longer virgins. They have been prostituted to, or raped by, American materialism. The "dead" (deserted) streets down which the poet walks are deserted probably because of the midday heat, but the adjective leads the poet to the reflection that the town is "dead" in another sense, having lost its soul to tourism. (The phrase "the first free port to die for tourism" ironically reverses a more familiar pattern of words often found on local monuments: the first citizen of this town to die for freedom.) Continuing his metaphor, the poet describes himself as walking at a "funeral" pace (slowly). One suspects a pun in the adjective "sun-stoned" (built of stones heated by the sun; drunk or drugged by the sun's heat). There is a complex verbal irony in the poet's use of "civilized" and "the good life" and a situational irony in the conjoining of "the good life" and "the American dream" with a rising crime rate. The empty condominium (paradoxically drowning in vacancy) gives evidence of a building boom in which the developers' eager anticipations miscalculated the actual demand. The roulettes spinning "rustily to the wind" evidence the same kind of overdevelopment at the same time that they testify to what "tourism," "the American dream," and "the good life" actually substitute for the speaker's "small-islander's simplicities": not only a rising crime rate, but cheap dreams of quick wealth made at the gambling casinos. In line 16 "trade" has the double meaning of trade wind and commerce. The spinning of the roulette wheels is related both by circular motion and monetary motivation to the "revving up" of motorboats and yachts headed for the "banks" (fishing banks and money banks) of "silver" (silver-sided fish and silver coins). And if "silver" is related to coinage, perhaps "green" is associated with dollar bills. LP

252. *Marilyn Nelson Waniek* OLD BIBLES (page 305)

Marilyn Nelson Waniek, a black poet, here gives a gently humorous portrait of a speaker with an amusing dilemma—what to do with a "sacred" object which one no longer wants. The speaker would like to get rid of her old torn-up, scrawled-on, cover-chewed Bibles, but fears that to do so would be a sin. She has therefore let them accumulate till they occupy a "whole shelf."

Perhaps the chief problem in reading the poem is to make a correct determination of its tone. Is this a portrait of a pious and perhaps slightly crazy woman who regards throwing an old Bible away, "stepping on a crack" on the sidewalk, and failing to "cross" one's fingers when telling a fib as *sins*! Or is the speaker an intelligent woman who is slyly poking fun at herself for her inability to throw away a worn-out Bible? The vocabulary, the images, and the comparisons in the poem all, in my opinion, support the latter interpretation.

Dropping an American flag, even accidentally, is also a sin, the speaker tells us—a sin that she herself had once committed. She had felt guilty for weeks afterwards. "A gaunt bearded stranger / in tricolored clothes" (Uncle Sam) had come to *get* her. But since there is no real Uncle Sam, these events clearly occurred in her imagination. She makes Uncle Sam the embodiment of her self-accusing conscience. But did she really feel that much guilt and for that long? Or is she not humorously exaggerating—"embroidering" on the truth, we might say, and possibly without crossing her fingers—making a joke at her own expense?

The speaker is a religious person. Her very possession of so many Bibles is evidence of that, but she is not so religious that she cannot perceive and laugh at her own foibles. And thus, throughout the poem, she exhibits a sometimes subtle and always delightful sly wit: the suggestion that Bibles may have souls "like little birds fluttering / over the dump / when the wind blows their pages"; the statement that Bibles are holy, like "kosher."

This is not broad humor, however. Not slapstick. In the last section, which is the most poetically resonant in the poem, the humor is so interwoven with true religious feeling that the two are inextricable. LP

253. *Robert Penn Warren* **BOY WANDERING IN SIMMS' VALLEY** (page 306)

The poem begins with exploration; it ends with a revelation.

The speaker, whom we may not unfairly identify with the poet (who grew up in rural Kentucky), is an adult recalling an incident from his boyhood. There are several time levels in the poem, and it is important to get them straight. First, there was a time (barely implied in the poem) when Simms brought his wife to live in the isolated valley farm and together they were able to keep the place "trim" (she the house, and he the fields). Then the wife fell sick and became bedridden, and "for long years" Simms had to bear the burden of working the fields and nursing her, while the place went gradually "to wrack." When the wife died, Simms let out his "spindly" livestock to forage at will, lay down beside his wife, and shot himself. So isolated was the farm that their bodies were not discovered till two years later, and then only by accident. A hunter, sitting down to rest on the porch-edge, was disturbed by the smell, began to "prowl," found two bodies in an advanced state of decomposition in the upstairs bedroom, and "high-tailed" to town. The town officials (we assume) gave the bodies a decent burial but were unable to find a purchaser even at auction ("tax-sale") for the rundown, isolated farm. The time of the boy's visit is many years later, and the property has continued to deteriorate. There has been time for maples about eighteen inches thick to grow in the remoter fields. The barn is down, the house itself is "ready to fall," the "place" is being reclaimed by the wilderness. "Lonely and forgotten," it has had few if any visitors since the burial of the farmer and his wife. Its furnishings are undisturbed by human pillage; nature has been the destructive agent.

In stanza 1 the speaker, describing his entry into the valley, gives some idea of its inaccessibility (though there must have been easier access somewhere, some road by which Simms took produce to market and fetched supplies from town). He also subtly foreshadows, with his mention in the first line of "love-vine" and the fact that he was "well blooded" (deeply scratched by thorns), the two questions that will be raised in the final line of the poem concerning "love" and "life" (for which "blood" is a metonymy). In stanzas 2-3 he relates what he knew (had been told) about the suicide of Simms and the finding of the bodies. Stanza 4 opens with a generalization—"A dirt farmer needs a good wife to keep a place trim"—as the boy reflects about the delapidation of the farm and the hardships of Simms' life after his wife became ill. Stanza 6 finds him standing in the upstairs bedroom, noticing further deterioration, and reflecting on the events that had taken place there. In stanza 7 the sinking sun brings him out of his near-trance, and he prepares to leave. But casting a last glance around, he suddenly sees "the old enameled bedpan, high on a shelf," and is brought again to a halt. In a final line, set off by itself and breaking the stanza pattern, we are told the questions that arose in his mind.

It is the bedpan which furnishes, in the full Joycean sense, the "epiphany" of the tale. It takes the boy deeper into the meanings of the events than his reflections had yet gone; it makes him ask and partially realize "what life is, and love, and what they may be"—what they are in essence, and what they may become in extreme cases, such as the Simmses'. Though the poem leaves us with a question, not an answer, it provides some of the materials needed for an answer. It tells us at once how terrible life can be, and how great human devotion can be. For Simms the latter part of life had been struggling, without help, to keep a poor farm going, the fields plowed and planted, the stock fed, and the crops harvested; and love had been emptying bedpans for a sick wife—as revolting and filthy a task as one can imagine (and certainly no part of "love's sweet dream"). Yet life was worth living for Simms only so long as he could carry those bedpans for his wife. When she died, he took his life, not in the fields or in the barn but by her side, not because the burdens of life had become too much for him (they could only be eased by her death) but because, when he had no one to care for, he had nothing to live for. He did it deliberately, taking thought first to let the livestock free to forage.

The poem is written in stanzas riming *abab*. Though there is no sharply definable meter, the rhythm flows loosely through five-beat lines—except for the last, which has six. The language (but not always the syntax) keeps close to the colloquial—".12 gauge" (8), "to jaw" (9), "high-tailed" (12), "his old lady" (14). LP

254. *Walt Whitman* A NOISELESS PATIENT SPIDER (page 306)

The situation of a man accepting the energies of a spinning spider as an example to himself should recall the famous story of the fourteenth-century Scottish king Robert the Bruce (Robert I), who in apparent defeat retired into a cave for refuge. There he watched the tireless effort of a spider which despite repeated failure refused to give up spinning; the king resolved to continue in battle—and was victorious. By the nineteenth century this anecdote had become a moral exemplum of the virtue of pertinacity (a narrative version of "If at first you don't succeed, try, try again!").

In its earliest unprinted version this poem had as its theme the poet's sense of loneliness as he searches for love in a world of "fathomless latent souls of love." [See Gay Wilson Allen, *The Solitary Singer* (New York Univ. Press, 1967), p. 342.]

The present version transforms both the moral tale and the earlier unprinted poem, changing the subject to the soul's yearning for spiritual truth. "In measureless oceans of space," the soul seeks security, an "anchor." Despite the traditional symbolism of an anchor as Christ or as the hope for salvation (see Hebrews 6:19), the poem does not openly suggest that Christianity is the answer to the speaker's problem. In fact, a "ductile anchor" attached to a "gossamer thread" suggests fragility and plasticity, rather than the security of a defined, systematic religion.

In Whitman's image, the spider resembles a fisherman, unreeling his lines as he launches them forth. The vocabulary of the poem tends to corroborate an implicit nautical or fishing context: *promontory, launched, unreeling, oceans, bridge, anchor.* Though the speaker seems not to be consciously aware of it, the imagery itself suggests a Christian solution to his problem—the anchor of Christian salvation, with the speaker's search evoking the church's role as a "fisher of men."

While the poem draws an explicit comparison between the spider's activity and that of the spiritually questing man, there are clearly implied contrasts as well: the contrast of size and perspective (a spider's promontory is indeed "little," and the area of exploration may seem to it to be a "vacant vast surrounding," but the range of "measureless oceans of space" inhabited by man is considerably grander); the spider's patience is in contrast to the "musing, venturing, throwing, seeking" of the man; the noiselessness of the spider may be contrasted to this verbal outpouring from the human being; and of course the spider's actions must be read literally, the man's metaphorically.

The poem should be examined for examples of alliteration, assonance and consonance, as poetic devices providing a replacement for regular rhythm and rime. Overstatement, particularly in the spatial references, emphasizes the need to recognize contrasts within the overt comparison. TRA

255. *Walt Whitman* THERE WAS A CHILD WENT FORTH (page 307)

If students have studied Tennyson's "Ulysses" (page 90), they might be asked to consider the difference between Ulysses' claim that "I am a part of all that I have met" (line 18), and Whitman's statement that "that object he became, / And that object became part of him" (lines 1-2). The two phrases of Whitman's statement refer to two related but different psychological processes, one we would call "identification" or "empathy," the other "memory." The first, operating at the moment of perception, projects himself outward into objects, the second extends the perception and empathy forward in time, absorbing and collecting his experiences. Neither is a particularly intellectual process. The implication is that the more sensitively he projects himself, the more inclusive his memory. Furthermore, the poem implies that the growth of the individual child relies upon this combination of projection and collection, and only at one moment (lines 27-30) is there an overt reference to the powers of the child to reason or judge.

Each of the five verse-paragraphs consists of a single sentence (the question marks at lines 29-30 are parenthetical, the long fifth sentence ending only with the predication in line 39). After the introductory summary sentences, the finite verb forms occur at the beginnings of sentences 2 and 3, and at the ends of sentences 4 and 5. The rest of the poem consists of catalogues of noun-phrases listing the "objects" that "became part of him."

The four sentences following the introduction present stages of increasing complexity in the child's perception: first, a perception of details of the natural world, then of persons, then in a generalized way of his parents, and finally of his parents in detailed actions arousing emotional responses. In line 27, the child experiences his first doubts about what is real or unreal, and whether his trusting eyes have been reporting objective truth. These questions are followed by a review, in reverse order, of the objects of perception—back through the human world and its activities to the natural world of water and sky. The tone of the last lines, 31-39, emphasizes distance and the perception of variety and beauty.

The essential structure of the poem is thus a collection of objects perceived, moving from the natural to the human; a turning point at which the child raises intellectual questions about reality; and a generalizing recapitulation emphasizing beauty—as if the doubting questions had to be ignored in a willed act of perceiving the grandeur which individual "specks" yield when seen from a distance.

A final line which universalized this process to include the reader was dropped by Whitman in 1867: "And these become of him or her that peruses them now." Although the poem may seem more directly autobiographical without that conclusion, Whitman seems to have trusted that the process he presents will strike readers as being true of themselves even without the line. TRA

256. *Walt Whitman* WHEN I HEARD THE LEARN'D ASTRONOMER (page 308)

This poem expresses a conflict which may seem even more cogent today than when Whitman wrote it: precise scientific knowledge is an assault on the cherished mysteries of the universe. Feelings similar to Whitman's were voiced in the wake of man's first steps on the surface of the moon on July 20, 1969; as the cameras of rocket probes send back close-up photographs of the more distant planets in our solar system, the skies may seem to lose their appealing wonder.

Whitman's ironic contrasts are readily perceived because of their directness and abundance, and though it may be a violation of his attitude toward "charts" and "columns," they may be indicated as paired lists:

crowd in lecture room	individual man
much applause	silence
mathematical counting	"unaccountable" feeling
lighted room	dark night
indoors	outdoors
approving audience	tired and sick poet
sitting	rising and gliding, wandering
scientific precision	random looking, "from time to time"
scientific thought	poetic feeling

These ironic contrasts make the speaker's decision seem more natural, more attractive, more human. The initial repetition of "when" in the first four lines has a hypnotic sameness, imitating the poet's boredom with the regularity of scientific proofs; and the redundancy of "proofs, figures, columns, charts, diagrams" and "add, divide, measure" reinforces the sense of repetitiousness and—for the speaker—the meaninglessness of such data about the universe. The phrase "perfect silence" in the last line ironically comments on the supposed perfection of scientific knowledge: genuine perfection is not mathematical or measurable, but is the harmonious response of perfect feeling to perfect stars.

The poem presents Whitman's distaste for precise, rational knowledge and his love of emotional, instinctive wonder at the mysteries of nature. His choice of the word "mystical" rather than "mysterious" extends his preference into a claim that his experience surpasses the astronomer's knowledge in a religious sense as well. His insight into the wonders of heaven seems to him to penetrate the merely mysterious and to reach to supernatural wisdom. TRA

257. *Richard Wilbur*   THE MILL (page 309)

The death of a friend must always move us to questions that we cannot answer, and leave us with a sense of emptiness and waste, especially if the friend's life did not end successfully, if life in some way defeated him. What has become, we may ask, of his memories, his appreciations, all his investment in living and experience? In the lost, abandoned mill with its wheel still turning and turning. Richard Wilbur has found the perfect symbol for those haunting, unanswered questions, that sense of emptiness and waste.

The organization of the poem emphasizes the passage of time. It begins with the "spoiling daylight," the late afternoon sun dying and for a moment coming in at such a slant that every mote of dust in the air is made visible and glistening. Then the friend recalls places in his past—"the names of streets, the exact look / Of lilacs" in Cincinnati in 1903, the turning mill wheel in an isolated valley in Brazil or Tennessee. The friend remembering is presented by the poet remembering. But the poet has already forgotten whether the millwheel was in Brazil or Tennessee, and when he, too, dies, all of these memories will be gone. What will it matter, then, that these places ever existed? Time needs human life and human memory to give it significance. "Time all alone and talking to himself" has no more meaning than a mill wheel which continues to operate when it serves no human purpose.

Wilbur's choice of words for sound and meaning is uncannily precise. The "spoiling daylight" refers not only to fading daylight but to the passage of time that "spoils" all. The friend's voice that "rose from the shades" of the darkened barroom blends into the dead friend that rises from the shades of death in the poet's mind. The word *sound* in "Your dead life's sound and sovereign anecdote" serves both as noun and adjective having two quite independent meanings, and *sovereign* not only means supreme but gathers in the meaning of a British gold coin from its association with "round sums" and "pocket change." The onomatopoetic verbs and repeated *k* sounds of the "crazy buckets / Creaking and lumbering out of the clogged race" reproduces the very sound and motion of the buckets; the word *rattle* is onomatopoetic and suggests a meaningless sound—talk that has no meaning. In the last line it is not only the mill wheel which "turns and turns," but the mind itself which turns this memory "over and over." Sound, position, and arrangement all serve the economy of meaning.* LP

*Reprinted from Laurence Perrine and James M. Reid, *100 American Poems of the Twentieth Century* (New York: Harcourt Brace Jovanovich, 1966), pp. 206–61.

258. *Nancy Willard* A WREATH TO THE FISH (page 310)

Hamlet riddlingly insults King Claudius with another such "wreath" as he shows the "progress" of a king's corpse: "A man may fish with the worm that hath eat of a king, and eat of the fish that hath fed of that worm." But unlike Willard's, Hamlet's wreath is logically connected, a causal sequence. Willard's poem seems to progress merely associatively, apparently following no development except that an idea or image used in presenting one thing will then be a subject for further development—with no end in sight. So the "mail" (scales) of the fish protects it against the cold of the stream, the stream leads to fishermen's lines, the lines to the hook, the hook to the caught fish, the fish to the Pope, and the Pope back to the opening question, "Who is this fish?" Each of the topics is explored poetically, through metaphor and metonymy, but chiefly through personification. The fish is an armor-clad dweller in the stream, his only wealth the suit of mail made of "thin coins." The stream is a slightly mad woman who "lolls all day in an unmade bed" (one of many puns in the poem, which also seem to have associative energy—as later the fishermen's lines lead to the written lines of scrawling eel). The hook is a "fanatic who will not let go," and the fish, finally, is "transfigured" into a "little martyr," so that the title itself contains a pun as a figurative wreath of glory is bestowed on it.

All of this wit springs from the speaker's playfully musing question, "Who is this fish," the "who" representing the germ for the flowering of personifications. But, the poem implies, once you start wondering about the meanings of little things, you may find yourself on a long and convoluted path, with little to guide you but your wit and your ability to find links and connections. It is almost "a little miracle" that the poem manages to close the circle. TRA

259. *Miller Williams* **A POEM FOR EMILY** (page 310)

The best approach to this poem about "arithmetic and love" is probably through the standard questions: Who is the speaker? To whom is he speaking? What is the occasion?

The speaker is a grandfather, age 53, speaking to his granddaughter, age less than one full day. The occasion is the birth of the grandaughter. But is the speaker literally addressing the child or is he apostrophizing her? Since she is asleep and would not understand his language even were she awake, he is apostrophizing her. At the same time, however, he is putting his thoughts and feelings into a poem (this poem) which, many years later, even after he is dead, she may read and understand and be warmed by. The message is: "I stood and loved you while you slept."

But between the beginning and the end there are intermediate times to think about, and some paradoxes to probe. The first paradox occurs, in fact, in the first two lines. The speaker, only "a hand's width" away from the child, calls it the "farthest one" from him. The paradox, however, is easily solved. At that moment he is, of all his kin, nearest the baby in space but farthest from her in time. They are separated in time by 53 years (two generations).

Ten years later, he muses, the child will be "neither closer nor as far." The first phrase can be read in two ways. The ten-year old will be no closer in space nor in time (they will still be separated by 53 years), but whichever way we read it, the second phrase offers a paradox. She will *not* be separated "as far" in time as she is now. The paradox is resolved by realizing that chronological time and psychological time are not the same. When the granddaughter is ten, she and her grandfather will have a common language in which they can converse and she will have learned something about arithmetic and love, thus shortening psychologically the distance in time between them.

In stanzas 3 and 4 the speaker projects himself even farther into the future: when he "by blood and luck" is 86, she will be 33, with children of her own. (The word "luck" alters the initial "When" into something more like *If*.) By then, he is sure, she will have read her children (his great grandchildren) this poem, so they will know he loves them (and says so) and loves their mother (his granddaughter, Emily, whose birth inspired the poem). In the final stanza (beginning with the last two words of the fourth) the speaker both projects himself into an even more remote time in the future and returns to time present where he stands beside the new baby's bed. In this distant future, when the baby is old and the speaker is dead, this poem, "a thing that might be kept / a while," will tell her what he would have said then, and says now in the poem.

The speaker asserts in stanza 4 that "whatever is / is always or never was." True things last forever; false things die. The true thing celebrated in the poem is love.
LP

260. *William Wordsworth*   I WANDERED LONELY AS A CLOUD (page 311)

The subject is typically Romantic and Wordsworthian: the speaker in an idle moment, alone in nature and feeling detached from it and from the social world, comes upon a natural event that moves him so deeply that his future life is shaped by it, and the memory of it can spontaneously return to him, to renew the emotion of the original experience. But why *should* a scene of natural beauty have such an effect? Is there more to this than the portrayal of the emotional response of a sensitive person? Does he *do* anything or only passively receive a gift from nature?

First, the speaker's condition before the event: wandering, alone, but also "lonely," an emotional state in which he regrets his isolation, and yet in his simile also glories in it—"lonely as a cloud that floats on high," superior to the valleys and hills of earth. And the simile contains another figure as well, personification, so that the opening situation is an example of poetic perception: the self compared to a cloud, the cloud given two human attributes, loneliness *and* superiority. So the speaker sets out from a point of poetic creativity even while he feels himself to be idly uninvolved.

As soon as the daffodils are visible, the poetic imagination shifts into a higher gear. The first impression, "crowd," is immediately and spontaneously revised into a more reverberative "host," the daffodils are "golden" in more than color, the rhythm takes on a lilt as the tetrameter line is broken in half with "Beside the lake, beneath the trees" (*beside* and *beneath* establishing a different spatial relationship from "high o'er"), and the daffodils are given costume and dance motions. What we might judge to be a serene and dispassionate emotional state in lines 1-2 suddenly leaps into creative energy which continues through line 14.

The major figure of the second stanza is overstatement, revealing the speaker's need to capture the intensity of his excitement—the flowers seemed infinite, heavenly, brilliant, "never-ending"; the speaker's sensitivity enabled him to see "ten thousand . . . at a glance." They seemed all to be dancing in unison, and the waves seemed to mimic (but of course fell short of) them in dancing.

At line 15, the submerged self-consciousness that has been implied by the spate of poetic devices finally comes to the fore: the "poet" must examine both his response and the external stimulus to it. He discovers that despite his reluctance ("could not but be" implies that he has tried to avoid it—perhaps that's what he was consciously doing by wandering "lonely as a cloud"?), he feels cheerful being in the "jocund company" of the daffodils. Unlike the "sparkling waves," he does not try to dance with them, but only gazes and gazes, storing up the emotion of the moment without knowing or thinking that the "golden daffodils" brought him more wealth than the single experience.

The additional wealth is the ability to relive that experience, not only as a memory but as an emotion, even—what he did not do in the past—to the extent of letting his heart figuratively "dance with the daffodils." But notice again the emotional straits that he is in when they come to him: alone, lying on his couch, "in vacant or in pensive mood," looking into himself with "bliss" that comes from solitude— then once again, unbidden and unexpected, the merry daffodils "flash upon that inward eye."

But what is really flashing is his own creative power—for, in fact, the daffodils cannot be jocund, cannot feel glee, do not dance. The lively, bright beauty of a surprising natural sight was the starting point for a poet's imaginative creativity; *that* is what can fill his heart with pleasure. TRA

261. *William Wordsworth*   THE SOLITARY REAPER (page 312)

The poem relates the awakening of the speaker's imaginative response to an experience of wordless expression and the extended effect of the experience on him. Apparently on a walking tour in the Highlands of Scotland, the speaker sees and hears a girl gathering grain while she sings a native song. Moved by both her solitude and the sorrowful melody, the speaker tries to find correspondences between the unintelligible song and other human experiences, but finally acknowledges that whether he understands it or not, it has moved him deeply enough to live on in his memory.

In accordance with his theories about poetry as the "spontaneous overflow of powerful feelings," a power which he attributes to the singing girl, Wordsworth frequently strives to give his poems both immediacy and the sense of personal experience. In this case, however, his starting point was not at all personal; the poem is based on a passage from a friend's manuscript account of a Scottish tour. Thomas Wilkinson had written: "Passed by a female who was reaping alone, she sung in Erse as she bended over her sickle, the sweetest human voice I ever heard. Her strains were tenderly melancholy, and felt delicious long after they were heard no more." The poem reports this (with direct quotation and verbal echo) as if it had happened to the speaker, achieving immediacy in the first three stanzas by using the present tense.

The opening lines emphatically establish the solitariness of the girl, and awaken parallel feelings in the speaker: "single" (1), "solitary" (2), "by herself" (3), "alone" (5). He has, or imagines, companions whom he exhorts to "Behold" and "listen," demanding excited attention; yet this he balances against the injunction to remain quiet so as not to disturb the girl's song and to preserve her sense of being alone. What strikes him most in the opening stanza are her solitude and the "melancholy" nature of her song, which seems to overflow the deep valley in which she works (the Scottish Highlands are for the most part barren and sparsely inhabited, with arable land restricted to the valleys).

In the second and third stanzas, as he listens to the music in a foreign tongue, the speaker imaginatively searches for corresponding situations that will explain the emotions with which he responds. The second stanza offers two comparisons, both suggesting relief from the hardships of natural surroundings. The singer is like two very different kinds of birds in two contrasted geographical locales, implying the universality of the experience: the nightingale singing in an oasis in the parched Arabian desert, promising cool comfort to exhausted travelers; or the cuckoo signaling the coming of spring to the stark, rocky islands battered by the seas in the northernmost reaches of Scotland. Both scenes are isolated, forbidding and lonely; both are momentarily relieved; and both imply that the speaker feels himself isolated, wandering in a wholly uncongenial natural setting, momentarily restored by the beauty of the song he hears.

The third stanza moves from geographical extremes to contrasts of time and social rank. The song might be a traditional lament expressing grief for ancient, heroic battlefield defeats or it might refer to the "natural sorrow, loss, or pain" of ordinary daily life in the present. Just as loneliness and weariness were universalized in stanza 2, stanza 3 universalizes melancholy here and everywhere, now and in the past.

The third stanza has asked for intelligible fact: what is she singing about? In the final stanza, the poem suddenly shifts into the past tense, in its first line denying the possibility (or even the necessity) of understanding exactly what the girl was saying. As it turns out, the speaker's inability to understand the meaning of the song has been an advantage. He has found in the melody and in the singer's isolation the occasion for his own imagined creation of the universal themes of loneliness and melancholy. Looking back on this experience, he has discovered that his imagination was revitalized, and that his profound feelings have persisted even after he has mounted up from the scene of her singing.

A full, suggestive reading of this poem is in Geoffrey H. Hartman's *Wordsworth's Poetry, 1787-1814* (New Haven: Yale Univ. Press, 1964), pp. 3-18. TRA

262. *William Butler Yeats*   SAILING TO BYZANTIUM (page 313)

In his book *A Vision,* Yeats wrote that if he could be given a month of antiquity and leave to spend it where he chose, he would spend it in Byzantium about the year 525 A.D. Byzantium (later known as Constantinople and presently as Istanbul), the eastern capital of the Holy Roman Empire, was in that period notable for the flowering of its art: painting, architecture, mosaic-work, gold and silver metalcraft, book illumination, etc. For this reason, it represented for Yeats a holy city of the imagination.

The title "Sailing to Byzantium" would seem to indicate that the poem is about a voyage; but line 1 (*"That* [not *This*] is no country for old men") together with lines 15-16 (". . . therefore have I sailed the seas and come / To the holy city of Byzantium") indicates that the voyage has already been completed. It is an imaginary voyage, of course, for it has been made not just across space, from Ireland to Byzantium, but backwards through time, from the twentieth century to the sixth. The important considerations, therefore, are not the voyage itself, but why the poet made it; and not Ireland and Byzantium, but what they represent.

The poem deals with the antitheses of the physical and sensual world versus the world of intellect and imagination, the mortal versus the eternal, nature versus art. Modern Ireland represents the first term in these oppositions, Byzantium the second. The poet, growing old (he was 63 when this poem was published) can no longer engage fully and unreflectively in the life of the senses, and longs for something beyond the life of the senses, for the life of the senses is mortal and dies. He finds what he is looking for in works of art ("monuments of unaging intellect"), which are eternal. The poem may be looked on as a kind of prayer: Let me leave this country of the young, the unreflective, the sensual, and the dying, and sail to the city of imagination and unaging intellect. There let my next incarnation be as an artificial gold-and-enamel singing bird that cannot decay as my body is decaying now but which will exist eternally. Let me be a work of art rather than a man!

Yeats thus seems to be elevating art above nature, the eternal above the mortal. But there is a catch here. What will this gold-enameled bird sing about? It will sing of "what is past, or passing, or to come"—a line that echoes line 6: "Whatever is begotten, born, and dies." Art celebrates the mortal world—the world of process, change, decay, and death. The poem thus has a circular movement in which the last line returns us to its beginning. The poet presents us, not with a preference but with a dilemma. He wishes to escape from life into art, but as a work of art he will celebrate life. Art is both superior and inferior to life. Though not subject to decay, it is an "artifice," without life. The dilemma is comparable to that presented by Keats in "Ode on a Grecian Urn" (page 277). LP

263. *William Butler Yeats*   **THE SECOND COMING** (page 314)

In 1919, the year this poem was published, Ireland was in the midst of a bloody civil war; World War I had only recently ended (November 1918); and Russia was engaged in civil war following its Revolution of 1917. All these events portended for Yeats the approaching end of the Christian era, the historical cycle begun almost two thousand years earlier with the birth of Christ. In Yeats's historical theory the transition from one historical era to another was always marked by an epoch of violence and disorder.

The poem is divided into two sections. The first gives the poet's impression of the present. The second presents an apocalyptic vision of the future.

His description of the present is terrifying. The opening two lines present a symbol of a world out of control. In the ancient art of falconry the falcon was trained always to return upon a signal to the wrist of the falconer. But in Yeats's image the falcon has flown beyond the hearing of his master's signal. The adjective "Mere" (4) here retains its obsolete meaning of *absolute, entire, sheer.* "Ceremony" (6) had for Yeats particular value as connected with orderly and civilized living (see "A Prayer for My Daughter," which follows immediately after "The Second Coming" in Yeats's *Collected Poems*). The closing lines of this section describe a familiar crisis situation where good people, by nature moderate and tolerant, are uncertain what should be done, while the bigots, the terrorists, and the assassination squads are full of "passionate intensity"—all too certain in their ignorant minds that they know exactly what is needed.

The opening lines of the second section seem to sound a note of hope. "Surely," the poet declares, "some revelation is at hand"—the word "revelation" suggesting a divine manifestation; "Surely the Second Coming is at hand"—the words "Second Coming" reminding us of the Second Coming of Christ prophesied in the Bible. Things can hardly get much worse; therefore these violent actions must be auspices of change, signs of the shifting from one historical era to another. No sooner has the poet uttered the words "Second Coming" than he has a vision. An image arises to consciousness (not just from his own unconscious but from the racial unconscious underlying it) of the stone sphinx in the Egyptian desert slowly coming to life and "moving its slow thighs." The vision is vivid. Yeats depicts not only its gaze "blank and pitiless as the sun," but the reactions of the desert birds to this amazing phenomenon. In indignant clamor they "reel" in circles above the slowly awakening sphinx; but Yeats with marvelous poetic economy depicts them only through their shadows (thus giving us in one picture the shadows, the birds that cast them, and the bright desert sun that causes them). The vision is brief, but now Yeats knows (or claims to know) that twenty centuries of "stony sleep" (the sphinx's) were "vexed to nightmare" by "a rocking cradle" (a metonymy for the infant Christ), and he also knows what "rough beast, its hour come round at last, / Slouches toward Bethlehem to be born." The vision is a vision of horror. The new era, its time come to replace the old one, is symbolized by a "rough beast." (The question asked in the last two lines is rhetorical, as shown by the ambiguous syntax of the sentence, in which "and" indicates the presence of parallelism but in which "what" can logically be linked only with "that" (19) ["I know that . . . and what . . ."], making "what" not an interrogative but a relative pronoun calling logically for a period at the end of the sentence. But when was logic ever the most direct way to poetic power?)

Our expectation, set up by the title and by lines 9-10, that the poem would concern the Second Coming of Christ are shattered by the last two lines of the poem. It is the coming of Antichrist which is prophesied. Legends tell us that Antichrist will be born in Bethlehem, and Antichrist is referred to recurrently in the New Testament as the "beast." It is Yeats, however, whose genius has assimilated Antichrist with the desert sphinx and given him new dimensions of horror and evil by his use of the adjective "rough" and the verb "slouches."

Surely, this poem derives its greatness from the feeling of evil and horror it so powerfully evokes. Yet the most controversial critical question regarding the poem occurs just here. Scholars familiar with Yeats's historical theories (expressed most fully in his book *A Vision*) have pointed out that the era Yeats expected to follow the Christian one was more amenable to him than the Christian era, and that therefore the advent of the "rough beast" is to be welcomed. As Marjorie Perloff has pointed out, "The basic argument is whether the poem should be read as an independent text, in which case its language suggests that the 'rough beast' is bringing a new dispensation of nightmare and terror, or whether it should be read in the light of *A Vision*, in which case one may argue, as Helen Vendler does, that 'Yeats approves intellectually, if not emotionally of the Second Coming. . . . The Beast is a world-restorer.'" LP

264. *William Butler Yeats* THE WILD SWANS AT COOLE (page 315)

Both his theory and his practice point to the need to read an individual poem by Yeats in the context of the rest of his poetry and of his life. A full understanding of this poem requires at least a reading of Donald A. Stauffer's analysis in *The Golden Nightingale* (New York: Macmillan, 1949, pp. 48-79). But even without the richness of the Yeatsian context, the poem has beauty and power that are available to the sensitive reader.

Both actually and superficially it is a meditation on nature and on the passage of time which alters the human observer but leaves nature essentially unchanged; it thus resembles Wordsworth's "Tintern Abbey" and Keats's "Ode to a Nightingale" (page 278), poems in which the response of the man is both intensely present and also intensely subjective and retrospective. External natural facts elicit feelings and memories and desires, and time present is contrasted with time past, human and natural. Nature undergoes cyclical changes and keeps returning to its same condition; the human being undergoes progressive changes which include decay and death, but also memories of earlier states. Nature is permanent and always in the present, man is transient but contains his own past, his sensitive present, and his predictions of the future.

The elegiac tone of this poem is established in the first stanza—autumn, dryness, twilight, stillness. But paradoxically the poem also contains terms that contrast with these: beauty, mirror-like clarity, brimming water, clamorous wings. Yeats maintains the tone, and also the contrasts, throughout the poem, summing up his inability to understand the swans in the simple declaration that they are "mysterious, beautiful" (26). Although he attributes much to them, they cannot be wholly captured in his language or his imagination, justifying the recurring Yeatsian strategy of the conclusion—a rhetorical question (for other examples, see "Leda and the

Swan," page 124, "The Second Coming," page 314, and "Among School Children.") The questions in these poems are not really questions, for the poem has implied the answer, as it does here. The speaker does not really wonder where the swans will be (in fact, they will most probably be where they are now, in the streams and lake of Coole Park, and if not these particular swans then their indistinguishable offspring). Nor does the question really mean "what other men will be delighted by them," for any man who sees them will be delighted; nor does it mean "where will *I* be when 'I awake some day / To find they have flown away,'" for the answer to that is implicit too: since the swans represent to him the continuity and permanence of the natural world, any awakening that discovers them gone will be an awakening out of nature, into death.

The number "nine-and-fifty," phrased archaically and with an implied hint of magic, first introduces the "mystery" of the swans: although they seem paired "lover by lover," the number is odd. The mystery of this number is augmented by the other one, nineteen; both of them are prime numbers, both end in nine, and both sound so very precise that a reader inevitably asks their significance. Is there a meaningful link between 59 and 19? The speaker has carefully kept track of the number of years he has been returning to this spot, and has carefully counted the swans, year after year—and yet, as he reports, even on that first count he had not finished counting before they flew up off the water. How can he know their precise number? As they suddenly mounted into the air, perhaps disturbed by his presence, perhaps even reluctant to be numbered, they scattered (suggesting random motion) yet wheeled; they flew in rings but the rings were "broken." What this succession of images suggests is a precise but uncountable number, a patterned movement that remained incompleted: a contrast between the human desire to discover number and geometric shape, and nature's reluctance to be comprehended in such intellectual undertakings.

From this perspective, we can see that the qualities attributed to the swans in the remainder of the poem are human interpretations: their wings beat like bells (tolling the passage of time, to the observer?), they are lovers, the water is "companionable," they are "unwearied," their hearts do not grow old, and—a clear indication that the qualities are not inherent in the swans—"passion or conquest" *attend* them. They are therefore genuinely mysterious, for the poem has not penetrated their mysteries, but seen in them parallels and contrasts to the human condition, revealing the impossibility of understanding them for what they are.

The natural world, then, is impenetrable to the human observer. What remains in the poem is the situation in which this places him—seeing the swans in their continuity, recognizing in himself the changes that time brings, confessing the pain that these changes have caused, and projecting further loss in the future. As the final question indicates, there will be other men to fill his place (as in fact there have been other swans to replenish the flock), but there is no consolation for the man in that fact, nor does his verbal tactic of thinking of his future as an awakening lessen the sense of loss. TRA